Death

by a thousand cuts

Death

by a thousand cuts

THE FIGHT OVER TAXING

INHERITED WEALTH

Michael J. Graetz and Ian Shapiro

PRINCETON UNIVERSITY PRESS

Princeton and Oxford

Published by Princeton University Press, 41 William Street, Princeton, New Jersey 08540

In the United Kingdom: Princeton University Press, 3 Market Place, Woodstock, Oxfordshire OX20 1SY

LIBRARY OF CONGRESS CATALOGING-IN-PUBLICATION DATA

Graetz, Michael J.
   Death by a thousand cuts : the fight over taxing inherited wealth / Michael J. Graetz and Ian Shapiro.— 1st ed.
      p.   cm.
   Includes bibliographical references.
   ISBN 0-691-12293-8 (alk. paper)
   1. Inheritance and transfer tax—United States.   2. United States—Politics and government—2001–   I. Shapiro, Ian. II. Title.
   HJ5805.G73 2005
   336.2'76'0973—dc22   2004024431

British Library Cataloging-in-Publication Data is available

This book has been composed in Adobe Garamond and Helvetica

Printed on acid-free paper. ∞

pup.princeton.edu

Printed in the United States of America

10 9 8 7 6 5 4 3 2 1

For Boris I. Bittker

Whose writings on the estate tax almost cost him tenure

CONTENTS

An American Story

A Political Mystery

At the heart of this story lies a mystery about politics and persuasion. For almost a century, the estate tax affected only the richest 1 or 2 percent of citizens, encouraged charity, and placed no burden on the vast majority of Americans. This tax was grounded on a core American value: that all people should have an equal opportunity to pursue their economic dreams. Yet it became so despised and generally unpopular that a wide majority of Congress voted to repeal it. How, in a democratic society, did this happen? And what does its demise signal about our future?

A law that constituted the blandest kind of common sense for most of the twentieth century was transformed, in the space of little more than a decade, into the supposed enemy of hardworking citizens all over this country. How did so many people who were unaffected by the estate tax—the most progressive part of the tax law—and who might ultimately see their own taxes increased to replace the revenues lost if the estate tax disappeared, come to oppose it? Who made this happen?

The answers to these questions reveal a great deal about how American politics actually works in the age of polls, sound bites, think tanks, highly organized membership organizations, and single-issue coalitions. The standard depiction of policy-making in Washington tends to focus on the incestuous relationship between the nation's lawmakers in Congress and the slick, well-heeled lobbyists who ply their trade between Capitol Hill and K Street by day and grease political wheels through campaign contributions and fundraising parties by night. The tale of the estate tax's demise—an epic whose final chapter has yet to be written—is different. It defies what we think of how big money influences politics. And the forces that killed this tax are now poised to take on much larger prey.

Contrary to conventional wisdom, inside-the-beltway machinations from Gucci Gulch did not send the estate tax to its grave. Rather, the movement to kill the "death tax" (as its opponents very effectively renamed it) first started, and until the mid-1990s operated almost exclusively, outside the nation's capital. The tax's assailants ranged from farmers to florists, from cattle ranchers to newspaper owners, from the humblest of small businesses to some of the largest fortunes in the nation. For years Washington insiders viewed the movement to repeal the tax as a pipe dream. They tinkered at the tax's edges, hoping to ease its burden here or there. But the outsiders never wavered in their quest to eliminate the tax entirely, picking up support in Congress slowly but steadily. The force that brought this change about drew its strength, if not from the grassroots, at least from the grasstops of a large swath of American society.

To be sure, repeal would not have happened if this incredibly broad coalition of outsiders had not eventually come together under centralized leadership, deploying savvy Washington representatives and ideologically sympathetic insiders. By the late 1990s, this band of outsiders had united with Republican antitax philosophers, activists, and legislators, who regard all progressive taxation as morally obnoxious and economically destructive. Seeds of this movement date back to the late 1970s. It flowered a bit during Ronald Reagan's presidency, but it did not gather genuine political strength until the Republican takeover of the House in 1994. Since then, eliminating all taxes on wealth or income from wealth has become a matter of Republican orthodoxy. Indeed, as stunning as the estate tax repeal was, it is a bellwether of a larger conflict—over the future of progressive taxation in America. Estate tax repeal is one important strand of a looming effort to strip from our nation's tax system the very idea that those who have more should shoulder a larger share of the tax burden.

Many observers, who have become cynical about the role money now plays in our nation's political process, will not be surprised that the interests of the wealthy triumphed here. But money did not lubricate this particular legislative change in the way that most people would expect. Tax policy has always been a prime area where moneyed interests attempt to work their wiles on willing politicians. Yet in the estate tax debate, the big money players who stood to gain the most from repeal—the multimillionaires and billionaires looking to escape future taxes—remained in the background, giving relatively small campaign contributions and refraining from direct lobbying. The large sums of money that facilitated repeal did not buy legislators' votes. Money did play a crucial role, but a more indirect one, a role that cannot be curtailed within the American constitutional system.

The political movement to repeal the estate tax achieved a great victory with the passage of George W. Bush's massive 2001 tax-cutting bill. That unprecedented piece of legislation began a decade-long phaseout of the estate tax, culminating in a repeal scheduled for 2010. But the entire 2001 tax law "sunsets"; the repeal disappears in 2010 unless subsequent legislation extends it or makes its changes permanent. Because a new law is needed, Democrats remain complacent. Having failed to learn any lesson from their trouncing in 2001, they are in danger of losing the larger war.

Conceived at a time of huge projected surpluses in the federal budget, the 2001 tax cuts are now caught in a kind of limbo: with the surpluses gone, replaced by deficits as far as the eye can see, final repeal of the estate tax is by no means certain. But Democrats underestimate the power of the forces working to eliminate progressive taxation in America. The coalitions and their leaders are working as hard as ever. Their agenda for progressive taxation in America is simple: death by a thousand cuts.

This is a story about how power in this country actually works today. The unexpected and often counterintuitive events that led to the 2001 repeal have important implications for lawmaking—not just lawmaking about taxes and the redistribution of wealth or income, but about the entire machinery of persuasion that goes into creating legislation in twenty-first-century American politics. The stakes in this battle could not be higher. At issue is what kind of government we shall have and who shall pay to finance it.

The law at the center of this tale is simple enough. When a person who is among the very wealthiest in this country dies, his or her estate has to pay a portion of the value of its assets to the United States government before the rest of the estate can be passed on to children or other heirs. But there are several important caveats. If the estate is passed to a spouse, there is no tax. If the person leaves the money to a charity or sets up a charitable foundation, as so many of America's wealthiest individuals have over the years, none of the money donated is taxed. Depending on where the person lives, state estate taxes may also apply, although, until the 2001 legislation, most of these payments could offset what the estate owed the federal government.

Until the passage of the 2001 tax bill, the tax affected only individuals with assets of more than $650,000, or married couples with assets of more than $1.3 million—figures known as "the exemption." That is to say, the first $650,000 of any individual's estate was "exempt" from the tax, and the exemption was scheduled to rise to $1 million by 2002. Any amount above that would be taxed. In 1999, just 2.3 percent of all estates were taxed by the federal government; the other 97.7 percent of adults who died that year owed no estate tax. The average size of the estates taxed that year was $2.5 million. The average estate tax paid was $469,000, for an average tax rate of just under 19 percent. Combined, the taxes collected from these estates totaled $24.4 billion. This amount would fund nearly one-half of the total spending in 2004 of the Departments of Homeland Security or Education and is more than twice the size of annual Pell grants, the federal government's largest expenditure to help students attend college. Of the total revenue from the tax, more than half came from the richest 7 percent of taxable estates, those valued at $5 million or more, the wealthiest 0.1 percent of our society. Nearly one-quarter of the total revenue—$5.7 billion— came from the 550 estates with $20 million or more of wealth. And nearly two-thirds of the wealth taxed by the estate tax is publically traded securities and other liquid assets, not family business or farms.

First adopted in the nineteenth century to fund various wartime government revenue shortfalls, the estate tax in its modern form has been on the books continuously since 1916. While the tax rate levied on large estates went up and down over the years, the tax itself was, until the movement we describe, generally considered an uncontroversial means of raising federal revenue from those most able to pay. Perhaps the most amazing accomplishment of the network of coalitions that worked to repeal this tax is the way in which it changed so many people's opinions about who was affected by the tax and its fairness as a means of funding government. One poll showed 77 percent of the population believing that the estate tax affects all Americans. Many polls show that more than one-third of Americans believe that they themselves will have to pay the tax.

As effective as the repeal forces were, they benefited greatly from an inept and inattentive opposition. The more traditionally liberal forces, who thought they could defeat the repeal movement simply by pointing out the fact that only the richest 2 percent are taxed, utterly misread the political dynamic at work.

Why did appeals to economic self-interest fail? One reason is Americans' enduring belief in the personal attainability of great wealth—our enduring optimism. In the 2000 presidential race, speaking before rallies of middle-class citizens across the country, George W. Bush again and again received his most enthusiastic applause when he declared his intent to end the death tax. It was a political lesson that he and his advisors would not forget.

It would be wrong, however, to think that the president, the coalitions, and business groups merely hoodwinked people into mistaking the interests of the super-rich for their own. They also managed to win in the court of public opinion, by making a philosophical argument over the very legitimacy of taxing large accumulations of wealth. The death tax was brought to its knees by a decade-long assault on its political support, its philosophical underpinnings, indeed, its moral character. The philosophical argument about fairness and justice that was marshaled on behalf of repeal animates the entire story this book tells, and its origins run at least as far back as the founding of the country.

Is inheritance a natural right or a social privilege? That is a long-standing question. Is the wealth that is accumulated during a lifetime, either through work or investment, the sovereign possession of its current owner to dispose of entirely as he or she chooses? Or does society have some claim on it from having provided the markets, the rules of law, the security, and the enforcement that allowed the wealth to grow and develop? If inheritance is a natural right, government has no business taxing it. Such a levy would represent what repeals forces call "double taxation," because the money is taxed once when it is earned and again when it is passed on to the next generation.

But if inheritance is a privilege in a society that has helped the wealth come into being, then the government can legitimately tax it as it has throughout most of our history. Indeed the failure to tax large inheritances of wealth threatens the fundamental American value that everyone deserves an equal opportunity to succeed—an equal shot at the American Dream.

This argument, while in principle applicable to any and all inheritance, has in practice focused only on the legitimacy of taxing large fortunes. No one, not even the most ardent advocate for the estate tax, believes that middle-class Americans should have to pay the government any portion of whatever savings or assets they have managed to accumulate when they die. The question is and always has been how to treat the wealthy and the super-wealthy.

When he endorsed the idea of a tax on inheritance back in 1906, Theodore Roosevelt said that its "primary objective should be to put a constantly increasing burden on the inheritance of those swollen fortunes, which it is certainly of no benefit to this country to perpetuate." Andrew Carnegie agreed, believing unfettered inheritance of huge fortunes makes people idle and profligate. In the early part of the twentieth century, when the nation's images of wealth came from Rockefellers and railroad barons, the general public also tended to agree. They didn't like the idea of an economic aristocracy perpetuating itself generation after generation in a country founded on the idea of equal opportunity for all.

Today, the images—if not the realities—of wealth have changed. Despite the well-publicized greed of the Dennis Kozlowskis, Martha Stewarts, and Kenneth Lays, our most famous rich citizen is a computer entrepreneur who started his business in a garage and became a billionaire. If Bill Gates can do it, so can you—at least that is how the thinking goes. And if you start the business, work the long hours, earn the money, and pay income tax on it, why should the government get anything when you die, no matter how rich you become?

Moreover, we have become a nation of capitalists and wanna-be capitalists. Although the financial assets of most are quite small, more than half of all Americans—70 percent of those who vote—now have some stock market investments through their retirement plans. When Ronald Reagan became president, the number of investors was closer to 20 percent. And if, as George W. Bush has suggested, a portion of Social Security taxes is allowed to be invested rather than paid over to the government, the number of people with some stake in the stock market will grow dramatically. Protecting one's wealth is no longer a concern of only the upper crust.

Taking advantage of this changed view of wealth, and sometimes manipulating it, repeal forces effectively turned their cause into a moral crusade. Once the issue became one of abstract fairness to all rather than the best policy for treating giant accumulations of wealth in a democratic society, the philosophical argument had been won. Opponents of repeal were then on the defensive—never a good place to be in politics.

Within the larger mystery—how this change in the climate of opinion and political fortunes occurred so quickly and unexpectedly—lie two further mysteries. How did the coalitions for repeal stick together even after they were offered compromises that most observers would have expected to splinter them? And why was the opposition to the repeal incredibly paltry, late, and disorganized? Why were the Democrats and other groups who opposed repeal unable to stop the repeal juggernaut? Why was there no modern Teddy Roosevelt to warn the public of the dangers of rewarding dynastic wealth in America? What does the opposition's failure here tell us about their ability to thwart the coming attacks on progressive taxation in this country?

By the time the 2001 tax bill was being negotiated in Congress, Democrats and other repeal opponents were willing to raise the estate tax exemption well above $650,000 to $3 million, $4 million, or even $5 million. At this level the tax would have applied to only a miniscule slice of Americans, about the top one-quarter of one percent, but it would have still generated significant revenue. The vast majority of the small businesses that comprised the National Federation of Independent Businesses (NFIB), one of the most important and effective advocates for repeal, would have faced no tax liability whatsoever. Nor would most of the members of the other trade associations that had banded together to seek elimination of the tax. The number of farmers still subject to the levy would have been tiny. The choice became stark: an immediate, substantial increase in the estate tax exemption offered by the Democrats, or the Bush plan— a slowly phased-in repeal, with outright elimination postponed until the year 2010.

But by the time these reform proposals appeared as realistic legislative alternatives, the movement to repeal the death tax had already been absorbed into a larger Republican antitax crusade, an effort to reduce the size and functions of American government. The leaders of this wing of the Republican Party regard the tax issue, not the wedge issues of social policy, as the linchpin to a long-term Republican majority. One of its most effective and outspoken leaders, Grover Norquist, insists that taxation is "the central vote-driving issue." "You win this issue," he says, "you win—over time—all issues." The antitax forces and their strategists have no intention of stopping with the estate tax. How they won this campaign tells us much about what may lie ahead in the most contentious upcoming battles over tax policy.

The antitax zealots bided their time during the 1990s, winning votes and support wherever they could, patiently awaiting their next opportunity. By 2001, estate tax repeal provided just such a chance. The repeal coalitions had built up broad-based support among the voters and won over a majority of Congress by the late 1990s. When the 2000 presidential election brought us George W. Bush—a president who was willing to support repeal and who also subscribes to the more fundamental antitax philosophy—the stage was set. Not only did the conservative antitax zealots embrace estate tax repeal, an issue they had come to late, but they also fused the death tax coalition, which had been a single-issue movement, with their broader attack on taxation as we know it.

Once we understand the place of the estate tax in the long-term war against progressive taxation, it becomes easier to see why even a long-delayed and uncertain repeal became preferable to a certain and substantial reform. Accepting reform would have meant conceding the justice of the estate tax. But the antitax movement has built up a powerful philosophical attack on the very concept of progressive taxation that underpins the estate tax. And by 2001 their attacks on progressivity had fundamentally changed the nature of tax politics in America, reviving a debate that had seemingly been settled in the first decades of the twentieth century. The antitax fighters wanted to get repeal on the books, no matter what the form. They were willing to gamble that they would be able to take the next step and make repeal permanent. The story of how and why this occurred, based on extensive conversations with the players and powerbrokers on both sides, unmasks the hidden dynamics of lawmaking.

The opposition's mysterious weakness is another aspect of our story, and in unraveling it we see a mirror image of the repeal movement's "perfect storm," with its motivated activists, grassroots organization, articulate spokespeople, and eventual presidential backing. Opponents of repeal, such as they were, were completely outmaneuvered. They never saw repeal coming until it was well on its way down the tracks. They consistently underestimated the diverse array of forces—including minorities, gays, and environmentalists, as well as farmers and small businesses—that would press for repeal. When they offered any responses at all, they answered moral attacks with numerical and tactical replies. "But you don't pay the estate tax!" was their battle cry. An opposing philosophical case was never made. Those who wanted to retain the tax mainly played catch-up and closed stable doors. If the stories of the organized coalitions and their drive for repeal constitute a textbook for effective political action, the disarray of the opposition is a cautionary tale about relying on stale assumptions and diffuse preferences in a battle against intense and organized opponents.

Well beyond the particulars of the estate tax, the American public stands to learn a great deal from understanding what happened in this endeavor. Regardless of ideological or political commitments, whatever one's stand on this tax or any other, the public needs to know how power and politics actually operate in Washington today. And, whatever the final outcome, one thing is certain: this contest has radically altered the political landscape. The broader antitax force is marching forward in Washington and in the great heartland. The fundamental principle of progressive taxation is under attack. The movement to repeal the estate tax has been the vanguard in this crusade. How this occurred is, in the end, a peculiarly American story peopled by buccaneering newspapermen, political climbers, crusaders and ideologues, farmers and entertainers, beer distributors and billionaires. This is a story about the carnival of politics in the United States in the twenty-first century, and how it is shaping the world in which we all live.

Genesis of the Repeal Coalition

If politics is the art of the possible, political creativity involves seeing what is possible when others miss or it—or dismiss it. How the repeal proponents navigated the waters of the possible will concern us later. First we attend to the creative pioneers—those who believed the estate tax could be repealed and began working toward that goal as far back as the late 1980s. Why would anyone who could see straight imagine that a tax paid by only 2 percent of the wealthiest Americans could be abolished? When the repeal movement began, the Democrats had been firmly in control of the House of Representatives for a generation and showed no sign of losing it. Even when there had been administrations—such as Ronald Reagan's—with mandates for tax-cutting and tax-reform, abolishing the estate tax did not make it onto the agenda. Conservative economists expect a much bigger bang for the buck from cutting taxes on corporate earnings, dividends, and capital gains and from lowering the top income tax rates for individuals. All of these options also have larger natural political constituencies than estate tax repeal. To anyone who noticed the early advocates of estate tax repeal at all, they seemed eccentric, if not quixotic.

Those who knew their history understood the odds. The last time the modern estate tax had been seriously challenged was in 1925–26. Then, as now, Republicans controlled the White House and both houses of Congress—and repeal had failed. But the situation then was much different. Far from a long-coordinated groundswell against the tax, this earlier repeal movement was spearheaded by one of the richest men in the country, Andrew Mellon, who happened also to be Calvin Coolidge's treasury secretary. Mellon philosophically opposed the tax, but he also stood to gain a great deal from its repeal. He and his main ally in Congress, Reed Smoot, who later became famous for the Smoot-Hawley tariff, nearly succeeded. Yet, as we shall see later, these earlier repeal advocates were able to achieve only a reduction in the rate of the tax, not its elimination. Thus, history gave no succor to the early players in our story who envisioned removing estate taxes entirely from the tax code.

The pioneers for repeal of the late 1980s and early 1990s are easily forgotten from the perspective of what the main pro-repeal group, the Family Business Estate Tax Coalition (FBETC) later became. By the time of the 2001 tax act, the coalition included over a hundred member organizations representing some six million individuals and businesses. It had, by all accounts, run one of the most effective legislative campaigns in recent times—flawless in organization and execution, adept at managing internal tensions, professional in its public relations, and formidable in delivering constituency pressure to key politicians in time for critical votes. But this juggernaut for repeal was a creature of the last few years before the legislative victory. As recently as 1997, the leaders of the National Federation of Independent Businesses (NFIB)—the single most important coalition member—believed repeal unrealistic. As they saw it, reform geared to reducing the rates and increasing the exemption was the only serious option. They inhabited a very different universe from the disparate collection of individuals and groups that had been crusading for abolition, against apparently overwhelming odds, for the better part of a decade.

One early and passionate toiler was Jim Martin, president of "60 Plus Association," a seniors' organization dedicated to saving Social Security and killing the death tax. A University of Florida graduate who looks as if he could as well belong to a "70 Plus" or perhaps even "80 Plus" group, Martin is an intense, wiry man whose chiseled features sometimes cause people to confuse him with Ted Turner. Yet Martin's politics are the polar opposite of the CNN magnate's. Martin has worked for Republican causes and candidates for decades—indeed, he is proud of having given George W. Bush his first political job as a staffer in 1968. Bush calls Martin "Buddha." The 60 Plus Association membership base is largest in California, Florida, and Texas—where it can often count 2,000 members in a single congressional district. But the national organization runs on a shoestring out of a small suite of no-frills offices in Arlington, Virginia. The group presents its "Ben Franklin Award"— a plaque sporting the famous line that life's only certainties are death and taxes—to politicians who take its antitax pledge at photo ops, but after the cameras disappear Martin must retrieve the plaque to use with the next awardee. 60 Plus Association is really Martin's one-man operation—as the cheap nameplate on his desk underscores: "James L. Martin, Guiding Guru."

Death tax repeal—he was one of the first to urge adoption of the label—has been Martin's obsession since the early 1990s. In a series of conversations with Republican members of Congress in 1993 and 1994, the idea was hatched to form a "Kill the Death Tax Coalition" and begin sponsoring legislation in Congress. Martin's allies on Capitol Hill included Christopher Cox of California, Phil Crane of Illinois, Don Sundquist of Tennessee, and Bob Livingston of Louisiana. Crane had been sponsoring repeal bills since the 1980s, and Cox took the baton from him in 1993. But Martin understood early on that building a truly powerful coalition meant more than just multiplying cosponsors for legislation on the Hill: he would need support from a broad cross-section of organizations and interest groups, even though many saw his plan as nothing more than a pie-in-the-sky idea. Although the coalition was formed in 1993, by early 1997 at the latest, the pie had moved a little closer to earth. The Kill the Death Tax Coalition counted 42 members, including not only small business groups, trade associations, and the usual suspects for conservative causes but also organizations such as Concerned Women for America, Women for Tax Reform, the African American group Project 21, and Minority and Women-Owned Business in the DC metropolitan area. Not quite a rainbow coalition, perhaps, but one built on an understanding that success would mean making common cause with strange bedfellows.

Another early champion for estate tax repeal was Harold Apolinsky. Like Martin, Apolinsky came to the cause out of moral conviction and ideological commitment; neither of these men are wealthy individuals who stand to gain personally from repeal. Indeed, Apolinsky, an estate-tax planning attorney out of Birmingham, Alabama, is fond of saying that death tax repeal would put a considerable chunk of his firm out of business—but that he could no more oppose it than an oncologist could oppose finding a cure for cancer. A suave gentleman who sports polka-dot bowties atop finely cut suits, he has been described as a "Southern Paul Revere" for his fearless assault on the death tax. Indeed, Apolinsky has been building networks and coalitions to get rid of the tax since the 1980s, logging what he estimates as 125,000 hours of unpaid time. For years many colleagues dismissed his quest as quixotic, but he was fortified by his wife's observation, "I bet that's what people said about Orville and Wilbur Wright."

The year 1994 ushered in a new era in estate tax politics. The Republicans triumphantly took over the House of Representatives, and estate tax reform became part of their "Contract with America." By the following January, reform had worked its way onto the agenda of Congress's Small Business Committee, and Apolinsky was one of 11 experts invited to testify. He saw this invitation as his chance to start changing the terms of the mainstream debate from reform to repeal, even though he was the only one on the panel to advocate outright abolition. Even the business groups that were supporting him continued to behave as though they were humoring a well-intentioned eccentric.

Apolinsky understood that moving repeal into the realm of the possible required two things on Capitol Hill: communicating what was at stake for people who faced the tax in moving human terms and finding credible research to back up the individual stories. He had gripping stories first-hand from clients who had confronted estate tax liability along with terminal illness. One such death tax victim was the prominent Alabaman developer John Harbert, and Apolinsky recites his story with poignancy and passion. One of the wealthiest men in Alabama, Harbert was given six months to live and was then devastated to discover the estate tax's implications for his powerplant business. Six weeks before his death in 1995, Harbert began contributing to Apolinsky's fund for research to support repeal. Some 40 other families pitched in as well, giving Apolinsky $200,000 to fund a study by Bill Beach, a senior researcher at the Heritage Foundation. Beach's study, "The Case for Repealing the Estate Tax," became Heritage's core paper on the issue, and it spawned other research geared to showing that the estate tax is inimical to economic growth and costs more to comply with and administer than it generates in revenue. From then on Apolinsky raised about $200,000 a year for the repeal effort. Funders included the American Family Business Institute, a dozen or so of Apolinsky's individual clients, and a man named Frank Blethen, owner and publisher of the *Seattle Times*.

The *Seattle Times,* founded in 1896 by Blethen's great-grandfather, is now Washington state's largest daily newspaper with half a million readers. It employs more than 3,000 workers and is valued at $350 million. The holding company, in which Blethen is the majority owner, is structured to keep ownership of the paper in the family.

Blethen is so passionate about the *Times* that he has its logo tattooed on his leg. Meeting him, you wouldn't think he was the tattoo type. With his twinkling blue eyes, elfin nose, and white beard, this 50-year-old newspaper publisher looks more like an undersized Santa Claus than a hard-boiled professional lobbyist. Blethen is gentle and earnest, energetic and determined. Capitol Hill is now familiar terrain to him. He has been there often since the early 1990s, crusading against the death tax. He insists that he and his family have no personal stake in repeal: they have done enough planning, corporate restructuring, and gift giving, he says, to make certain that "we've got no dog in this hunt." However, he deeply resents the $150,000 he spends each year on life insurance to fund potential estate tax liabilities.

So why does Blethen care so much? "I just believe passionately in small family businesses," he says. He hates the consolidation of American businesses, especially newspapers, and he blames the estate tax. He insists that "Gannett built their chain on the back of the death tax," by buying up newspapers that were sold to pay the levy. And his ire extends far beyond the newspaper business. "You see the same thing with RiteAid in the state of Maine—local drugstores closing down. But big isn't always beautiful. Now RiteAid is bankrupt, and the people that run these places, the newspapers in particular, are MBA types, that's their lingo, business, not newspapers. They don't think about winning Pulitzers, they're just thinking about the bottom line." Blethen regards himself as a political liberal. "In all of this," he adds, "you have to remember that the system is really stacked against family businesses. I just find it intuitively unfair that the government should take what you've earned and paid tax on once already."

By all accounts, Blethen has been one of the most effective advocates of death tax repeal. He created the deathtax.com website, a key resource for repeal advocates, and he promoted the effective Death Tax Summits, where reform advocates gathered in Washington to pump up the troops and lobby members of Congress. It was Blethen who first saw the value of involving minorities, gays, environmentalists, and other unlikely groups in the repeal campaign, and he mobilized newspaper owners across the nation to oppose the tax.

Apolinsky credits Blethen with bringing anti-repeal forces from around the country together in 1995. At that time there were as many proposed remedies for the ills of the tax as there were opponents. A carve-out for family businesses, for example, which eventually became law in 1998, was first proposed by Republican Senator Bob Dole of Kansas, who was acting at the suggestion of his former tax aide, Rich Belas—an advocate for the National Cattlemen's Beef Association, another early pro-repeal group, nicknamed "the Don Quixote of tax reform" by the media. Other suggested fixes included generous provisions for delays in paying the tax, increases in the exclusion, decreases in the rates, and exceptions for family farms and small businesses. Proponents of all these various remedies shared an antipathy for the death tax, but as yet lacked any common vision of what to do about it. For Blethen, Apolinsky, Martin, and the other early repeal advocates, to transform their disparate visions into a single guiding force would take resources, organizational skill, and the wherewithal to persevere over time. These building blocks were provided by Pat Soldano.

A small, well-groomed woman in her fifties with bright blue eyes, Soldano had her own inspiring personal stories to add to the cause. She began managing the assets of Frederick Field, the heir to the Marshall Field's department store fortune, in 1980. Since then she has added a select number of wealthy families to her portfolio, establishing family offices for them, managing their investments, and doing their accounting and tax planning—a formidable task, given that a typical client has a minimum of $25 million in liquid assets. In 1987, Soldano established a family office for the Brown family of California, whose wealth came from oil and gas properties. The office was called Cymric Family Office Services—named after the Brown's California oil-producing territory—and Soldano became its sole owner in 1996. The Brown family remained a client, and she took on several others. Families such as the Plimptons of New Jersey, the Mars family, the Gallo wine family, and the heirs to the Campbell's soup and Krystal fast-food fortunes may not be Cymric clients, but they all contributed money to Soldano's efforts to eliminate the estate tax. Melding business with personal ties is Soldano's hallmark characteristic. Cymric's website proclaims, "It is our mission to help families define and achieve their personal and financial goals."

Soldano's intense personal empathy for her clients is reflected in her account, published by the Newspaper Association of America, of the untimely death of Tina Brown. Diagnosed with ovarian cancer at the age of 38, Brown was "brilliant, beautiful, and a caring American who loved life," Soldano writes. "Once she knew that her time was short, she was told even more bad news! If she did not want the assets that she had been recently gifted from her grandfather to be taxed at a 55 percent rate of tax, she could not let her German-citizen husband be the trustee of her assets." Resolving these issues consumed many of Brown's final days and hours, the story continues. "Tina died after complying with the death tax laws, spending her last weeks and days doing something that she hated to do even when she was alive." Compounding the family tragedy, Tina's mother Pat was stricken with lung cancer five years after she had watched her daughter die. "Even though she had done her best to divest herself of her assets by donating to over 70 different charities on an annual basis," Soldano writes, "she still had substantial assets from the business that her father and mother built." Pat Brown died three months later. The federal government subsequently received "a very large check" covering the Browns' estate tax liability, for which substantial family assets had to be sold. Pat Brown's surviving children spent months winding up her estate, which required a six-inch-thick tax return. The Brown family saga, according to Soldano, revealed the fundamental inequities of the death tax. "Families work hard, build businesses and create jobs. Why at death should they be penalized for doing that?"

But wrenching personal stories of the costs of the estate tax to America's wealthy are just the tip of an iceberg. The families that Soldano represents have battled long and hard to get Washington to reduce their estate tax liability. The Gallos, in particular, have long invested in contributions to politicians of both political parties while searching for special estate tax treatment. In 1978, California Democratic Senator Alan Cranston, to whom the Gallos had given over $3,000 in the 1974 campaign, pushed a Gallo wine amendment: the Gallo heirs received ten years to pay off estate taxes, instead of paying the full amount immediately upon inheritance. Eight years later, Senator Dole supported another "Gallo amendment" to be included in the 1986 tax reform bill. During one week while the bill was being written, Dole received four $5,000 Gallo-family contributions, and in July of that year he received $29,000 from the family for a Los Angeles dinner he sponsored. Dole's amendment would have let the Gallos pass on $5 million to each grandchild without incurring estate taxes. It did not pass, but a $2 million per grandchild "Gallo exemption" was approved.

Given this success with death tax lobbying, why did the Gallos need Pat Soldano or an organized repeal movement? Well, the Gallo amendment's exclusion was subsequently reduced to $1 million per grandchild, underscoring the limits of ad hoc solutions and the wealthy families' desire for Soldano's efforts at repeal. Since the 1990s, the Gallos and the Mars family have reportedly contributed tens of thousands of dollars to both Soldano's Center for the Study of Taxation, a not-for-profit lobbying and research group she formed to address the estate tax, and the Policy and Taxation Group, the lobbying organization dedicated to estate tax repeal that she founded in 1992. The liberal Center for Responsive Politics reports that the lobbying income for the group, largely derived from the Mars and Gallo families as well as some other large privately held companies, added up to $256,500 in 1997 and $266,000 in 1998. In 1999, the group's lobbying expenditures totaled $493,307, and $345,244 in 2000.

In the movement's early days, however, Soldano's efforts weren't nearly as elaborate or well organized as they were to become. Washington insiders confirm her claims to have been a political innocent in the early 1990s, when she first started visiting the nation's capital from Orange County. "I didn't even know how to meet a staff person," she says. Soldano gives the impression she relied on the kindness of strangers. "People in Washington are so nice, so very helpful. They're always willing to tell you who you should meet with."

Many lobbyist-lawyers make a living in Washington by telling others who to meet with. The Patton Boggs law firm is legendary for its lobbying skills, and Soldano hired them to help her meet people and strategize about repealing the estate tax. "People don't always take calls from California," as Soldano says. Her early meetings in the Capitol were mostly with staffers. Occasionally she brought family office clients, but mostly she traveled alone.

Thanks to her wealthy clients, Soldano had the financial wherewithal to get attention in Washington, but money buys only access—not guaranteed results. From time to time it might help buy ad hoc exceptions such as those enjoyed by the Gallos, but it does not put together coalitions or ensure ambitious legislative successes on the scale envisaged in the aspiration to abolish the estate tax.

In 1992, when Soldano first began her lobbying efforts, repeal was an exceedingly long-shot proposition. Patton Boggs's competitors in town regarded success as so unlikely that they often joked that the firm was taking Soldano's money for guiding her on tours of the nation's capital. Soldano, Blethen, and the others contemplating repeal had to face the reality that both houses of Congress were then controlled by Democrats and that Bill Clinton, the newly elected Democratic president, was utterly without sympathy for their cause. But necessity is the mother of invention. Precisely because the odds were stacked so heavily against them, the early repeal advocates had to ready themselves to be effective should the political climate change. They began to think creatively about unlikely allies who might be induced to support their cause.

Soldano and Blethen were true visionaries. They both understood from the beginning that success would depend on distinguishing estate tax repeal from other conservative agendas: it had to appeal to a variety of non–traditionally Republican constituencies. Realizing that first-generation minority business owners would be vulnerable to the tax, for example, Soldano was one of the repeal leaders, along with Blethen, to start courting their support. She talked to the Black Chamber of Commerce and other minority groups, and reached out to gays and lesbians through opinion pieces pointing out how the lack of a marital deduction compounds their potential estate tax liability. Perhaps Soldano's most natural sell was to a group that could intimately relate to her: female business owners. A successful businesswoman in her own right, Soldano was keenly aware that the nation now had a large cohort of women with significant assets, many of whom might be mobilized for repeal. She herself represents Women Impacting Public Policy, whose members own over 300,000 small- to medium-sized businesses across the country. She gives out her business card for this organization when she meets with people about the estate tax.

Mobilizing women, minorities, gays, and lesbians required that estate tax repeal not become sullied by association with other controversial political agendas in which these groups might have stakes. Affirmative action, social programs, gay marriage, child care—these would all be off limits for what had to be, and had to be seen as, a single-issue campaign. They would lose unless they kept their eye on the ball.

Soldano and Blethen also knew that any coalition to repeal the estate tax would fail if it was seen as a tool of the ultra-wealthy. Popular support could be garnered only if people could empathize with those who were vulnerable to the death tax—not only with terminally ill multimillionaires such as Tina and Pat Brown, but also with ordinary people who had worked hard all their life to build a nest egg that was about to be smashed by a voracious federal government. The working rich, not the idle rich, had to become the poster children of the movement. Soldano was one of the first to float the oft-repeated argument that the ultra-wealthy can take care of themselves through foundations, trusts, and other financial instruments; in other words, Soldano and her allies worked hard to ensure that the public would see the estate tax as a small- and medium-sized business issue.

Blethen brought a different populist twist to this agenda, pushing his claim that the death tax fosters corporate consolidation. Family-owned newspapers, vulnerable because they might well have a net worth of many millions but few liquid assets, are bought up by the likes of Gannett when sold to pay the estate tax. Similar arguments about family farms and supermarkets could pull their trade associations into the repeal coalition while legitimating members' concerns as something to which middle Americans could readily relate. People like Soldano's families could help bankroll the coalition and its efforts, but they would need to stay in the background. The foot soldiers would have to look like middle America—or at any rate they would have to look like what middle Americans respect and aspire to become.

Of course, this is not to say that the super-wealthy ever lost their stake in the repeal coalition. Soldano estimates that 65 wealthy families now support her research and lobbying groups for repeal, the Center for the Study of Taxation and her Policy and Taxation Group, including some of her wealthy Cymric clients. Overall, there are people in 25 states involved in her Policy and Taxation Group. Many of them remain invisible, preferring the public face of the repeal effort to be an owner of a small but growing business, preferably an African American, a Hispanic, or a woman.

By the mid-1990s, Soldano's individual work had borne fruit, and she was ready to pass the reins to the professionals. She helped form the Family Business Estate Tax Coalition which, together with the NFIB, began to coordinate the repeal movement. Typically, Soldano has spent 30 to 40 percent of her time on this lobbying effort.

The FBETC, out of all the various ad hoc groups and committees formed by the early visionaries, was the one that developed traction and staying power. Established in 1995, it was initially composed of some 45 business and trade associations led by the NFIB, the National Association of Manufacturers (NAM), the American Farm Bureau, the National Cattlemen's Beef Association, the Food Marketing Institute (FMI), the Newspaper Association of America, and Soldano's Policy and Taxation Group. The FBETC came to serve as the main anti–estate tax information clearinghouse. Its leaders would run monthly coordinating meetings, gather and disseminate information, organize spokespeople, work to answer critics, and activate constituency pressure. In 1995 the FBETC was little more than a shoestring operation, funded with $500 annual contributions from each member. But it had great potential as a political instrument. The most important of its leaders was the NFIB, widely regarded as the most influential business organization in Washington—and ranked third overall among *Fortune* magazine's "Washington's Power 25," behind only the National Rifle Association and the American Association of Retired Persons. The NFIB has 600,000 small business members, many of which are in fact quite small. Nearly three-quarters of NFIB's members employ fewer than ten people, and almost 80 percent have less than $1 million in annual sales. The National Association of Manufacturers (itself one of *Fortune*'s top ten lobbying groups) represents about 14,000 businesses, two-thirds of which are small and mid-sized. The Food Marketing Institute represents food wholesalers and retailers, more than half of which are family- or privately owned. The American Farm Bureau, widely regarded as the most influential farm group in Washington, is known for its ability to generate grass-roots support for its policies. The National Cattlemen's Beef Association is the trade association for cattle farmers and ranchers, and it would play a particularly important role in the Senate. The Newspaper Association of America represents family-owned newspapers; it helped formulate ads and other media opportunities for publicizing the coalition's efforts. Even before joining the estate tax fight, many of the FBETC's members maintained Washington offices with full-time lobbyists and support staffs. Most knew one another, having worked together on small business issues before. They all had the capacity to identify quickly, communicate with, and mobilize members in vital constituencies.

Before the FBETC could do any real work, its various members had to agree on their goal and then stick to it in the face of countervailing political forces. As the absence of the word "Repeal" from the organization's name indicates, the member groups may have shared estate tax problems, but they lacked a common vision of what to do about them. Some disagreements flowed from competing views of what was politically feasible, with the NFIB leadership in particular convinced that political realists should go for some combination of reduced rates and an expanded exemption. But some of the disagreements stemmed from deeper conflicts of interest. An exclusion for family farms, for example, had obvious potential to hive that sector off from the rest—as would eventually occur to the Democrats. But more on that later.

There were subtler conflicts as well. It was widely agreed inside the beltway that estate tax repeal would involve getting rid of the so-called step-up-in-basis—the tax law provision that allows the revaluing of inherited assets at their fair market value at death for the purpose of assessing capital gains tax liability. Eliminating the step-up-in-basis would be exceedingly costly for those family businesses—most commonly newspapers and farms—where the assets had been held for many decades, greatly appreciating in value. But without this quid pro quo, the claim that the estate tax amounts to double taxation would not sell. Despite these potential wedge issues and centrifugal forces, the FBETC stuck together and even prevailed.

As we leave these early days of organizing and move on to one of the main events that made eventual repeal possible—the Republican takeover of Congress in 1994—it is worth remembering just how unlikely a prospect total repeal of the estate tax was when the pioneers of the movement whom we've described here—Martin, Apolinsky, Blethen, and Soldano—began their work. Mellon had failed in the 1920s under a Republican president. Bill Clinton occupied the White House now, and even some of the main advocates for repeal didn't believe it possible. If there is an answer to the mystery of how this tax was brought down, a large part of it lies in understanding the crucial role of true believers and crusaders, those who began not from a place of practicality but from one of conviction and even anger. The energy and determination that these people brought to their work would eventually catalyze a much larger movement.

Squall or Sea Change?

The Republicans swept both Houses of Congress in November 1994 for the first time in a generation. Dan Balz described them in the *Washington Post* as riding a "tidal wave of voter discontent." R. W. Apple in the *New York Times* put it down to voter dissatisfaction "with President Clinton, with liberalism, with the Democratic Party, and with Washington in general." These assessments were accurate, but they left unanswered the larger question: Did this election mean an end to the Democratic congressional dynasty that had been entrenched in Washington since the Eisenhower administration?

Certainly many Democrats behaved as if 1994 were a temporary interregnum in a natural order that soon would be restored. Showing an imperviousness unimaginable in any other democracy, those at the party's helm would continue in control for nearly a decade, without any discernible changes in strategy or tactics or, indeed, without indication that such changes were judged necessary. After 1994, there would be no turnover in the House or Senate Democratic leadership until they had lost the next four congressional elections—and then only when Dick Gephardt decided to run for president in 2004.

For Republicans, 1994 could not have been more different. Hungry for power after decades in the wilderness, their victory was both the culmination of an insurgency within the party and a key moment of a revolutionary odyssey to redefine the shape of American national politics. They saw it as a potential sea change rather than a squall or even a tidal wave. Yet they did not take the new waters for granted. One of the main behind-the-scenes players in the Republican takeover, Grover Norquist, likes to repeat Winston Churchill's insistence that when the tide first turned in World War II, it represented the end of the beginning, not the beginning of the end. The statesman's phrase captures well the essence of the post-1994 Republican revolutionary ethos: critically important victories must be recognized, even memorialized, but they must also inspire renewed commitment to meet the greater challenges that lie ahead.

Newt Gingrich, who led the House Republicans to victory and authored their manifesto, the "Contract with America," was a close confidant of Norquist with a similar eye for the big picture and the goal of producing irreversible change. With a doctorate in history from Tulane University and having authored books with titles like *To Renew America* and *Window of Opportunity*, as well as creating a satellite TV course on "Renewing American Civilization," Gingrich was the main force behind the House Republican Party's transformation. First elected to Congress (on his third attempt) in 1979 at the age of 36, the precocious Georgian immediately got himself appointed to a task force to plan for a GOP majority. Gingrich was always a controversial figure, plagued by charges of financial and other ethical improprieties. A strong partisan of the view that the best defense is a good offense, he ascended rapidly within the GOP in good part via relentless attacks on Democratic leaders for their ethics violations—indeed, he eventually brought down House Speaker Jim Wright, in 1989. That same year, Gingrich was elected minority whip by two votes in a bitter fight that was seen as a victory for the Young Turks over the GOP old boy networks. The fight was on to transform the wilderness opposition into the party of government.

Gingrich's ascendance to the top of the House GOP heap reflected a conscious reformation of the party's strategy. For much of the 1980s, the Georgian had been widely seen as verging on the political lunatic fringe, even by many congressional Republicans. Yet their inability to challenge the Democrats seriously even during Ronald Reagan's ascendancy (they suffered severe midterm losses in 1982) eventually forced the party to come to grips with reality: the go-along, get-along leadership of the moderate House Republican leader, Bob Michel from Illinois, was not going to get them into the majority. Under Michel, the House GOP's response to its long-term minority status had been to search for bipartisanship. To participate in legislation, the party may have had no other choice. Bill Frenzel, a respected Republican moderate from Minnesota who served in the House minority for 20 years, explains that there is no other way to have influence in the House when you are not the majority party. Majority status matters less in the Senate, where voting rules—particularly the possibility of filibusters—empower individual senators even when they are in the minority.

In any case, the Republicans had controlled the Senate from 1981 through 1986, and often seemed close to winning it again. But by the late 1980s the situation of House Republicans seemed all but hopeless. They had been out of power for so long that radical rethinking was needed if things were going to change. Accordingly, as little as Frenzel liked Gingrich's scorched earth, take-no-prisoners approach to politics, he ended up nominating the Georgian for the Republican leadership as one of his final acts before retiring in 1990.

Gingrich certainly brought a new style to Republican House politics, geared to confrontation rather than finding a middle ground. As Frenzel puts it, "Until 1994 everyone accepted that tax policy was made on the margin." The name of the game was tinkering and incremental change to a structure that was largely accepted as legitimate. Even major legislation, such as the 1986 tax reform act, was geared to the ideologically unexceptional goal of tax simplification, and it had to be both revenue and distributionally neutral. Republicans pulled in one direction and Democrats in another, to be sure, but everyone understood that the result would be some form of splitting the difference.

Gingrich and the Young Turks signaled that this brand of politics was over in 1990 when they refused to participate in the elder George Bush's deficit reduction package, which involved raising taxes—and breaking the president's "no new taxes" pledge of his 1988 campaign. "They may have been right," Frenzel was later quoted as saying of the Gingrichites, underscoring his ambivalence about them. "But they've never had the responsibility of running the government," he said. "What they were offered here was a small share and they turned it down. That little act of insurrection cost us about $20 billion in spending cuts." He added ruefully, "It is what happens when you decide to be pure rather than practical."

When the 1990 deficit-reduction act became law, Gingrich refused to appear with the president and the other congressional leaders in the Rose Garden to announce the compromise—distancing himself from Bush for the remainder of his administration. This gesture was a portent of things to come. A few years later, House Speaker Gingrich would refuse to include House Democrats—now in the minority—in a bipartisan budget agreement, leading eventually to a confrontation with the Clinton White House that would shut down the federal government.

Gingrich's antipathy for the moderate Republicanism of Bob Michel and George H. W. Bush bound him to his allies in the emerging House Republican leadership. Tom DeLay, a Houston millionaire who had made his money in a pest-control business and was elected to the House in 1984, would become majority whip with the Republican takeover a decade later; Dick Armey, also elected from Texas that year, would become majority leader. DeLay, nicknamed "The Hammer," is famous for confrontational politics and for such memorable one-liners as calling the Environmental Protection Agency the "Gestapo of government." Armey sponsored a resolution condemning Bush for breaking his tax pledge. He has a Ph.D. in economics from the University of Oklahoma and was the author, along with Gingrich, of much of the "Contract With America." It is notable in an institution famous for being dominated by lawyers that none of the Young Turk leadership came from the bar. They were either businessmen such as DeLay, or conservative intellectuals such as Armey and Gingrich. Their background and agenda made them Grover Norquist's natural allies, bound together by the common goal of massively shrinking the federal government.

Unlike the Young Turks who took over the House in 1994, Norquist is not well known outside the beltway. Yet he has become a towering figure in Washington's conservative circles since the Reagan years and was integral to the 1994 Republican takeover and to its tax-cutting agenda. President of Americans for Tax Reform (ATR), which "opposes all tax increases as a matter of principle," Norquist has spent two decades fingerprinting politicians with his Taxpayer Protection Pledge demanding opposition to "any and all" tax increases (signed by 212 representatives and 37 senators by 2003). He believes in advancing on a broad front, pushing as many tax cuts as possible to see which ideas gain political traction. His goal? "To cut the government in half in 25 years, to get it down to the size where we can drown it in the bathtub." Norquist works closely with conservative foundations such as Olin, Scaife, Heritage, and Bradley, some of which have joined a variety of corporate backers in funding his activities. Gingrich describes Norquist as "the most creative and most effective conservative activist in the country," and "the person who I regard as the most innovative, creative, courageous, and entrepreneurial leader of the anti-tax efforts and of conservative grassroots activism in America."

Norquist is a bearded, owlish man in his mid-forties who paces like a 20-year-old. His second-floor corner office in ATR's L Street headquarters

is functional, yet large enough for him to move around while he talks—
and divides his attention between us and his mail. We find ourselves peri-
odically at the other end of a giant Bowie knife that he uses to open his letters, and which he thumps vaguely in our direction when he wants to make
a point. His demeanor is more middle America than eastern establishment,
but he speaks with an unstinting confidence that reflects his Harvard undergraduate and MBA degrees. As he flits from topic to topic, striding back
and forth like a caged tiger in front of the medication box on his desk (labeled for days of the week), we cannot help but wonder momentarily
whether he is chronically hyperactive—or perhaps a sufferer of attention
deficit disorder.

But this is wrong on both counts. Norquist is legendary for his steely-
eyed focus and his relentless determination to achieve an irreversible re-
alignment of American politics. He carries a timeline around in his pocket
that runs from 1980 through the mid-twenty-first century on which he
has neatly laid out his legislative agenda—for everything from abolishing
affirmative action and privatizing Social Security to renaming a building
for Ronald Reagan in every county in America. Described by the *Wall
Street Journal*'s Paul Gigot as "The V. I. Lenin of the anti-tax movement,"
Norquist is widely—if somewhat grudgingly—acknowledged as a major
and continuing force behind the reorientation of the Republican Party and
an important player in the George W. Bush administration. "We is them
and they is us," he has said on Pat Robertson's "700 Club" and elsewhere.
"When I walk through the White House, I recognize as many people as
when I walk through the Heritage Foundation." Norquist makes no secret
of his determination to use this influence to move America as far down
his timeline as possible, and he is adroit at pulling in potential allies along
the way.

His strategy is inclusive. Not himself a social or religious conservative,
he has been as careful as Ronald Reagan was not to alienate them. Norquist
sits on the board of the National Rifle Association and the American Conservative Union, and he seldom misses a chance to launch barbs, leavened
with his memorable wit, at their liberal antagonists. Where other conservatives question whether abolishing the death tax will really reduce charitable giving, as many claim, Norquist retorts that he would rather see the
wealthy drink their money away "like the Kennedys" than create foundations to be run by their liberal heirs. "America does not need another twenty

Ford Foundations" he says, punching that Bowie knife for emphasis. He predicts that this will indeed be the result if the new wealth created in the 1990s remains subject to the present tax code.

Norquist built ATR into a spearhead of the conservative movement during the first Bush and Clinton presidencies. He had no love for either of those two chief executives, but he backed George W. Bush early in the 2000 Republican presidential primaries as the best potential standard-bearer for his cause. Norquist has worked closely with both the younger Bush's White House and the Republican leadership on the Hill to craft and build support for tax cuts since 2000. He holds invitation-only "Wednesday Meetings" at which about 100 conservative lobbyists, politicians, and opinion-leaders meet to exchange information and plan legislative strategy. The Wednesday Meetings are now mimicked in 39 states—he promises that it will eventually be 50—where ATR sponsors and coordinates state and local antitax efforts, orchestrating grassroots support for Norquist's national agenda.

Critics such as the *New York Times*'s Paul Krugman often point out that Norquist, the New Republican Turks, the George W. Bush administration, and the conservative movement always advocate the same policies (deep cuts in taxes, particularly on wealth or income from capital) regardless of the political-economic climate. Whether the economy is growing or in recession, whether the federal budget is running a surplus or a deficit, whether the country is at war or at peace—the proffered remedy is always the same. Democrats are quick to cite this consistent refrain as evidence of either Republican disingenuousness or lack of sophistication. Yet this very objection underscores how little the critics grasp of the revolution in the GOP and its leaders' aspirations since 1994. The ascendant conservatives have no interest in politics on the margin or in managing the next recession or the one after that. They see themselves as engaged in a cumulative and historic project to reorder the nature and goals of American government. Bill Frenzel remarks that the Democrats continue to behave as if the basic questions of distributive politics in America were settled 70 years ago, while the Republicans who took over in 1994 have been determined to put the questions back on the agenda and resolve them differently. One Republican staffer summed up the divergent perceptions: "Democrats were put on earth to raise taxes; Republicans were put here to stop them."

Listening to Norquist makes you realize why some political observers now distinguish Republicans from Democrats by suggesting that Democrats want to be right, while Republicans want to win. It is not that Norquist doubts he is right. On the contrary, he exudes an almost fanatical aura of certitude about the wisdom and justice of his cause. But his relentless focus is on how to move the ball down the field. Everything he says assumes that there will be forces arrayed against him that will need to be vanquished, not persuaded or compromised with. He is happy to take help from any quarter, so long as cooperation does not mean negotiating over the core principles of his "center right" coalition. He reportedly identifies bipartisanship with "date rape" (a line that originated with Dick Armey when the Republicans were in the minority), insisting that conservatives cannot advance their agenda without taking principled stands and drawing lines in the sand. The confrontational stance of the Young Turks who took over the Republican Party on the Hill in the early 1990s was music to his ears, and he has worked effectively with them to craft their legislative agenda and get it enacted.

Rejecting compromise does not mean rejecting pragmatism for Norquist. In fact, he is quite open to incremental advance. His overall goal is to abolish all taxes on capital and move America to a consumption or wage tax, but he realizes that the federal tax law cannot be rewritten in one fell swoop. However, he is interested in piecemeal change only if it clearly advances toward his goal. On the estate tax he has been unequivocal from the start that he "would not cross the street" to reform it by reducing the rates or expanding the exemption. Such reform, he is sure, would be undone by inflation and the passage of time, ultimately reinforcing the status quo. More seriously, it would involve conceding the legitimacy of the underlying tax, and therefore abandoning the moral high ground. How can it be acceptable to have a death tax for people above a certain wealth threshold but not for those below it? What principled basis could possibly justify treating farmers differently from the rest of us? Norquist is certain that there are no winning answers to these questions.

In the early years Norquist was skeptical of the feasibility of a repeal, but he could not see the point of getting behind anything less—though the "Contract with America" took a different tack. In this respect, sweeping innovators that they were, even the authors of the contract underestimated how radical the possibilities might be. They called for reform of the estate tax, not its abolition, and the legislation they first proposed in 1995 envisaged gradual expansion of the exclusion from $600,000 to $750,000 over three years, after which it would have been indexed for inflation. Norquist, on the other hand, thought it better to take a page from the environmentalists' playbook and sign up cosponsors for a bill that no one takes seriously just to get it onto the agenda. If you get enough sponsors, the unthinkable can become thinkable. As a result, even when few apart from the likes of Jim Martin, Harold Apolinsky, Frank Blethen, and Pat Soldano took the possibility of repeal seriously, Norquist thought the pioneers had the right approach. It fit into his overall agenda of restructuring the entire tax code over the long haul.

The Republican takeover of Congress in 1994 indeed turned out to be far more of a sea change than a squall. Nonetheless, the 1994 revolutionaries' treatment of the estate tax again demonstrates just how extreme an idea total repeal was: even Newt Gingrich and his fellow Turks, usually impatient with compromise, could not envision getting rid of the tax altogether.

Before the quest for repeal would take hold of the Republican majority, at least one compromise would have to fail and the cause would need to acquire a strong congressional advocate, someone to pick up the repeal banner and drive it to the finish line.

An Opportunity Missed

If you wish to conquer, first divide. Few political issues better demonstrate the power of this approach than the battle over taxing American inheritances. And yet the opposition to repeal of the death tax, diffuse and disorganized, missed its golden opportunity to do just this. By the mid-1990s, groups such as the Family Business Estate Tax Coalition and their allies had managed to bring together an unlikely combination of super-wealthy families and working farmers, scions who had inherited all their money and car dealers who had worked for every penny. If the interests of the more numerous but less wealthy members of these coalitions—the farmers and small business owners, who were crucial in the contest for votes in Congress—could be satisfied by some kind of compromise, the charge for repeal would have faltered soon enough. In unraveling the mystery of how a tax affecting the rich was successfully transformed into a populist issue, there is no underestimating the damage done by a failed attempt to reform the tax rather than eliminate it.

When the anti–estate tax coalition first came together in the early 1990s, outright repeal seemed a hopeless quest. Bill Clinton, a Democrat not sympathetic to repeal, had moved into the White House in January 1993, a time when his party also controlled both houses of Congress. The federal budget was in deficit, and projected to remain so, far into the future. Budget rules adopted in 1990 required that any tax cuts must be paid for either by offsetting tax increases or by cuts in specific categories of government spending. Bill Clinton's priority was to raise taxes to put the federal government's financial house in better order, not to lower them. Even estate tax reductions seemed a pipe dream.

But savvy Washington insiders recognized the potential political power of a coalition of associations of small business owners, farmers, and ranchers. They also understood the irresistible appeal of their main argument: burdensome estate taxes, with rates topping out at 55 percent, would frequently force the liquidation or sale of a family business built up over a lifetime or more. As the repeal proponents often would say, "On the day the owner of the business dies, the government becomes the majority shareholder."

Facing an unfriendly climate for repeal in the early days of the Clinton White House, the coalition decided to channel its energy and dollars toward a more realistic alternative. The estate tax has long contained some minor provisions to aid small business owners and farmers. They may, for example, delay payment of the tax for as much as ten years and pay only a discounted rate of interest; another rule allows farmers to value their land for estate tax purposes at its working-farm value, rather than at the higher market price that the land would get if sold off for suburban housing. The coalition decided to press for an expanded exemption and lower tax rates for small businesses and family farms. Washington insiders convinced those who preferred pushing for repeal that this step was the only realistic alternative and that it would move in the right direction. Repeal proponents had little enthusiasm for the effort, but they went along.

In 1993 and 1994, the National Cattlemen's Beef Association, represented by Richard Belas, a former staffer for Senator Robert Dole, laid the groundwork. Northwestern lumber interests joined in, as did the NFIB, the American Farm Bureau, and other small-business trade associations. Soon they had constructed a bandwagon.

In July 1995, Senators Dole and David Pryor, a Democrat from Bill Clinton's home state of Arkansas, went to the Senate floor and introduced the American Family-Owned Business Act of 1995. This bill would have created a special $1.5 million exemption for family businesses and farms and would have taxed any excess over that at half the normal estate tax rates, thereby creating a maximum 27.5 percent rate. When first introduced in mid-summer, the Dole-Pryor proposal had 32 senators as cosponsors; by October, Dole and Pryor had added 12 more. In winning colleagues to his side, Senator Dole had listed for them the groups that supported this legislation. The list included the NFIB, the National Cattlemen's Beef Association, the U.S. Chamber of Commerce, and more than five dozen other small business associations representing soybean and cotton growers, truckers, florists, vintners, oil drillers, wholesalers and retailers, restaurants, and contractors, to name a few. The leaders and members of the Family Business Estate Tax Coalition were also there. The Dole-Pryor provision, with a new $10 million cap on property eligible for the lower tax rate, made it into the budget act passed by Congress in 1995. But that legislation was vetoed by President Clinton and never became law.

In 1996 the bill's two main cosponsors left the Senate. Dole ran for president as the Republican nominee; Pryor, as it turned out, would become trustee for Bill Clinton's Legal Defense Fund. Senators Charles Grassley of Iowa and Max Baucus of Montana, subsequently to be chairmen and ranking minority members of the Senate Finance Committee, took up the bipartisan cudgel for estate tax relief for family businesses and farms. In March 1997, they introduced legislation, similar to the Dole-Pryor bill, to provide an estate tax exemption for the first $1.5 million of family-business assets and a further exemption for half of the next $8.5 million of property. The Grassley-Baucus bill had already taken one wrong turn: it offered less relief than the original Dole-Pryor proposal.

When he introduced this new legislation, Senator Grassley made an offhand remark that foreshadowed the train wreck to come. "In some places," he said, "we have made technical improvements suggested by the tax experts." Technical improvements indeed.

With further modifications, Grassley's legislation, now known as QFOBI (Qualified Family Owned Business Interests) was included as part of the Taxpayer Relief Act of 1997, the first tax cut enacted under the Clinton presidency. QFOBI received additional changes in the IRS Restructuring and Reform Act of 1998. By the time Congress was finished, nearly 2,600 words of confusion had been added to the estate tax law. QFOBI now occupies 265 lines in the federal tax code, probably more than the number of businesses that have managed to take advantage of the tax break it offers. Its longest sentence is 344 words and 28 lines long; four sentences alone total more than 1,000 words.

QFOBI's text is long, but the benefits it provides are short. The estate tax savings never exceeded $675,000 for any decedent, and this amount phases down over time to $300,000 before disappearing altogether. The unlimited tax reduction of the Dole-Pryor bill, already restricted to the first $10 million of a business's assets by the Grassley-Baucus bill, was cut down to a maximum of $1.3 million of assets by the time the legislation finally passed Congress. Then even this limited benefit was diminished by increases in the estate tax exemption that were made available to all estates.

Worse yet, to get even the limited tax break promised by QFOBI, family businesses must jump through more hoops than a circus dog. Tax legislation, you see, is written by a bunch of well-meaning lawyers sitting around a table in the basement of the Longworth congressional office building. These tax lawyers collectively imagine all the ways that accountants or other lawyers might conspire to take advantage of a tax relief provision. One of the drafters might ask, "What if someone buys a small business while on his deathbed?" Another might ask, "What if the heirs sell the business anyway?" A third person will ask, "How can we give this relief to a company that is publicly traded?" "Why should we benefit people who have plenty of other liquid assets to pay the tax?" "What if somebody simply takes their liquid assets and puts them into a family corporation?" "Do we want to give a tax cut to people who are not American citizens or residents?" "How about businesses operating abroad?" "What if the decedent did not really operate the business?" And on and on. In the tax-law boiler room, the motto is "Anything worth doing is worth overdoing."

So, if your family member was not the sole owner of the business when he died, in order to benefit from the QFOBI he and your family would have to have owned at least 50 percent of the business at the date of death; or 30 percent if at least 70 percent of the business was owned by two families or if 90 percent was owned by three families. Otherwise you lose. If any interests in the business were publicly traded in any of the three years prior to death, you lose. If more than 35 percent of the business's income derived from dividends, interest, rents, or royalties, you lose (unless the business is a bank). If the owner was not a U.S. citizen or resident when he died, you lose. If the business has its principal place of operations outside the United States, you lose. If the business accounts for less than half the value of the entire estate, you lose. If, for any five of the eight years before the owner died, he or a member of the family did not "materially participate" in the business, you lose. If your family did not own the business for five of the eight years prior to the owner's death, you lose. Need we go on?

Notwithstanding its shortcomings, many of the key players in the repeal effort at first hailed QFOBI as a major victory. Both the NFIB and the congresswoman who would eventually become the strongest advocate for total repeal, Republican Jennifer Dunn of Washington, applauded its adoption. But as time passed, it became clear that the law would not achieve the benefits for family businesses and farms that its sponsors had intended. One coalition member put it well: "There are a lot of fixes you can do that don't

hit the social policy objective of the estate tax. One is to increase the exclusion. Another is to defer taxes." "But the problem," he continued, "is
that those who wanted solutions like this came up with dysfunctional rules
for it. People who write laws are really nervous that if they change the law,
the wrong people will drive through it. But in this case, they didn't let the
right people drive through it. That led to a palpable disgust on the part of
people in the coalition."

Everyone now agrees—regardless of which side of the issue they are
on—that QFOBI has been a complete and utter failure. Coalition members describe it as "complex," "convoluted," "worthless," and "a mistake waiting to happen." They view it, at best, as a "modest, well-intended attempt,"
a "politically expedient solution." It did not solve anything. QFOBI has so
many requirements, so many strictures and pitfalls, that very few family
businesses have obtained any tax relief at all because of it. Thus, the provision failed in its stated purpose to protect family farms and businesses from
having to be sold to cover the family's estate tax liability. More important
to our story here, its unrealized promise meant that small businesses and
family farms did not get the kind of genuine relief that might have stalled
their campaign to repeal the tax entirely.

In fact, QFOBI has had exactly the opposite effect. When asked why
they did not pursue—or settle for—an increase in the estate tax exemption
or a special exemption for family farms or businesses in 2001, repeal advocates frequently cite QFOBI to illustrate why they view the reform path as
a dead end. "It will never work," they say. And they believe it. QFOBI has
simply confirmed for them Will Rogers's adage that when Congress makes
a joke, it is a law.

QFOBI thus marked a turning point in the repeal effort. For more than
five years the coalition had worked to achieve some protection targeted to
small businesses and family farms. Not any more. QFOBI's false promise
made them believe that compromise is futile. Now they would work for repeal. At the time when QFOBI's promises were fresh and untested, it was
difficult to foresee the role it would play as an impetus for total repeal of
the tax. If the Democrats had realized then what everyone knows now, they
would have worked very hard indeed to ensure that this exemption for
small businesses and family farms really worked. Their diffident support
subsequently proved very costly. Once the idea of incremental improve-

ment in the tax became anathema to the coalition and to most of their congressional allies, the campaign for repeal picked up genuine momentum.

The QFOBI misadventure also had the effect over time of helping the new coalition coalesce its forces and organize itself into an effective force for repeal. During the years that the legislation moved through Congress, the Family Business Estate Tax Coalition and its members made and expanded valuable contacts with lawmakers on the Hill. They learned who their friends were and whom they had to sway to their side. The coalition also refined its own operations and added members. By 1999, there were 60 associations of small business groups, farmers, and ranchers; in 2001, the coalition's membership reached 100, more than double its 1995 size.

Knowledgeable Washington insiders had now taken the helm of the repeal effort. An executive committee, which included several of Washington's most powerful business organizations, now ran the coalition. In 1996, former chairman of the Senate Finance Committee Bob Packwood joined the coalition to fight for estate tax repeal on behalf of a group called "American Business Is Local Enterprise"—a group whose members Packwood does not identify. Packwood had left the Senate just one year earlier, resigning in shame at age 63 for sexual misconduct while in office. Eleven days after the expiration of his one-year ban on lobbying his former colleagues in Congress, Packwood formed his lobbying company, Sunrise Research Corporation. Packwood now runs this organization out of a nondescript office in a nondescript building on Wisconsin Avenue at the northern tip of Georgetown, a long cab ride away from Capitol Hill and several miles from Washington's famous K Street lobbying corridor.

Sitting behind a mahogany partners desk in the far corner of a large room, Packwood is surrounded by overflowing bookcases and photos from his halcyon days in the Senate: on Air Force One with the first President Bush; arm-in-arm with Democratic House Ways and Means Chairman Dan Rostenkowski, a *Time* magazine photo marking the successful completion of the Tax Reform Act of 1986 of which Packwood was a key architect. When the phone rings, Packwood answers it himself. When he hangs up, he expresses pride about his minimal overhead expenses. He looks good: he is thin, physically fit for a man his age, showing no scars from his final, ravaging Senate ordeal.

Agreeing that a $5 million exemption would have taken care of 95 percent of the coalition members, Packwood suggests that ultimately the story of repeal is more one of personal contacts than of campaign contributors seeking influence. "Senators like to listen to people who they went through the fire with thirty years ago, people who were on the city council with them, or in the military. They listen to former staff. They listen to people who give them time, the treasurer of their campaign committee, people like that." The repeal movement's great strength came from having so many of these people, community leaders and small businesspeople who knew congressmen or senators working on the issue.

One of the coalition members, Bill Nelson of the American Vintners Association, credits Packwood with focusing the coalition's efforts on repeal. "Up until Packwood came in, the group was focused on fixing business problems," Nelson says. "Then Packwood focused the group on repeal." Certain other members of the coalition minimize Packwood's role, insisting that they, not he, made all the difference.

Grover Norquist describes a meeting, arranged by Packwood in Mississippi Republican Senator Trent Lott's office early in 1997, in which many coalition members urged repeal. According to Norquist, the NFIB disagreed: "Just nick it because we know you can't eliminate the estate tax within the budget." Norquist adds, "This took the wind out of everything everyone else said. The NFIB thought they were being sophisticated. Their attitude was 'Clinton's going to veto it so why try to fit it into any budget, you morons!' Now they probably won't even remember they said that." Not only do they not remember, but Dan Blankenberg of the NFIB insists that it never happened. Nevertheless, Norquist's account sounds plausible. Indeed, although the NFIB may deny putting the brakes on repeal, Senator Lott went on record expressing the same budget concerns when Senator Grassley introduced his version of the bill that became QFOBI in 1997. "The estate tax is a monster that must be exterminated," Lott complained. "Unfortunately," he added, "our budget process does not allow us to completely repeal this tax all at once. We must do it in stages."

Bob Packwood himself told the *National Journal* that same year, "You might be able to get [repeal] in three Congresses, counting this as the first." But now, Packwood added, "you can only expect more modest relief." Packwood's prediction was right on the money. Congress first passed QFOBI in 1997; it passed repeal in 2001. Whatever disagreements may have persisted in the coalition during the late 1990s, once the practical failure of QFOBI became clear, the coalition never wavered in its quest for repeal.

As effective as the NFIB, NAM, Bob Packwood, and others were inside Washington's beltway, the most remarkable—and persuasive—operations of the coalition involved mustering grassroots support for repeal. Coalition members all stress the successes of the group in generating letters, e-mails, and faxes to members of Congress urging them to eliminate the death tax. The goal was to bring to Congress's attention real people facing genuine estate tax problems. As Bob Packwood says, "The stories were compelling, true, and graphic." He adds, "All the other side had to combat the stories were numbers about the distribution of the tax burden." Beyond reams of correspondence from voters across the country, the coalition also organized public testimony before congressional committees and private meetings with key legislators.

The coalition's steering committee kept a list of undecided legislators and urged its members to "activate your grassroots efforts" in the key states and congressional districts. The coalition urged its members to keep the message to legislators simple:

- Support repeal of the death tax.
- Stress that the death tax kills jobs.
- Oppose complicated carve-out provisions that would maintain or increase high compliance costs.
- Point out that 85 percent of Americans polled agree that inheritance taxes are extreme forms of taxation and that the 55 percent rate is unfair.

The coalition was also creative in its lobbying efforts. In 1999, the first annual Death Tax Summit took place in Washington. Frank Blethen, Harold Apolinsky, and a few others had organized the event as a way to bring repeal advocates together and lobby members of Congress. The summit was held one block from the Capitol at the Capitol Hill Club, whose lobby is festooned with portraits of Republican leaders, including the first President Bush and Dennis Hastert, Speaker of the House. While Blethen was able in 1999 to convince four Democratic members of the Washington State congressional delegation to make an appearance in this Republican haven, later summits would be even more inviting to the party associated with defending the estate tax: the event moved the following year to the Democrat's club and subsequently to neutral territory in various reception rooms in the Capitol itself or in House or Senate office buildings. These summits served two essential purposes: first, to rally the Washington troops, keeping them focused on the fight for repeal; and second, to provide an occasion for out-of-towners to meet with congressional supporters or wavering lawmakers to present the case for repeal. And this was just one of the coalition's methods for rallying nationwide support for repeal.

As the 1990s drew to a close, the Family Business Estate Tax Coalition had come a long way from its shaky and unrealistic start. Pat Soldano confesses, "Early on, we had a plan, but it wasn't a good one. We did a lot of spinning of wheels." By 1997, the *Washington Post* could describe the coalition's efforts as "an increasingly sophisticated form of lobbying that coordinates grass-roots work by influential members of local communities with a legislative plan masterminded by Washington strategists representing large associations." By 1999, as QFOBI began to reveal itself for the failed compromise that it was, the coalition had become a force not to be trifled with, a powerhouse for repeal. With Republicans in control of Congress and the best chance for dividing the coalition apparently missed, the ground was laid for a strong congressional advocate to convince her colleagues that now was the time to kill the death tax.

An Advocate for the Working Rich

As she sits in her wood-paneled corner office of the Longworth congressional building, dressed in her elegant, gray-flecked skirt-suit, its jacket adorned by a giant red carnation, Representative Jennifer Dunn barely resembles the soccer mom selected by the Republican Party to respond to President Clinton's State of the Union address in January 1999—just after the start of his impeachment trial. Her hair is perfectly coiffed and her ring finger is weighed down by a six-carat sapphire mounted on a thick gold band. It is a gift from her fiancé, the wealthy businessman Keith Thomson, who has recently proposed "at a fabulous restaurant"—The Inn at Blackbeard's Castle in St. Thomas, Virgin Islands. Her high cheekbones and upright posture explain why the 58-year-old Dunn was once described as "Margaret Thatcher with better clothes." She is indeed striking, utterly poised, and ready for any question.

On the occasion of her State of the Union response, Dunn had emphasized her struggles as a middle-class mother. Dressed in a white turtleneck and blue sweater, standing on a darkened balcony framed by the bright Capitol dome alongside another Republican rising star, Congressman Steve Largent of Oklahoma, she said, "I've been a single mother since my boys were little—six and eight. My life in those days was taken up with making ends meet, trying to get to two soccer games at the same time on two different fields, worrying about dropping the boys off early at school in order to get to work on time." She added, "I know how that knot in the pit of your stomach feels. I've been there." She then went on to bash the Internal Revenue Service, calling for a 10 percent across-the-board income tax reduction and elimination of the tax law's marriage penalties. In that winter of 1999, she also urged that "we must cut death taxes so that families don't have to sell their businesses and farms when Mom and Dad die."

Dunn has long since abandoned her call simply to cut estate taxes; now she will settle for nothing less than permanent repeal. A tireless advocate for the cause, she dismisses claims that the tax affects only the wealthiest 1 or 2 percent with a wave of her hand, just as she waves aside as inconceivable suggestions that repeal might diminish charitable giving. She is too stylish to reach for George W. Bush's favored phrase, "fuzzy math," but she might as well have. Her demeanor, as well as her language, makes it obvious that she sees the estate tax as immoral and unfair. Dunn even believes that if the leaders of the life insurance industry—which has much to lose from repeal—only understood the issue, they too would come around. It is easy to see why she is universally considered repeal's most effective congressional advocate. A cartoon on her office wall says it all: Jennifer Dunn stands in a lifeboat aiming her harpoon at a huge whale named "Death Tax," which is swallowing up a little fish labeled "small business." It was no accident that Jennifer Dunn stood directly behind President Bush when he signed the 2001 tax act. She had done a great deal to make that bill a reality.

In May of 1999, Dunn wrote an editorial for *Insight* magazine. In it she argued that the estate tax "has become less of a tax on wealth . . . and more of a tax on the accumulation of wealth of those who are trying to get ahead and save for the future." A subtle distinction, you might think, but with it she had found the sweet spot for estate tax repeal in American politics. Citing a recent study alleging to show that "the effective tax rate on the most valuable estates was actually lower than that on medium-sized estates," Dunn insisted that the truly wealthy can avoid estate taxes by "stuffing money away here and there at the suggestion of high-priced attorneys and accountants." She claimed that it is the working rich and, more importantly, the would-be working rich, who must live in fear of the tax. In short, the estate tax is at war with the American dream.

She is clear that she regards the stakes as high. "The policy choices we make surrounding the death tax," she says, "go to the heart not just of our tax system but of who we are as a society. How should we tax? Who should we tax? What should we tax? What values does our tax system reflect?" She answers her own questions. "Naturally our tax system is not neutral to social values," she says. "Look at the values that are penalized when a government imposes a death tax: Thrift. Conservation. Entrepreneurship. Ingenuity. Family Buisnesses. Family farms. Families."

Pitching her case in this way enabled Dunn to tap into emerging demographic constituencies, notably women and minorities, whose members had only recently begun accumulating significant assets. And they are just one constituency. The dot.com revolution and the massive stock market run-up in the 1990s—not to mention the explosion in real estate prices—meant that by the time the second George Bush ascended to the presidency, growing groups of middle-class Americans would no longer be shielded from the estate tax by the $650,000 exemption that was on the books at the time. Many of them might reasonably anticipate dying with a net worth well in excess of $1 million.

Dunn knows how to communicate with these groups. She "speaks eloquent suburban" according to the *Seattle Times*. *Business Week* calls her a "translator to women," though the conservative *Washington Times* notes with approval that she has avoided "being defined by 'women's issues.'" She is utterly in tune with her district, which contains a great deal of new wealth. Microsoft, headquartered there, is one of her largest contributors. Her older son is named Reagan for the former president. As a fiscal conservative Dunn gets top ratings from small business groups, even though her record on social and especially environmental issues is moderately liberal.

First-generation accumulators of wealth may lack the tax problems of those who find themselves inheriting large estates, but Dunn understood implicitly that these working rich are a fiery potential constituency for repeal. Entrepreneurs who have built up assets resent what they see as double taxation—not least when it is pointed out to them that they would have avoided estate taxes had they consumed their wealth rather than saving it. The inability to pass on assets provokes righteous anger, particularly in activities such as farming, where it can take several generations to build up a major business. From the perspective of farmers and owners of small businesses, estate taxes are inimical to family values as well as the work ethic.

By appealing to the newly affluent while seeming to distance herself from the super-rich, Dunn understood that she would win powerfully motivated allies. Perhaps more important, she would put her opponents on the defensive—backing them into denying the legitimacy of the American dream and wanting to punish those who have worked all their lives to achieve it. So she complained that, according to another study, today fewer "than half of all family-owned businesses survive the death of a founder and only about five percent survive to the third generation." The implication? "It is cheaper for an individual to sell the business prior to death and pay the individual capital gains rate than to pass it on to heirs." Family-owned businesses are one of the "foundations on which strong communities are built." It is "terrible public policy" to undermine them.

For all Dunn's grasp of the politics of the estate tax outside the beltway, her greatest contribution to repeal was serving as its champion in the House. She did not identify with this issue right away. Elected as Washington State's lone Republican in 1992, Dunn came into her own with the Republican takeover in 1994. She allied herself closely with Newt Gingrich's leadership and quickly became part of his kitchen cabinet. She was described by the *Seattle Post-Intelligencer* as one of Gingrich's "chief lieutenants." In keeping with the "Contract with America," Dunn initially backed reform, hoping for a bipartisan bill that President Clinton would have to sign, and she worked hard to get QFOBI enacted.

Dunn's close relations with the new House leadership gave her in 1994 a seat on the powerful Ways and Means Committee—through which all tax legislation must pass. That someone as junior as she could get onto the most powerful committee in Congress reflected Gingrich's leadership style: replacing the old seniority system, where committee chairmen presided over local baronies, with one that kept much more power in the hands of the House Republican leadership. As well as becoming the fifth woman in the history of the House to be appointed to Ways and Means, Dunn was the first to serve on the Joint Economic Committee, and in 1997, she replaced Susan Molinari as vice-chair of the House GOP Conference—making her the highest-ranking woman in the House. The George W. Bush administration considered her for several cabinet positions, including commerce secretary and secretary of labor, but avoided tapping her due to the expected difficulty of replacing her with someone as effective in Congress.

Dunn cut her teeth on Ways and Means by fighting successfully to get the luxury car tax phased out. This battle provided good training for estate tax repeal. Cutting luxury taxes benefits the wealthy almost by definition, yet the pressure for action came from family-owned car dealerships—just the type of constituents who would become critical for death tax repeal. The challenge for Dunn was to sell a tax on luxury purchases as an issue about employment and the survival of small businesses. Defenders of the tax might see it as a levy on only a tiny minority of America's wealthiest, but Dunn managed to portray the tax as a denial of basic fairness to small businesses—unfairly eroding their livelihood and costing the jobs they create.

It was partly this experience that convinced Dunn that estate tax repeal might actually be easier to achieve than reform. Like Grover Norquist, she saw that portraying a tax as fundamentally unfair does not supply an effective argument for trying to reform it at the margin. Moreover, there is an appealing simplicity to repeal. Arguing over the terms of reform means trying to get people to understand complexity. It violates the old adage that in politics when you are explaining you are losing. Better to let the other side explain complex formulae while you line up behind an easily articulated view.

Unexpected ammunition for Dunn's assault came from the QFOBI debacle. In her *Insight* editorial, Dunn wrote of a tax attorney who had told her that only 5 percent of family-owned businesses were actually eligible for the QFOBI treatment. "No amount of artful drafting will provide relief to only those Congress deems worthy," she insisted. The exception "creates 14 new definitions with which a business must comply before it is eligible for relief." Conceding that she thought the QFOBI reform a good idea in 1997 when it was enacted, the exemption "has proven to be nothing more than a boondoggle for attorneys and estate planners who are hired by families trying to navigate their way through these eligibility hoops." Radical surgery was now needed.

Dunn understood that success would require working with key senators and, eventually perhaps, with the White House. But her immediate challenge was to give life to the idea of repeal in the House. Since mid-1993, Republican Congressman Christopher Cox of California had been introducing bills to repeal the estate tax. A fiscal conservative from Pat Soldano's Orange County district, Cox managed to get 29 cosponsors for repeal in 1994 and 102 in 1996, yet he could not move the legislation. A Harvard Law School graduate who has been in the House since 1988, Cox is no lightweight. Yet the widespread perception among repeal advocates was that although his heart was in the right place, he was not good at coalition building. He lacked a seat on Ways and Means and the ability to win Democrats to the cause. Moreover, moving legislation in the Gingrich era meant getting it into the leadership's top ten priorities. This in turn meant convincing the party's top brass that a given bill could pass with enough support to give it a significant chance of surviving in the Senate and in the conference committee. Strong Democratic support in the House would also put pressure on the Clinton White House to sign the bill rather than veto it.

Over in the Senate, Jesse Helms of North Carolina and Jon Kyl of Arizona had been toiling away much as Chris Cox had been in the House. Helms introduced several repeal bills in the late 1980s and early 1990s, passing the baton to Kyl in 1995. But their efforts were largely symbolic politics; votes came down strictly along partisan lines through early 1999, without much chance of anything passing. Most of the Senate action centered around QFOBI and various other compromise proposals. In these tussles, Senate Democrats such as John Breaux of Louisiana, Patty Murray of Washington, and Byron Dorgan of North Dakota competed with Republicans Bob Dole of Kansas, Charles Grassley of Iowa, and Don Nickles of Oklahoma to shape an exception that would win the day.

It would not be until mid-1999 that any Democratic senators would begin cosponsoring repeal bills, and July of 2000 that the Death Tax Elimination Act would garner the support of nine Democratic senators—a number that grew to twelve by 2001. It was largely the coalition that managed to sway these senators, picking them off state by state. There was some coordinating from Trent Lott's office after the Mississippi Republican became majority leader in 1996, but Senate leaders simply cannot dictate the legislative agenda to backbenchers, who operate as semiautonomous feudal lords. In the House, by contrast, the leadership of the majority party runs the show. Jennifer Dunn's most important task was to get the attention of Republican leaders, convincing them that she could produce a bill that had a good chance of becoming law.

Cox was unable to deliver on these fronts, but Jennifer Dunn was. While still working on QFOBI and her own reform bills, Dunn signed on as a cosponsor of Cox's repeal bill in 1997. It was then referred to Ways and Means, where Committee Chairman Bill Archer of Texas, a staunch proponent of the view that we should "pull the income tax out by its roots and throw it away so it can never grow back," ensured that the bill was taken up the following year. Archer's desire for structural reform of the tax code and his confrontational style fit hand-in-glove with the agenda and approach of Gingrich and his fellow Texans in the Republican leadership. By 1998, death tax repeal had won 204 cosponsors, including, tellingly, the entire GOP leadership.

Important as Archer's support was, it was Jennifer Dunn's ability to deliver support from the Democratic side that convinced Armey, Gingrich, and others that death tax repeal had political legs. She successfully wooed a serious Democratic cosponsor on Ways and Means in the person of John Tanner of Tennessee, lined up support from liberal Democrats such as Neil Abercrombie of Hawaii and even African Americans such as Albert Wynn of Maryland. At that point, the House Republican leadership started to realize that what they had been saying but not really believing might actually be true: that death tax repeal could be given a bipartisan, perhaps even populist spin. Thus, when the Death Tax Elimination Act was introduced in February 1999, the bill was HR8—signaling that it was now in the leadership's top ten priorities. It was going to pass, at least in the House, with substantial Democratic support.

Part of Dunn's success stemmed from her superior political skill; she knew how to build unlikely across-the-aisle alliances by attending to critical nuances in what potential allies needed. For instance, Neil Abercrombie had to get a change in the definition of a family-owned business in QFOBI. The Hawaiian land magnate James Campbell's family trust in Abercrombie's district had been due to expire in 2007—20 years after the death of Campbell's last surviving daughter. At that point millions of dollars in estate taxes would be owed because, with 23 surviving beneficiaries, the family would be too large to qualify for the exception's special treatment. Dunn agreed to incorporate an increase in the maximum number of family members allowed for a small business to claim exemption to 45, bringing them within its ambit. The Joint Tax Committee estimated that the change would benefit some 3,000 families at the cost of $3.2 billion to the Treasury over ten years. By incorporating it into the legislation, Dunn secured Abercrombie's support for the overall bill.

Conventional logrolling of this sort was one piece of Dunn's approach. But the larger reason she succeeded was that, by reframing the death tax as a fairness issue especially for family-owned small businesses, she gave political cover to Democrats whose votes she sought. Abercrombie could talk about the Campbells' contribution to the local economy—not to mention the low-income housing on the Campbell estate that would be lost if the family had to sell the property. Albert Wynn could focus on the fact that his Maryland district has the tenth-largest number of small businesses in the country and the largest number of minority-owned small businesses. There might be little intense support for repeal in traditional Democratic constituencies, but these lawmakers and others like them were discovering that neither was there much opposition to it once repeal was construed as an issue about small business, jobs, and the working rich rather than the super-rich. No one was going to lose their seat for voting for death tax repeal. Supporting it in return for a benefit for an important local constituency amounted to a win-win proposition.

If Dunn and the House leadership made astute and creative use of cooperation where it could win them unlikely supporters, they also relied on the post-1994 Republican leadership's signature confrontational tactics. Conventional wisdom might suggest that estate tax repeal, which benefits only a narrow segment of the population, would show up in an omnibus bill in which votes for repeal are traded off against other priority items for different interest groups. But the Republican leadership realized that opposing popular tax cuts puts Democrats on the defensive. If death tax repeal could be reframed to take on a populist hue, then there would be no reason to bury it in omnibus legislation. Indeed, and to the contrary, a large tax cut bill would give opponents the wiggle room to vote "no," either because they balk at the sticker shock or they claim some other portion of the bill is objectionable. It is a measure of repeal proponents' success that they saw early on the wisdom of forcing stand-alone votes on death tax repeal in the House and the Senate. They knew that repeal would eventually wind up as part of an omnibus tax cut under the Senate's rules, but they wanted to ensure enough demonstrated bipartisan support for repeal to ensure that it could not be edged out by other tax cuts in conference or the final markup. A stand-alone vote would also fingerprint potential defectors with the threat of being accused of flip-flopping later.

If presenting death tax repeal as a bipartisan "fairness" issue did not work, the alternative was simple pressure. Both the House and Senate leaderships worked closely with the coalition to identify, and go after, individual members who had been identified as vulnerable on this issue in their states and districts. And they did it by appealing to the working rich and would-be working rich who were the footsoldiers in the coalition, using Dunn's arguments. Congressional staffers speak proudly of their efficient coordination with the coalition. If any targeted representative was being difficult in committee or showed signs of wavering on a key vote, calls from 30 or so constituents could be arranged within a matter of hours. The person on the other end would ideally be "the owner of the local hardware store," the kind of person the lawmaker "likes to be seen with," or has "known for thirty years."

As we shall see, the repeal effort is notable for its successful use of these "super-constituents," local business people or civic leaders who are not merely voters in the representative's district or the senator's state, but visible community members whose opinions influence other voters. In the popular imagination, the forces that influence lawmakers' decisions are either campaign contributors with special access or, perhaps on a particularly hot-button issue such as gun control, mass-mailing campaigns organized by special interest groups such as the National Rifle Association. The influence and personal lobbying of local notables is less often discussed, though it is potentially decisive. This activity goes on largely under the radar screen of the news media, which tend to focus on the large agglomerations of financial interests rather than the month-in, month-out personal visits like the ones that the repeal advocates organized.

Given Jennifer Dunn's well-coordinated efforts in the House and the coalition's effective and timely use of super-constituents, to whose stories we now turn, it is small wonder that proponents and opponents alike described the repeal campaign as unusually well run. In fact, it became one of the most effective legislative efforts many of them had ever seen.

Stories from the Grasstops

An old courtroom adage urges, If the law is on your side, argue the law; if not, argue the facts; if neither helps, sow confusion. On Capitol Hill, the wise advice is to come armed with a good story. The most effective story-teller is someone the senator or representative knows, a good friend or an old political compatriot. Congress frequently moves the law in response to anecdotes. Washington insiders know this well.

Bill Beach is one such insider, and this Heritage Foundation analyst was thinking strategically when he published "Death Tax Devastation: Horror Stories from Middle-Class America." It was August 1995, the same month that Pat Soldano founded the lobbying wing of her Policy and Taxation Group, and just a year after the establishment of the Family Business Estate Tax Coalition. Beach's paper quickly became widely used—Frank Blethen instantly loaded it onto his deathtax.com website, and it spread from there. It relates three "family farm horror stories" and twelve "family business horror stories," where the death tax always plays the role of the grim reaper coming after the hardworking business owner or farmer. In a particularly creative move, Beach adds a story illustrating that the death tax threatens the environment. This tale describes how the Hillard family's sale of 12,000 of their 17,000 southern Florida acres to pay estate taxes threatened the habitat of the Florida panther, an endangered species. Finally, Beach concludes his narrative exercise with five stories labeled "wasted resources" cases. This last batch is designed to convince readers that small business owners' efforts to minimize their estate taxes through advance planning—for example, through purchases of life insurance policies to provide liquid funds free of tax—cause only economic waste and job loss.

An abbreviated version of one of Beach's "horror stories" gives a sense of the sympathy for the working rich that he was trying to instill in his readers:

> For three generations, Barry's family ran their own business in Kentucky. Today they own 20 gas stations and convenience stores and em-

ploy about 100 people. However, Barry's father is growing older and would like to pass on the business. Barry likens the death tax to the old saying about sheep: "Slaughter your sheep and you will get dinner for a night. Shear them and you will get a lifetime of wool." According to Barry, his family has spent a significant amount of money on accountants and attorneys to prepare for shifting ownership of the business from his father to Barry's generation and the grandchildren. Family members have purchased insurance and have gone through rewriting several wills and trusts. "It's something you continually update. Every time a new grandchild is born, we have to revise the will and trusts."

Beach culled his stories from congressional testimony, newspaper articles, and conversations with death tax opponents inside and outside Washington. He has a practiced eye for finding convincing anecdotes for Capitol Hill: he and his Heritage colleagues have long been active in finding people who could be effective advocates in committee hearings and supplying them to congressional staff. "The staff always wants new witnesses, but often they only have a short list of who might testify," Beach says. He describes the resulting testimonies, which are often very emotional, as "wonderful resources that are little used." Heritage will republish the stories after the hearings. As Beach concludes, "Congress produces a lot of heat. If you can find a way of putting it in a bottle, you can reuse that over and over again. And it costs you very little."

The death tax horror stories—Beach's own little "Tales from the Crypt"—have enjoyed a good long run. They get recycled every time Congress debates the estate tax. The *Congressional Record* is filled with them. And Beach's chronicles provide standard fodder for speeches by repeal proponents.

Bill Beach, however, was not the only repeal advocate on the hunt for wrenching stories. As the estate tax debate heated up in the mid- to late-1990s, virtually all the members of the coalition sought sad stories about families whose breadwinner had died and who were struggling to keep their small businesses, farms, or ranches from being sold to pay the death tax. This quest became a critical task in the repeal movement.

During these years, the Family Business Estate Tax Coalition met frequently, using NFIB headquarters. Fifty or more people would gather around the oblong, hollow table that dominates the big, windowless conference room off the NFIB lobby. The walls are festooned with many large, framed color photographs of small business owners such as Sam Mahler of the Maid Brigade house-cleaning franchise business. Dan Blankenburg, NFIB's point man on the death tax, would chair the meeting from the head of the table. Blankenburg is a confident, plain-talking man in his late 20s or early 30s. With his square shoulders and jaw, short dirty blond hair, slightly scarred chin, and close-set eyes, he looks as if he might be the second baseman of some minor league baseball team. He doesn't speak in long, multi-phrase sentences—nor does he seem to understand them easily. His effectiveness as a political operative, however, is not in question.

Before a typical meeting, Blankenburg and the other FBETC leaders would have put together a list of legislators whom they considered important lobbying targets. Once the group convened, Blankenburg would go around the room asking for volunteers to lobby on a particular representative or senator, then another, and on and on. Representatives of organizations that had a connection with that lawmaker would take the assignment.

Bob Packwood, who attended the sessions, describes a typical interchange. Blankenburg, or another coalition member, would ask, for example, "Who knows Senator Cleland?" Then, Packwood says, "A member of the farm bureau, or the beer and wine wholesalers or the grocery wholesalers would say, 'I know a guy in Albany, Georgia, who was in the military with Senator Cleland.' Enough people like this made enough calls on enough members of the House and Senate to get the votes." Packwood adds, "If you're in Congress and no one is calling on the other side and you can do something for a friend or contributor, you would like to do it." David Rehr, president of the National Beer Wholesalers Association, confirms Packwood's observations: "I've been in Washington 22 years and I know that in the end it's not what the lobbyists say that counts, but hearing from constituents."

Of course, not all tax issues lend themselves to this sort of constituent pressure. Take, for instance, the Earned Income Tax Credit (EITC), which allows refundable tax credits to workers at the bottom of the income scale. Raising or lowering the EITC has now become something of a political football, with Democrats often arguing for its expansion, and Republicans usually fighting to hold the line. But given the demographic group whose interests are at stake—the working poor—representatives and senators are unlikely to receive visits from constituents concerned about EITC funding levels. On this issue, legislators hear almost exclusively from liberal advocacy groups. And even if constituent visits and stories were to be mobilized, they wouldn't be coming from the grasstops or from "super-constituents"; a poor working mother worried about losing part of her EITC refund is not the kind of person back in the home district whom the representative or senator is likely to know already.

To see just how personal lobbying worked in the case of the estate tax, it's worth going behind some of the individual stories to get more detail. Take the case of John Kearney, whose experience was first reported in the *New York Times*. Both his background and his eventual meeting with his congressman illustrate the repeal coalition's successful use of constituent lobbying.

Kearney, who is now in his mid-50s, until recently owned a Ford and Mercury dealership in Ravena, New York, 12 miles south of Albany. His father left school after the tenth grade; after that he picked oranges in Florida, held other odd jobs, always worked hard. In 1936, with the help of a mentor, he began working in the automobile industry, and in 1949 he started a Studebaker dealership on Ravena's main street. It was a family business. Kearney's father, his mother, and John, their only child, lived in an apartment above the automobile showroom. John's uncle ran the service department from an open lot in the back of the dealership, and John's mother did the books.

In 1954, Ford approached Kearney, Sr., and asked him to become one of their dealers. He agreed. A year later he added Mercury, becoming one of the first Ford and Mercury dealerships in the country. Kearney became a well-known local citizen. He once sold a car to Daniel Patrick Moynihan before he became a senator from New York. In 1959, as the nearby Highway 9 was being developed, Kearney relocated his dealership, leaving downtown for the highway.

His son John worked at the dealership part-time and during the summers. In 1970, John graduated from college and started to learn more about the business. All along the family expected to pass its business to him. John already knew what to expect; he says, the trick was always "keeping money, not making money." He recalls the 1970s as a bad decade of increasing regulatory burdens. He complains that the government did not seem to care what size business you were. His wife, the child of potato farmers in Maine, understood this feeling intimately. Scarred from this experience, John says, "Everyone has a hand out for donations, and the government has two hands out."

The family engaged in considerable estate planning, looking ahead to how they could keep the business in the family when John's father died. Over time, John gradually acquired 61 percent of the dealership company's stock through gifts from his father. Nevertheless, John laments that his father was something of a stubborn man. Despite advice, he, like many other businessmen, did not transfer as much to John as would have been wise to minimize the estate tax. The elder Kearney, for example, remained the sole owner of the dealership building, which the corporation leased, as well as the land. He also owned his own residence, a rental property, and a summer home in Maine.

In 1999, John's father died. John Kearney owed an estate tax of about $400,000. When the tax came due, it was January; business was slow. $400,000 was a huge sum for a business this size to have on hand, Kearney says, and he had to take $50,000 out of his son's college education account to meet that month's payroll. He was furious.

Having been a small business owner for sometime, John Kearney had joined NFIB many years ago. He always read their literature when it came in the mail. Whenever they asked him to write letters to his congressmen on an issue affecting small business, he would do it. The estate tax he had just paid, however, got him sufficiently angry that he decided on his own to write directly to President Clinton. He told the president the story of his father, who began with nothing, created a strong business, and passed it on to his son. In the letter, Kearney said that if Clinton really wanted a legacy, why not make it the elimination of this terrible tax?

He sent copies of the letter to his congressman, Democrat Michael McNulty, and to Roger Hannay of Hannay Reels, Inc., a man heavily involved in small business issues. Hannay liked the letter so much that he forwarded it to the NFIB. People there were so taken with Kearney's story that they sent a copy of his letter to all 100 senators. NFIB also asked Kearney if he would be willing to come to Washington for a day to help lobby the issue. He agreed.

Dan Blankenburg and another NFIB staffer, Liz Lyons, took Kearney around to various offices and meetings during a day of lobbying. The group met with John Ashcroft, then a senator from Missouri and a wholehearted supporter of estate tax repeal. They also attended a session where New York's Democratic Senator Chuck Schumer spoke to a large group about the issue, but Schumer disappointed Kearney when he said he favored raising the exemption rather than repeal. West Virginia Democrat Robert Byrd sat across the table from Kearney at this meeting—Byrd looked like "a more regular guy," says Kearney, and rolled his eyes when Schumer spoke. Kearney also met with Jennifer Dunn who, of course, was very supportive.

At the end of the day, the NFIB took Kearney to meet his congressman. Kearney and McNulty were friends who had known each other most of their lives. McNulty's father, Jack, had been mayor of a nearby town and was friends with John Kearney's father. Everyone in the area knew Jack McNulty, and his son had gone into politics as a Democrat and had risen to the U.S. Congress.

This meeting between the two friends began with Representative McNulty reminding John Kearney that he was mainly interested in balancing the budget, an objective he favored over eliminating the estate tax. Kearney responded by telling McNulty the story of the payment he had recently had to make to cover the tax for his father's estate. Kearney reports, "Mike's eyes opened up as wide as saucers. He knew my dad and our business. He couldn't believe it. This wasn't political, it was personal." McNulty changed his mind that day and voted for the repeal bill that passed in 2000, both in committee and on the floor. John Kearney, of course, was pleased. Dan Blankenburg and NFIB were impressed that Kearney had swayed a Democrat previously opposed to repeal.

However, when President Clinton vetoed the measure and the bill returned to the House, Mike McNulty did not vote to override the veto. Kearney was angry, and he contacted McNulty to complain. McNulty told him that the Democrats were proposing to raise the estate tax exemption to $5 million, which would take care of people like Kearney, and added that Kearney had to remember that McNulty "had other constituents." John Kearney and Mike McNulty are still friends, but they have agreed to disagree about this issue.

Kearney believes the 2001 tax legislation is a bad joke. The phase-ins of lower rates and higher exemptions suit him, and after a year or more his own estate will be exempt; but with the sunset provisions, it may all be taken away. After "kicking this around over beer with friends," John Kearney has come to believe that the end result will be something like the Democratic compromise, not full repeal. And he is not happy about it. "It's double taxation. I don't care if you're Bill Gates, it's an unfair tax."

Kearney has two children, a son and a daughter, neither of whom is interested in the business. "And I can't blame them," he says. "It's getting harder and harder to make money from a small business and the Ford people are pressing everyone to get larger, because independent dealers are a headache for them." Taking all these pressures into consideration, he decided to sell the business to a slightly younger man who wanted to own a dealership in his hometown. Kearney is now a consultant to the business, and he has made his assets more liquid. Still, he is determined that his children will not go through what he did with his father's estate. So he pays $6,000 a year for an insurance policy held by an irrevocable trust (which protects the life insurance proceeds paid at his death from the estate tax). The policy, a so-called last to die policy, will pay out $1 million after both Kearney and his wife die. Kearney does not know if the estate tax will be around or will apply to him then, but this policy will protect his kids if they do have to pay it. He acknowledges that the life insurance policy is also a good tax-free savings vehicle. If the estate tax doesn't apply at his or his wife's death, then his children will get a million dollars. Kearney likes that idea. So although he purchased the policy as a tactic to avoid the death tax, it doesn't seem like a terrible waste of resources to him.

Since John Kearney's lobbying efforts, NFIB has not contacted him again, but he keeps up with the ongoing developments on the death tax. This tax is the only issue that has ever taken him to Washington, a place he calls "Disneyland." At the end of his day of lobbying, seeing how the members of Congress spent their time rushing from meetings to votes to caucuses and back to meetings, he recalls turning to Dan Blankenburg and asking, "How does anything ever get done here?"

One answer, of course, is that things get done when people such as John Kearney come to visit. While Representative McNulty may not have voted to override Clinton's veto of estate tax repeal, he became far more favorable to the idea of repeal or serious reform after meeting with a friend, someone whose father had known his father. Kearney's story demonstrates a few important elements in the estate tax saga. First was the moral outrage he felt: as noted earlier, he doesn't care if it's Bill Gates or himself, the tax is just wrong. That this tax is immoral became a constant rallying cry for the NFIB and other groups in the coalition. Kearney's story also illustrates how the estate tax issue managed to foment anger, resentment, and eventually effective lobbying among a social and economic class with great potential influence on their senators and representatives.

Kearney's story, of course, might never have left Ravena, New York. It did not have to end up in the *New York Times* or in congressional transcripts. But Kearney's tale became part of a larger political campaign. Once that happened, the ends to which his experiences were put depended, of course, on the strategy employed by the various groups that were interested in mobilizing voices like his.

Let's take another example. David Pankonin, owner of Pankonin, Inc., Farm Supply in Louisville, Nebraska, wrote a description of his situation that made its way to the repeal groups and landed on the *Wall Street Journal* op-ed page, later becoming one of Bill Beach's tales of "horror." A closer look at Pankonin's background and position reveals much of the complexity in the relationship between those affected by the tax and the groups in Washington who cull their stories for congressional consumption.

The Pankonins have plenty of experience when it comes to passing a business from one generation to the next. The farm supply company that David now owns and operates in rural Nebraska has been in his family since 1883, when his great-grandfather started the business just a few years after arriving in the United States from Prussia. In a handwritten contract dated December 8, 1910, his great-grandfather conveyed the business to David's grandfather for $518.09. There was no estate tax at the time, and the sum involved would hardly have triggered the levy had there been one. A generation later the business had grown, and it was David's grandfather's turn to pass it on. In 1946 he entered into a partnership agreement with his son, David's father, this time a typed, two-page document that placed the value of the business at $8,912.66. The federal estate tax was in effect by then, but the Pankonin family's assets were well within the exemption and the tax wasn't a concern.

By the 1970s, things had changed. Starting in 1971, David's father began preparing for the estate tax through asset transfers and insurance purchases. When he died suddenly in 1975, David was just one quarter shy of his MBA degree at Northwestern University in Chicago. David came back for the funeral and decided to stay in Louisville to run the business. Under his father's will, all the assets had passed to his mother, and so she became his banker and extended him all his financing. David says proudly that Pankonin's Farm Supply is now the oldest business in the county, having been in continuous operation for 144 years.

David Pankonin is a soft-spoken man, gentle and deliberate in his speech. When he tells you that in the 28 years since he took over his father's business he has never taken a Saturday off, and that he works 20 Sundays a year, there is no hint of complaint. "In the summer and fall when the harvesting is on, servicing these machines for our customers is basically a 24/7 business," he says. Despite the grueling hours, David's son Paul, currently a bank employee in Colorado Springs, would very much like to inherit and run the business. Here's where Pankonin's estate tax problem arises. Like many of the farms it supplies, Pankonin's has a large inventory and small cash flow. With combine-harvesters on the lot that sell for $240,000 each, as well as the land, buildings, and other business assets, Pankonin's, Inc., is worth "somewhere in the seven figures," according to its owner.

"But you'd laugh if you heard what my wife and I took home last year," David says. Before taxes the business showed a profit of $58,000, he says. A drought in Nebraska meant hard times for the farmers and for their supplier Pankonin's. In 2004, David said that 1997 was the last good year he and his customers have had. Under present circumstances, if the business were to pass through David's or his wife's estate, it would not come close to generating sufficient revenue to pay the estate taxes—they would need to sell assets or engage in some other form of estate planning. David has 14 employees, and they and his customers ask regularly about his son Paul's plans for the future. If Pankonin's were to close its doors during lean times for farmers, David says it's not clear whether another supplier would take its place.

As a small business owner in a state dominated by the Republican Party, David has been involved in local politics for as long as he can remember. He was Republican Party Chairman for the county at a young age and has been mayor of his hometown of Louisville. And while he never gives thousands, he is a steady financial supporter of Republican candidates. "In a state of 1.7 million, if you're active in the dominant party for thirty years, you get to know the elected officials," he says. He counts his congressman, Doug Bereuter, as a friend, as well as the governor, Mike Johanns, and his wife. He knows Senator Chuck Hagel as well. But Pankonin's life remains local. He has spent time in Washington only once, in the summer of 1973 when he interned in the office of Senator Roman Hruska. "It was Watergate summer so there was a lot to see. Since then, I've always been interested in the process."

For 20 years David has been a member of the NFIB. In 1995, the year the Family Business Estate Tax Coalition was formed in Washington, the NFIB contacted him to see if he would be interested in writing a brief article about his family's business, its history, and his concerns about the estate tax as he thinks about passing the business on to his son Paul. The NFIB representative said the organization would get David's story placed in a newspaper. David agreed, and he included a call for change in the estate tax in his brief account of his family's circumstances. He was quite surprised to be told a month later that what he had written would appear the next day on the op-ed page of the *Wall Street Journal.* The day after David's op-ed ran, he received a call from Senator Bob Dole's office informing him that Senator Dole had taken the article to a meeting at the White House and given it to President Clinton. Sometime later, Chuck Hagel quoted from the article at an estate tax hearing held by the Senate Agricultural Committee. "Mr. Chairman," Senator Hagel said, "people like David Pankonin look to us for leadership—and for help."

Interestingly, David Pankonin's article did not call for repeal. "The best solution," he wrote, "would be to exempt the hundreds of thousands of small family businesses across this country from the estate tax altogether. Congress and the president could haggle over how small is small, but the principle would be carried into policy." He also tried to lay out a realistic legislative proposal. "If the political climate isn't right for a complete exemption, then President Clinton ought to adopt the proposals Congress has built into its budget plan: raise the federal tax exemption for family-owned business assets to $1.5 million, institute a $750,000 personal exemption and cut the tax rate for qualified small businesses in half for assets between $1.5 million and $5 million."

Today, despite the firm commitment of the coalition's leaders to eliminating the tax, Pankonin's own views have not changed. "In my personal opinion I'm not for total repeal. The limits need to be indexed. I told the NFIB guy that, but that's not what they wanted to hear." In his characteristically soft-spoken way, he doesn't seem particularly bothered by this difference of opinion. "They've done a good job with the issue, keeping the pressure on. What I don't like is the sunset provision, because one year you don't have to pay, then the next year the whole thing is back again." David credits the success of the movement thus far, as enshrined in the 2001 tax legislation, to many people across the country who must be just like himself—people who are worried about the issue and who, as local business people, know people in Congress and get involved.

Nearly a decade after his name entered the national debate, Pankonin, now in his fifties, is still planning for the estate tax. "Who's going to come in and invest in a business with this kind of cash flow? You've got to plan." He has several term life-insurance policies that are about to expire, but renewing them will be more expensive because he now has high blood pressure. He considers the costs of the insurance and what he pays advisors to handle all his estate planning "unproductive."

While Pankonin remains a member of the NFIB and has been active as the mayor of Louisville, he hasn't lobbied on this issue. Perhaps because he favors only raising the exemption and exempting small businesses, not total repeal, the NFIB has not contacted him again. Nor was he active on either side when the Democratic compromises were being considered in 1999, 2000, and 2001. He has not spent time in Washington since his Watergate summer.

Like Kearney, Pankonin is a classic grasstops constituent. He is a well-known local businessman who is on friendly terms with his elected officials, and is therefore well positioned to get his concerns not only heard but acted on. The way his personal story made its way through the political machinery is telling: solicited by a Washington lobbying group—the NFIB; placed through the group's contacts at the *Wall Street Journal*; brought from the pages of the *Journal* to the attention of Senator Dole, and eventually to President Clinton. In all, it was a well-run operation to use the opinions of relatively affluent constituents as leverage on lawmakers.

Pankonin is interesting for another reason as well. One of the mysteries of estate tax repeal is how the coalitions stuck together even when Democratic compromises would have satisfied the concerns of most members. One answer suggested by the story of this Nebraska businessman is that ordinary citizens' views were solicited and brought forth when they fit the Washington agenda, but more easily disregarded when they didn't. To this day, Pankonin doesn't favor total repeal of the estate tax; and to this day, the NFIB has not asked him to come to Washington. If, then, there was a national groundswell of opinion against the estate tax, it seems that there also came a point when the coalition's leadership in Washington gathered their wagons in a circle and ceased to communicate and vet alternatives to repeal with the broader membership. In practice, this meant that David

Pankonin ended up as part of a campaign to repeal a tax that he considered seriously in need of reform, but he did not actually believe should be eliminated.

As the work of Bill Beach illustrates, and as the NFIB and the other proponents of estate tax repeal know well, many people throughout the country have stories demonstrating how this tax affects real families. Marshalling these stories and presenting them to the American public through speeches and well-placed newspaper articles has been a critical and visible element of the estate tax repeal movement. Bringing the tales to the members of Congress who control the future of this tax has been equally vigorous work, but far less visible.

As Frank Blethen, Pat Soldano, Jim Martin, and other repeal advocates recognized, however, getting rid of a tax on well-to-do white business people, even if they weren't the super-rich, was a difficult cause to transform into a populist issue. If the coalition was to move the center of attention from those who would benefit most from total repeal—families like the Waltons, the Gallos, Mars, and others with huge fortunes—they needed more than grasstops stories, like John Kearney's and David Pankonin's, to humanize the struggle of small independent businesses. They needed to find a way to link estate tax repeal to broader American themes of fairness and justice.

Changing the Face for Repeal

On the morning of February 1, 1995, just nine months before David Pankonin's story would appear in the *Wall Street Journal,* in the cavernous hearing room of the House Ways and Means Committee an elegant, 83-year-old African American tree farmer from Montrose, Mississippi, moved into the witness chair. Chester Thigpen was a grandchild of slaves. He had come to Washington to urge these lawmakers to exempt most family businesses from the estate tax. Surrounded by large portraits of former Ways and Means Committee chairmen, all white, Thigpen looked up from the witness table to the dais where the legislators sat. He began to speak softly, but with conviction:

"Estate taxes matter not just to lawyers, doctors and businessmen, but to people like [my wife] Rosett and me. We were both born on land that is now part of our Tree Farm. I can remember plowing behind a mule for my uncle who owned it before me. My dream then was to own land." Thigpen then related how he began to realize his dream in the 1940s, with a couple of small land purchases and one inheritance. He continued, "Back when I started, the estate tax applied to only one estate in 60. Today it applies to one in 20—including mine. I wonder if I would be able to achieve my dream if I were starting out today."

Thigpen went on to describe his feelings about the farm that he had built. "It took us half a century, but Rosett and I have managed to turn our land into a working Tree Farm that has been a source of pride and income for my entire family. Our Tree Farm made it possible to put our five children through college." The farm, he said, "made it possible for Rosett and me to share our love of the outdoors and our commitment to good forestry with our neighbors. And finally, it made it possible for us to leave a legacy that makes me very proud: beautiful forests and ponds that can live on for many, many years after my wife and I pass on. We wanted to leave the land in better condition than when we first started working it. And we will."

Thigpen claimed that an essential element of his dream was being threatened. "We also want to leave the Tree Farm in our family. But no matter how hard I work, that depends on you," he said. "Right now, people tell me my Tree Farm could be worth more than a million dollars. All that value is tied up in land or trees. We're not rich people. My son and I do almost all the work on our land ourselves." But, he added, "My children might have to break up the Tree Farm or sell off timber to pay the estate taxes" when he died.

Then Thigpen came to the punch line. The tree farmer had turned into an advocate. "I am here today to endorse a proposal called the National Family Enterprise Preservation Act which would totally exempt over 98 percent of all family enterprises, not just Tree Farms, from the federal estate tax." He felt an exemption was especially justified for tree farmers. "Healthy, growing forests with abundant wildlife provide benefits to everybody. Without estate tax reform, it will become harder and harder for people like me to remain excellent stewards of our family-owned forests."

Having laid out his case, Thigpen concluded. "Mr. Chairman, a few months ago, Rosett and I were named Mississippi's Outstanding Tree Farmers of the Year. It was a great honor to be selected from among the thousands of excellent Tree Farmers in Mississippi. I'm told one reason we were recognized was because Rosett and I have been speaking out on behalf of good forestry for almost four decades." Thigpen suggested it was his environmental commitment that explained "why I made this trip to Washington: to remind the Committee that estate tax reform is important to preserve family enterprises like ours. It is also important for good forestry." In essence, Thigpen made his family and their farm into a symbol of industrious, hard-working, environmentally friendly minority-owned family businesses around the country that would benefit from estate tax exemption. "We just planted some trees on our property a few months ago. I hope my grandchildren and great-grandchildren will be able to watch those trees grow on the Thigpen Tree Farm—and I know millions of forest landowners feel the same way about their own Tree Farms. We applaud estate tax reforms that will make this possible."

Chester Thigpen and his tree farm soon became the epitome of the case for estate tax repeal. His testimony was cycled and recycled. It naturally became one of Bill Beach's horror stories—Family Business Horror Story #7. In 1996, after Republicans won control of the Senate and Mississippi's Senator Trent Lott became majority leader, Thigpen traveled back to Washington to pose for a picture with the senator. While there, he also met with other members of Congress, including Mississippi's Sonny Montgomery and Bill Thomas of California, now the Ways and Means chairman. That same year, Thigpen's son Lonnie, who later went to work for the U.S. Department of Agriculture, testified that the estate tax strikes "a mortal blow" to African American businesses, which are threatened with seeing "their hard work and earnings squandered." In a 1998 report "The Economics of the Estate Tax," Congress's Joint Economic Committee used Chester Thigpen's tree farm to illustrate "the burdensome nature of the estate tax" and to argue for its repeal. In the congressional debates over the tax, Thigpen was mentioned dozens of times.

In March 1997, two years after Thigpen's testimony, Edmund Peterson, chairman of a conservative African American tax-exempt organization, Project 21, devoted his entire speech to Thigpen at a press conference supporting repeal of the estate tax. He told reporters:

> I believe the freedom of the individual supersedes the might of a greedy Government.
>
> But apparently some of our political leaders do not agree. The death of an individual, while to many Americans is a time for mourning, is to some politicians a time for taxing. In addition to the grief of losing a loved one, today many families have to struggle to withstand the assault a greedy Government unleashes upon their inheritance.
>
> One such family going through this tragedy are the Thigpens of Montrose, Mississippi. A grandson of slaves, voted Outstanding Tree Farmer of the Year, a Mississippi Agriculture and Forestry Museum Hall of Famer, 84-year-old Chester Thigpen is so ill today he is unable to fly to Washington to testify before Congress. And while both God and Government may be smiling on Chester today, it's for two very different reasons. God sees the good he has done, and Government sees the land he owns. The calculators are out of the bureaucrats' pockets ready to ring up the bill. Chester's family knows when that bill comes, they'll have to sell the land to pay it.
>
> So a man who once plowed fields behind a mule finds that the little land he bought in 1940 and expanded to 850 acres today is at risk of existing no more. In effect, when Chester and his wife die, the govern-

ment will conduct a burial of its own—a burial of everything the Thig-pens worked for to pass on to their children. That's what the death tax does: it turns the American Dream into a Government-sponsored nightmare. Every time we think we're free, Government reminds us that it just isn't so.

Not long ago, the Underground Railroad took blacks to freedom. If the estate tax remains as is, the ride over the bridge to the 21st Century threatens not to lead us into greater freedom, but into slavery once again.

Even in 2003, eight years after Thigpen's original testimony, his story was still providing ammunition against the death tax. An April cover story in the Sunday *Washington Post Magazine* by Bob Thompson invoked Chester Thigpen's plight. Thompson wrote that "his children might have to sell [his tree farm] or at least harvest trees before their time, to pay the estate tax."

This claim, however—like the many others that had been made about Chester Thigpen—was not true. When the *Washington Post* article was published, Chester, at age 92, was in Mississippi, virtually incapacitated by a bleeding ulcer that had caused the removal of most of his stomach and a weight loss of more than 50 pounds. As Chester's son Roy puts it, "He doesn't get out much; he doesn't even have his license anymore." Chester's wife Rosett had died four years earlier. Roy says the press frequently exaggerated the Thigpen family's situation. He says that Chester's estate is not taxable, because the value of its assets is below the minimum threshold where the tax applies.

If that is the case, how did Chester Thigpen end up before the House Ways and Means Committee? The Mississippi tree farmer did not get there on his own. Jim Martin, the anti–death tax crusader of 60 Plus, brought Thigpen to Washington and toured him around Congress. When we asked Roy whether Chester wrote his own testimony, Roy gave a hearty laugh and said he thought that Chester's speech was written by "some professors." But we think it far more likely that an astute Washington hand penned Chester's testimony; it is far too compelling to have been crafted in the ivory tower.

Jim Martin himself loves telling Chester Thigpen's story; he has repeated it many times, most frequently in the *Washington Times*. Chester and his sons told Martin in 1999 that Chester's estate would not be taxable. Nevertheless, even in 2001, Martin was still getting good mileage out of the story. That year he did an interview for the liberal *American Prospect* magazine, leading reporter Joshua Green to observe that "Thigpen seems tailored for Martin's campaign." Martin apparently warmed to Green's suggestion that Congress rename the "Estate Tax Elimination Act" the "Chester Thigpen bill." Green quotes Martin: "The Chester Thigpen bill, huh? We'd make the *New York Times* and the *Washington Post* spend a paragraph each time they wrote about it, explaining that he is an African American, the grandson of slaves, who's being affected." Martin added, "I probably ought to send Congress a letter and ask them to do it right now. Hang on for a minute while I write this down." More recently, however, Martin has rarely mentioned Thigpen.

Looking back, Chester Thigpen, who was obviously sincere and genuinely concerned about the future of his family and his tree farm, seems to have been used by repeal advocates for their own purposes. Thigpen, a rural African American descendant of slaves, was a perfect poster child for the campaign. Opponents of repeal now regard him as a stalking horse in the debate, a front for wealthy white families who were financing the repeal machine.

Chester Thigpen aside, however, the coalition's effort to involve minority business owners in the repeal effort was real. Here Frank Blethen, the *Seattle Times* owner and publisher, played a crucial role. If there is any issue Frank Blethen cares about as much as the future of family and independent newspapers in America, it is racial justice and inclusion. He is proud of the diversity of both the content and the work force of his newspaper. Indeed, minorities comprise nearly a quarter of the *Seattle Times*'s employees, more than twice the national average for newspapers. In speeches, Blethen routinely scolds his media colleagues for "what a lousy job we have done on race." He explains, "We are the members of our society responsible for chronicling our nation's history, providing contemporary context, and looking to the future. But how can journalism reflect the faces of America when we lack the will to have our newsrooms reflect its faces? What does it say about our values-based profession that it still excludes countless citizens from our ranks because of their skin color, gender, cultural background, or sexual orientation?" Blethen then challenges his colleagues: "If there is a single crusade journalists in this country should be leading, this is it."

In the 1990s, Blethen's longtime support of racial diversity and inclusion coalesced with his passionate advocacy of estate tax repeal. He believes that the estate tax perpetuates the black-white wealth gap and is harmful "for minorities especially." He felt that the repeal movement should reach out beyond the white affluent circles in which it originated. "We had a bunch of middle-aged privileged white guys sitting around saying 'this tax isn't fair,' and I just thought to myself, this isn't going to work," he says. Blethen takes seriously his role as an image-maker for the coalition.

In 1999, shortly after he received an award from the Leadership Conference on Civil Rights for his work on behalf of affirmative action, Blethen contacted two other newspaper publishers who could help publicize minorities' interest in the death tax debate. Alexis Scott-Reeves is an African American and the publisher, president, and chairman of the *Atlanta Daily World Newspaper*; Alejandro Acquirre is deputy editor and publisher of *Diario Las Americas,* a Miami-based Spanish-language newspaper. Blethen enlisted both of them to aid and support the effort to abolish the estate tax. Adding minority advocates certainly changed the face of the repeal coalition as Blethen intended, and it also contributed to another important cause: the coalition's effort to secure Democratic votes.

Representatives Jennifer Dunn and Chris Cox, along with Senator Jon Kyl, had long emphasized the need for the coalition to attract Democratic support for repeal as a way of fostering at least a modicum of bipartisanship on the issue. Blethen, a self-described liberal who supported former Senator Bill Bradley's run for president in 2000, relished this task. When he told Cox and Kyl that he would get the votes of the liberal Seattle Congressman Jim McDermott and Washington's Democratic Senator Patty Murray, the two Republicans just laughed.

Enlisting the support of Alexis Scott-Reeves and Alejandro Acquirre was a master stroke. Scott-Reeves is the granddaughter of William Alexander Scott II, who founded the *Atlanta Daily World* in 1928. This family paper became the first successful African American daily in the nation, thriving on advertisements from companies such as Atlanta's own Coca-Cola and Sears. In 1944 one of the paper's reporters, Harry McAlpin, became the first African American authorized to attend White House press conferences. The Scotts have also long played a central role in Atlanta's political and cultural life. Alexis Scott-Reeves has been an active citizen in Atlanta, and she has been widely honored for her accomplishments. For example, she was one of fifty women included in an Atlanta History Center exhibit honoring the city's leaders, which opened July 4, 2003. And down in Miami, Alejandro Acquirre's paper, *Diario Las Americas,* plays an important role for the Hispanic community there, while Acquirre himself is active in community affairs, chairing the Florida Arts Council, for example. After the two publishers joined the repeal movement in 1999, many minority-owned family newspapers soon became active for repeal in San Francisco, Los Angeles, Chicago, Cleveland, New York, and other cities up and down the east coast.

After Blethen had spoken to Scott-Reeves and Acquirre, Wayne Henderson of the Leadership Conference on Civil Rights arranged meetings for all three of them with many members of Congress. Even focusing on the particular interests of minorities did not win all the legislators over to repeal. Blethen describes the reception they received, for example, from Charles Rangel, the Harlem congressman who is the ranking Democrat on the Ways and Means Committee, as polite but cool. Nor did the trio convert John Lewis, the civil rights hero from Atlanta, who also sits on Ways and Means. (Blethen, however, still describes meeting Lewis as "one of the highlights of my life.")

Blethen and his allies had surprising success, however, with other minority members of Congress. Sanford Bishop of Georgia, Harold Ford of Tennessee, William Jefferson of Louisiana, and Albert Wynn of Maryland, all Democrats in the Congressional Black Caucus, supported repeal in 2001. Wynn had a particular interest in small businesses' concerns. He chairs the Black Caucus's Minority Business Task Force, having represented since 1992 a district in Prince Georges and Montgomery counties that is inhabited by many federal workers and owners of small businesses. According to Wynn, the district ranks tenth in the nation in its number of small businesses. When the congressman talks about estate tax repeal, he sounds just like Hawaii's Neil Abercrombie in his concern for the tax's impact on his hard-working constituents. He views repeal as a "little guy's" issue. In his district, he says, the death tax affects auto dealers, gas station owners, funeral parlors, and local beer distributors. "I think the Democrats have missed the boat on small business issues generally," he says. "Most of my liberal colleagues don't get it," he adds, echoing Abercrombie. "It is very important to reach out to ethnic minorities, they are almost all very entrepreneurial."

Speaking in favor of estate tax repeal on the floor of the House of Representatives, Sanford Bishop of Georgia, who attributes his support for repeal to the advocacy of peanut farmers from his southwest Georgia district, sings from the same songbook. In one speech he said,

> The "death tax" represents all that is unfair and unjust about the tax structure in America because it undermines the life work and life savings of Americans who want only to pass along to their children and their grandchildren the fruits of their labor and the realization of the American Dream. In my state of Georgia, farmers, many of whom are widowed women and the children of deceased fathers, are faced with losing their family farms because of this harsh tax. Employees of small- and medium-size businesses, many of whom are minorities, are at risk of losing their jobs because their employers are forced to cut costs because they cannot afford the unfair "death taxes" levied upon them. Funeral homes, newspaper publishers, radio station owners, garment manufacturers are all affected—all across the demographic spectrum. Although reasonable minds can differ on this issue, I believe that the "death tax" is politically misguided, morally unjustifiable, and downright un-American. Let us vote today to finally eliminate the "death tax" and return to the American people and their progeny the hard-earned fruits of their labor.

The Clinton White House was caught completely by surprise when members of the congressional Black Caucus voted for repeal. Whatever its other fictions, we have it on extremely good authority that the following excerpt from "The West Wing" accurately depicts the confused reaction in President Clinton's White House:

> LEO: They have the votes for repeal?
> JOSH: They have 218 without breaking a sweat.
> TOBY: It's 290 to override.
> LEO: Where are they getting them?
> JOSH: The Republicans are calling an "all-hands," we're assuming they'll get the full 226 plus Fayette, Genesee and Trent. . . .
> TOBY: We lose about another 13 votes from rural districts. Maybe 3 of them will switch back to us if it was close but they'd get killed next November and I wouldn't ask them to do it.

LEO: That's 283. Where are the other 7 votes against us?
JOSH: That's the thing.
TOBY: It's from inside the Black Caucus. That's where the 7 votes
   are. . . .
JOSH: These are members of the Congressional Black Caucus. . . .
   Can you think of any reason why they'd oppose the estate tax?
LEO: Sure.
JOSH: What?
LEO: The first generation of black millionaires is about to die.

Pat Soldano also played an important role in the effort to enlist minorities to the cause. We have already seen how she effectively reached out
to women business owners. She also recruited the Black Chamber of Commerce, and in 1999 its president, Henry Alford, labeled the estate tax a
"legacy killer" for blacks. Alford offered two purportedly death tax–induced bankruptcies as prime examples: that of the "great Sammy Davis's"
wife and of the "*Chicago Daily Defender*—the oldest Black-owned daily
newspaper in the United States." Alford also saw in the repeal movement a
tremendous chance to rid the country of this inequity: "Fortunately, we
now have an opportunity to get the 'legacy killer' out of our lives and future. . . . Call your applicable congressperson or senator and tell them you
support these bills to end the 'death tax.' Tell them it is alright for Black
folks to begin building wealth in this country. It is not against the law and
it certainly is more enjoyable than poverty." If you click on "taxation" on
the Black Chamber of Commerce website, you will find precious little other
than messages opposing the death tax.

In May 1999, Henry Alford, Alexis Scott-Reeves, and Alejandro Acquirre appeared at a morning press conference at the National Press Club
with several owners and representatives of minority-owned businesses, including George Herrera, president of the U.S. Hispanic Chamber of Commerce; Pete Homer, president of the National Indian Business Association;
and Terra Neese on behalf of the National Association of Women Business
Owners. None of the major national or regional papers, or the inside-the-
beltway dailies *The Hill* or *Roll Call*, or even the *Washington Times* printed
a word about this press conference. Nevertheless, it sent an unmistakable
message to both repeal advocates and opponents that the repeal effort was
no longer comprised of just "a bunch of middle-aged privileged white guys."

A story from the 2000 presidential election shows just how thoroughly the strategy of enlisting support for repeal from racial minorities had spread. Late in the campaign, in the basement of the St. Matthew Christian Methodist Church in Milwaukee, Wisconsin, representatives of the candidates met a group of African American voters to describe what their campaigns offered the African American population. Al Gore's representative talked about poverty relief and initiatives to encourage and stimulate home ownership. In contrast, Angela Sailor, representing George W. Bush, highlighted his commitment to eliminating the death tax as a way to help African Americans. Somehow the Bush campaign had determined that this issue was crucial to African American voters. This conclusion is curious, given that the disparity between white and African American wealth is considerably greater than the income gap. In their 1995 book *Black Wealth/ White Wealth,* Melvin Oliver and Thomas Shapiro show that while middle-class African Americans now earn 70 cents for every dollar earned by whites, they have only 15 cents for every dollar of white middle-class wealth. A more recent book by Thomas Shapiro says the latter number is only 10 cents. The odds are therefore extremely high that none of the African Americans at that St. Matthew church meeting would be subject to the estate tax. Nevertheless, the repeal campaign had successfully spread the message that the death tax was a key issue for minority voters.

But this does not mean that African Americans are wrong to be concerned with their ability to pass their wealth on to future generations. Here is how the magazine *Black Enterprise* describes the goal and the obstacles:

Leaving a legacy for future generations is a key motivation for pursuing entrepreneurship, particularly for African Americans. But achieving that legacy isn't easy. Only one in three family firms survives two generations; only one in six survives three generations. The challenge is not starting a family business, but being able to pass it on from generation to generation.

And the financial planning book *The Black Woman's Guide to Financial Independence* emphasizes the barrier created by the estate tax. "Estate taxes are the most expensive taxes you will ever have to pay," it says. "The federal estate tax has graduated rates ranging from 40–55%. The more you have, the higher the tax rate. This is money you have earned and should be passed on to your heirs instead of to the federal government."

The repeal coalition's minority recruitment efforts did not stop with African Americans. By April 2001, Pat Soldano could report to the House Ways and Means Committee that "many new voices have called for the elimination of the death tax, including the National Association of Women Business Owners, National Black Chamber of Commerce, National Indian Business Association, U.S. Hispanic Chamber of Commerce, U.S. Pan Asian American Chamber of Commerce, National Association of Neighborhoods, and Texas Conference of Black Mayors."

During the summer of 2004, repeal advocates focused on mobilizing Hispanics to oppose the death tax. In July, Pat Soldano's Policy and Taxation Group was able to tout the results of a poll and focus-group survey of Hispanic business owners conducted by IMPACTO Group, an organization founded by Leslie Sanchez, after she left George W. Bush's White House staff. Sanchez had headed the National Republican Committee's marketing campaign to attract Hispanic voters in the 2000 presidential campaign. The surveys concluded that 71 percent of respondents said they will support candidates who want to eliminate the "death tax" and that 83 percent of Hispanic small business owners surveyed believe that the "death tax" is unfair. Moreover, more than one-third (36 percent) of respondents said that they believe they can escape "death taxes" by taking their assets out of the country before their death, and one out of four said that they believe their heirs would be forced to sell off part of their businesses to pay the tax. Needless to say, repeal advocates held a press conference to herald these results and peddle them to both Republican and Democratic members of Congress.

Years earlier, Jill Mackie, a bright, dedicated woman, who has worked on the estate tax issue for Frank Blethen for more than a decade, had suggested to Soldano that the gay and lesbian community might also be brought on board. So on July 21, 2001, Soldano spoke in Chicago at the Liberty for All National Leadership Conference, telling the gathering that "gay and lesbian couples are not entitled to the 'marital deduction,' so the 55 percent tax is assessed immediately at the time of death—and then assessed again at the time of the second spouse's death. In other words, in a gay or lesbian family, you are taxed twice." She concluded, "So, without a doubt, the death tax is about you. And if you're gay or lesbian, it is a discriminatory tax that can bankrupt your loved ones at the worst possible moment—the time of your death." An innovative political twist: turning the inability of gays to marry to the cause of estate tax repeal.

Polling data suggest that Soldano's arguments took hold. Frank Luntz reports that 61 percent of self-described gays and lesbians who voted for Al Gore in 2000, when presented in a survey with the arguments on both sides of the estate tax issue, indicated they would support a candidate who believed that the estate tax was unfair and should be eliminated. Luntz concludes that "elimination of the estate tax is a bipartisan issue." He says, "While cutting or eliminating taxes has traditionally been seen as a Republican issue, 83 percent of gays and lesbians that support death tax repeal were 2000 Gore voters." Moreover, "these same Gore voters overwhelmingly support a candidate that calls for the elimination of death taxes." Luntz insists that "no tax reform package is easier to explain than the repeal of the death tax. Gay and lesbian respondents clearly understood it and 72 percent of them believe it is 'discriminatory.' When asked if they would support a law to eliminate the estate tax, even though they knew they may not benefit, 82 percent stated they would."

As a result of all these outreach efforts, the coalition for estate tax repeal no longer had to rely on endlessly repeating Chester Thigpen's lament to suggest that estate tax repeal was not an issue affecting only wealthy whites. A veritable rainbow coalition of minority groups was now actively urging repeal. Many Democrats were stunned. As one of Washington's most plugged-in players on the left put it, the organization of minority support for repeal took place "below the radar screen."

In solving the mystery of the allure that repeal has held for a majority of Americans over the last decade, we should not underestimate the degree to which the repeal campaign altered public perceptions about who would profit from the demise of the death tax. Long before George Bush's tax legislation was signed in 2001, the anti–death tax campaign was no longer primarily associated with repeal's largest beneficiaries, the super-rich; indeed, by the mid-1990s, it was no longer even seen as solely the concern of the white, male, "grasstops" whose stories were being so effectively mobilized during this same period. From Jim Martin's possibly cynical use of Chester Thigpen to Frank Blethen's and Pat Soldano's apparently more sincere efforts, the anti–estate tax groups had fully succeeded in changing the face for repeal. As we shall now see, this new diversity coincided with a determined and well-researched effort to alter not only the public face of the issue, but the very words and phrases used to understand and describe it.

Talking the Talk

When Abraham Lincoln was a young Illinois legislator, he unsuccessfully urged his state to impose a graduated tax on real property. Such a levy would be "equitable within itself," he argued, because it would burden the "wealthy few"—who, he emphasized, "are not sufficiently numerous to carry the elections." More than a century and a half later, congressional Democrats opposed to estate tax repeal regarded Lincoln's point about the limited political power of the wealthy few as adequate protection against the forces for repeal. To repeal advocates, however, this point was irrelevant. They knew full well that the wealthy still are not sufficiently numerous to carry elections. To win, they needed to sway the masses to their side. To accomplish this, the repealers had to emphasize again and again the connection between the tax and the event that everyone, rich and poor alike, must confront—death. The repeal coalition had to make the American people believe that the *cause* of the tax was death itself rather than the size of one's fortune.

Major tax policy debates in the United States have historically been fought over big ideas. Ambrose Bierce, writing in 1911, five years before the modern estate tax came into effect, famously described politics in his *Devil's Dictionary* as a "strife of interests masquerading as a contest of principles," the "conduct of public affairs for private advantage." The tax law is always produced in this context. In contrast, Stephen Weisman, in his book *The Great Tax Wars,* regards tax policy debates as a contest between two fundamental, conflicting principles: "justice" on one side, and "virtue" on the other. Justice, according to Weisman, is taxation based on ability to pay, with progressive taxes on income or wealth "soften[ing] the edges of the distribution of wealth in the interest of justice and fairness," acting as a "kind of leveler." Virtue, by contrast, views "wealth as a product of hard work, thrift, ingenuity and risk-taking," something the state should encourage and protect.

The battle between virtue and justice has often raged in political battles over taxes—in debates, for example, over whether to raise income tax rates or lower them and in arguments over the appropriate level of tax on capital gains. The debate over estate tax repeal, however, was unique. Repeal advocates managed to muster arguments of *both* fairness and virtue to their cause. Opponents responded essentially with a plea to self-interest, arguing, "This tax will not affect you; it burdens only the wealthy few, so you should support it."

Those favoring repeal of the estate tax advanced a straightforward argument: This is an unfair double tax, imposed at the worst time—the death of the family's breadwinner. It attacks the American dream by destroying family businesses and family farms. Yet for all this destruction, the repealers argued, the money raised is only a small drop in the huge bucket of federal revenues which, as far as anyone can tell, will be wasted by Washington bureaucrats anyway, lost in the swamp of excessive government spending.

Those who wanted to retain the tax fashioned no equivalent reply. Their constant refrain was that the tax burdens only the wealthiest 2 percent of Americans who die in any given year. The message was directed to the majority of voters, making a weak attempt to boost the plea to self-interest with an implicit claim of fairness: since this is a tax on the wealthy, not on you, it must be fair. Repeal advocates promptly labeled this argument "class warfare."

Repeal's adversaries also endeavored to link estate tax revenues to the funding of popular federal programs. Democratic Representatives Dick Gephardt and Henry Waxman in 1992 proposed using estate tax revenues to finance long-term care and some Medicare enhancements. Subsequently two other Democrats, Senator Paul Wellstone and Congressman Barney Frank, tried to use estate tax revenues to fund a prescription drug benefit, an item that had long been on retirees' wish list. OMB Watch, one of the liberal Washington think tanks that support the tax, suggested on its website that retaining the estate tax could keep certain federal programs, such as Head Start and child-care grants, fully funded. But no one ever believed that the future of these programs turned on retention of the tax. Nor did those who wanted to save the tax ever succeed in earmarking revenues for a specific type of spending. These feeble efforts to link the tax to popular spending programs never really got off the ground.

How did the estate tax repeal movement capture both the language and the forces of justice and virtue? Many people helped shape and sharpen the message, among them Bill Beach, Frank Blethen, Jim Martin, and Jennifer Dunn. As we shall see, however, arguably the most important player in re-shaping the rhetoric of estate tax politics was the Republican pollster and policy entrepreneur Frank Luntz, whom Pat Soldano's group of wealthy families hired to conduct research on the issue.

Success, of course, has a thousand mothers. When it comes to the shift in terminology from "estate tax" to "death tax," a linguistic move that be-came a central component of the repeal coalition's strategy, there seem to be as many authors as there were advocates for repeal. In 1993, for exam-ple, Jim Martin began crusading to substitute the label. He created a "pizza fund" by fining office workers at his 60 Plus Association one dollar each time he heard them utter the words "estate tax." Martin claims that his pizza-fund technique spread to the NFIB, to other death-tax repeal lobby-ing shops, and even to some congressional offices. In his characteristically excessive manner, he also likes the terms "grave-robber's tax," the "grim reaper's tax," or the "vulture tax," to name only a few of his choicest sug-gestions. But—with the exception of the CATO Institute, which used the grave-robber label twice in the titles of publications opposing the tax—these epithets failed to catch on. "Death tax" it was. Martin's favorite slo-gan is "Kill the death tax!"

Isn't this fuss about the choice of words just semantics? Not according to Martin, who stresses that "language popularizes issues." Indeed, by 1999, even CNN—often scorned by repeal advocates for its liberal incli-nations—had accepted the "death tax" label. Other networks had also accepted the nomenclature. More importantly, the public changed its vo-cabulary. An African American taxi driver in Boston, complaining to us in the summer of 2003 about the economy and George Bush's tax policies generally, did see one redeeming factor in the president's economic plan. "At least he wants to repeal the death tax," this former policeman said. Jim Martin boasted to *American Prospect* magazine about the success of the death tax terminology: "Liberals have lost the battle over popular percep-tion. Conservatives have managed to control not only the tax's image, but the very language used to describe it."

But Martin is not the only one who tries to take credit for popularizing the "death tax" label. Rush Limbaugh began attacking the "death tax" in the early 1990s. Dan Blankenburg of the NFIB and Alan Soba of the National Cattlemen's Beef Association told Family Business Estate Tax Coalition members always to use the phrase. Frank Blethen named his website of repeal resources "deathtax.com."

Moreover, politicians' rhetoric moved in step with that of the lobbyists and pundits. In 1995, House Speaker Newt Gingrich urged his colleagues to deploy the label. Ways and Means Committee Chairman Bill Archer also fired off a memo to House Republicans telling them to use only the term "death tax." Jennifer Dunn admits she was "reluctant to use it at first," principally because "it didn't go over well with women," but she soon relented. "It worked well with those we needed to influence," she says. Dunn adds, "That was a real turning point. Death tax is a good name because it emphasizes you cannot prepare for it."

California Republican Congressman Christopher Cox is right when he insists that "no pollster or lobbyist can take credit" for the "death tax" epithet. As he notes, the phrase was not invented recently. In the nineteenth century, inheritance taxes were routinely called death taxes. W. M. Kiplinger used that label in a 1926 *New York Times* article discussing that year's legislative changes. The prominent tax lawyer Louis Eisenstein used the death tax phrase in an influential 1956 article in New York University's *Tax Law Review* and in a 1955 report for Congress's Joint Economic Committee. Ronald Reagan used the term in his 1980 campaign speeches. Examples abound. But Cox's emphasis on the ancient lineage of the death tax pseudonym is quite beside the point. Its many antecedents in no way diminish the impact of the death tax label in this repeal campaign.

A key staffer to a high-ranking congressional Republican stresses the role played by the shift in labels. "Republicans," he says, "put a high level of importance on the death/estate tax language—they had to work hard to get members to act in unison, including training members to say 'death tax.'" The staffer traces this campaign to mold lawmakers' language to Newt Gingrich, stressing that the label sends a particular important message to constituents. "Estate tax sounds like it only hits the wealthy but 'death tax' sounds like it hits everyone. They focus grouped this a lot, and people viewed a 'death tax' as very unfair. You don't have to be really rich to be worried about a death tax."

A prominent Washington journalist agrees. "Repeal advocates found a winning formula," he says. "Call it the death tax and make it appear that many more people have to pay it than actually do, appeal to the Republican anti-tax sentiment and make it a moral issue, and spread the gospel to politically powerful constituents who in reality didn't have the stake in it that they thought they had." Former House Republican Majority Leader Dick Armey goes so far as to claim that "the nomenclature turned the debate." Washington political pundit Norman Ornstein agrees. "Republicans," he says, "moved the rhetoric from 'taxing the rich' to taxing at death. The image was of a tax collector coming to the door of a family grieving." One member of Congress spoke to a lobbyist opposing repeal as if the death tax label had magical powers: "Where I am from, no one will ever be subject to the estate tax, but when I feel my support waning, I say 'I'll get rid of the death tax to protect you, your families, your farms'—and I get cheers. Why should I try to educate them?"

The battle to win repeal-converts by changing the terms of the debate, however, went far beyond simply relabeling. As Frank Luntz's work on the issue demonstrated to Republicans, this name change would have to be accompanied by an entirely new rhetoric.

Luntz, who regularly relies on his raffish charm to rescue him from trouble, has always been a political junkie. He claims to have begun reading news magazines by age six. By the end of high school, this son of a Connecticut dentist had become state chairman of Teen Age Republicans. In 1987, after receiving his doctorate in politics from Oxford University, Luntz took a job with Ronald Reagan's pollster, Richard Wirthlin. Luntz credits Wirthlin with having pioneered the "instant response" focus-group technique that Luntz has since transformed into an art form. That year Luntz also opened his consulting firm, Frank I. Luntz and Associates, in Arlington, Virginia. (Its successor, Luntz Research Companies, has worked on repeal of the estate tax for Pat Soldano and represents the NFIB and other key estate tax opponents, including the U.S. Chamber of Commerce and the National Association of Manufacturers.)

Beginning in the late 1980s, Luntz tried to combine an academic career with his role as a political pollster and consultant. He taught politics at the University of Pennsylvania until 1993, when the university cancelled his classes. He blames that unhappy ending on the reaction of the university's brass to a heavily publicized Luntz poll that described Penn as last in the Ivy League academically, but first in promiscuity. But the poll may just have been the straw that broke the university's back. Two years earlier, Luntz had gotten into a campus controversy over his assignment to his students to get elected to the Undergraduate Assembly. When the Nominations and Elections Committee (NEC) of the student government blocked this gambit, Luntz told his class, "I will be damned if I'm going to allow a student government body that wasn't elected and doesn't represent anybody . . . [to] tell me what I can and can't teach." He added, "I will not fuck up my class by buckling in to the NEC."

Frank Luntz's start in Republican politics was also a bit rocky. In 1991 he tried to work for President George H. W. Bush but was turned down. He then found employment with two men seeking to unseat the president, Pat Buchanan and Ross Perot. When both failed in their election bids, Luntz made a Nixonian exit from politics, saying, "I have seen too much from the inside. All I really want to do is teach." In September 1992, this master of political spin published a tirade in the University of Pennsylvania's *Daily Pennsylvanian,* announcing,

> We are a nation cynical about politics, with much to be cynical about. We desperately seek straight-talking candidates where there are none. . . . We ask for substance, but all we get are polls. We expect reality, but in politics, there are only perceptions. . . . [E]ven when a presidential campaign decides to "address an issue," the primary goal is to create a visual image. . . . That is why most so-called issue-oriented debates are so high on rhetoric and so low on substance. . . . Yes, the American voter has a declining attention span. . . . Yes, they buy this trash. But this is why more content, not less, is needed.

With the benefit of hindsight, we wish that Luntz had concluded this column with the famous refrain from the Pogo comic strip: "We have met the enemy and they is us."

The 1994 midterm election, which made Newt Gingrich speaker of the House, also catapulted Frank Luntz into the forefront of American politics. Gingrich had hired Luntz to work on his "Contract with America" after seeing one of the pollster's presentations on what Perot voters wanted. Whether or not Luntz deserves as much credit for the contract as he claims, he clearly influenced Gingrich to rank the document's ten items in order of their importance to Perot voters. Then, on October 1, 1994, Luntz became one of the first to predict a Republican takeover of the House of Representatives. A month later his forecast was vindicated, and he was labeled the Republicans' "boy wonder," an appellation that received confirmation in the mainstream media. In December 1994, *USA Today* listed Luntz as one of the nine most influential minds in the Republican Party and *Time* included him among "50 of America's most promising leaders aged 40 and under." Since then Luntz has had more staying power than his friend Newt Gingrich.

Luntz fancies himself something of a scientist. His trademark is the "instant response" focus group, where people listen to information, phrases, or speeches and immediately register their positive or negative responses with hand-held measuring devices. "The way I do it, usually, is to hear the words of somebody else," Luntz says. "I can't give you a single example of a word I actually created. The way my words are created is by taking the words of others—average Americans, not politicians." Luntz says he moderates more than 100 focus groups and 30 instant response sessions—"the ones with the dials"—each year, and has done so for a long time. "I show them language I've created. Then I have a line for them to create language for me." He believes he is discovering new territory from the American voters. "The goal of a focus group," he says, "is to gain access to private noncommercial uncensored feelings and emotions." To make sure no one underestimates his importance, he adds, "The single greatest component of a successful focus group is the moderator."

Luntz converts these focus-group tidbits into detailed playbooks for Republican politicians. There are many versions. In the 1990s, he condensed his 222-page *Language for the 21st Century,* which he says weighed "about three pounds," into a 75-page pamphlet, *Conservatively Speaking: How to Use the Language of the 21st Century to Win the Hearts and Minds of the American People.* Apparently, the longer title made up for the discarded pages. In the year 2000, he published a five-pound, 406-page binder, *A Conversation with America 2000,* and a pocket-sized version called *Right Words.* Luntz no doubt hopes that Republican politicians will carry the latter with them everywhere so as never to be at a loss for words, the "right words."

These manuals vary in size, but not in style. They are filled with advice both about what to say about the issues of the day and how to say it. Little boxes throughout contain snippets in bold type entitled "Language that Works" or "Words that Work." Luntz insists that these claims are grounded in hard evidence. "As with every memo we provide, we have used the same scientific methodology to isolate specific words, phrases, themes and messages that will resonate with at least 70% of the American audience. The language [used here] will help you secure support from a large majority of Americans."

Regardless of the issue, Luntz emphasizes similar themes: "Every issue must have a moral component." "The best-performing sound bites mention children, families and democratic values." "Talk about real people," he advises.

When Luntz says "talk about real people," he is using a turn of phrase. You are supposed to talk about specific people whether they are real or not. He elaborates:

> People like to know about people. The more personal and specific the anecdote, the better. A story about a little old lady who was mugged by a parolee doesn't really hit home until you learn that the lady was in Philadelphia visiting her family, that her name is Nellie Smith, that she has snow white hair and walks with a cane, and that she was on her way home from the local toy store where she had just picked up an Elmo doll for her granddaughter.

Luntz concludes, "A compelling story, even if factually inaccurate, can be more emotionally compelling than a dry recitation of the truth." Remind you of the Chester Thigpen story?

When Luntz applies his science to taxes, he says, "Personalize tax relief. Don't talk in numbers. The IRS is still the most hated institution of government. You cannot overdo it when it comes to attacking the IRS." Here is his advice about the death tax from *Conservatively Speaking*:

> No proposal is easier to explain than repeal of the estate tax—what I like to call "Death Tax." From "taxing the American dream" to "you shouldn't have to visit the undertaker and the taxman on the same day," the language of Death Tax repeal is easy to understand. It is important to explain the "principles" behind your desire to repeal the Death Tax. . . . If you get the principles right, support will follow. Otherwise, you open yourself to accusations of selfish behavior.
> Start with four "common sense" principles:
>
> 1. It is the wrong tax. It provides just one percent of the nation's revenues, and it costs more to collect than any other federal tax.

2. It comes at the wrong time. People shouldn't be burdened at the most difficult time of their lives.
3. It hurts the wrong people. If you saved for the future, put away money for your children, built a small business, ran a family farm, or achieved the American Dream in other ways, the Death Tax punishes you.
4. It helps the wrong people. The only people helped by the estate tax are the fancy lawyers and expensive tax accountants—and IRS agents.

Finally, Luntz offers the following paragraph as part of a "good two-minute conclusion," incorporating virtually all of his prior advice:

> The Death Tax is simply unfair. It tells every American that no matter how hard you work or how wisely you manage your affairs, in the end the federal government is going to step in and take it away. The estate tax is double and, in some cases, triple taxation. It punishes hard work and savings, it fails to raise the kind of revenues that might conceivably justify some of the damage it causes. It has been destroying businesses and ruining lives for four generations. Let us not make this mistake with our children. End the Death Tax now.

Frank Luntz understands that repeal advocates have garnered the momentum. "Years ago," he says, "the death tax was thought of as a chance to recoup money from the richest Americans. Today it is one of the most unpopular taxes. Even a plurality of Democrats support its repeal."

Luntz warns that Americans "are particularly sensitive to any kind of apparent dogma or canned prescriptions." He insists that "if they hear you repeating the exact same words over and over again, they will come to distrust your message." But his Republican disciples seem to believe repetition is the sincerest form of flattery. Bill Archer, chairman of the House Ways and Means Committee, said in 2000, "No one should have to visit the undertaker and the IRS on the same day." While Speaker of the House Newt Gingrich, always an original, changed it to "the same week." J. C. Watts, now Luntz's business partner, kept to the script when he was a congressman. "Furthermore," he added for emphasis, "nobody should be forced to visit the undertaker and the IRS in the same day." On the floor of the House of Representatives, two dozen legislators have repeated the same phrase.

And across the Capitol on the Senate floor, Iowa's Republican Senator Charles Grassley, subsequently chairman of the Senate Finance Committee, added his variation: "No taxpayers should be visited by the undertaker and the tax collector at the same time." The active verb associated with a dead person was apparently too much for this Midwesterner. A half-dozen other senators also chimed in with the undertaker bit.

Repetition of the undertaker refrain is nothing compared to the characterization of the death tax as a tax on "the American dream." A casual reading of the *Congressional Record* reveals more than 50 incantations of the death tax shattering the American dream in the House of Representatives and nearly a dozen in the Senate. Ignoring his own advice, Luntz himself can't stop worrying about threats to the American dream. In his little book *Conservatively Speaking,* it is not only the death tax that assaults "the American dream." Luntz says that the budget debate also should be cast "in terms of 'the American dream.'" Lawmakers should tell their constituents that a "secure retirement" with private accounts substituting for Social Security is what "you deserve to fulfill your vision of the American Dream," and that when invoking "the children," the question is, "How will your *solutions* help the next generation achieve the American Dream?" Fatigue set in; we cannot tell you how many times the American dream is invoked in Luntz's larger volumes on behalf of conservatives' proposals.

One may feel manipulated by Luntz's scientific experiments. He tests how people react to specific language and then shapes our nation's political debate to gain traction on behalf of conservative dogma that a fully informed public might or might not endorse. But one cannot deny the effectiveness of his technique. Even if one believes that most of Luntz's scientific pretensions are a bunch of hooey, it has become clear that those fighting to repeal the death tax are tapping into a few tenets widely felt by the American public: distaste for imposing a tax when the family's breadwinner dies; desire to mark one's success in life by building up wealth—a legacy—and passing it on to children or grandchildren; admiration of entrepreneurship, small businesses, and family farms; and the inherent unfairness of "double taxation."

The defenders of the estate tax have lost this debate. Shouting "the richest 2 percent" over and over has failed. No one has effectively made the case that Theodore Roosevelt did nearly a century ago on behalf of taxing inheritances. Roosevelt's claim that the "man of great wealth owes a peculiar obligation to the state, because he derives special advantage from the mere existence of government," now seems quaint. Today it would quickly be labeled "class warfare." Consider the case he made in 1910 for a narrowly targeted inheritance tax:

> The absence of effective state, and, especially, national, restraint upon unfair money-getting has tended to create a small class of enormously wealthy and economically powerful men, whose chief object is to hold and increase their power. . . . The really big fortune, the swollen fortune, by the mere fact of its size acquires qualities which differentiate it in kind as well as in degree from what is possessed by men of relatively small means. Therefore, I believe in a graduated income tax on big fortunes, and in another tax which is far more easily collected and far more effective—a graduated inheritance tax on big fortunes, properly safeguarded against evasion and increasing rapidly in amount with the size of the estate.

Roosevelt added, "We are bound in honor to refuse to listen to those men who would make us desist from the effort to do away with the inequality, which means injustice; the inequality of right, opportunity, of privilege." It is the rare Democrat or Republican who today would dare utter such words.

The coalitions and their leaders have helped to drastically redefine the debate over this tax in moral terms. They have enlisted both virtue and justice in their cause. Their strategic genius gives distinction and originality to their venture. Their opponents have been back on their heels, denying, contesting, and counterpunching in the repealers' terms and on their terrain. In democratic politics, this defensive fighting is a recipe for defeat.

Yet, the organizational and intellectual advantages that the repeal movement possesses are of more than just the devotion of well-funded activists and their pollsters. Behind the success of the movement lies a much larger trend in American political culture. To understand the counterintuitive rise in the popularity of estate tax repeal, one has also to understand the increasingly important role that think tanks have come to play in the lawmaking process in our nation's capital.

Exploiting the Think Tank Gap

Our tale thus far has emphasized the crusaders who led the charge against the death tax and the grasstop constituents who most effectively sold the case for repeal to their legislators. But working alongside these individuals, a powerful group of policy-oriented research organizations played a crucial supporting role in our drama. Washington think tanks have become major players in the political game. Indeed, death tax repeal might never have made it onto the political agenda but for the revolutionary transformation of think tanks since the early 1970s.

A handful of these Washington think tanks and research groups had existed since the 1930s, but the number has mushroomed in recent decades, growing to some 200 by 1985, and 305 by 1996—two-thirds of them focused on national policy-making. The ideological hue of think tanks has also changed markedly, reflecting the growth of the conservative movement that we have encountered elsewhere in our tale. Between 1976 and 1995, almost twice as many conservative think tanks emerged as liberal ones. Moreover, with a couple of exceptions, the conservative think tanks are substantially better funded. This growing think tank gap strengthened the hand of the repeal forces considerably.

Think tanks did not play much of a part in moving the 2001 tax legislation forward; the coalition members and the political entrepreneurs such as Jennifer Dunn were decisive in that effort. In fact, the most important think tank that promoted repeal—the Heritage Foundation—was already gearing down its expenditures on the issue by the late 1990s when the repeal bill took off. However, the think tanks were important earlier, and less obtrusively, in shaping a climate favorable to repeal. They created what Robert Bothwell, president of the National Committee for Responsive Philanthropy, aptly describes as the "echo chamber" in which the arguments for death tax repeal would resonate.

Until the 1970s, Washington think tanks were sleepy affairs. They were "universities without students," as people in our line of work describe them—not without a little envy. Some have been around for decades. Perhaps the best-known organization is as old as the modern estate tax. Founded as the Institute for Governmental Research in 1916 by millionaire businessman and philanthropist Robert Brookings, it was a product of the Progressive impulse to evaluate government policy using social science research methods. The institute grew steadily in size and stature, developing a reputation for rigorous analysis of government policy during the New Deal and thereafter.

Today the Brookings Institution's 120 scholars, who are mostly Ph.D.s in one of the social sciences, consume an annual budget of over $35 million in plush accommodations—an imposing, eight-story building on Massachusetts Avenue near Dupont Circle, not far from the original site at 26 Jackson Place. The marble-tiled lobby is abuzz with perpetual activity, as purposeful people come and go to meetings and seminars, head for the large cafeteria to the right of the lobby, or frequent the bookstore, which is chock full of recent Brookings publications and books by affiliated scholars. The Brookings ambiance is one of efficient professionalism dedicated to the public interest.

Similar stories can be told about the other mature think tanks. The Urban Institute, for example, began life in 1968 as a committee appointed by President Lyndon Johnson to evaluate Great Society programs and initiatives. UI has grown steadily since then, eventually becoming the biggest kid on Washington's think tank bloc, with a staff of some 400 analysts, who mostly hold Ph.D.s from major research universities. Eight senior fellows, drawn primarily from high-ranking government positions, oversee the staff's work. From 1991 to 2003, its annual operating budget grew from about $20 million to almost $80 million. The current president, Robert Reischauer, exemplifies UI's personality. He has a Ph.D. in economics, is a former Brookings fellow, and directed the nonpartisan Congressional Budget Office from 1989 to 1995, the time from the elder Bush's White House into the Clinton administration. Like Brookings, UI has always had a policy-wonk image. Its mission statement avoids ideological commitments, instead expressing its philosophy through seven motivating principles: UI aspires to "pick the right issues, choose/create the right methodologies, assemble the right team, follow the facts wherever they lead, find the right words, subject findings to outside review, and reach the right audiences."

Like the career staffs on congressional committees, the researchers who populate think tanks often see themselves as professionals with a strong commitment to providing objective analysis. They have political views, to be sure, but their professional self-image is basically technocratic. As with many liberal policy analysts in the nation's colleges and universities, they are often civic-minded people with a public-spirited commitment to social improvement, but they like to think that they operate above the political fray—working for a better America in their area of expertise.

Conservatives have often taken a different view of the traditional DC think tanks. For them, the incrementalism of places such as Brookings and UI legitimates the main contours of the welfare state; they view these institutions as tinkering with its margins. For people philosophically at odds with the welfare state as it has existed since the New Deal, this is not a sufficiently critical perspective. From their point of view, the supposedly independent think tanks—501(c)(3) organizations that are prohibited from lobbying—have been captured by their object of study. It does not escape the critics' attention that over half of UI's vast budget comes from government contracts. One can almost hear Grover Norquist opining that these think tanks are a symptom of bloated government, not objective analysts of it.

Conservatives have responded from time to time by organizing think tanks of their own, but it was not until the 1970s that they achieved a sustained change in the think tank landscape. As long ago as 1937 the Tax Foundation was established in response to concerns over the tax increases resulting from the New Deal. Though billed as independent and unaffiliated, with a mission to "educate the public about taxes," the Tax Foundation has always had an aggressive antitax agenda. Today it is best known for its annual calculation of "Tax Freedom Day"—when the average taxpayer's annual obligations to the government have allegedly been met. (This day moved forward through the calendar each year of the Clinton administration, from April 19th in 1991 to April 30th in 2000, but started moving back again after George W. Bush came into office, to April 11 in 2004, the earliest date since 1967.) Perhaps too busy advocating fiscal discipline in government, the Tax Foundation needed some lessons in thrift itself: it went badly into debt in 1989 and was bought by the antitax advocacy group Citizens for a Sound Economy, which promised to maintain the foundation's separate identity and preserve the "objectivity and credibility of its publications." But the Tax Foundation is relatively small potatoes in any case.

The earliest consequential conservative answer to the "neutral" policy-wonk think tanks came from the American Enterprise Institute. Located on Seventeenth Street, a stone's throw from the White House, AEI has become integral to the conservative movement in recent decades. It occupies the top three floors of a modern office building and does not advertise its presence to the public. Without even a sign downstairs, visitors have to search for the group on the building directory on the wall. But everyone in policy circles in Washington knows about AEI. The scholars and fellows include a veritable who's who of the conservative chattering classes. Walter Berns, David Frum, Glenn Hubbard, Irving Kristol, Charles Murray, and Michael Novak are among the more notable—not to mention staple figures of the Republican scene such as Second Lady Lynn Cheney, Richard Perle, and Newt Gingrich.

AEI had a rocky start. Founded in 1943 as the American Enterprise Association, it initially lived on the margins of the Washington think tank universe. While Brookings and UI prized their reputation for scholarly neutrality, AEI made no secret of its free market, anti–big government orientation. Its mission statement gears the organization to "promoting freedom" by limiting the role of government, strengthening national defense, and encouraging private enterprise. In the early years its mission hampered AEI's credibility in the policy world. The institution's close ties with Barry Goldwater's 1964 presidential campaign led to a subpoena of AEI's tax records by Congressman Wright Patman's House Subcommittee on Small Business, followed by a two-year IRS audit to see whether the group had violated its nonprofit status by lobbying. This scare led AEI's executive vice-president, William Baroody, to back away from an activist role and even appoint some token liberals.

Like the CATO Institute, which was founded in 1977 by millionaire businessman Edward Crane, AEI retained its free market orientation but distanced itself from direct involvement in politics. Instead it nurtured an "academic" image as the Brookings of the right-of-center, without any strict Capitol Hill agenda. This distance from politics diminished some when the AEI became caught up in the revitalization of the conservative movement in the Reagan years, but to some extent the legacy continues even today. On the estate tax, despite the staunch pro-repeal stance expressed in vari-

EXPLOITING THE THINK TANK GAP 89

ous briefs produced by some AEI economists, Ben Wattenberg and Norman Ornstein wrote op-eds against estate tax repeal from their AEI perches in the late 1990s. But there is no doubt that AEI's center of gravity is to the conservative end of the spectrum.

The real pivot that blurred the line between advocacy groups and think tanks came from the Heritage Foundation. In the mid-1990s this colossus of ideologically focused conservatism, with an annual operating budget in excess of $30 million, would play a major role in moving estate tax repeal into the realm of the politically thinkable by producing backgrounders and position papers years before the think tank's counterparts on the left took the issue seriously. In doing this, Heritage mirrored the momentum among the lobbyists and interest groups—moving the ball a long way down field before the opposition even realized the game had begun.

Heritage was founded in 1973 by Paul Weyrich and Edwin Feulner, who had been Republican staffers, Weyrich for Colorado Senator Gordon Allott, Feulner for Illinois Congressman Phil Crane. With characteristic British understatement, the *Economist* describes Weyrich, an architect of both the Moral Majority and the Christian Coalition, as "one of the conservative movement's more vigorous thinkers." His sunny demeanor and cherubic cheeks make it easy to imagine Weyrich performing alongside Trent Lott and John Ashcroft in the "Singing Senators" (when Ashcroft was a senator, that is). He would certainly have harmonized with them ideologically. Like others in the vanguard of the conservative movement, Weyrich has insisted that "we are radicals, working to overturn the present power structure of this country." Among his more notable causes have been urging the United States formally to declare a war on drugs, so that suspected offenders could be treated as prisoners of war. Weyrich eventually became disillusioned with political activism as the Religious Right's agenda lost ground in the second Reagan and first Bush administrations. President Clinton was anathema to him and, when the Senate refused to deliver a conviction in Clinton's 1999 impeachment trial, Weyrich began telling the Moral Majority to "drop out of this culture, and find places . . . where we can live godly, righteous and sober lives."

But in the 1970s this retreat from political activism lay far in the future. Along with Grover Norquist, Weyrich and Feulner initially cut their teeth as visionaries of the emerging conservative movement. Less flamboyant than Weyrich but more formidable intellectually, Feulner would become

Heritage's first president. Feulner, who holds a doctorate from Edinburgh University, has long been identified with such conservative groups as the Mont Pelerin Society and the Council for National Policy. He is a syndicated columnist and the author of books with titles including *Looking Back, Conservatives Stalk the House, The March of Freedom,* and *Leadership for America.* In 1989 President Reagan described him as a "leader of the conservative movement" when awarding him the Presidential Citizens Medal.

Initially the Weyrich-Feulner venture seemed like quixotic political fringe activity. After all, 1973 was far from a propitious time for a conservative revival. The Nixon administration was falling apart. Gerald Ford had stepped in for Vice President Spiro Agnew, who was run out of office amid swirling corruption allegations even before the Watergate scandal broke. Ford would soon replace Nixon, and would be hamstrung by the reality that he had not been elected to the number two position, let alone to the presidency. Democrats controlled both houses of Congress and showed no sign of losing their grip on either. By 1976 there would be a Democrat in the White House as well—Jimmy Carter defeated President Ford, who, to the public's mind, had lost whatever legitimacy he brought to the presidency by pardoning Richard Nixon within months of taking office. Despite the contrarian predictions of a few isolated commentators such as Kevin Phillips, the conventional wisdom held that conservatives were on the run in American politics.

Facing this difficult situation, Weyrich and Feulner put their energy into reshaping the ideological terrain for the long haul rather than working to elect the available Republican candidates. They found soul mates, and vast financial backing, in three ultraconservative multimillionaires: Richard Mellon Scaife, an heir to the Mellon family fortune made largely in oil and banking; Oklahoma oil and gas magnate Edwin Noble; and Joseph Coors of Coors Breweries. Coors had been a Reagan supporter since the late 1960s, and a Goldwater devotee before that. His brother describes him as "a little bit right of Attila the Hun."

Heritage may have worked in relative obscurity during the 1970s, promoting ideas that few outside right-wing political circles took seriously, but it was not alone for long. In 1977, the former National Libertarian Party chair, Edward Crane, founded the CATO Institute, funded mainly by Kansas billionaire Charles Koch, to promote libertarian ideas in national political debate. CATO's trapezoidal six stories of glass and steel soon became a fixed star in the emerging conservative constellation on Massachusetts Avenue. While considerably smaller than Heritage—by 1991 CATO's operating budget would reach about $3.7 million, compared with $16.7 million at Heritage—it quickly developed an important place in conservative circles. Other, smaller conservative think tanks, such as the American Council for Capital Formation, also emerged in the late 1970s. But it was after Ronald Reagan's election to the presidency that right-wing think tank activity began growing exponentially, elbowing its way into the political mainstream.

The dramatic impact of Reagan's election is evident in the story of the Heritage Foundation. Indeed, the Reagan administration became the vehicle for mainstreaming Heritage. The transition began with Heritage's highly influential 1980 "how-to" manual, *Mandate for Leadership,* the first of a series that became a blueprint for the early years of the Reagan presidency and jolted many other think tanks into a more activist stance. Heritage staffers and supporters gained access and influence within the administration, even as they criticized the Reagan camp for being insufficiently conservative. As early as 1982, Feulner was promising potential $1,000 contributors to Heritage, "You will be provided with an access to Washington policy makers which cannot be had at any price. I have no doubt that you will find your membership fee returned to you many times over." By 1985, Heritage was collecting $10 million in donations each year; by 1995, it had an operating budget of $30 million, up from less than $1 million just 20 years earlier. As these figures suggest, Heritage continued growing even during the Clinton years, celebrating a triumphant twenty-fifth anniversary in 1997 in the midst of a successful $85 million fundraising campaign.

In 1983, the *Washington Post* described Heritage's newfound role as follows:

> Let the scholars and the other think tanks sweat to produce the important books that nobody in Washington has time to read. Heritage's 100 young activist-researchers will grind them up and spew them out in brief, fact-packed reports keyed to major events and trends. Then Feulner and his lieutenants will route them to every key congressman and senator, make the phone calls that get them to the right aides.

Researchers at traditional think tanks chose what they would work on, published their research pretty much after the fashion of academic journals and university presses, and took seriously the injunction against lobbying.

Heritage's political mission, however, requires a different approach. The foundation is run more like an army than an academic department, or even a traditional think tank. It has a command structure in which the leadership decides priorities, sets the agenda for the troops, and devotes huge amounts of energy to promoting that agenda in the halls of Congress.

In fact, as the 1983 *Post* article implies, often Heritage does not even do research. Rather, its experts scour what others have done and repackage the material to suit their own agenda. Once the leadership has identified a topic for attack, they deploy a five-part strategy. The first step is publication of a comprehensive "foundational" paper incorporating relevant research from law, history, economics, sociology, and elsewhere. The foundational document then becomes the basis for two- to three-page papers, used to highlight different aspects of the issue for different purposes: to serve as a marketing plan designed to get the attention of the 2,000 politicians and support staff on the Hill who are Heritage's primary audience; to provide tailored congressional testimony by Heritage's in-house experts; and to advertize major events, often held in the Capitol or nearby, organized in cooperation with key congressional allies on the issue.

Heritage is strategically located a few hundred yards from the Senate office buildings, just off Columbus Circle on Massachusetts Avenue. Its wide structure looks from the outside like a run-of-the-mill office building—even a bit drab. It could easily be home to a faceless corporation or insurance company. A large American flag flies from the flagpole. Blue awnings seem a little incongruous beside a well-manicured lawn, bordered by hedges and red and white gentians. Heritage is in the process of taking over a slightly smaller building next door, giving a hint of its expanding activity and influence. Otherwise it looks unremarkable.

Things change once you go in. You find yourself in a modest-sized lobby. The floor—part marble, part carpeted—is lit by a chandelier. The place seems to be straining, not altogether successfully, for a degree of sumptuousness—with dark wood paneling in the entryways, doors, and desks. Large placards sporting the names Coors, Noble, and Scaife confront you above the central hallway. If you didn't know who these men were, you might think Heritage had forgotten to take down the sign from an old law firm that had previously occupied the building. Each of the main rooms off the lobby is named for a donor, with the Lehrman Auditorium on the left and the Van Andel Center on the right. A gilt mirror graces the wall behind the receptionist, in Federalist style. A large reproduction painting of the Constitutional Convention dominates the far wall, fronted by a glass plate covered with the gold-etched names of donors to the Heritage expansion capital campaign.

Entering the elevator, it becomes clear that this is not your mother's think tank. Gold letters on the side wall proclaim Heritage's motto: "Building an America where freedom, opportunity, and civil society flourish." For anyone who doesn't get the point, the full vision statement is posted in the main corridor: "The Heritage Foundation is committed to rolling back the liberal welfare state and building an America where freedom, opportunity, and civil society flourish." There is no question about where this group is coming from, or where it hopes to take America.

Heritage may have catapulted into the mainstream when Ronald Reagan moved into the White House, but it acquired unprecedented access to power with the election of George W. Bush to the presidency in 2000. Weyrich crowed over the organization's growing influence to the *New York Times* the following year: "I've been through five Republican administrations, and the effort to communicate with conservatives and to understand our concerns and address our concerns and involve us in the process is [now] the best of any of the Republican administrations, including Ronald Reagan. In fact, far superior to Ronald Reagan." Currently, Heritage maintains over $100 million in assets, a large operating budget, and 200 employees. About 70 of them are policy experts, most of whom have come from government positions. A few have doctorates.

Heritage does not quite lobby politicians, but it sails as close to the edge of the law as possible without violating it. It is, indeed, a measure of how the limits of acceptable conduct have shifted that Heritage manages to engage in notably more activist partisanship than what got AEI into hot water in the 1960s. Its congressional liaisons will accompany a professional lobbyist on a visit to a senator or congressman, supplying the economic or otherwise "technical" analysis of the issue under discussion. The lobbyist then takes over, concluding, "And so that is why you should support our position." Brookings and the Urban Institute do not even have congressional liaisons. Small wonder that in a 1999 *Washington Post* poll in which Capitol Hill staffers ranked Heritage as the ninth most credible think tank, they also ranked it as the single most influential. Heritage is, as Feulner has said, "an activist version of Brookings."

Estate tax repeal was an early and intense preoccupation at Heritage. After 1996, the organization committed one full-time and one half-time analyst to it, with Senior Fellow Bill Beach taking the lead. We have already seen how influential Beach's "Death Tax Horror Stories" would become. He himself comes across as a colorless, mousy figure who would be more comfortable as a back-room operative than a public advocate. Yet this ex-litigation economist is remarkably astute politically. He took on the issue very early, and in addition to the "Horror Stories," he published a foundational paper on "The Case for Repealing the Estate Tax" in August 1996. In it Beach reviewed the history and theory of the tax, crafting pithy rebuttals to all the arguments that have been adduced in its support.

This paper—step one in Heritage's traditional five-step plan of attack—pounds away relentlessly at the tax's harmful impact on investment, on the cost of capital, on job creation, on savings, and on personal income. It attempts to quantify the perverse incentives that the estate tax calls forth in all of these areas. But Beach also emphasizes the tax's failure to raise federal revenue, its destructive effects on small businesses and employment, and the ways in which it encourages tax avoidance. He even tries to show how the tax violates the principles of justice defended by the liberal political philosopher John Rawls. This paper set the tone for subsequent Heritage work on the death tax and for other pro-repeal economic analyses.

The Rawls argument belonged to a larger strategy that the repeal forces would subsequently use with great success. Like the lobbyists and congressional managers of the repeal effort, Beach understood from the start that a coalition of strange bedfellows would be needed to accomplish repeal, and that different supporters would be moved by different arguments. Accordingly, he was as comfortable citing Rawls or Edward McCaffery, a USC law professor who bills himself as a liberal opposed to the estate tax, as he was relying on supply-side economic theory. In a similar vein, Heritage publications repeatedly claim that the estate tax hurts women and minorities, and that it fails to raise the revenues needed for federal social programs. In this tactic Beach and his associates come across more like attorneys than scholars. They line up argument after argument in favor of the proposition at hand—even if these arguments contradict one another or other Heritage commitments. After all, who ever thought that Heritage cared about funding social programs?

Like Pat Soldano and Jennifer Dunn, Beach was acutely aware that demographic changes were expanding and reshaping the potential constituency opposed to the estate tax. In the early 1990s, two economists then at Cornell University, Robert Avery and Michael Rendall, had produced a much-cited study predicting that the largest intergenerational transfer of wealth in the history of the world was around the corner, with the baby boom generation expected to pass on some $10 trillion by 2040. The numbers of Americans who stood to inherit wealth would rise, they showed, from 1.5 million heirs in 1995 to 2.2 million in 2000, and 3.4 million by 2015.

The substantial and increasing concentration of wealth at the top of the income distribution would still keep the vast majority of families out of the estate tax's range. The average size of inheritances was expected to reach only $56,000 in 1995, $65,000 in 2000, and $99,000 in 2015—well south of even the $650,000 threshold. But Beach understood that this particular reality was much less politically important than another reality: millions of baby boomers would begin thinking seriously about inheritance for the first time, in many cases without knowing exactly what their estates would amount to or where the estate tax would begin to bite. Moreover, significant numbers of the new "merely rich" would be women, and some would be minorities. It caught Beach's attention that in a 1996 conference of women in business held in the Clinton White House, the estate tax was rated the number one concern. Progressive-sounding messages might resonate better with such groups than would the usual Heritage fare; and so the repeal bastion needed to canvas arguments emanating from all parts of the ideological spectrum.

Plausible as Avery and Rendall's $10 trillion prediction was in the early 1990s, it turned out to be too modest by at least a factor of four. As the decade unfolded, America saw one of the largest bursts of economic growth in history, driven in large part by the dot.com revolution in the technology sector and an unprecedented run-up in the stock market. The bull market produced unanticipated trillions in new wealth. By the end of the decade, modest estimates held that the coming intergenerational wealth transfer would total at least $41 trillion by mid-century, and possibly as much as $136 trillion. The economic downturn and stock market retrenchment that began in March 2000 brought reality closer to the lower end of this range, but in the mid-to-late 1990s that reality check lay in the future. The net worth of middle-aged "haves" was growing at an astonishing clip, and their stock options, million dollar homes, and bulging 401(k)s would pre-dictably make them keenly attuned to the costs of estate taxes. Many of these new economy beneficiaries might not reach the top 1 or 2 percent who are truly vulnerable to the tax. But Beach and his Heritage colleagues understood that polls routinely show that some 20 percent of the Ameri-can population *believe* that they are in the top 1 percent, and another 20 percent believe that they will soon reach that echelon.

Beach, as well as being one of the first to comprehend the meaning of America's changing demographics, also acted early on the political truth that we saw with the use and promotion of stories from the grasstops: poignant anecdotes often move legislators more than economic theories and statistical studies. Starting in 1996, just a year after the Family Busi-ness Estate Tax Coalition had formed, Beach began sharing the stories he found with others in a collection of think tanks and advocacy groups that became known as the Working Group for Death Tax Repeal. The group met monthly, by invitation only. It numbered about 20 to 25 organizations, including think tanks such as CATO and AEI, but also hybrids including Americans for Tax Reform and lobby groups such as the 60 Plus Associa-tion, United Seniors, and the NFIB. The Working Group coordinated the production of think tank essays, became the main forum for talking over events and publications, prepped friendly congressional staffers and sup-plied them with people to testify at hearings, and disseminated "bottled" testimony to others in the repeal movement.

In all this activity, one nagging question remains: Where was the think tank opposition? As we shall see, the same question can be asked of con-gressional Democrats and traditional liberal pressure groups. Part of the an-swer in the think tank world is obvious. The growing gap in funding, par-ticularly with respect to the new activist think tanks, gave the pro-repeal forces a huge advantage. Well-heeled, traditional, policy-wonk think tanks such as Brookings and the Urban Institute do not come within a country mile of the kind of activism in which Heritage and the others in the Work-ing Group engage. In recent years, these old-school think tanks have made some modest attempts to market the results of their research in shorter and more user-friendly papers aimed at policy-makers. But they only go so far: active lobbying is an affront to their professional self-image. They will not try to do for the left what Heritage does for the right.

There is one exception, but it is an exception that proves the rule when viewed from the perspective of death tax repeal. The most substantial activist think tank on the anti-repeal side was the Center on Budget and Policy Priorities, established by Bob Greenstein in 1981. Unlike the policy-wonk organizations, CBPP was a self-conscious liberal response to the explosive growth of activist, conservative think tanks. Its mission is to publish research on issues affecting low- to moderate-income families. Its 35 fellows focus on federal tax policy, income support programs such as welfare and the Earned Income Tax Credit, unemployment insurance, and poverty relief.

CBPP's offices are part of a large complex just west of Capitol Hill, which also houses many of the TV news organizations in Washington. It shares a new, albeit rather drab, 11-story building along with CNN—a fitting arrangement, since CBPP is the think tank equivalent of a liberal breaking news channel. CBPP fellows are known for deluging Hill staffers with e-mail and for crunching data on the policy implications of legislative changes within hours of their being proposed. They are also aggressive about calling congressional offices for information and bending ears among Democratic staff. They are unabashedly liberal in their analysis, though they do have a reputation for accuracy and quality work.

Greenstein has the low-key presentation of a college professor. In fact, he did teach high school history for three years before going to work for Ralph Nader. His salt-and-pepper beard disappears into his nondescript tie and gray jacket. Yet he is quite high-powered—in 1996 he received a coveted MacArthur Fellowship, awarded to individuals for "extraordinary originality and dedication in their creative pursuits." He has long-standing, close ties to the Hill, having served on President Clinton's 1994 Bipartisan Commission on Entitlement and Tax Reform. Before founding CBPP, he served as Administrator of the Food and Nutrition Service at the Department of Agriculture, directing a staff of 2,500 with a $15 billion budget. His operation is much smaller now. CBPP's $8 million operating budget pales by comparison with those of Heritage and AEI—it is Pop's Grocery Store next to Stop and Shop. On the estate tax, its main allies were the liberal Bob McIntyre's one-man tax policy shop and the tiny OMB Watch on the north side of Dupont Circle. Greenstein himself says that his group was a peanut compared to the pro-repeal coalition.

Yet he also concedes that resources were only part of the story and that, like the Democrats on the Hill, CBPP was caught asleep at the switch on the estate tax. The publishing history says it all. CBPP did not start working on estate tax repeal until the summer of 1999. This entry into the debate came three years after Bill Beach's major backgrounder advocating repeal, which had spawned the flood of activity at Heritage and the Working Group and had been so effectively exploited by the repeal coalition. Indeed, by the time CBPP was gearing up for the fight on the estate tax, Bill Beach and Heritage were already cutting back their work on it—confident that the key hearts and minds on Capitol Hill had been won over.

By all indications, the pro-repeal movement's activities were not invisible to Greenstein and CBPP or other possible allies for retaining the tax. Rather, the estate tax's defenders continually underestimated the seriousness of the threat. In 1999, everyone on the anti-repeal side counted on Clinton to veto any eventual bill containing death tax elimination. Others wouldn't get involved until later, betting on a Gore victory in 2000 and at least another four years under the protection of a Democratic veto. More was the pity for them. As in the case of the think tanks, and the other liberal political forces that we turn to next, assuming the safety or permanence of the status quo turned out to be a very bad gamble indeed.

Disorganized Democrats

The conservative think tanks' influence on congressional Republicans is easy enough to perceive. It is more difficult to calibrate just how much the lack of opposing liberal policy groups disarmed the Democrats before the fight was even joined. One thing, however, is clear. Democrats in Washington at first ignored the repeal movement and eventually flailed against it with remarkably little effect. The House and Senate Democratic leaderships made no secret of their hostility to estate tax repeal, yet they could not prevent substantial defections from their own ranks when the time came to vote in the final Clinton years and in the 2001 tax legislation. Neither were they able to line up their troops behind an alternative to repeal that might split the coalition—or at least take the wind out of its sails. The Clinton White House, famously adept at stealing Republican thunder by "triangulating" on issues from NAFTA to welfare reform and deficit reduction, proved notably devoid of political creativity on estate taxes. The Democrats' passivity became particularly harmful after it became clear that QFOBI had failed to halt the push for repeal. President Clinton's promise to veto any repeal bill was not accompanied by any serious effort to pass a workable compromise reform. Indeed, the Democrats did not even float an alternative to repeal until July of 2000, when it was already clear that nothing would happen before the election.

Hindsight is often said to be 20/20, yet we are not just playing Monday morning quarterback. Over and over again, the repeal forces read the signs about the possibilities for change differently and—as it turned out, more accurately—than did the Democratic leadership. Some of this blindness stemmed from the larger Democratic denial of the extent of the political change that had occurred in 1994. Refusing to admit how low they had fallen, the Democrats were unable to come to grips with what they would have to do to regain a measure of influence on the Republicans' anti-tax agenda. While the Republicans were marching forward, the Democrats were assuming the issue would go away.

But the Democrats had blind spots about estate taxes long before 1994. If American voters actually supported heavy taxes on large estates, then George McGovern's 1972 proposal to abolish all inheritances above $500,000 (about $2 million in 1995 dollars) would not have run into the buzz saw of popular opposition that it did. Nor would 64 percent of Californians have voted to abolish their state inheritance tax, paid by only a tiny minority, in 1982. By the same token, had Americans been strongly in favor of curtailing inherited wealth, there might have been substantial opposition to the ten-fold increase in the estate tax exclusion—from $60,000 to $600,000—during the period 1977–87 or to the unlimited marital deduction for estate and gift taxes, enacted at the start of the Reagan administration. All along it has been clear that there is little political support for an estate tax that limits the bequests of anyone but the very rich.

Even ignoring that history, the more recent experience of Dick Gephardt and Henry Waxman should have alerted Democrats—as it did Republicans and members of the repeal coalition—to the widespread antipathy toward estate taxes in America. In 1992, the two Democratic lawmakers proposed cutting the estate tax threshold by two-thirds, to $200,000, to fund long-term care for low-income disabled Americans. They proposed this reduction in the exemption in exchange for Medicaid reforms, because Medicaid trusts were allegedly being used to avoid estate taxes. The bill had six cosponsors (including one Republican, Benjamin Gilman of New York), and was referred by the Democratic leadership to several House committees, including Ways and Means. But it ignited a firestorm of protest from small businesses and from conservative radio talk-show hosts, who insisted that the Democrats were trying to get rid of the exemption altogether. The proposal died in committee without ever coming to a vote, and the official legislative summary was changed to say nothing about the proposed legislative change. It simply vanished.

One senior Republican staffer identified the Gephardt-Waxman debacle as "the early sign of how volatile the issue was"—a sentiment repeatedly echoed by others on and off the Hill, who said that this failed effort emboldened them to think for the first time about pushing for full repeal. Indeed, this episode was one of the catalysts behind Pat Soldano's decision to form her Center for the Study of Taxation to begin working for repeal.

Yet if Gephardt and the Democratic House leadership learned anything about the "third rail" character of estate taxes from this incident—other than to back off—none of their new wisdom showed up in anything they said or did. The period between 1992 and the 1994 midterm elections was surely their greatest missed opportunity, a time when they could have read the same demographic information that Dunn, Soldano, and Beach were reading, and when they still controlled both Houses of Congress and the White House. At any point before 1994, they could have taken repeal off the table by increasing the exemption threshold or passing a bill that carved out significant workable exceptions for farmers and small businesses. Instead, through their inaction they ceded the initiative to the pro-repeal forces—who were busily pulling out creative stops to mobilize support for their side.

The 1994 election losses put Democrats on the Hill on the defensive. From that point on, the Clinton White House became the logical place for those opposed to repeal to regroup and to try to find viable strategies for deflating the antitax balloon in Congress. Yet the Clinton administration showed no more imagination in dealing with the estate tax than had the Democratic leadership on the Hill. The White House even had their own version of the Gephardt-Waxman fiasco in the spring of 1997, and like their congressional counterparts, failed to learn much from the experience. The debacle started when Deputy Treasury Secretary Lawrence Summers made an off-the-cuff remark that "there is no case other than selfishness" for cutting the estate tax.

Summers is no wilting violet. At the age of 28 he had become Harvard's youngest-ever tenured professor following a meteoric rise through the ranks in MIT's Economics Department. The *Washington Post* described this burly future Harvard president as "the intellectual powerhouse of the Clinton administration's economic team." Although this might have been a bit over the top, he was widely seen as a major player—not to be trifled with.

But when Summers stepped into the estate tax debate, within 24 hours his remarks brought forth attacks from Gingrich and 18 other GOP lawmakers, who called the comment "irresponsible" and "an insult to hardworking families." Senate Finance Committee Chairman Bill Roth accused the administration of instigating class warfare. Ways and Means Chairman Bill Archer called it the kind of comment "that people who believe in socialism would make," and Senate Majority Leader Trent Lott complained that Summers had undermined the possibility of bipartisan tax policy. "The Republicans," as conservative commentator Patrick Buchanan put it with characteristic vividness, "landed on Summers with both feet." None of this vitriol was surprising. Nor were the calls for Summers's resignation in conservative organs such as the *Washington Times*. But the intensity of the assault clearly unnerved the White House, which cut and ran; they left Summers, as Buchanan noted, twisting in the wind.

Summers turned on a dime, conceding that "I should not have used the term 'selfishness' to characterize positions in the debate over estate taxes. . . . There is room for honest disagreement on this issue. . . . It is wrong to question the motives of others in policy and policy debates." His mea culpas might have been good practice for his subsequent dealings with the complaints of African American Studies Professor Cornel West in Summer's post-Washington career, but they failed to get the GOP off his back. Two years later, Republican National Committee Chairman Jim Nicholson was still lambasting him over the remark when Summers was up for confirmation as treasury secretary. Nicholson invited Summers to explain to taxpayers "why he thinks it's selfish for them to want to leave their businesses and farms to their families when they die—rather than have government confiscate the fruits of their life's labors."

There the Clinton administration left the matter. Though Summers continued to declare himself well disposed to less costly tax breaks for small businesses instead of estate tax repeal, neither he nor anyone in the White House thought it worth trying to get ahead of the curve on the issue—let alone refocus the debate to an agenda that they would find more congenial than repeal. Certainly they never proposed a bill that might give anyone in the coalition reasons to think about jumping ship or might supply vulnerable Democrats on the Hill with political cover to resist repeal. Nor did the administration make any overtures to moderate Republicans who were unhappy with the Gingrich/Lott scorched-earth approach to tax policy, and who might perhaps have been hived off for a reformist agenda. That such people existed would become clear with Senator Jim Jeffords's defection from the GOP in June of 2001, which returned control of the Senate to the Democrats until the 2002 midterm elections.

One episode provides a striking indication of how disengaged the administration remained. When 65 House Democrats voted for the Dunn-Tanner repeal bill in June of 2000, Summers, then the treasury secretary, discounted the result by agreeing with Democrat Congressman Charles Rangel's euphemistic gloss that the president's promised veto made this one a free vote. Both on the Hill and in the White House, Democratic leaders seemed uninterested in why so many of their members would feel the pressure to vote for repeal, or what this substantial defection might signal about the consequences of further inaction. They continued to behave as though, if only they could keep repeal at bay for long enough, in the fullness of time it would go away.

Nor can it be said that astute observers sympathetic to blocking repeal did not warn the Democrats. In April of 1997, political scientist-cum-commentator and pollster Norman Ornstein, a moderate at the AEI, published an article in *USA Today* entitled "Boomers Beware: Estate Tax Now Not Just for the Rich." It should really have been called "Beware of the Boomers," because Ornstein was warning the Clinton administration about this constituency. He admonished Democrats to stop blindly resisting estate tax repeal as a windfall for the rich, and to start paying attention to the "dramatically different economic circumstances of baby boomers, including those in their 40s who are in their peak earning years and those in their 50s planning for retirement." Ornstein pointed out that for the first time a "large swath of middle-age, middle-class people own their own homes, have savings building in pension plans like 401(k)s and IRAs, and in many cases have small businesses or professional offices." Apart from the doctors, lawyers, and entrepreneurs, he pointed to the appreciation in real estate values and to the growth of defined-contribution pension plans. "While just under 2 percent of estates pay taxes now, when baby boomers start to retire, their savings will total in the many trillions, making $600,000 estates common," he said. "If the current system stays in place, a lot more people than the Rockefellers and Mellons will feel the heavy bite." Though still a minority, he added, "the numbers of people with assets large enough to be affected by estate taxes will certainly swell into the millions over the next decade or two."

For Ornstein the implication was inescapable: watch out, because these aging boomers will be easily mobilized by Republicans once they see what's coming down the pike. Indeed, the working rich to whom he referred were exactly the constituency that Jennifer Dunn was seeking to mobilize and represent. As Ornstein put it, there will soon be "a slew of politically active middle-class voters, proud that they have built up assets by saving and investing." Unless the law is changed significantly, they will have to confront the possibility "that all they have sacrificed to accumulate may be virtually confiscated. They heeded the rules and norms—saving, not spending. Their reward is to have it snatched away before their kids can touch it. These are not people who consider themselves rich. They will not be happy that politicians have labeled them as such." Ornstein opposed repeal, but he was unequivocal that the tax must be reformed to ward off the perception that it punishes middle-class success. Otherwise, Democrats would find that "voters who usually don't mind hitting the rich" would line up at the barricades beside them to fight for repeal.

Why were the Clinton administration and the Democratic leadership on the Hill so inattentive, and then so ineffective once they started paying attention, that they would lose 65 backbenchers in the House and 12 senators in the 2000 vote? The White House story is surely part of a larger one about the administration's misreading of the electorate, from its earlier gambits with gays in the military and universal health care, to tripping up in the midterm elections while looking beyond them to 1996. Perhaps they were confident that Gore would succeed Clinton, or that, even if he didn't, enough Senate Democrats would continue throwing enough sand in enough wheels to keep repeal from becoming law. Whatever the reason, the Republicans—partly due to their early discovery of the populist resonance of the issue, and partly, perhaps, in anticipation of Democratic triangulation—were shifting the goalposts from reform to repeal and digging in. "Our strategy was simple," one senior Republican Senate staffer said. "We were going to start from total repeal and negotiate down to total repeal."

At the best of times, controlling backbenchers in Congress involves difficulties akin to herding cats. Senators can be a particularly unruly bunch, because the Senate's voting rules often make the committee assignments that leaders control less valuable than in the House, and because threats to run primary challengers against uncooperative incumbents are less credible. The herding cats problem was especially acute for Democratic leaders on death tax repeal—as ultimately reflected in the large numbers of Democratic defections with virtually none on the Republican side. Large budget surpluses took away the main potential fissure in Republican ranks, between tax cutters and deficit hawks—making it easy for the party in 2001 to rally round a tax-cutting agenda.

The Democrats, in contrast, fought against plenty of centrifugal force. Blue Dogs and other fiscal conservatives faced a particular quandary: they had either to support tax cuts or explain why they were not big government spenders. True, they could make arguments about the national debt (as distinct from the deficit) or the future solvency of Social Security, but the inherent complexity of such arguments inevitably puts their proponents on the defensive. Moreover, it was not just the conservative Democrats who were picked off, as we have seen. The Neil Abercrombies and Albert Wynns succumbed as well. Things might have been different had there been a coordinated effort from the Clinton White House and the Democratic leadership to move a serious reform alternative early on—giving Democrats a proposal to rally around and providing leverage with which to pressure moderate Republicans. The complete lack of Democratic creativity on the issue was underscored by the Democratic staffer who candidly admitted to first learning that the pro-repeal forces had lined up members of the Congressional Black Caucus when he turned on the TV and saw them holding a press conference.

Democrats who had not been identified early on as hostile to repeal became targets for pressure both in Washington and from their constituents back home. And here another factor came into play: lawmakers are usually a good deal closer to the grasstops in their constituencies than to the grassroots. The Senate is filled with millionaires. Consider Senator Diane Feinstein of California, who voted for repeal twice in the last years of the Clinton administration and for Bush's 2001 tax cut that made repeal law. Feinstein sits toward the liberal end of the Democratic Party spectrum on most distributive issues, but she grew up in a wealthy family and her social milieu consists of exceedingly well-to-do—albeit liberal—California families. As she flies back and forth, first class, between Washington and San Francisco, she might well find herself sitting next to someone concerned about estate tax repeal. The odds that she will find herself talking to an avid proponent of retaining the tax are vanishingly small.

And the grasstops' influence on congressional decisions extended beyond Feinstein. As Congressman Rangel noted at the time of the 2000 vote, if someone a congressman knows personally has felt the bite of the estate tax, that may be all it takes. Unfortunately for the tax's defenders, Rangel added that "everyone in the House knows one person who's affected." The same statement surely applies to the Senate. On the death tax, small numbers of wealthy families have a huge amount at stake. No doubt many of these families have strong personal relationships with their members of Congress, and it is surely worth their while to communicate to their senator or representative what the personal cost to their families will be. Soldano, Blankenburg, and others in the repeal coalition made it their business to see that this communication happened. Moreover, a senator or congressman will not hear wrenching personal stories from anyone on the other side, given how widely dispersed the costs of repeal are. We were told of several cases where a representative initially opposed repeal but found the pressure to support it irresistible for just this reason.

The Democratic leadership on the Hill faced an additional difficulty once repeal became the unambiguous Republican goal. They were fighting a foe that had a well-defined purpose behind which its troops were united. By contrast, particularly after the botched QFOBI, the Democrats were unclear about what their own goal should be, let alone how to make a convincing case that it could be implemented even if they could agree. This failure partly explains why they remained back on their heels trying to impede Republican progress rather than trying to achieve a solution of their own—they didn't have any solution of their own to achieve. Indeed, talking to the strategists from both sides left the indelible impression that the Democrats facing the repealers were like the Yale football team trying to take on Ohio State.

But another major piece of the story was the pervasive Democratic disbelief that repeal would actually happen, which persisted until the Republicans had the ball a long, long way down the field. John Tanner, who cosponsored Jennifer Dunn's repeal bill in the House, believed and expected that a compromise reform proposal would eventually emerge, and he was disappointed when none did. Democrat after Democrat told us of reckoning it unthinkable that the estate tax would be repealed, of being unprepared and blindsided by the relentless Republican push, and of the constituency influence that was so well orchestrated by the coalition. But if the Democrats were so disorganized, one has to ask, where were the interest groups that might have pressured them to act?

Pushing against an Open Door

As we have seen, Republican effectiveness on the Hill was partly due to the party's superior organization, leadership, and focus, but it also stemmed from the relentless pressure exerted by pro-repeal forces off the Hill—the think tanks, the grasstops, and the lobbyists who constituted or worked with the coalition. Coordinating with one another, and with House and Senate leaders, these groups managed to get repeal onto the agenda when few people took it seriously and then keep it there. They built momentum, sustained it through critical votes, and ensured that repeal remained a significant part of President Bush's tax cutting agenda that eventually became law in 2001.

A large part of the mystery surrounding repeal concerns why no countervailing pressure developed on the other side. Many stood to lose, directly or indirectly, if the estate tax was done away with. Some stood to lose a lot. Eventually, an organized movement of anti-repeal interests would surely arise. But, like the Democrats on the Hill, the private opposition was of the dollar-short-and-a-day-late variety. First we need to understand why, from the beginning, the repeal coalition found itself pushing against an open door.

The estate tax is the most progressive part of the Internal Revenue Code. When President Bush proposed in 2001 to eliminate $138 billion from this tax over ten years (rising to $600–$700 billion over the next ten) to benefit the wealthiest 2 percent, traditional forces of the organized left surely should have been expected to rush to the barricades in its defense. So where was organized labor? Why didn't they throw themselves into the fray? Whatever the merits of arguments about farmers and keeping small businesses in the family, what did the rank and file of the AFL-CIO and other constituencies of the left care about such niceties?

Some of these groups indeed came to favor tax cuts in the new political and economic context after the mid-1990s. When Democrats and budget deficits on Capitol Hill were replaced by Republicans and budget surpluses, it became all but inevitable that tax-cutting of some kind would be on the agenda. Reading the obvious tea leaves, some on the left were determined to limit the regressive character of any cuts, and perhaps even ensure that they would be progressive. The Clinton administration understood the stakes well enough after the Republican takeover. Following the president's reelection in 1996, the White House made a point of getting behind at least one tax cut every year to avoid being tagged as big spenders who always resist tax cuts.

Many potential tax cuts would have benefited organized labor's constituents. Some of these possibilities, such as the child tax credit and reductions in marginal income tax rates, eventually wound up in the 2001 Bush tax cut bill. Others—most obviously cuts in the payroll taxes, which for most workers are now more burdensome than income taxes—did not. In these circumstances, what was remarkable was the deafening silence from organized labor long before estate tax repeal was bundled with any less regressive tax changes that might muddy just who was benefiting. We have seen that there was plenty of legislative activity on the estate tax before 2001: the various Cox and Kyl bills gained increasing numbers of cosponsors in the mid-1990s; the Dunn-Tanner bill was introduced and referred to Ways and Means in May 1998; and stand-alone repeal bills were voted on in 1999 and 2000 in both chambers. During this entire time, organized labor did nothing. Nor did other traditionally left-leaning lobbyists or public interest groups emerge to mirror the work of groups such as Grover Norquist's Americans for Tax Reform or Pat Soldano's Center for the Study of Taxation.

The important exceptions were Chuck Collins's United for a Fair Economy (UFE), formed in 1995, and OMB Watch, a liberal advocacy group that has been monitoring the federal budget since the Reagan administration. But like the anti-repeal think tanks, these two groups were overshadowed by the repeal coalition and its allies. OMB Watch eventually organized Americans for a Fair Estate Tax, which brought together various labor, civil rights, child welfare, and liberal groups to promote reform instead of repeal—but this did not happen until after President Bush had come to power in 2001. Chuck Collins was quicker off the mark. Toward the end of 1997 he formed UFE's "Responsible Wealth" project to combat repeal; the project was a response to the increasing numbers of cosponsors for repeal bills on the Hill, even though Collins still considered repeal to be a stretch. They lobbied on the Hill to ensure that Clinton's veto of the 2000 bill would be sustained. But most of their intense work came after the 2000 election when they teamed up with Bill Gates, Sr., with whom Collins would eventually write *Wealth and Our Commonwealth,* published two years after repeal was enacted.

The main commonality between OMB Watch and UFE is how few people have heard of them. Part of this anonymity comes down to geography. Located on Connecticut Avenue past Dupont Circle, OMB Watch occupies a rabbit warren of offices in a decrepit building that looks more like off-campus student housing than a professional office. If you couldn't tell that it operates on a shoestring before you got there, you wouldn't be in much doubt afterward. UFE in some ways is even worse off; it is crammed into run-down quarters over 400 miles away in Boston—which says volumes about its capacity to get things done on Capitol Hill. The contrast with Grover Norquist's spacious war room on L Street, or the opulent Heritage Foundation lobby, or the coalition members' main offices dotted around DC's political district, could not be starker. Even Pat Soldano, who works out of Orange County, California, understands that out of sight is out of mind. She spends a week each month camped out in a Washington hotel traipsing from office to office on the Hill, jawboning waverers, and keeping the repeal issue on members' front burners. People know who she is.

The lobbying gap between the two sides mirrors the think tank and contributor gaps, but it may matter more. Lobbying is the most important of the three forces in passing—or stopping—legislation. It has a "squeaky wheel" quality that stems from lobbyists' intense commitments to their task. If nothing else, the very fact that lobbyists are working an issue tells the congressman, senator, or staffer that the outcome is important to a given constituency. Moreover, lobbyists, like grasstops constituents themselves, are able to personalize issues. Real or imagined, the stories like Tina Brown's that people such as Soldano orchestrate and recycle move politicians, providing them with reasons for acting as well as political cover when they do.

Lobbyists against repeal lacked compelling constituents to whom they could point, let alone mobilize, for the obvious reason that there is no individual whose life would be devastated by death tax repeal. Chuck Collins tried to move farmers to action by claiming that Republicans "only care about you when you die." But this rhetoric produces no identifiable victim; in any event, the only group he managed to snare was the National Farmers Union and its 300,000 small farmers. They came out against repeal in 2000, but Collins admits that it has never been a front-burner issue for the group. As with OMB Watch and UFE itself, this farmers' union is notable for our story because no one in Washington has heard of them as defenders of the estate tax. Among the more than 150 people we spoke to on and off the Hill, there was universal belief that farmers had been lockstep behind repeal.

Organized labor has substantial representation and resources in Washington, but it was ill suited to work against estate tax repeal. Particularly in recent years, labor has relied less on lobbying and more on soft money, PAC contributions, and its large membership for political influence. Public sector unions ranked 56th in lobbying expenditures, for example, among all industries and other reportable interests in 1997–98, far below their top-ten spot in federal campaign contributions. In 2000, labor ranked eleventh out of thirteen reporting sectors in lobbying spending, though it was seventh in campaign contributions. Labor was out-lobbied by finance, insurance, real estate, "miscellaneous business," health, communications and electronics, energy and natural resources, transportation, ideological and single-issue groups, agribusiness, defense, and "other" interests. Workers thus face a distinct disadvantage in generating the focused activity around particular bills that is the sine qua non of lobbying.

Outflanked on the lobbying front, organized labor's political influence depends mainly on turning out its membership to vote and, to a lesser extent, on its campaign contributions—which outnumber its lobbying expenses by a ratio of about three to one. But tax issues excite notoriously little interest among labor-oriented voters. Tax issues do not move workers much even at the voting booth; much less do they motivate them to contact their political representatives. This reality shapes the lobbying activity that organized labor does engage in. Of the AFL-CIO's eight full-time lobbying staff, only one, David Medina, has responsibility for tax issues—but he also deals with health care, labor law, pension reform, trade, budget, appropriations, civil rights, education, campaign finance reform, and election reform. Medina reckons that he spends no more than 25 percent of his time on all tax matters. He opposed the 2001 Bush tax cut in its entirety, but he made no particular effort on the estate tax.

Small wonder, then, that politicians on the Hill report that they found it impossible to mobilize organized labor on the estate tax. When they tried, labor responded that tax issues divide their members. Although this need not have been the case with the estate tax, labor lobbyists believed that the ways in which rank-and-file members of organized labor stood to lose from repeal were too indirect for it to be worth their time to get involved. In any case, organized labor is just not set up to deal with tax issues. They assume that their energy is best focused on regulatory issues, labor relations, protecting federal expenditure programs that matter to their members, and, above all, international trade. We unearthed one letter that the municipal workers' union AFSCME sent to members of the House and Senate registering opposition to permanent estate tax repeal in 2003. But we found no lobbying activity of any kind.

Organized labor's strategy of ignoring tax issues might seem myopic, but it is in fact a logical response to their needs; lobbying must take a back seat to collective bargaining and, most important, organizing new workers. If the Democrats on the Hill have been on the defensive in recent years, their plight pales by comparison with organized labor. Decimated membership tells the story. In 1955, 31.8 percent—nearly a third—of the American work force was unionized. This figure has fallen steadily: to 28.6 percent in 1960; 23.2 percent in 1980; 16.1 percent in 1990; 13.5 percent by the end of the century; and it continues to decline. When John Sweeney replaced the ousted Lane Kirkland as head of the AFL-CIO in 1995, his main task was to arrest the decline. Though he has yet to succeed, this goal has inevitably redirected resources from lobbying to organizing. In a recent interview Sweeney said he has urged affiliates to spend at least 30 percent of their budgets on organizing. "Our hope is that we'll be able to increase that goal in the future to 50 percent."

This reorientation began in the late 1990s, just as the battle over estate tax repeal was heating up. In Sweeney's first years, AFL-CIO lobbying expenses had continued to grow, from $3.2 million in 1997, to $4.2 million in 1998, and $5.2 million in 1999. But the budget then took a precipitous drop to $3.3 million in 2000. These numbers only hint, however, at the lobbying gap that now exists between business and labor. The entire labor sector's lobbying expenses basically tracked inflation in the late 1990s, going from some $20.8 million in 1997 to $27.3 million in 2000. These numbers pale by comparison with the lobbying expenses of the miscellaneous business groups, which grew from $150.3 million in 1997 to $224.2 million in 2000. The absolute differences are startling enough, but the increasing differential is even more dramatic.

A measure of the desperation in labor's situation is the positive spin that their allies, such as economist Paul Harrington of the Center for Labor Market Studies at Northeastern University, try to put on it. Minimizing the disadvantages of trying to play David among lobbying Goliaths, labor's sympathizers say that the unions were misguided to invest in lobbying and applaud the return "to their roots" in organizing and mobilization.

So we have found the answer to our original question, "Where was organized labor?" Their absence from the death tax battle now seems less perplexing. It's a bit like asking why someone in urgent need of a transfusion is not waiting in line to give blood. In the last decade, organized labor has had more pressing priorities than preserving the estate tax—like trying to survive. They have had shrinking resources to spend on lobbying precisely because they have had to look to rebuilding membership and concentrating on hot-button issues such as trade policy, which the unions widely blame for the steady loss of jobs to developing countries.

If the threats to farmers' organizations, labor unions, or their rank-and-file were too indistinct to motivate a focused effort to stop repeal, what of others who had more direct interests at stake? One such group is the non-profit community of charities, foundations, and private universities—the smorgasbord of 501(c)(3) organizations, many of which have thrived because of the estate tax's unlimited charitable deduction, which induces wealthy taxpayers to give large chunks of their estates to charities that they care about while diminishing their federal tax liability. The disappearance of the estate tax would substantially reduce wealthy people's incentives to be philanthropic. Without the estate tax it would cost them no more to pass assets to kith and kin than to make a charitable bequest. Will there be another generation of Carnegie, Ford, and Gates Foundations in the absence of an estate tax? The extent of the likely reduction in charitable giving is much debated, ranging from about 10 to 60 percent of total charitable bequests depending on the study, but it is hard to imagine the nonprofit sector concluding that the losses would be negligible. Surely they would have an interest in mobilizing opposition to death tax repeal. Blood is thicker than water; it is also thicker than named university or museum buildings.

Many in the world of nonprofits were indeed greatly troubled by the anticipated effects of repeal—and completely unimpressed with conservative economic studies purporting to show that it might actually increase charitable giving. Some 8.2 percent, or $15.6 billion, of the $190 billion given to charities each year comes from estates—the bulk of it from estates over $2.5 million and over a third from estates of over $20 million. Indeed, taxable estates give at twice the rate of nontaxable ones. Moreover, these numbers fail to capture the charitable gifts that people make during their lifetimes to obtain income tax as well as estate tax reductions.

But what were the nonprofits to do about this real and substantial threat? Their difficulty was that while repeal was potentially dangerous to charities and foundations, it was quite popular among the wealthy donors to which these institutions owed their livelihood. How does a university president come out against repeal without angering potential donors? This is not to mention the university's trustees, who often include millionaire philanthropists within their ranks. The same is true of many other nonprofits, ranging from museums and foundations to churches, nongovernmental organizations, and environmentalists. This don't-bite-the-hand-that's-feeding-you problem plagued the nonprofit sector's lobbying organizations throughout the debate. They found themselves deeply divided on what, if anything, to do in response to the repeal threat. The normally low-key, friendly meetings of the Council on Foundations, a nonprofit umbrella group with more than 2,000 members, became unusually crowded and contentious when the estate tax came up. The board was eventually forced to organize a retreat devoted to the repeal problem—but not until June of 2001, after the Bush tax bill had already passed.

After much hand-wringing, the council chose not to take a position, sticking with its policy of advocating only on issues that affect philanthropy directly. They worried about division within their ranks. They worried about not having the resources to make a difference in any case. They worried about a slippery slope: If you oppose estate tax repeal because of its effects on charitable giving, must you also oppose cuts in marginal income tax rates? Where would that path lead them? They also worried about seeming too liberal—already a sore spot, ever since conservatives "troubled by an increasing lack of political and intellectual diversity within parts of the philanthropic community," as their website puts it, had peeled off to form the Philanthropy Round-table in the late 1970s. And finally, they worried about alienating powerful people on the Hill.

This last concern should not be underestimated, as shown by the experience of one group that waded farther into the estate tax debate than most nonprofits. The Independent Sector, which represents over a million charitable, educational, religious, health, and social welfare nonprofits, eventually came out against repeal in February 2002 and joined OMB Watch's Americans for a Fair Estate Tax coalition. The nonprofits were feeling the pinch after the 1990s stock market bubble burst and charitable giving suffered, and repeal seemed to be another blow that they couldn't afford. But they found it difficult to advocate on the estate tax without antagonizing members. Nor could they decide on the particulars of a reform proposal to support. As a result, they have tried to avoid getting too far out front on the issue, restricting their activities to signing letters and meeting with "holdout" politicians like Senator Mary Landrieu of Louisiana. It is far from clear what this tepid opposition to repeal has achieved, other than forcing Independent Sector to take stands on other controversial tax issues and alienating Ways and Means Chairman Bill Thomas. Since coming out against repeal, they have found him less than responsive on other issues, like itemized deductions, that may matter to some of their members more.

Aside from these delicate political issues, the nonprofit sector had difficulty fashioning its argument to challenge repeal. Nobody believes that the purpose of the estate tax is to encourage philanthropy. Defending it on this ground is a bit like trying to defend the space program because it has produced Velcro and nonstick frying pans. When you add to this fundamental problem further difficulties with mixed motives, divided memberships, reliance on donors and board members, lack of a coherent policy to support, and slippery slopes, it is scarcely surprising that organized philanthropy sought mainly to duck the fight over the death tax. Preserving philanthropy as a reason for opposing repeal, as they say, is a dog that won't hunt.

Not only the philanthropic community had a hard time fighting repeal. Consider the life insurance industry. After all, much of the life insurance industry is devoted specifically to estate planning. And life insurance representatives certainly know how to work lawmakers: one legislative aide describes them as "the only competent lobbying group that was anti-repeal."

Perhaps so, but they soon found themselves behind the eight-ball. As a senior life-insurance lobbyist admitted, opposing repeal was like the Bayer Corporation trying to scuttle a cure for headaches. And there were at least as many difficulties with the messenger as with the message. The life insurance lobby is very Republican, deeply enmeshed with the GOP on other issues, and its members are reflexively antitax. Opposing any tax cut affronts their sensibilities. To make matters worse, some of the life insurance executives in the estate-planning business are themselves wealthy individuals worried about their own tax liability.

The industry is also divided by interests. Fewer than 10 of the 383 members of the American Council of Life Insurers are so heavily into selling estate-planning life insurance that they might actually go paws-up if the tax were repealed permanently. Moreover, the ACLI's polling revealed that its members lacked a winning reform proposal. Increases in the exemption were the most viable mode of reform, but here's the rub: with an exemption much above $3 million, ACLI members who were oriented toward estate planning were also concerned that there would not be much of a market left for their product.

Taking all these factors together, it is easy to see why the life insurance industry produced no groundswell against repeal. Moreover, many insurance agencies (as distinct from companies) are family-owned small businesses that belong to the NFIB. The Insurance Agents and Brokers of America have dozens, if not scores, of members in every congressional district in America. They were active members of the Family Business Estate Tax Coalition working for repeal. So if a representative or senator ever heard from lobbyists about the problems that repeal posed for life insurers, this message would likely be muddied by contrary messages emanating from back home.

So it is scarcely surprising that life insurance lobbyists who did come out for repeal were reduced to making disingenuous arguments. The American Association of Life Underwriters (AALU), a trade association whose members sell insurance to wealthy clients, was the most active anti-repeal insurance lobby. It rallied around the banner of "consistency." It claimed that although permanent repeal might be best for the AALU's members, reform would create a more predictable world and facilitate estate planning because the three previous occasions of estate tax repeal were each followed by subsequent reinstatement. Hence the association called for a "permanent estate tax reform that enables the clients of our members to plan for their futures with certainty."

These lobbyists did not trumpet the fact that they were referring to the "certainty" of the nineteenth and early twentieth centuries for evidence about what will likely happen in the twenty-first, even though the tax code has changed out of all recognition in the interim. They also evaded the inconvenient reality that, although the federal estate tax has "consistently" existed since 1916, it has been anything but stable. Huge variations in the rates and the exclusions have resulted from changing revenue needs during wars and the Depression—not to mention the vicissitudes of politics. Increasing the top rate from 20 to 45 percent, as occurred in 1932, created many more dollars worth of new estate-planning headaches than "reinstating" an estate tax with a 10 percent top rate in 1916. Other changes over time have frequently made a great many estate-tax plans archaic. It is not easy to accept that a reform would lead to more predictability for estate planners than would a repeal. Death and taxes might both be certain, but there can be no certainty about what death taxes will be. That the AALU based its case against repeal on such tortured logic is eloquent testimony to the obvious conclusion: they found no plausible argument against repeal to advance—other than self-interest.

Charities and the estate-planning life insurance industry were hamstrung in the public domain by their awkward motives. But why didn't they do more to oppose repeal below the radar? One difficulty here is how late they came to the issue. It is much easier to work behind the scenes to keep something off the agenda than to oppose it once the curtain has gone up. Like the congressional Democrats, the charities and life insurance lobbyists were in denial about the repeal movement's viability for far too long. This blindness is especially remarkable with respect to the life insurers. They found their members reluctant to commit even modest funds for research or to support anti-repeal efforts in any other way, even after the Clinton veto in 2000 showed that repeal was just a Republican president away from becoming law. A senior insurance lobbyist explained that the recession had made money tighter, and that in any case the industry thought Gore would win the election. She seemed oblivious to the irony of this risky bet coming from people who sell insurance—like someone insisting he does not need health insurance because he is not sick.

Behind-the-scenes action ceased to be a serious option once death tax repeal was in the limelight. There are few secrets in Washington, and even fewer that endure for long. The people pushing for repeal and their allies on the Hill made it their business to know who was working on the other side—as Independent Sector discovered to its cost. Whether due to lack of foresight, fear of politicians or clients, or personal concerns with estate taxes, the life insurers who had a stake in preserving the estate tax failed to have a quiet impact when they might possibly have done so. And once the battle was joined there was little they could do.

As momentum for repeal built, many of its advocates were taken aback at how little resistance they met—at the degree to which they found themselves pushing against an open door. Now we know why they should not have been surprised. Like the Democrats on the Hill, the forces off the Hill who might have opposed repeal remained in denial for a long, long time. Once they saw what was happening, they were too poor, too weak, too distracted, too compromised, and too divided to have much chance of influencing the result. The one group that looked as if it might live to fight another day was Chuck Collins's Responsible Wealth project at United for a Fair Economy in Boston. But it remained to be seen what, if anything, it might do that had not already been tried.

The story of the opposition to estate tax repeal in the years leading up the Bush tax cut bill is a tale of too little, too late. From outnumbered and undermotivated think tanks, to disorganized Democratic responses, to a disarmed labor movement, to incapacitated charities and foundations, and a lone inept business lobby potentially opposed to estate tax elimination, the interests aligned in favor of progressive taxation of inheritance in this country were left choking on the dust kicked up by the pro-repeal movement as it advanced toward its prize.

And yet regardless of how well-organized a lobbying machine the various coalitions had assembled, the fact remained that this tax applied to only the wealthiest 2 percent of the nation. Did Americans really support getting rid of a tax collected from so few? As it turns out, the old consensus that estate taxes were a fixed element of sound tax policy had become so strong that no one had bothered to ask what the public actually thought. When the question was finally posed, everyone was in for a surprise.

The Running Room of Public Opinion

Opinion among political elites, lobbyists, think-tank researchers, and other inside-the-beltway types is one thing; what middle America thinks is another. Unfolding the mystery of estate tax repeal demands an answer to the question: Why would the public broadly support repealing a tax paid by only 2 percent of America's wealthiest taxpayers? Indeed, no repeal effort ever got off the ground during the Ronald Reagan and George H. W. Bush administrations largely because most Washington insiders assumed that abolishing the estate tax was politically impossible. According to the orthodox wisdom, the vast majority of Americans would oppose repealing a steeply progressive tax that they would never themselves pay. It was not until the Gephardt-Waxman fiasco in 1992, when their gambit to cut the threshold to $200,000 blew up in Democrats' faces, that conservatives became alert to the possibility that they might have missed something.

In fact, the supposition that repeal would be a political nonstarter was not based on any evidence. The assumption that there would be little public support was so widespread that no one had done any polling on the issue. Michael Franc, vice president for Governmental Relations at Heritage, recalls that in 1992 or 1993 he assumed that pushing repeal would be devastating for conservatives. He was subsequently surprised by the same thing that surprised everyone else: appeals to the American majority's economic self-interest—the "class warfare" argument, as Franc and other conservatives dub it—turned out to have no traction when Democrats tried that tactic in seeking to muster public opposition to repeal.

Franc draws a moral from this episode: many more Americans than he had realized buy into the dynamic vision of the economy favored by conservatives, rather than the static vision that he attributes to liberals. While proponents of the static view worry about the distribution of income and wealth at any given time, the dynamic view focuses attention on economic growth and the potential for individual upward mobility. This perspective leads people to think prospectively about where they might get to, given a proposed policy change, not where they currently are or what they can get via transfers from the government. The dynamic theory supplies impetus to the American dream.

Franc is partly right about how Americans assess their economic situation. Poll after poll reveals that the great majority of Americans believe themselves to be better off than they actually are relative to others, and most expect to get wealthier over the course of their lives. Franc points to a *Time/CNN* poll in 2000 revealing that 39 percent of Americans believe that they either are already in the top 1 percent of wealth or will be there "soon." A year earlier, a similar *Newsweek* poll had put the number at 41 percent, with a mere 26 percent believing that they had no chance of becoming wealthy. One might think these numbers unrepresentatively high, since they came at the end of one of the most explosive decades of wealth-creation in the nation's history. But sociologists have been aware for decades that large numbers of Americans are unrealistically optimistic about their relative and absolute economic circumstances. They underestimate the levels of inequality, overestimate their own wealth compared to others, and exaggerate their likelihood of moving up significantly and getting rich.

History provides another clue as to why the class warfare argument made so little headway in the fight against estate tax repeal. One might suppose, as many people on both sides of the issue evidently did, that a period of substantial economic growth would lead to pressure to make the tax code more progressive, not less so. Growth takes the budgetary pressure off governments by increasing revenues, reducing deficits, and even creating surpluses—all trends that became evident during the Clinton administration. Pressure for downward redistribution should be particularly intense when significant increases in inequality accompany growth. In 1990 Kevin Phillips made this prediction in *The Politics of Rich and Poor*, arguing that the enormous concentration of wealth in the United States during the previous decade had led to a new Gilded Age that would soon provoke a backlash among ordinary Americans.

But in sharp contrast to his prescient 1969 classic, *The Emerging Republican Majority*, this time Phillips could not have been more wrong. He was correct about the facts and, indeed, the public perception of those facts. Assessed by any measure, inequality did rise between 1975 and 1995. In a 1994 poll commissioned by *Time* and CNN, some 64 percent of respondents said that the income gap between rich and poor in the United States was widening, while 25 percent thought that it was stable and only 6 percent believed that it was shrinking. Polls by other nonpartisan groups revealed similar perceptions. By the mid-1990s, not only had the gap between rich and poor widened significantly since the mid 1970s, but most people knew it.

But Phillips was quite wrong in supposing that knowledge about the growing income gap would translate into class-based demands for progressive changes in the tax code, let alone resistance to regressive changes. Although in 1978 a poll by the University of Chicago's National Opinion Research Center had found 30 percent of respondents agreeing that "the government should reduce income differences between rich and poor" and 20 percent disagreeing, 20 years later the number believing that government should try to close the gap had fallen to 24 percent, with 27 percent believing that it should not.

A little wider historical perspective might have alerted Phillips to why the dynamic of the 1990s might in fact be the opposite of his predicted backlash. Throughout American history, most of the significant increases in taxes on the wealthy have occurred during wars and other times of national crisis. Indeed, going all the way back to the nineteenth century, estate taxes have been instituted only when the nation has been at war or facing imminent war (admittedly, after the last estate tax introduction in World War I, it took another 86 years for the tax to be repealed). Moreover, significant increases in estate taxes have been possible only during episodes of crisis such as when Herbert Hoover raised them during the Depression.

Indeed, good times produce overwhelming pressure to cut taxes on the wealthy right along with the less fortunate. Americans think that they are going to join the party, so they don't mind paying for the drinks. Ronald Reagan famously insisted in 1983 that "what I want to see above all is that this country remains a country where someone can always get rich." This comment resonates powerfully with the public. Americans may support income floors, such as a minimum wage, but they are exceedingly reluctant to endorse any government-enforced limits on wealth—even when CEOs, Hollywood celebrities, and sports superstars are paid in the tens and hundreds of millions of dollars. A 1997 survey commissioned by the Democratic Leadership Council showed fully 71 percent of Americans agreeing that the government should "foster conditions that enable everyone to have a chance to make a high income"; only 22 percent thought it appropriate for government to "redistribute existing wealth." Asked more specifically whether "government should work to redistribute income to close the gap between the wealthy and the poor," about a third agreed, but 64 percent instead indicated that "government should work to create opportunity, but not redistribute wealth."

In attributing the public opinion about estate tax repeal to widespread acceptance of his dynamic economic view, Michael Franc is only partly right. An equally important factor is that most people care remarkably little about tax policy, even when they know what the parties stand for—which is rare. It is true that in 2000, the Bush campaign was as surprised as everyone else that the Texan's strongest applause line at rallies was so often his promise to get rid of the death tax. But most voters don't go to political rallies. If not merely conservative activists, it is activists plus the small minority of Americans with a strong partisan interest in politics who show up at political rallies—the talk radio crowd. For Republican political junkies, getting rid of the death tax was red meat in the same way that being pro-life or pro-choice is red meat for activists on both sides of the abortion question.

For most voters, however, tax policy—like abortion—is not a primary or even secondary concern. Whatever their view on a given tax, it will not likely determine how they vote. Politicians must stay attuned to the intensity of voters' preferences on different issues—a failure to do so can be exceedingly costly. The British Conservative Party learned this lesson the hard way, when, despite poll after poll showing large majorities supporting its opposition to replacing sterling with the euro, the Tories still failed to get political mileage out of the currency debate. The reason? On many other issues that matter to people much more than keeping the pound—education, local government, the National Health Service—they favor Labour's stance.

The much-reported widespread public support for repeal played a part in producing the eventual result; we attend to it shortly. More important, however, was that the pro-repeal forces understood the contours and intensity of public opinion about the estate tax earlier and more fully than those on the other side. This early lead gave them the running room to shape the terms of the debate, and to hone and then deploy "findings" about public opinion to mobilize activists, grasstops, and coalition members while cowing potential opponents.

It is common knowledge that public opinion is multifaceted—even contradictory—and that, depending on how an issue is framed, majorities of the public can be alleged to hold very different views. Again, the comparison with abortion is instructive. Polls show repeatedly that most Americans think that abortion is murder, and that substantial majorities are pro-choice. How, if at all, people square the tensions inherent in holding these two views simultaneously is a complex matter that activists on neither side of the issue try to resolve. Instead, they advertise the aspect of majority opinion that is favorable to their case. In the hurly-burly of political conflict, opinion polls are less authentic measures of public opinion than they are rocks that activists throw at one another. Having structured a poll to get people to say what they want to hear, activists then use the results to rally the faithful, get media attention, and intimidate potential opposition.

Public opinion about taxes is particularly susceptible to manipulation. People's views are not intense to begin with, and the subject is inherently complex. In the late 1990s, for example, many opinion polls revealed substantial majorities—often upward of 70 percent—agreeing that the estate tax should be repealed. At the same time, polls on how to "spend" the surplus revealed only a third or fewer favoring tax cuts. Substantially larger numbers thought it more important to make Medicare and Social Security more secure, increase spending on education, and provide prescription drug benefits for seniors.

The tensions in public opinion did not dissipate in the new millennium, as the economy moved from boom to recession and the surplus was replaced by large deficits. Substantial majorities continued to affirm that the estate tax is unfair, agreeing that it should be repealed. At the same time, between a half and two-thirds thought balancing the budget more important than any tax cuts. If the question posed was how best to stimulate the economy, two-thirds or more favored tax cuts. Then again, support for tax cuts plummeted to around 18 percent if they were married to cuts in domestic spending.

Partisan and nonpartisan polls made it clear that, within the universe of possible tax cuts, getting rid of the estate tax was not particularly important to people. A June 1997 NBC News poll revealed that more people would prefer to see a child credit, a tuition credit, or a capital gains cut than a reduction in estate taxes. A year later, larger numbers were telling the same organization that that they preferred cuts in payroll taxes, rates for married couples, and capital gains taxes. The only option that the estate tax beat was a corporate tax cut. By July 1999, an NBC News poll on people's tax-cut priorities found a paltry 4 percent of Americans advocating cuts in the estate tax; 34 percent chose tax reductions for moderate- and low-income Americans, 31 percent wanted tax cuts for all Americans, 17 percent favored elimination of the marriage penalty, and 7 percent supported capital-gains tax cuts. These priorities remained stable in NBC's polling through the 2000 election and the passage of the 2001 tax act. Indeed, in 2003 Frank Luntz's polling was telling him that 10 percent or fewer chose estate taxes when asked what tax Congress should cut if it were only able to reduce one tax.

It has thus been common knowledge all along that the public accords low priority, and even that with low intensity, to estate tax cuts. But repeal proponents understood that in politics you must play the hand that you are dealt, and they did so no less brilliantly with respect to public opinion than with other aspects of their campaign. Frank Luntz and his associates were careful to do a great deal of well-publicized polling of the estate tax as a stand-alone issue, framing it as a question of basic fairness. Describing it as double-taxation, as President Bush would do in his campaign, helped—as did the "death tax" nomenclature.

Frank Luntz has a better read on what moves public opinion about the estate tax than does Michael Franc. Theories of how the economy works and its impact on people's prospects for upward mobility play into public opinions, but economic theories are less important than Americans' underlying perceptions of fairness. Partisan polls by the pro-repeal group Americans Against Unfair Family Taxation and others have yielded results in which about half the respondents agree that the estate tax hurts the economy, but nonpartisan polls suggest that this perceived impact cannot be the compelling reason why voters support repeal. A poll by three business professors that appeared in *Tax Notes Today*, for example, revealed that only one-third believe the tax reduces economic growth, almost 40 percent believe it does not, and over a quarter have no opinion.

One of the first estate-tax polls, taken in 1981, gave an early signal that factors other than perceptions of economic self-interest drive opinion on the subject. Fifty-seven percent of those polled supported an increase in the estate tax exclusion to $600,000—taking it beyond anything the vast majority of them would ever accumulate. And although people have unrealistic ideas about their prospects for upward mobility as we have seen, there is substantial evidence that this distortion does not account for their hostility to the tax, or at any rate not exclusively. Polls by partisan groups such Luntz Research, Americans Against Unfair Family Taxation, McLaughlin & Associates, and the NFIB are not the only ones showing substantial majorities convinced that the tax is unfair regardless of the likelihood that they themselves will pay it. Zogby International in 1999 found 86 percent believing that a 50 percent tax on estates over $1.2 million is unfair; 91 percent of Hispanics in California held that belief! A March 2001 survey published in *Tax Notes Today* showed over 76 percent convinced that the estate tax is unfair to family businesses and farms, despite the fact that these latter groups constitute a small minority of taxpayers. Even a partisan poll on the anti-repeal side by Greenberg Research found that explaining to people who it is that actually pays the tax reduces support for its repeal, but only from 59 percent to 47 percent—with 46 percent opposed to repeal and 7 percent undecided.

The finding that the estate tax was widely seen as unfair was fed back to the activists in the coalition and the entrepreneurs in Congress with great efficacy, as we have seen. Frank Luntz, Frank Blethen, and their allies in the media also ensured that the "death tax" label and fairness arguments were widely deployed on the talk show circuit, in advertising, and in editorial writing. In one memo Luntz urged Republican members of Congress to stage press conferences at their local mortuary. "I believe that this backdrop will clearly resonate with your constituents," he said. "Death is something the American people understand." As Joshua Green subsequently observed in *The American Prospect,* "Republicans have employed the term 'death tax' so aggressively that it has entered the popular lexicon. Nonpartisan venues like newspapers and magazines have begun to use it in a neutral context."

Indeed, by 2003 the fusion of "death," "inheritance," and "estate" taxes was so complete in the public mind that Luntz was finding that it scarcely mattered which term was used. Over 70 percent thought the tax either "somewhat unfair" or "completely unfair" (with more than half in the latter category) no matter which terminology was used. So Luntz was able to crow, "Sure, when the phrase 'Death Tax' is used, you get a more hostile response to the tax and greater support for its abolition. But even when 'inheritance' and/or 'estate' tax questions are posed, the results are almost the same. The American people simply oppose on principle the concept of anyone—even the children of wealthy parents—being taxed on the death of their parents." This contention fit well with the impressions of others in the coalition and on the Hill. Pat Soldano and Jennifer Dunn both insist that while the "death tax" terminology provided good public relations, fired up activists, and made some difference in public opinion at the margin, it mattered less than is often claimed in actually changing people's minds or shaping public opinion.

The main political effect of the "death tax" label may have been to keep the Democrats on the defensive—running scared of the issue. For one thing, associating the tax with "death" made it much more difficult for them to disabuse people of the notion that most people don't pay it. Everyone dies, whereas inheritances and estates are beyond most people's experiences. A (perhaps apocryphal) vignette has an airport baggage handler asking Senator Durbin when he would repeal the death tax, "so I won't have to pay it." Regardless of the authenticity of this particular baggage handler—recall Frank Luntz's instructions to talk about "real people," regardless of the truth of their existence—many congressmen, senators, and staffers recounted similar calls to their offices and questions on the stump from working-class people who are never going to be within a country mile of any estate tax.

Americans' misperceptions are remarkably resilient. One Democratic poll by Greenberg Research in 2002 found that supplying people with accurate information about who pays the tax reduces the number who think that they or someone in their household will pay it—but only from 37 percent to 30 percent, nowhere near the 2 percent who actually pay. Nonpartisan polling suggests that almost half of Americans believe that "most" families have to pay the estate tax, while only a third believe that "only a few" families have to pay it. A poll by Americans Against Unfair Family Taxation in 1999 revealed 84 percent thinking that the tax affects groups besides the wealthy, 77 percent believing that it affects all Americans, and merely 9 percent saying it affects only the wealthy. In 2003, more than half of Americans apparently believed incorrectly that the estate tax is assessed on transfers to a surviving spouse.

Why does the public's exaggerated perception of the estate tax's reach matter, if it was arguments about the tax's inherent unfairness that swayed people in favor of repeal more than appeals to economic self-interest? Actually, the belief that many people do in fact have to pay bolstered the perception that the injustice in question is widespread.

But the misperception about who pays the tax was most important, perhaps, because it spread to the small business owners who were the backbone of the repeal coalition. Fully one-third of small business owners indicated in surveys a belief that they would pay the estate tax. One 1995 poll revealed that 90 percent of minority business owners thought they would be vulnerable to the tax. A survey the following year found more than 60 percent of family-owned businesses reporting that paying estate taxes would limit business growth and threaten their survival, with a third believing their tax liability would require them to sell all or part of their business. In a 1998 study by Congress's Joint Economic Committee, 98 percent of the heirs of small business owners cited the need "to raise funds to pay estate taxes" when asked why family businesses fail. This finding seems especially exaggerated with respect to farms, given that neither the American Farm Bureau nor *New York Times* reporter David Cay Johnston's research could turn up a single case of a farm that had actually been sold to pay the estate tax. Even if repeal advocates are correct that both AFB and Johnston got it wrong, the number of farms that have been required to be sold to pay death taxes is tiny. As one Senate Democratic staffer put it, "There is a lot of ignorance about this, but ignorance is something you deal with in politics."

While the Democrats were neglecting to deal with public misperceptions, Republicans were exploiting the low intensity of public opinion about the estate tax. Americans' relative apathy on the issue allowed conservatives to obscure the relative unpopularity of estate tax repeal when compared to other possible tax relief or paired with specific spending cuts. One obvious tactic was to flood the media with stand-alone polls on the unfairness of the tax. In addition, Luntz and other conservatives were highly creative in polling groups that had traditional ties to Democrats. Luntz was thus able to report in April 2001 that 61 percent of self-described gays and lesbians who had voted for Al Gore the previous year would now support a candidate who believed the estate tax was unfair and should be eliminated, that 72 percent of gays and lesbians believe the tax is discriminatory, and that 82 percent would support a law to get rid of it even though they knew that they might not benefit.

One could, of course, explain that it is not the estate tax that is discriminatory here but rather the laws prohibiting gay marriage, because it is married couples who benefit from the unlimited estate tax marital deduction. Needless to say, Luntz and his associates would never think of advising Republican candidates to support gay marriage so as to protect gays and lesbians from missing out on a multitude of tax and other economic advantages—of which the estate tax marital benefit is only one. But in politics, when you are explaining, you are losing. In any case, the Democrats seem to have been too shell-shocked even to try. As with the staffer who commented that he first realized that the Republicans had lined up members of the Congressional Black Caucus when he saw them holding their press conference on TV, it seems not to have occurred to anyone on the anti-repeal side that gays and lesbians could be lined up for repeal—until after it had occurred.

With respect to opinion outside the beltway, the Democrats were misled by the low levels of intensity on the estate tax, which they should have known about from both nonpartisan and Democratic polling since at least 1997. The low priority that Americans accorded to the issue seems to have lulled the Democrats into thinking that the estate tax could safely be ignored. It is as if they forgot that although public opinion does not pass legislation, the way in which it is portrayed in the media, among activists, and to politicians and staffers is important in shaping agendas on the Hill and creating momentum to move legislation. Political scientists sometimes describe the exercise of political power as the mobilization of bias. By the time the anti-repeal forces began mobilizing, the other side had already done such an effective job in marshaling the available biases that the anti-repeal Democrats were now fighting a battle they couldn't win.

In stark contrast to the multitude of well-publicized polls on the Republican side, the Democrats did almost nothing to try to use the facts about the contours and intensity of public opinion to undermine the Republican case or to push a more progressive tax reform agenda. Our exhaustive search of published polls through 2003 revealed 31 nonpartisan polls, 20 Republican polls—virtually all of which had asked about the estate tax as a stand-alone issue—and a mere 4 polls by Democratic organizations and pollsters. And three of the latter came after the 2000 election, by which time the die was substantially cast.

It was not until 2002 that OMB Watch finally commissioned the Democratic pollster Greenberg Research to do a poll on the issue. This survey revealed that upon hearing "balanced arguments on both sides," 58 percent of respondents supported a reform that protects small business and family farms from the estate tax, compared to only 37 percent supporting repeal; this latter number drops to 27 percent "when voters learn more about the issue." Some Democratic pollsters insisted to us that their private polling and focus groups had been producing similar results since the mid-1990s, as well as confirming the NBC and *Wall Street Journal* polls in which estate tax repeal consistently ranked last among voters' tax cut priorities. Others candidly admitted that they had done no polling on the issue until the close Senate races of 2002, where making estate tax repeal permanent had become an issue. What is beyond question is that the public Democratic response to the blizzard of endlessly recycled Republican polls was thundering silence.

Part of the explanation for this response—or lack thereof—is that focus groups and partisan polls are usually conducted by and for candidates seeking to win elections. Inevitably they zero in on issues that will be critical in an upcoming campaign in a particular district. If a Democrat knows that preferences about taxes in general and estate taxes in particular are not intense in his or her district, there is no reason to waste money running polls on the issue. Campaigns in a few close House and Senate races would become important to the coalition as the battle was joined on Capitol Hill by the late 1990s, but it was the organized interests and grasstops that really mattered, as we have seen. The campaign for public opinion was more about building momentum for the legislation, not about individual races. It was about creating the impression in the media that estate tax repeal was a populist issue, about supplying cover to politicians who needed it, about rallying the troops in the coalition with the feeling that they were making progress, and about fostering a general sense of unstoppable momentum for the repeal. It was in this quest to shape public perceptions that Pat Soldano, Frank Blethen, and groups like Americans Against Unfair Family Taxation poured resources into conducting the stand-alone polls that would make their case look good and publicizing the results.

Like most effective tools in politics, good polling is expensive. The 2002 Greenberg Research poll cost OMB Watch $80,000—a large amount for a tiny organization that is run on a shoestring. Chuck Collins's United for a Fair Economy in Boston had a similar problem. They were constantly scrambling for money, frustrated because well-heeled groups that could have been funding opposition research, such as the nonprofits and insurance interests, were hamstrung by their internal conflicts, while organized labor was manning other barricades. Wealthy individuals might have helped, but those who actively opposed repeal, including Bill Gates, Sr., George Soros, and Steven Rockefeller, did not get involved in the fight until 2001. Even then, they were tight-fisted when it came to writing checks for OMB Watch and UFE as opposed to orchestrating a few news conferences and ads.

There certainly didn't seem to be any similar cash pinch on the pro-repeal side. By all accounts, the repealers' campaign for and management of public opinion was relentless. As they were building support for repeal on the Hill in the late 1990s, coalition members could conveniently point to polls showing high and increasing public support for repeal—reinforcing the perception of momentum. While 65 percent of respondents to the Zogby International poll had favored repeal in 1998, 71 percent were in that camp in the same organization's poll in 2000; a similar rise occurred in Pew Research polls for the same years, with the number who supported repeal going from 69 percent to 71 percent. A 1999 Americans Against Unfair Family Taxation poll showed 89 percent agreeing that it is unfair to tax a person's earnings "while it was being earned and then again after death." This number increased to 92 percent in their 2000 poll. A similar "double taxation" poll in 2000 by McLaughlin and Associates produced an 83 percent majority agreeing that the tax is unfair, rising to 88.5 percent by 2001. On abolishing the tax, McLaughlin found 68 percent in favor in November 2000, rising to 78.5 just two months later.

Even the rare comparative polling, which usually reveals the truth about the softness of support for estate tax repeal, was affected by this public opinion campaign. In NBC News/ *Wall Street Journal* surveys, the percentage of voters polled who said that the estate tax was their priority for a tax cut in the next year almost doubled (admittedly from only 4 to 7 percent) between August 1999 and January 2001.

By the time of the November 2000 election, the momentum had built to the point that stand-alone measures to abolish state estate taxes had worked their way onto ballots in South Dakota and Montana, where they passed by majorities of 79 and 68 percent, respectively. Jonathan Weisman was not exaggerating when he wrote in *USA Today* the following

May that the repeal movement had become "a massive lobbying effort that has swayed public opinion, altered the terms of the debate and proven unstoppable."

A liberal monthly, the *American Prospect,* could do little more than lament that Democrats had been "unable to sway public perception" or gain support for proposals that would utilize the revenue generated by the estate tax to fund social programs or finance a prescription drug benefit. The pro-repeal forces had occupied the running room of public opinion so completely that their opponents lacked even a vocabulary with which to resist their arguments. And the irony was, as the *American Prospect* correctly noted, that the pro-repeal forces achieved this feat even though "research shows that once voters understand the implications of the estate tax and who pays it, they tend to support the Democratic position."

If one of the central elements of our mystery is how public support could be achieved for eliminating a tax as steeply progressive as the levy on large estates, we can see more clearly now how this was achieved. By separating repeal from the context of the overall federal budget and spending priorities, and thus isolating the "death tax" as a stand-alone issue of fairness, repeal advocates were able to manipulate a low level of interest in the general public. People who would rather have used the surplus for other ends somehow got transformed through opinion polls into ammunition for a focused attack on the morality of this one provision in the tax code. Both the structure of the coalition's polls and the constancy of their efforts to distribute and promote the results can be seen as a virtual playbook on how to forge low-intensity preferences into a sword wielded by those with a high-intensity desire for a particular outcome.

Indeed, the sword is still being held aloft. Even after the passage of the 2001 tax bill, which we turn to next, Pat Soldano still travels to Washington every few weeks. On her agenda one week: a meeting with Paul Gigot, editorial page editor of the *Wall Street Journal,* to share with him new poll results—courtesy of Frank Luntz—the results demonstrating, despite recession and massive job losses, widespread popular support for making Bush's elimination of the death tax permanent.

The Battle for Passage

The Missing Link

For both advocates and opponents of estate tax repeal, the 2000 presidential election was a make-or-break contest. In the 1996 campaign, Republican running mates Robert Dole and Jack Kemp had proposed changes that by 2000 seemed modest: to "increase the estate tax exemption from $600,000 to $1.6 million and eventually eliminate the estate tax on family-owned businesses, farms and ranches." But in the intervening four years, the forces for repeal had picked up momentum, especially following the QFOBI debacle. After the favorable votes in Congress in 1999 to repeal the tax, it became clear that the main ingredient missing was a supportive president. The coalition and its allies had mustered a majority for repeal in both the House and Senate, but not the 60 necessary to stop a Senate filibuster or the two-thirds necessary to override a presidential veto.

The opponents of repeal understood the situation well. In January 2000, for example, the Association of Advanced Life Underwriting—a group of life insurance sellers whose livelihoods were threatened by the prospect of estate tax repeal—issued a *Washington Report* which argued that the "most devastating political development, with respect to this specific subject, would be the election of the Republican nominee for President, coupled with a Republican sweep of the House and Senate." If the Democrats retained control of the White House, however, AALU was comfortable that "repeal, as contrasted to modification, would be very unlikely to occur." Jennifer Dunn, along with Georgia's Republican Senator Paul Coverdell, responded with a scolding letter, asserting "deep disappointment" with the AALU for opposing Republican control of both the executive and legislative branches. Dunn and Coverdell urged the underwriters to "embrace" repeal, saying they found it "devastating" that the AALU would "work so clearly and unequivocally against the interests of estate planning clients in order to protect your own members' livelihoods." Devastating, maybe, but surely not surprising, given how much the life insurance industry stood to lose from repeal. Dunn and Coverdell also asserted that the AALU's concern was "contrary" to the AALU's members' "fiduciary responsibilities to their clients," and concluded by urging the AALU to "alter its view of the death tax and join the national groundswell of support for a tax system that mirrors America's value of building a legacy for our children." Not a chance; the AALU refused to join the cause.

The Democratic campaign for the presidency, unsurprisingly, promised four more years of White House opposition to repeal if the Democrats prevailed. Bill Bradley said virtually nothing about the estate tax. Al Gore, who secured the Democratic nomination, proposed increasing the value of a small business or family farm that could be bequeathed tax free to $2.5 million per person, $5 million for a couple—in other words, doubling the amount eligible for the QFOBI benefit. To repeal advocates, this proposal was insulting. QFOBI had done little or nothing for them; two times nothing is still nothing. Gore emphasized that his plan would cost the federal government little in lost revenues, less than 10 percent of the cost of repeal. The small revenue cost reflected the limited nature of the relief offered, and even this estimate was probably excessive.

Despite the AALU's well-founded forebodings about what a Republican White House would portend—since estate tax abolition had become a totem of Republican dogma by 2000—repeal was not unanimously embraced in the fight for the Republican presidential nomination. Arizona's unorthodox Senator John McCain, who was George Bush's most formidable competitor, dissented. On the stump, McCain advocated a much smaller overall tax cut than Governor Bush; he simply was not prepared to forego the entire estate tax revenue. Instead of repeal, he proposed increasing the estate tax exemption from $1 million to $5 million (from $2 million to $10 million for a married couple). This change would have substantially diminished the number of families subject to the estate tax while preserving most of the estate tax dollars received by the federal government. The AALU's *Washington Report* summarized the impact of this alternative: "Senator McCain's program, if enacted as articulated, would not be a happy occasion for AALU members; alternatively it would not necessarily be a catastrophe."

By the winter of 2000, in contrast, George Bush had become a strong advocate for repeal. Early in his campaign—until the summer of 1999—Bush had concentrated his efforts on amassing a huge campaign war chest, raising more money than any previous presidential candidate at that stage of the game. He refused to begin campaigning in earnest until June 1999, after the Texas legislature adjourned for that year. The governor had taken brickbats for his reticence to campaign, receiving a scolding from the other Republican candidates, for example, for not participating in a New Hampshire debate a month earlier. Impervious to the pressure, the Bush campaign had merely set up a booth in New Hampshire offering people bags of fresh popcorn with a sign that read: "Coming attractions: Governor George W. Bush. Coming this summer to a neighborhood near you."

Bush finally hit the campaign trail in Iowa in the second weekend of June 1999, formally acknowledging what had been known for months. He immediately surprised his opponents by announcing that he would participate in an upcoming Iowa straw poll. Bush remained cautious on the issues, however. Although he had signaled his desire for tax cuts, his actual plans remained mysterious. A few days later in New Hampshire, he indicated that his party—and his opponents—would have no better luck coaxing out the details than they had in coaxing out the candidate. "I know everybody's waiting with baited breath for the specific tax plan. And I'm going to be laying it out here on my timetable, and a timetable that sets to the pace of the campaign." The governor made a few other campaign appearances in June and July 1999, but no major speeches. Compared to the other Republican candidates, Bush was virtually silent on the major issues of the primary campaign.

When he first traveled to Iowa in early June, George Bush's campaign website described estate tax "reform" as one of his goals. In July, an article in the *Dallas Morning News* criticized Bush for being deliberately vague about his position on the estate tax. But by the end of August, the campaign website had upped the ante by calling for a phasing out of the "death tax." And by September 1, 1999, Bush had given a speech in Iowa calling for repeal. From that point on, according to his campaign aides, proposing an end to the death tax would garner Bush the greatest applause from his audiences during his campaign stump speeches.

While no surprise, exactly what caused George Bush's switch from estate tax reform to repeal remains something of a mystery. This change has almost as many people claiming credit as for the "death tax" label itself. One lobbyist for beer and wine distributors insists that Texas beer distributors friendly with Bush persuaded him to support repeal. Others—perhaps more plausibly—pin the change on his early trips to Iowa, where Bush was told that advocating repeal was essential to gaining the support of Iowa's farmers. Several Washington trade associations also claim a role in getting Bush into the repeal camp.

Some Bush aides and many repeal advocates give much of the credit to Jennifer Dunn, who was an early supporter of the governor. Indeed, Dunn herself says that she was determined to see that death tax repeal move high up on Bush's list of campaign priorities—and stay at the forefront of his agenda. And she was well-positioned to make her case. Dunn was a key congressional member of Bush's exploratory committee at the behest of his political guru Karl Rove. She was also one of the governor's "Pioneers," a group of supporters who raised at least $100,000 for his campaign. She talked to Karl Rove; Larry Lindsey, Bush's key economic advisor; and Bush himself, urging repeal. Anytime she saw or heard of the Bush campaign using the word "reform" rather than "repeal," she says, "I would get on the phone to Karl Rove and say 'we need to change this language.' We want repeal." Dunn insists that George Bush himself understood the issue well and strongly favored repeal. She attributes any confusion about the campaign's position to miscommunication, not to uncertainty within the Bush camp.

Surely the Bush family has had enough experience with estate planning and estate taxes that George W. Bush needed no lessons on the subject. In any event, after August 1999, the candidate never wavered in his support for estate tax repeal. In accepting the presidential nomination at the GOP convention in July 2000, Bush left no doubts: "On principle, everyone should be free to pass on their life's work to those they love. So we will abolish the death tax."

Repeal of the death tax was just one part of an economic plan that George W. Bush had begun to shape long before the convention. In 1997, when he began seriously to consider mounting a presidential campaign, George Bush asked his long-time friend and Harvard Business School classmate, Al Hubbard, to help him put together a number of policy teams. Hubbard, an Indiana businessman and former chair of the Indiana Republicans, had been Vice President Dan Quayle's deputy chief of staff in the administration of George H. W. Bush. He had also run the senior Bush's Council on Competitiveness, a group that sought out regulations seen as adverse to business interests, which the administration would then attempt to terminate or loosen. George W. Bush, notwithstanding his two terms as

Texas governor, which had included serious attempts to restructure that state's tax system, told his old friend, "I don't know anything about economics, you have to teach me."

Hubbard selected Larry Lindsey to be George Bush's principal economics tutor and advisor. Lindsey, with an economics degree from Harvard, had a good relationship with the influential Harvard economist Martin Feldstein, who had served as Chairman of Ronald Reagan's Council of Economic Advisors. In the early 1980s Lindsey had joined the Reagan administration as a staffer for Feldstein, and the two men later worked together back in Cambridge. In 1989 Lindsey returned to Washington to serve as a White House economic advisor during the first Bush administration. In 1992, President Bush appointed Lindsey a governor of the Federal Reserve, where he served from 1992 to 1997, heading the Fed's efforts at community development.

Larry Lindsey, like George W. Bush himself, admits to "youthful mistakes": Lindsey voted for George McGovern for president. Larry Lindsey has long since become a convert to supply-side Republicanism—he wrote a book strongly defending Reagan's 1981 tax cuts during his sojourn back in Cambridge in the 1980s. But he has maintained his concern for the poor, what he describes as his "populist streak." Indeed, Lindsey's parsimonious populism fit well with Bush's "compassionate conservatism." Lindsey also shares Bush's easy-going, upbeat affability, but in physical style Larry Lindsey and George Bush could not be more different. In sharp contrast to Bush's physically fit, immaculate appearance and his disciplined manner, Lindsey is overweight and routinely disheveled. Larry Lindsey seems constantly to be engaged in a battle to keep his shirt tucked in. Nevertheless, this odd couple of Lindsey and Bush hit it off well when they first met in a three-hour meeting with Hubbard in Austin, Texas, in October 1997. For the next five years, until December 2002, Larry Lindsey would serve as Bush's chief economic advisor.

Lindsey and Hubbard did not work on Bush's economic policy by themselves. They assembled an impressive economic team to advise the governor, a team that helped fashion both his tax cut proposal and his position on Social Security. But the two men had a means of exercising their influence on the team: Hubbard would chair all the meetings so that Lindsey would be free to express his own views forcefully. Other members of the team included Lindsey's Harvard mentor Martin Feldstein; Martin Anderson, Ronald Reagan's domestic policy chief; J. D. Foster, the conservative chief economist for Washington's Tax Foundation; Columbia University economics professor Glenn Hubbard, another Feldstein protégé, who had served in the Treasury Department's Office of Tax Policy in Bush's father's administration; John Cogan, a former budget official in the Reagan White House; and Stanford University economics professors John Taylor and Michael Boskin, former chairman of the first President Bush's Council of Economic Advisors.

The Texas governor's team of economists, along with his political advisors, quickly agreed that a large tax cut proposal should become a central campaign plank. The political benefits from this position were clear: advocating a major tax cut helped Bush secure support with fervent Republican activists as well as with the many Republicans and Independents who feared that the large ongoing federal budget surpluses, which were amassing toward the end of the Clinton administration, would be tapped for additional government spending. Bush was well aware that important GOP figures such as Newt Gingrich and Grover Norquist had abandoned his father when he agreed to raise taxes as part of the 1990 budget agreement. That agreement, many would argue, set the stage for the surpluses that George W. Bush had to work with when he took office. Nonetheless, the elder Bush had suffered a great political cost for the tax increase, and his son's political advisors were determined to establish firmly the new Republican candidate's conservative bona fides with a solid tax-cutting position.

The economic team regarded an across-the-board cut in income tax rates as the best economic prescription. The economists were particularly anxious to lower the top rate, which President Clinton had raised from 31 to about 40 percent. The precise components of the tax cut proposal depended, of course, on its overall size. Bush himself always favored a large number, and he ultimately settled on a $1.3 trillion reduction over ten years.

Making estate tax repeal part of the package, however, was a political decision, not an economic one. The economic team generally cared little about the estate tax, regarding it as not particularly important to the overall economy. They would have preferred a deeper cut in income tax rates. But the candidate and his political advisors decided on death tax repeal early in the game, months before the campaign's overall tax plan was revealed on December 1, 1999. The only flexibility they gave the economic team was to postpone the date of repeal as a way of keeping its ten-year cost down, thereby making room for larger income tax rate cuts. Bush's final campaign proposal called for the estate tax to be repealed eight years after the legislation was enacted.

George Bush's tax proposal had four main components: (1) a reduction in income tax rates—taking the top rate from 40 to 33 percent, the lowest rate from 15 to 10 percent, and some reductions across the board; (2) an increase in the income tax credit for children—doubling its size from $500 to $1,000 per child and increasing the income levels at which it could be claimed; (3) a reduction in the income tax "marriage penalty" for some middle-income couples; and (4) the slow elimination of the estate tax. When asked how he arrived at the overall size of his proposal, Bush claimed that his goal was to return a quarter of the projected ten-year, $4.56 trillion budget surplus to taxpayers. During the campaign, he frequently said, "I want to take one-half of the surplus and dedicate it to Social Security. One-quarter of the surplus for important projects. And I want to send one-quarter of the surplus back to the people who pay the tax bills."

The Bush proposal was carefully designed so that he could accurately claim that it included some benefit for all Americans who pay income taxes. And to rebut contentions that his plan was tilted too much in favor of the rich, Bush had included across-the-board income tax rate cuts and a sufficiently large increase in child tax credits to allow him to describe large tax reductions for middle-class families of four. These elements did not, of course, stop Democrats from complaining about the largest tax breaks going to the rich, but they meant that George Bush always had a ready response.

Indeed, during the presidential campaign, Al Gore frequently charged that Bush's tax cut proposal "would spend more money on tax cuts for the wealthiest one percent than all of the new spending [Bush] proposed for education, health care, prescription drugs and national defense, all combined." Emphasizing the point, the Democrat usually added, "I think those are the wrong priorities." In response, George Bush not only pointed out the tax reductions he offered to middle-class families of four, but he also often charged his opponent with using "phony numbers" or, more frequently, "fuzzy math." Although this detail was never grasped by the American public, whether Gore's charge was accurate turned entirely on how one assessed the impact of estate tax repeal. Gore's claim was based on an analysis by Robert McIntyre's liberal tax policy shop, Citizens for Tax Justice.

McIntyre treated virtually all of the revenue lost from estate tax repeal as benefiting taxpayers with the highest 1 percent of income. While widely accepted among experts, this conclusion was a bit controversial among some economists. Supporters of estate tax repeal claim, for example, that a significant portion of the death tax burden falls on employees of small businesses whose jobs are jeopardized when their employers are vulnerable to the tax—although they would also concede that most of the benefits from repeal will flow to those with substantial wealth.

In a September 2000 speech to a group of California Republicans, Bush attacked Gore's economic policy ideas, describing them as "tired even when his career began." On the estate tax specifically, he lambasted his opponent's proposals. Bush said Gore's proposed estate tax reform would require the decedent to participate in the business for five of the eight years before death and heirs to participate for the ten years after death, echoing the conditions of the failed QFOBI provisions. Al Gore, in turn, claimed that both Bush's assumptions and his math were faulty.

The single best opportunity for the American public to assess the differences between the two candidates' positions on the estate tax came on October 7, 2000, during their third and final debate. Bush had responded to a question about what he would do to help America's farmers in part by citing his desire to get "rid of the death tax," claiming it "is a bad tax," one "that taxes people twice" and "penalizes the family farmer." The moderator, Jim Lehrer of the Public Broadcasting System, then asked the candidates to explain their differences concerning "the inheritance tax." Gore, who went first, claimed that he supported "a massive reform of the estate tax or the death tax," using—intentionally or not—the repeal proponents' lingo. He added that under his proposal, "80 percent of all family farms" and the "vast majority of all family businesses" would be "completely exempt" from the tax. But, he hastened to add, he did not favor eliminating the tax for "the wealthiest one percent." He insisted that repeal would produce "an extra-heavy burden on middle-class families" who, he claimed, would have to "make up" the lost revenues.

Lehrer then asked Bush, "What's the case for eliminating the tax, completely for everybody?" The Republican did not hesitate. "Because people shouldn't be taxed twice on their assets," he said. "It's either unfair for some or unfair for all." Bush then attacked Gore's plan for picking and choosing winners and for having "a lot of fine print," adding, "I'm not sure 80 percent of the people will get [Gore's] death tax [benefits]." Bush concluded, "I know this: 100 percent will get it if I am the president. I just don't think it's fair to tax people's assets twice regardless of your status. It's a fairness issue. It's an issue of principle, not politics."

Later, both on the campaign stump in 2000 and in private White House conversations with his aides in 2001, Bush would frequently return to this principle, the unfairness of double taxation, as he remained steadfast in favor of repeal. And in 2003, he would again invoke the same "double taxation" mantra in an effort to eliminate the individual income tax on corporate dividends.

The 2000 election was one of the closest in American history. The outcome was fateful for estate tax opponents. Al Gore won the popular vote but lost by five votes—one state—in the Electoral College. George W. Bush became the first president since 1888, when Benjamin Harrison defeated Grover Cleveland, to win the presidency after having lost the popular vote. The result was not finally known until December 12, 2000, when the Supreme Court halted a Florida vote recount. Gore conceded the next day. Had Al Gore carried even his home state of Tennessee, he, not George W. Bush, would have been the 43rd president of the United States. The estate tax would not yet have been repealed.

Great skepticism about Governor Bush's ability to be an effective leader followed his controversial victory. Many commentators wondered about how he would navigate a polarized Washington political scene. When Bush assumed the presidency on January 21, 2001, Republicans controlled the House of Representatives and, for a brief while—until the May 2001 defection of James Jeffords of Vermont—the Senate. But the Senate majority was as slim as could be: with its 50 Republicans and 50 Democrats, Republicans were in control only because of Vice President Dick Cheney's ability to cast tie-breaking votes.

George W. Bush had, however, campaigned emphasizing his ability to get things done with a divided and sharply partisan Congress. He decided that his first priority must be to enact his tax cut plan. This task would be the first big test of his presidency. Dick Cheney knew a victory on taxes was important: if Bush lost, Cheney warned, all people would talk about was how he had lost the popular vote. Grover Norquist elaborated the stakes: "If Bush gets his $1.6 trillion, two things happen: his stature and power in town is greatly enhanced and it makes the rest of his agenda more likely to pass." Dirk Van Dongen, president of the National Association of Wholesale Distributors and a close Bush ally, put it a bit more colorfully: "In my judgment, this president is either going to make his bones on this, or we find out we have an administration that cannot easily advance its agenda in this city." Considerably more than the fate of the estate tax hung in the balance.

Building a Strong Offense

George W. Bush's ascendance to the presidency in January 2001 certainly enhanced the prospects of repeal, but neither his election nor the hard work of the Family Business Estate Tax Coalition and its allies, like Jennifer Dunn, would be sufficient to put estate tax repeal into the tax code. More than a little help was needed from others. A powerful economist, a college dropout, an Iowa hog farmer, a California political scientist, a high school wrestling coach, a Montana lawyer who prefers his Harley-Davidson to his car, America's first African American billionaire, and a Louisiana party animal who had become Congress's consummate dealmaker were among those who played important roles in getting repeal enacted in 2001. And, as they had throughout the 1990s, repeal's enemies both inside and outside the Congress proved ineffective in the battle.

Repeal proponents caught their first good break in January 2001 when both the administration's Office of Management and Budget and its counterpart on the Hill, the Congressional Budget Office, predicted much larger federal budget surpluses than previously suggested. During his campaign, Bush had relied on CBO's earlier estimates of a budget surplus of about $4.5 trillion in fashioning his roughly $1.3 trillion proposed tax cut. By the time of his inauguration, however, CBO raised its estimate of the forthcoming decade's federal surplus to $5.6 trillion, giving the president more than an additional $1 trillion to work with. More than half the increase—$600 billion—came simply from dropping the year 2001 from this new ten-year forecast and adding the year 2011. The balance was due to more optimistic economic assumptions.

With the benefit of hindsight, we know that these predictions were wildly off the mark. By 2003 the federal deficit was nearing the $400 billion mark, and in January 2004 President Bush announced it would exceed $500 billion that year—the highest dollar amount in U.S. history. Back in January 2001, however, no one in government foresaw the massive loss of income tax revenue from capital gains and stock options resulting from the precipitous stock market decline that had begun in March 2000. Nor had government forecasters yet realized how much sluggishness was haunting the nation's economy. And, of course, the substantial increase in government spending for both homeland security and the military that followed the attacks of September 11, 2001, was completely unpredictable. But relying too much on predictions of how the federal budget will look in the years ahead has always been a risky venture. The 1995 CBO forecast for the year 2000, for example, had missed the mark by nearly $600 billion—more than one-third of the total federal budget for that year.

A second stroke of good fortune for advocates of a large tax cut occurred on January 25, 2001, when Alan Greenspan told Congress that a large tax reduction was fitting. In testimony before the Senate Budget Committee, the widely respected head of the Federal Reserve provided economic legitimacy for a plan that Democrats and a few Republicans—including Bush's rival for the presidency, Senator John McCain—had decried as reckless. Chairman Greenspan did not claim that George Bush's tax proposals would stimulate the economy. Instead, he expressed his fear that large federal surpluses would not only enable Washington to pay off its entire debt, but would also require the government to start purchasing private assets such as corporate stock, an idea that Greenspan abhorred. Again, hindsight makes Greenspan's fear seem laughable. By 2004, the federal debt was growing like summer grass, and the CBO was predicting it would continue to grow until 2013 and probably for some time thereafter.

But as Congress commenced its legislative session in 2001, the Greenspan testimony gave the new president's tax plan a kickstart. Not even Democrats would any longer contest the propriety of a large tax reduction. The dispute between the two parties had been over whether to enact a tax cut; it now dwindled to an argument over how much to cut and whose taxes to cut the most. Once the argument shifted to one about numbers, George W. Bush held the high cards. In his address to a joint session of Congress on February 27, 2001, he transformed Alan Greenspan's testimony into a trumpet for immediate action: "We must act quickly. The chairman of the Federal Reserve has testified before Congress that tax cuts often come too late to stimulate economic recovery."

It is ironic that the new president's good fortune had come in the person of Alan Greenspan, a man who had been a thorn in the side of George

W. Bush's father during his presidency. Many key members of George Herbert Walker Bush's administration blamed Greenspan for not acting soon enough to lower interest rates to head off or shorten the recession of the early 1990s, which greatly aided Bill Clinton's campaign to defeat the elder Bush. But whatever his relationship with the new president's father, Alan Greenspan gave a major boost to the size and substance of the White House tax plan and created a catalyst for its enactment.

Bush—along with those who had toiled so long for estate tax repeal—also caught a break in the composition and leadership of the Congress in 2001. Republicans controlled the House of Representatives. The speaker was "Denny" Hastert, a former Illinois high school teacher and wrestling-coach-of-the-year who led his team, the Yorkville Foxes, to the Illinois State Wrestling Championship in 1976. Hastert himself had wrestled in college, and the former athlete has not lost his competitive edge. The quiet but affable Hastert is a can-do guy and an often underestimated legislative strategist.

Denny Hastert lets it be known that he was born "in the Illinois cornfields," and he is proud to represent the suburban Chicago district that houses the boyhood home of Ronald Reagan. Hastert, who had pledged not to drink, smoke, or watch movies while attending the evangelical Wheaton College in Illinois, married his wife Jean when they were both teaching at Yorkville High. When Denny was first elected to Congress in 1986, Jean refused to live in Washington. To this day she remains in Illinois, where Denny returns nearly every weekend. In 1999, Hastert rose to the speaker's post following the successive departures of Newt Gingrich and Robert Livingston, the GOP's first choice to replace Gingrich but who resigned from Congress following disclosures of marital infidelities. When Hastert was selected, many Washington insiders regarded his main qualification for the job as being neither Newt Gingrich nor a philanderer.

In a town where most people's politics have become remarkably easy to peg, Denny Hastert remains enigmatic. Jonathan Franzen, writing about Hastert in 2003 in *The New Yorker,* calls him "an irrelevant, indispensable, modern, old-fashioned, moderate, conservative, nobody somebody."

Consider Hastert's chameleon-like transformation in 2001 from moderate bipartisanship to hard-line partisan politics. During his two years of working with the Clinton administration as speaker, Hastert got along reasonably well with Democrats in the House and with the Democratic president. He broke long-standing tradition by inviting the Democrats' leader Dick Gephardt to participate in celebrating his first day in the leadership post, and he began his term with a call for bipartisan cooperation and the end to "a pool of bitterness." His economic priorities were not too far removed from those of centrist Democrats: he seemed more of a mainstream fiscal conservative than a tax-cutting zealot. As late as 2003, for example, Hastert still emphasized the accomplishments of his cooperation with the Clinton White House, claiming credit for "balanc[ing] the budget" and for "lock[ing] away 100 percent of Social Security and Medicare dollars to be spent solely on Social Security and Medicare—not other government programs." By that time, he had helped push both of those accomplishments into the trash bin.

If the moderate side of Hastert came to the fore during the Clinton presidency—when some cooperation with Democrats was a political necessity for the Republicans—the conservative side has reigned since George Bush became president. House Republicans, under Hastert's leadership, have not hesitated to use all of the advantages that the House rules award the majority party to stifle the Democratic minority. Unlike the Senate, where 60 votes are often necessary to stop a filibuster and thus to pass legislation, the House of Representatives can be governed by a simple majority. And, since late in the nineteenth century, the House rules have been fashioned to allow the majority party both to set and enact its legislative agenda. As the Republican architect of these rules, Congressman Thomas Brackett Reed, explained in 1880, "The best system is to have one party govern and the other party watch; and on general principles I think it would be better for us to govern and for the Democrats to watch." That sentiment precisely captures the mood and the intention of the Republican House leadership in January 2001. Throughout the presidency of George W. Bush, by keeping the Republican troops in line, the House leadership has been able to exclude Democratic representatives from any serious role in fashioning legislation.

Following Bush's election, Hastert's term as speaker spawned new levels of rancor between the parties. Washington insiders often attribute both the partisan bitterness and the lockstep votes of House Republicans to the iron hands of Hastert's Texas lieutenants (some say henchmen), Dick Armey and Tom "the Hammer" DeLay. But notwithstanding his paeans to bipartisanship, firm control of a voting majority suits Denny Hastert just fine.

Of course, Hastert was thrilled in 2001 to have a Republican president to work with. But he caused considerable consternation in the Bush camp weeks before the inauguration by suggesting that Bush's tax legislation not be brought to the House floor all at once. Instead he insisted on splitting the proposal into smaller bites. This idea may have inconvenienced the White House, but Hastert's reasoning was shrewd. He knew that if the package were brought to the House floor for a single vote, Democrats— and, he feared, some Republicans—would vote against it solely on the ground that it would create too large a hole in federal revenues. He had seen this sticker-shock problem provide Democrats cover for voting against tax cuts in 2000. In addition, a massive tax-cutting bill would focus the public's attention on the overall cost.

But the "too big" argument would be much more difficult to muster if the bill were broken into smaller pieces. Members of Congress worried about the size of the tax cuts would have to vote separately against income tax rate cuts, reductions in marriage penalties, enhanced tax credits for children, and repeal of the estate tax—all items that individually were very popular, even among a substantial group of Democrats.

Hastert held firm on his strategy, and ultimately the White House went along. At a meeting in the White House Cabinet Room in early February, President Bush secured a promise from Denny Hastert that if the tax package was broken up for House consideration, the income tax rate cuts— which Bush regarded as the most important and vulnerable of his proposals—would be voted on first. As it turned out, the House vote on estate tax repeal would come last.

Once the Republican leadership backed the Bush tax plan, estate tax repeal faced only one other major stumbling block in the House of Representatives. This human barrier was the volatile chairman of the Ways and Means Committee, Bill Thomas of California. His committee, which has responsibility for tax, trade, and much health care legislation, is the oldest committee in the House. The press so often refers to it as "the powerful House Ways and Means Committee" that many people must think "powerful" is part of its name. As a new president moved into the White House and as Congress opened its session in 2001, a new chairman also took charge at Ways and Means.

Bill Thomas did not rise to the top of the Ways and Means Committee in the natural order—that is, simply by waiting to become the committee's most senior member on the majority side. Instead, the House leadership picked him over his more senior colleague Phil Crane of Illinois. Crane had long been regarded as quirky, unpredictable, and, most importantly, uncontrollable. The House Republican leadership regarded Bill Thomas as the less risky choice, but only a little less risky. Everyone had confidence that Thomas, a bright and hard-working former political science professor from California, would master the details and complexities of the important issues within the committee's jurisdiction. The question was whether he could control his irascible personality long enough to get legislation passed. Thomas's feistiness was no secret. The *New York Times* has described Bill Thomas as "one of the most revered and reviled members of the House." The *Washington Post* has called him "a spirited policy wonk known for berating allies and enemies alike." On January 5, 2001, the day after Thomas was elected to head the committee, the *Los Angeles Times* quite accurately said that Thomas was "known for his mastery of complex matters . . . but also for his occasional fits of temper."

Fits of temper indeed. In July 2003, the Democratic members of Ways and Means were upset that, without consulting them, Thomas and his Republican colleagues had rewritten a supposedly bipartisan pension bill the night before it was due for a committee vote. The Democrats stormed out of the Ways and Means hearing room to protest this and gathered to caucus in an adjacent library. But Thomas, their chairman, called the Capitol police to roust them. A few days later—after many consultations and exhortations by his Republican colleagues—a tearful Thomas apologized on the House floor, confessing, "As my mother would have put it, when they were passing out moderation, you were hiding behind the door." This emotional outpouring was a remarkable occurrence in any legislative session, and a stunning confession from one of the House's most self-satisfied members.

So as President Bush's tax bill went to the House of Representatives in 2001, it was this unpredictable character and his powerful committee that needed to agree with his plan. The big question was whether Bill Thomas would rubberstamp the Bush plan, as the White House hoped, or whether he would use his first opportunity as Ways and Means chairman to reshape it in order to put his own mark on the bill. Estate tax repeal advocates were particularly worried. On the one hand, Bill Thomas represents one of the nation's largest and most productive agricultural districts in the nation. California's Kern and San Luis Obispo counties, most of which fall within Thomas's constituency, produce more than $3 billion of crops and livestock annually. Surely he would be sensitive to the interests of the farmers who were well represented in the repeal coalition. Nevertheless, Thomas's top priority was reducing marginal income tax rates, not repealing the estate tax. When asked his position on estate tax repeal on February 15, 2001, Thomas told reporters, "I'm listening to all the options." A few days later, he privately informed lobbyists that they should prepare an alternative to full repeal. However, by the time the Ways and Means Committee met on March 21, to consider estate tax repeal, Thomas was singing Jennifer Dunn's tune. He told the committee, "The death tax should be repealed for one reason, which is simply that Americans should not be taxed when they die."

Once Thomas and the Ways and Means Committee were fully on board, passage of estate tax repeal on its own in the House was a foregone conclusion: a "Dunn deal." The real action would take place in the Senate. But moving Bush's entire tax package intact through the House of Representatives—a far easier task than winning Senate passage—was not as simple as it looks in hindsight. George Bush himself deserves a lot of the credit.

First, Bush assembled a cohesive and effective team to win congressional support. His longtime political advisor Karl Rove was the quarterback. Everyone agrees that Rove is a savvy political strategist who has become one of the most influential presidential advisors in history. A 30-year veteran of Washington battles who never graduated college, Rove claims to have first become a political junkie—and a Republican—at the ripe age of nine, when he decided to support Richard Nixon over John F. Kennedy for the presidency. Rove also enjoys a long history with the Bush family. He was the first person whom George H. W. Bush hired to help run his 1980 presidential campaign against Ronald Reagan. In George W. Bush's successful run for the Texas governorship in 1994, more than half of the money he spent in the first three months of the campaign went to Karl Rove. Money well spent. Not only did Bush defeat the Democratic incumbent Ann Richards, but all six candidates whom Rove worked for that year in Texas won election. Indeed, Rove is widely credited with reshaping Texas politics so that by the end of the 1990s, all statewide offices were occupied by Republicans. One Democratic political consultant calls Rove the "Bobby

Fisher of politics. He not only sees the board, he sees about 20 moves ahead." George W. Bush calls him "Boy Genius" or, somewhat less flatteringly, "Turd Blossom."

As his principal liaison to Congress—the assistant to the president for legislative affairs—George Bush hired Nick Calio, who had headed the White House Office of Congressional Affairs for Bush's father. Calio, who would fight featherweight if he were a boxer, is a "hail fellow, well met." You cannot help but warm to him. He is a charming, longtime Washington lobbyist, as popular among Democrats as among Republicans. To take but one example, during the legislative tug of war over the 1990 budget act, Bill Archer, then the ranking Republican on Ways and Means who would become its chairman from 1995 to 2001, asked Calio to convey a point to Democrat Dan Rostenkowski, then the committee's chairman. As Archer put it to Calio, "You have a better relationship with Rosty than I do." A Republican senator well described Calio's relationship with the members of Congress. "He's done an outstanding job. He's always available and he's responsive," she said. In addition to getting along well with members and staff, Nick Calio is an excellent vote counter, and his long-standing and widespread congressional contacts served the White House well during Congress's consideration of the 2001 tax legislation.

Calio was faulted, however, for failing to anticipate or learn in advance about Vermont Senator Jim Jeffords's disavowal of the Republican Party just as Bush's tax bill was wrapping up in May of 2001. Jeffords voted for the bill, but his switch to an Independent allowed the Democrats to retake control of the Senate. And Calio somehow caught the blame from many Republicans for Jeffords's defection. That unhappy event notwithstanding, Nick Calio worked closely on the tax bill with George Bush, Karl Rove, and many others inside the administration, including the White House Chief of Staff Andrew Card, who also knows his way around Capitol Hill, having been General Motors's chief lobbyist before coming to the White House. "The Bush team was really unified on getting this bill through and worked well together," Calio says. "This was a sharp contrast to the first Bush administration, which had a lot of well-publicized in-fighting. What's more, the President was willing to travel a lot and meet with many people on the issue."

One of Calio's compatriots in the effort to get Bush's tax package through Congress was Mark Weinberger, assistant secretary of the Treasury for Tax Policy. In filling this post, George W. Bush had broken with a long-standing tradition of selecting well-known tax law experts for the job. Not that Mark Weinberger was a novitiate in the tax law. Before coming to Treasury, he had worked as a Senate staffer for Jack Danforth, a moderate Republican from Missouri; been chief of staff of the 1994 President's Commission on Entitlement and Tax Reform; and served as an advisor to a commission on economic growth and tax reform headed by Jack Kemp, Bob Dole's vice presidential running mate in the 1996 campaign.

But it wasn't just these policy credentials that got Weinberger his job in the George W. Bush administration. Weinberger is best known around Washington for his prowess as a successful lobbyist for large multinational corporations: he co-founded the tax lobbying firm Washington Counsel, Inc., which later became affiliated with Ernst and Young. Unlike his predecessors, who liked nothing better than working through the details of hundreds of pages of tax regulations, Weinberger is far more comfortable with people, including the lawmakers and staffers on Capitol Hill. And working with Congress would be his principal assignment for George Bush. Mark Weinberger came to Treasury committed to stay in the job only a year—until the Bush tax plan passed Congress and was signed by the president.

A Texan by residence and at heart, George W. Bush began his presidency knowing well the ways of Washington from his father's time in the White House. In 2001 he not only assembled an impressive team to help him win congressional approval, but, unlike his father, he was willing to travel far and wide proselytizing his plan. To sell his tax proposals, Bush reprised his successful campaign strategy of repeating virtually identical speeches over and over throughout the country. His tax speeches followed a standard format. They always began with a thank you to the host of the event and a joke, maybe two. Next, Bush would talk briefly about the economic issues facing the country before launching into the details of the tax plan. The order in which he listed his proposals varied. Sometimes he would lead with the marginal income tax rate cuts, always mentioning the reduction in the bottom rate from 15 to 10 percent before the cut in the top rate from 40 to 33 percent. But often the proposed increase in the child credit from $500 to $1,000 headed the litany; in any event, it was always near the beginning of the speech. Bush would then mention marriage penalty relief and repeal of the death tax—if these items made the speech at all. He ended with an example of how his plan would help a particular middle-class working family. Frequently the family was present. Bush called his examples his "tax families." He invited a number of them to the White House when he announced his tax plan and again to the Rose Garden ceremony when he signed the 2001 bill into law. If none of his "tax families" were present, Bush usually invoked a hypothetical waitress supporting two children on $25,000 a year to illustrate how his plan would benefit the middle class. Bush's speechwriters tinkered a bit with the speeches to fit with the day's location and audience.

It took Bush only a few weeks to launch into his tax campaign. In his inaugural address on January 20, 2001, Bush made only a general reference to his goal of cutting taxes. After a week of heavy campaigning around the country for his tax plan, George Bush sent his detailed tax proposals to Congress on February 8 and gave his first Rose Garden speech urging their passage. He did not mention his proposal to repeal the estate tax in that speech. The same day the head of Bush's Office of Faith-Based Initiatives, John Dilulio, complained publicly that repeal of the estate tax would be devastating for private charities.

For the next three weeks, Bush gave no speeches on taxes, but on February 24 Bush advanced his plan in his weekly radio address. Three days later he detailed his tax proposals to a joint session of Congress. There the president offered his main refrain in favor of repeal. "It is not fair to tax the same earnings twice—once when you earn them and again when you die—so we must repeal the death tax." From that point on, the death tax became a staple in the president's speeches. Typically Bush would emphasize the tax's burdens on small businesses, farmers, and ranchers.

In the two days following his address to Congress, Bush made four speeches urging support of his tax cuts—in Omaha, Nebraska; Pittsburgh, Pennsylvania; Council Bluffs, Iowa; and Atlanta, Georgia. Over the next month he didn't let up. In March alone he gave Air Force One a workout, hawking the tax cut in Illinois, North and South Dakota, Louisiana, Florida, New Jersey, Maine, Montana, Missouri, and Michigan. He also gave speeches in Washington to the National Conference of State Legislators, the National Newspaper Association, the Hispanic Chamber of Commerce, groups of small business owners, and groups of women and African American business leaders. Bush picked his spots carefully, campaigning in states where Democratic senators were facing reelection in 2002. This tactic put pressure on senators such as Mary Landrieu of Louisiana, Max Cleland of Georgia, Tim Johnson of South Dakota, and Jean Carnahan of Missouri. He also picked states where he could shore up support from key players, especially Democratic Senators John Breaux of Louisiana and Max Baucus of Montana, and Republican Chuck Grassley of Iowa.

In sum, George W. Bush put an experienced, effective, and collegial legislative team together in the White House. He installed a persuasive lobbyist in the Treasury's key tax policy post. And he made extraordinary personal efforts to sell his tax plan to the country. The president's personal barnstorming, particularly in those states where key senators held office, emphasized how much was at stake for him and signaled his determination to get his tax plan through Congress.

Given all this work, what were the president's prospects? Bush enjoyed a Republican majority in the House, to which the Constitution awards primacy in initiating tax legislation, assuring him a good start. The House leadership stood firmly in his corner and speaker Denny Hastert had developed a strategy to maximize the likelihood of success. Even so, a favorable outcome in the House was not completely wired. More importantly, the 50-50 split in the Senate, along with the prospect that Senate rules might require 60 votes for passage, made success turn ultimately on securing some real help from Democrats. Another key piece of George Bush's campaign for enactment had to be put in place.

The Birth of a New Coalition

When President Bush hit the road in 2001 touting all the ways he believed his proposed tax cuts would help the American people, one element was conspicuously missing from his list: the plan contained no tax relief for corporations. The reason is simple enough. The administration's proposal came straight from the presidential campaign, and urging corporate tax cuts does not help anyone—particularly Republicans—garner votes in a national political election. Indeed, opposition to corporate tax breaks is the one place in American politics where the "class warfare" argument seems to work consistently. So the Bush plan contained no reduction in the corporate tax rate, nor did it propose more rapid write-offs of business plant and equipment purchases, the other item heading big business's wish list.

This politically necessary omission in 2000, however, became the greatest potential threat to the enactment of the Bush tax plan in 2001. Large corporations wield considerably more power on Capitol Hill than they do with the electorate. The White House was properly concerned that big companies and their representatives might attempt to influence Congress to reshape the legislation, diverting Bush's tax priorities to their own purposes. The faltering economy, which had become indisputable by February 2001, also added to the pressure, because many economists, including conservatives, believe corporate tax cuts are far more likely to stimulate a lagging economy than the ideas Bush was advancing.

In these circumstances, it was no doubt tempting to the White House to try somehow to sneak corporate tax breaks into the legislation, away from the glaring spotlight they would have received during the election. However, given the large revenue costs of the Bush proposal and widespread concern in Congress about its overall size—particularly among Democrats, but also some Republicans—expanding the tax cut to accommodate corporate relief was not a genuine option. If the corporate community were to throw its considerable political clout into seeking tax relief, the entire composition of the bill would be up for grabs. The prospect of a vigorous corporate campaign thus threatened to knock out key elements of the Bush plan—and, in turn, to deprive George W. Bush of the legislative victory he desperately needed to get his presidency off to a good start. The administration needed to get Corporate America on its side or, failing that, at least neutralize it.

This White House certainly didn't lack corporate contacts. Vice President Dick Cheney had headed Halliburton, Inc.; Andrew Card, the White House chief of staff had come from General Motors; Paul O'Neill, the former chairman of Alcoa, was Bush's treasury secretary; and Don Evans, the commerce secretary, who had chaired the Bush-Cheney campaign, had been CEO of the Texas Energy Company Tom Brown, Inc. These boardroom veterans, along with Karl Rove and Larry Lindsey, all made phone calls and met with business leaders. But the president himself needed personally to signal his firmness about the details of the package—and an unwillingness to budge. On Wednesday, February 7, the day before he sent his tax proposals to Congress, George Bush had lunch in the White House with 22 business leaders, including Jack Welch of General Electric, Enron's Kenneth Lay, General Mills's Stephen Sanger, Gap's Donald Fisher, and more than a dozen others. The guests also included a few key Washington players, such as Jerry Jasinowski, president of the National Association of Manufacturing, and Charls Walker, a longtime Washington advocate of more rapid write-offs of corporate purchases of equipment and capital gains rate cuts, neither of which George Bush was proposing.

Walker, a tall, down-home Texas Republican whom everyone calls Charlie, had first worked at the Treasury back in the Eisenhower administration. After a stint at the American Bankers Association, he had returned to be Richard Nixon's deputy treasury secretary. When he left government in 1973, he formed the first Washington lobbying firm headed by a non-lawyer, the enormously successful Charls Walker and Associates. A little over a year later he founded the American Council for Capital Formation, an organization funded by businesses and business groups with a mission to promote corporate and capital gains tax cuts. ACCF has long been one of Washington's most effective proponents of lower taxes on capital income. Walker's first big legislative achievement came in 1978, when Congress cut capital gains taxes. At that time, Walker says, "on a tax issue, if you had the agreement of the chairman of Ways and Means, you could go off and play golf." In the decades since, getting tax legislation through Congress has become a considerably more arduous endeavor. Now, according to Walker, "you can't rest easy unless you've worked all the members." Over the years, Walker has worked them often and worked them well, achieving important business and capital gains tax cuts in both the Reagan and Clinton presidencies.

Not surprisingly, given the corporate-friendly makeup of the Bush White House, Charlie Walker also had excellent connections to the new administration. Both Andrew Card and Paul O'Neill had served on the ACCF board, and Larry Lindsey had written economic papers financed by the organization. Walker was also a longtime friend of the Bush family. When George W. Bush had been governor of Texas, he had unsuccessfully attempted a major restructuring of that state's business taxes along lines that closely resembled a plan presented to him by Charlie Walker.

When George W. Bush moved into the White House, however, Charlie Walker was 77 years old and essentially retired. But with more than a trillion dollars of tax cuts in the offing, Walker decided to return to the fray in search of one final legislative victory. On February 6, the day before he attended the president's lunch, Walker announced that he had formed a new business coalition to seek specific tax changes favorable to multinational corporations. His ideas would have added more than $300 million to Bush's $1.6 trillion package through, among other things, expanded retirement savings incentives and either a reduction in the corporate tax rate from 35 to 25 percent or more rapid write-offs of business investments in new equipment. During the morning of February 7, Walker and members of his coalition met with Larry Lindsey and Don Evans to press their case.

Compounding the pressure from Walker, the Business Roundtable (BRT), an association of CEOs from about 150 of the nation's largest companies—some of whom would also partake of the president's lunch—tried to push the administration in a similar direction. The BRT announced that it would urge Congress to reduce the corporate income tax rate by $1 for every $5 of individual tax cuts. This idea would have added 20 percent, another $320 billion, to the president's plan.

Before the February 7 lunch with these corporate representatives, George Bush had already had a busy morning. He had spent some time trying to sell his ideas to 21 members of the House Ways and Means Committee. Jennifer Dunn reports that in the face of some skepticism, the president showed the legislators "the strength of his backbone." Switching gears entirely, Bush had also gathered at the White House that morning more than 20 of the "tax families" who had served his campaign by bringing to life his tax plan's claims about the benefits to working families. These were middle-class working people and their children, George Bush's very own rainbow coalition of waitresses, secretaries, auto repair technicians, and the like. The Republican National Committee had paid to fly them into Washington from around the country. Between the Ways and Means Committee and the hungry corporate executives, these tax families presumably provided a welcome respite for the president.

With Walker's group, the BRT, and sundry other powerful corporate interests holding their hands out, the lunch in the West Wing's Cabinet Room was not simply a social gathering. Bush brought these corporate scions together as part of his campaign to get them to keep their hands off his tax bill. And the president was not satisfied just to call the dogs off; he was determined to turn them into *his* dogs. To that end Bush may have hinted, but never promised, that if the economy continued to exhibit weakness he would advance a second tax cut proposal containing breaks for corporate investments. His luncheon guests were also reminded that their companies had important stakes in a wide variety of other policies that the White House either controlled or heavily influenced. Most immediately, it was essential to make clear that the corporate executives in the room had a real interest in securing an effective start for the Bush presidency. Those in attendance also had a lot to gain personally from the individual tax cuts that Bush was proposing, even if the companies they were representing had no horse in this particular race. These people were among the most highly paid executives in the land, and both the cuts in the top income tax rate and estate tax repeal would give the IRS a much smaller chunk of their wealth. In the parlance of the craps table, Bush was asking these corporate leaders to bet on the come, to support his tax plan now with the expectation that they might pick up a large batch of chips on subsequent rolls of the dice.

After lunch, during the first news conference of his fledgling presidency, George Bush indicated that he was sticking firm to his tax cut plan. "I have made it clear to the business interests that the best tax policy is one that reduces taxes on the people." The next morning the president would detail his tax plan in his first Rose Garden event and Paul O'Neill would hand-deliver the president's proposal to Congress. The battle for enactment had begun in earnest.

Behind the scenes, meanwhile, Bush's staff was working to muster business support for the president's tax plan. Karl Rove and his assistant Kirk Blalock had recruited a consummate Washington insider, Dirk Van Dongen, president of the National Association of Wholesale Distributors (NAW), to help in this task. They agreed that Van Dongen would create and head a new business coalition to help push the president's plan through Congress. Numerous conversations ensued among Van Dongen and Rove, Blalock, and Nick Calio. In mid-February, Dirk Van Dongen laid out his plans for a new business initiative at a White House lunch with Karl Rove, Kirk Blalock, and Bush's Director of Public Liaison, Lezlee Westine. They planned a kickoff event for the group for later in February.

The choice of Van Dongen to form and head the Tax Relief Coalition (TRC) marks a transformation of the repeal movement in 2001. Once a Republican president was in the White House, and repeal became part of a tax plan that he wanted to enact on his terms and schedule, the main force of the movement moved inside the beltway. Van Dongen, for instance, is hardly known outside of Washington. Although NAW represents more than 40,000 U.S. companies in Washington, it is a dwarf compared to the major Washington trade associations. The U.S. Chamber of Commerce, for example, claims three million members; NFIB has 600,000. But NAW is not a nobody. It brings together small businesses worth an annual $3 trillion. Nearly 80 percent of its members are Republicans.

Dirk Van Dongen came to NAW in 1968 from a position in AT&T's marketing department. His principal job then was to boost the organization's membership. He succeeded and has been there ever since. He is a prolific fundraiser for Republicans, reportedly responsible for having raised more than $10 million for GOP candidates over the years. Van Dongen and NAW were early supporters of George Bush's presidential candidacy, and Van Dongen qualified as a George Bush "Pioneer," the title reserved for those who raised $100,000 or more for the campaign.

Dirk Van Dongen and George Bush form a mutual admiration society: Bush calls Van Dongen "my good buddy" and has bestowed upon him one of his trademark nicknames, "Dirkus"; in turn, Dirkus tells people that George Bush "is a great president for the business community." Van Dongen is also close to Karl Rove, and he taught Nick Calio the art of effective lobbying when Calio became NAW's lobbyist in the 1980s, long before Calio became chief lobbyist for both presidents Bush. Calio and Van Dongen remain close friends.

Jeffrey Birnbaum of *Fortune Magazine* does not exaggerate when he reports that Van Dongen has a "place on the White House's speed dial" and has used his "golden Rolodex of insiders to score legislative victories on everything from tort reform to OSHA deregulation." Van Dongen is legendary in Washington for both his personal and political skills, and with his close White House ties backing him up, he is a formidable force. To White House insiders, Van Dongen was a natural choice to head the new Tax Relief Coaliton. As Grover Norquist puts it, "Dirk fights outside his weight."

This was not the first time Van Dongen had been enlisted to help a Republican president win tax cuts. In the battle between large and small businesses over Ronald Reagan's 1986 tax reform legislation, Van Dongen led a coalition of small business owners to victory in achieving major reductions in the top individual income tax rates (a benefit to small businesses, which often operate as proprietorships, partnerships, or "S" corporations, all of which have their income taxed at the rates applicable to individuals). In 2001, a cut in the top income tax rate was again a centerpiece of the president's plan. And once again, Van Dongen would put together a coalition to help sell the rate cut as small business relief. President Bush's proposal also contained another boon for Van Dongen's small business coalition: estate tax repeal. Van Dongen himself is a firm advocate for eliminating the estate tax and, as we have seen, repeal headed the tax agenda for many small business owners.

The kickoff of the TRC came on February 23, 2001. The president had formally announced the details of his tax proposals just over two weeks before, and four days later he would deliver his tax speech to a joint session of Congress. George Bush, Treasury Secretary Paul O'Neill, Larry Lindsey, Karl Rove, Lezlee Westine, and Kirk Blalock were all there. Their invitees included nearly 50 business representatives and lobbyists, all of them advocates for the Bush tax cuts. The meeting took place in the Indian Treaty Room, the most ornate room in the Executive Office Building next to the White House. This large space had originally served as the Navy Department's library and reception room, and a few important treaties (though, as far as anyone knows, none with Indians) have been signed here. The Ital-

ian and French marble walls are adorned with shells, seahorses, and dol-
phins, surrounding a compass at the center of the nineteenth-century tile
floor and navigation stars in the ceiling—a motif suggesting that one
should endeavor not to go astray here. But the Indian Treaty Room con-
veys a sense of warmth and friendliness along with its signals of importance.

During the gathering, the president, Larry Lindsey, and Paul O'Neill sat
at one end of the room. The businesspeople and K-Street heavyweights sat
in two rows of semicircles around the other walls. The inner circle was made
up mostly of people who ran small- to medium-sized businesses and were
there as the elected heads of their respective trade associations. Their Washington lobbyists sat directly behind them. Dirk Van Dongen sat at the far
end of the room opposite the president.

The meeting had been well scripted in advance. As agreed with Van
Dongen over the previous weeks, its purpose was to establish a new business coalition to support fully and enthusiastically the administration's tax
plan. The agenda began with Paul O'Neill and Larry Lindsey briefly explaining the president's plan and why it would be good for America. The
president arrived a bit later, welcomed everyone, and emphasized the importance of his plan. Over to his left sat Denise Marie Fugo, of the National Restaurant Association and the owner of Sammy's Catering in Cleveland, Ohio. She had on her lap a pile of letters endorsing the president's
plan from the more than 20 trade associations represented in the room. She
presented them personally to the president.

Denise Marie Fugo is exactly the sort of person George Bush wanted
pushing his plan. She has a business degree from the University of Chicago
and is a civic leader in Cleveland. She was the first woman to intern at Goldman Sachs and the first woman elected to head the Restaurant Association
in more than 40 years. She is also the mother of three daughters. She and
her husband founded Sammy's together, using $40,000 they had gained
from a real estate investment. Sammy's is widely credited with introducing
fine dining to Cleveland, with specialties including veal with a porcini and
basil sauce and roasted rack of lamb with a pistachio nut coating. The
Cleveland Plain Dealer reports that when Sammy's first opened in 1980 in
one of the city's "less-than desirable" areas, "the words 'fine dining' and
Cleveland fit together about as well as lobster and peanut butter."

Denise strongly favors repeal of the estate tax, which she claims "creates
a climate of fear that taxes will be too great when the time comes to pass

on the business." She regards the tax as the "main reason many businesses don't make it to the next generation." In mid-March, when George Bush held another White House event to push his tax plan, she stood on the speaker's platform right behind him.

Shortly after Denise Fugo presented her pile of letters to George Bush, the meeting broke up. Everyone left feeling exactly the way a hypnotist likes people to wake up: feeling good, happy, energized. The Tax Relief Coalition had been launched. Notably, Pat Soldano, Harold Apolinsky, Frank Blethen—the pioneers of the movement for estate tax repeal—had not been in the room. The action had shifted to Washington powerhouses.

Dirk Van Dongen was named "executive secretary" or, to some, "president" of the TRC. But he was not alone at the head of the table. Along with NAW, three other groups stepped forward to lead the coalition: NFIB, the U.S. Chamber of Commerce, and, surprisingly, the National Association of Manufacturers (NAM). NFIB was a natural. It had already made clear its strong support for the president's plan, and it had major clout both on Capitol Hill and in the White House. Its tight link to the Family Business Estate Tax Coalition was also a valuable asset.

The U.S. Chamber of Commerce was also a natural member of the leadership group. The Chamber was founded in 1912, after President Taft told Congress that the nation needed a "central organization in touch with associations and chambers of commerce throughout the country" to advance "purely American interests." Today it is America's most venerable and largest business organization. Although large Fortune 500 companies are members and are often quite influential in the group's policy positions, 96 percent of the members are businesses with fewer than 100 employees. The Chamber of Commerce thus had no difficulty rounding up small- and medium-sized businesses hungry for cuts in income tax rates and for estate tax repeal. The chamber also represents more than 3,000 state and local chambers of commerce and more than 800 business associations. It can generate a massive outpouring of grassroots support or opposition in Congress at the click of a mouse. And, like the NFIB, the Chamber of Commerce has members in every state and congressional district who have close personal ties to their representatives and senators.

NAM's place at the head of the TRC was a bit surprising. Like the Chamber of Commerce, NAM represents both large and small businesses. But although NAM describes 10,000 of its 14,000 members as small or mid-sized companies, its policy positions are typically dominated by its Fortune 500 members. Its tax policy agenda, for example, has long emphasized a big businesses' tax cut menu: incentives for business investment, such as more rapid writeoffs of business equipment purchases; additional tax breaks for business research and development expenses; and an international tax and trade system more favorable to American manufacturing. President Bush's 2001 tax plan contained nothing on this list. But Jerry Jasinowski, NAM's head at the time, cannot stand to be left out of the action, and he could not resist Dirk Van Dongen's invitation to help lead the TRC.

By including NAM at the top of the TRC letterhead, George Bush sent two important signals to members of Congress and to other business lobbyists. First, and most importantly, the business community—large and small—had united behind the president's plan. There would be no point in attempting to muster support for alternative ideas by substituting corporate tax goodies for Bush's proposals. This message would greatly help the president's case in Congress, which was still seen as potentially vulnerable to corporate lobbying. It was especially helpful in alerting Bill Thomas, the new head of the Ways and Means Committee, that this was not the moment to exhibit his intellectual prowess or creativity. Secondly, NAM's position at the head of the TRC signaled to large businesses that this was no time to freelance. It counseled patience and made a statement that it was better to be on the president's bus than on the sidewalk. Many Washington insiders said that NAM's leadership role also offered a strong hint that the Bush administration would likely include corporate tax breaks in any subsequent tax proposals.

Charlie Walker got the message. He abandoned his effort to add corporate tax breaks to this tax bill.

On February 28, only five days after the Indian Treaty Room meeting, the Business Roundtable (BRT) joined the TRC. What was curious about this move was that the BRT had been founded in 1972 largely due to concerns of big business executives that their companies' interests were inadequately represented by the U.S. Chamber of Commerce or even by NAM. The addition of this corporate heavyweight to the TRC left little doubt that businesses large and small had rallied behind the president's tax reduction proposals. (Ultimately, the large corporations' patience would pay off, and they would obtain tax cuts from George Bush. The events of September 11, 2001, delayed a second Bush tax bill until 2002, but the hopes and expectations of large businesses were fulfilled in that bill, again in Bush tax cuts of 2003, and tax legislation in 2004.)

Representatives of business organizations had dominated the gathering in the Indian Treaty Room, but they were not the only people invited to join the TRC. Grover Norquist was there, representing Americans for Tax Reform and the tax-cutting zealots of the Republican Party. Likewise, Citizens for a Sound Economy (CSE), another well-connected Republican organization of passionate tax-cutters, was there. After he left Congress in 2002, Dick Armey, the House Majority Leader during the 2001 tax battle, became the head of CSE.

A couple of weeks after the meeting in the Indian Treaty Room, on March 7, 2001, the Tax Relief Coalition sent an open letter to all members of Congress urging "enactment of the President's proposal to provide $1.6 trillion of tax relief, beginning with HR 3." HR 3 was the bill containing income tax rate cuts, the part of the Bush plan that Denny Hastert had agreed to bring to the House floor first. After the rate cut, Hastert would secure votes on Bush's proposals for marriage penalty relief and expanded tax credits for children, saving estate tax repeal for last. TRC's letter was signed by 175 organizations, including many state and national trade associations and several other well-known advocates of the president's plan. The list provides impressive evidence of how Dirk Van Dongen and his allies had rapidly succeeded in expanding the size and scope of the coalition.

While full of the usual suspects, the TRC alliance now also included many lower profile groups as well, such as the Republican Jewish Coalition. Although it is not as well known as organizations such as the U.S. Chamber of Commerce, this group has close ties to the White House and many important contributors to Republican candidates. RJC members have received plum ambassadorships, such as Nancy Brinker in Hungary, Mel Sembler in Italy, and Stuart Bernstein in Denmark. The organization is headed by billionaire Sam Fox of St. Louis, Missouri, a major Republican contributor and, unsurprisingly, a passionate advocate for estate tax repeal. In 2000, Fox hosted a record-setting GOP gala that raised over $21 million in one night. The TRC was bringing together the president's strongest supporters and giving them a unified purpose and a vehicle to advance the president's plan.

The TRC's March 7 letter to Congress was just the beginning—and the most public element—of the new coalition's efforts in support of George Bush's tax plan. Over the following weeks and months, the TRC would prove enormously effective in rallying grassroots—or, more accurately, grasstops—support for the president's tax proposals. And it would not stop with the 2001 victory. During George W. Bush's first term in office, TRC members generated thousands of phone calls, e-mails, and letters from constituents asking members of Congress to enact the president's tax proposals. They produced "grassroots action kits" containing "target lists" of key legislators, talking points in support of the proposals, sample letters to Congress, and letters to newspaper editors. They placed supporting editorials in many newspapers and magazines, issued countless press releases, and arranged numerous radio talk show appearances and some television spots by advocates of the president's tax proposals. TRC also harnessed the Internet to its cause. The Chamber of Commerce, for example, developed pop-up ads for Yahoo, MSN, AOL, and a variety of financial websites aimed at small businesses; the ads allowed the user to click to a website called "economicgrowthnow.com," which urged and facilitated contact with members of Congress. State-based organizations, which are also members of the TRC, trained their sights on their state's representatives and senators, organizing contacts and personal meetings—principally between small business owners and key members of Congress.

The TRC's efforts were closely coordinated with the White House. The key White House contact was Karl Rove's youthful but skilled assistant Kirk Blalock. Blalock, who looks fit enough to play football but would be undersized anywhere except in the Ivy League, was enthusiastic, energetic, and focused on rallying the TRC whenever he thought it helpful. His relationship with the leaders of the coalition became so close that when he left the White House staff in 2003 to join the Washington lobbying shop Fierce and Isakowitz, the TRC became one of his first clients. Dirk Van Dongen and Nick Calio also regularly compared notes, especially about wavering representatives and senators, and they coordinated the pressure on Congress from the White House and important constituents back home. The TRC and the White House were in constant communication as the 2001 act made its way through Congress.

While business coalitions for favorable legislative or regulatory actions crop up routinely in Washington, the TRC is unique, and not just because of its size or its relatively rare confluence of large and small business interests. What made TRC unusual is that it was unambiguously the Bush White House's coalition. As Dirk Van Dongen puts it, "The Tax Relief Coalition is an administration coalition. It was brought into existence for the express purpose of supporting the president's package." He insists that members must pass a "litmus test" in being "willing to work on behalf of the president's proposals." So that you not miss the point, he adds, "There is an umbilical cord to the White House." "TRC is not a debating society," he says. "You either support the administration's proposals and only those changes the administration agrees to, or you leave the team." Then, as if to disabuse us of the notion that he is leading a group of sheep, Van Dongen adds, "One of the attributes of this president is that he does listen to what real people say to him, and he takes it into account." The parentage and the patronage of the TRC is crystal clear.

Van Dongen and his allies in the TRC view getting legislation through Congress as a team sport. He is completely unfazed by the number of people who want to claim credit for the enactment of the president's tax proposals—he has seen it all before. And he appropriately attributes the 2001 victory to "a huge team effort." He regards the NFIB as his closest ally and agrees with the general consensus that it is the foremost Washington lobbyist for small business issues. The TRC also "worked closely with the Family Business Estate Tax Coalition (FBETC)," according to Dirk. "We didn't supplant them," he says. "They laid much of the groundwork for death tax repeal." Moreover, there was much overlap between the membership of TRC and the FBETC. Most importantly, the FBETC's convener, NFIB's Dan Blankenburg, became the legislative director of the TRC. This linkage made it easy for the two groups to coordinate their efforts to convert legislative targets. Picking the right people to call on members of Congress and getting them to meetings either in Washington or back home was not difficult. It is clear, however, that during the debate over the 2001 act, the most important private sector player was the Tax Relief Coalition. And the TRC headed off a potentially destructive dogfight between large and small businesses.

The TRC has been an energetic and effective ally for George Bush. It stayed in existence after 2001, according to Dirk Van Dongen, to make all of President Bush's 2001 tax cuts permanent. It has also grown dramatically. By the time the debate over the 2001 legislation really heated up in Congress, TRC claimed about 500 members. Two years later, in May 2003,

TRC sent a letter to selected "target" senators on behalf of George Bush's 2003 tax cut proposals in which it claimed over 1,000 members, representing 1.8 million businesses. Listing all these members would now fill 21 pages, so, unlike TRC's first epistle in March 2001, the letter was signed by a somewhat enlarged "TRC Management Committee." The signatories were familiar, although the management group had now expanded to 11. From the original cast, there were Dirk Van Dongen and Grover Norquist, Dan Danner on behalf of NFIB, Bruce Josten for the U.S. Chamber of Commerce, Mike Baroody for NAM, John Castellani, president of the BRT, and Paul Beckner, then president of Citizens for a Sound Economy. The list was filled out by organizations representing mostly small businesses: the Food Marketing Institute, Associated General Contractors, the International Foodservice Distributors Association, and Denise Marie Fugo's National Restaurant Association.

Given this expansion, have the TRC's tax priorities changed over time? Dirk Van Dongen insists that permanent repeal of the estate tax remains the coalition's first priority. And despite the influx of big business allies, TRC remains "overwhelmingly a small business coalition," Van Dongen says.

But for Van Dongen, the estate tax issue involves far greater stakes. This elegant, soft-spoken Washington insider sounds exactly like the peripatetic crusader Grover Norquist when he insists that the fight over the Bush tax cuts of 2001, 2002, and 2003, and the subsequent battle to make them a permanent fixture of the tax landscape, is about the size of the American government and how it is funded. For Van Dongen, this contest harks back to the heady tax cut fights at the beginning of the Reagan administration— a struggle that he recalls as marked by "tremendous passion, tremendous human energy, on both sides." In his words, "That was a battle over the size of government, a time when people were mad at Washington and wanted to cut taxes to cut government—to cut nasty unpleasant things—down." The Bush administration is so exciting for Van Dongen because he views this passion as having dissipated by the late Reagan years, but he believes it has just begun to reappear. The small burst of enthusiasm, which he saw reemerge when Newt Gingrich took over the House, wasn't sustained, Dirk says. But today, we are engaged in "a quasi-national referendum over the size and method of funding of the government." Nevertheless, Van Dongen has not yet felt quite the Reagan-era level of passion on either side. "It is a just fraction of what we saw before," he says. However, he excludes the committed advocates for estate tax repeal from this assessment; they are genuinely zealous.

Every one of the Bush tax cuts of 2001, 2002, and 2003 is scheduled to expire between 2003 and 2013. If as time passes it becomes clear that not all of these cuts will be extended permanently, how will Congress choose which of the sunsets enacted in the first three years of the Bush administration should take effect? As lawmakers come to weigh the various options, the extraordinary lobbying coalition that the Bush administration created in 2001 may not hold together. If the debate over making individual measures permanent dissolves into a more typical competition over who gets tax relief and who doesn't, the business community, large and small, will find it difficult to maintain a united front. Even Dirk Van Dongen may not be able to fight the centrifuge of tax politics as usual.

No matter what happens down the road, however, George W. Bush hit a home run in 2001, and a couple of triples in 2002 and 2003, in getting his tax proposals through Congress. These achievements were due in no small part to the contacts, energy, and political skill of the Tax Relief Coalition. The Bush administration showed great foresight and ability in pulling the group together and in using it effectively. In our nation's capital, coalitions crop up all the time advocating one set of positions or another. What made the TRC different was its unswerving devotion to the White House's tax policy, no matter how that policy evolved. This commitment was truly unusual, and it demonstrated the business community's overall faith in the president's tax-cutting agenda. The TRC proved an invaluable ally to George Bush. It married the authority of the presidency to the legislative expertise and political pull of American businesses and their very effective Washington representatives.

Before this powerful combination could achieve its goal, however, a group of some of America's richest men would try to halt the forward momentum of repeal.

Billionaires Battle

By the time George Bush became president in January 2001, Democrats in Congress were not doing well in opposing estate tax repeal. Due to the inattention and ineptitude of the opposition forces, they were not getting much help either. Organized labor took a pass. Charities were silent. The life insurance industry's efforts were half-hearted and ineffective. Liberal Washington think tanks were outmanned. On Capitol Hill you cannot beat people with shadows.

And repeal proponents had plenty of people working to kill the death tax—wealthy, powerful, successful, well-organized people invoking the "American Dream." The Tax Relief Coalition and the Family Business Estate Tax Coalition had produced a phalanx for repeal, pulling together Washington powerhouses and mobilizing constituents from outside the beltway. The coalitions had key allies in the conservative think tanks, including the Heritage Foundation and the CATO Institute. Republican policy operatives such as Grover Norquist were the torch bearers. And they had connected real people to their representatives in Congress, people like Nebraska's David Pankonin, who was struggling to figure out how to pass his farm supply business on to his son Paul. Inside the government, repeal's allies were well positioned, powerful, and determined. And after January 2001, both the Republican majorities in Congress and the White House were on board. Finally, repeal advocates had rallied public opinion to their side. Could the opposition find any immovable object to halt this irresistible force? Who could save this tax from extinction?

Just after George Bush took over the White House and the pallbearers began preparing to take the death tax to its grave, a cavalry of would-be saviors appeared. At the head of the opposition coalition—and they insisted it was a coalition—stood an unlikely warrior: William Gates, Sr. (He was born William Gates, Jr., but he changed his name in order not to be confused with his son Bill—William Gates III—the world's richest man.) A retired lawyer who towers at six feet six inches, the elder William Gates co-chairs the Bill and Melinda Gates Foundation. With the foundation's endowment of $24 billion, Gates spends his days deploying billions of dollars of his son's wealth to good causes. Nothing could be further from the mind of this father than how to pass assets on to his son Bill. Free from any personal interest, William Gates became the spokesman for a group of America's best-known wealthy, leading the charge, such as it was, against repeal.

William Gates knows first-hand about the American Dream. His grandfather was a delivery man who moved his family to Alaska during the gold rush of the late nineteenth century. He failed to strike it rich, so the former delivery man returned to Bremerton, Washington, to run a hotel and then a furniture store, which was eventually taken over by Gates's father, who himself had only an eighth-grade education. William Gates was born on November 30, 1925. An Eagle Scout as a teenager, he enlisted in the army during World War II, serving in the Philippines and Japan. He returned to Washington to attend college and law school and, after practicing law in Seattle for more than a decade, founded his own successful and ultimately prestigious law firm. Now, he is giving back. Even the *Seattle Times* owner Frank Blethen, an arch-enemy of Gates on the estate tax, acknowledges Gates's charitable works. "Basically, instead of doing whatever it is retired attorneys usually do, he's doing an awful lot of good. It's tough to fault a guy who's passionate about families, higher education, K–12 education, and social services."

In his battle to halt estate tax repeal, William Gates's chief strategist was Chuck Collins of Responsible Wealth, a project of Collins's Boston-based United for a Fair Economy. Collins knew that he lacked the name recognition to grab the media's attention, and so he recruited Gates to take the lead.

A month after Bush's inauguration, as the president was launching the fight for his tax bill, Chuck Collins and William Gates made national headlines by announcing that they had accumulated the signatures of 120 of America's richest individuals on a petition favoring retention of the estate tax. The list included the billionaire financier George Soros; media mogul Ted Turner; Ben Cohen, the owner of Ben and Jerry's Ice Cream; the actor Paul Newman; and a handful of Roosevelts and Rockefellers. Warren Buffett supported the group but never lent it his signature—not because he had any doubts about preserving the estate tax, but because he felt the petition didn't go far enough for him to support it. Buffett explained to the *New York Times* that the petition needed to do more to describe "the critical role" played by the estate tax in promoting economic growth and "a society based on merit, not inheritance."

An advertisement containing this petition first appeared on the op-ed page of the *New York Times* on February 21, 2001, and it subsequently ran in major newspapers throughout the nation. The group concentrated its ads in nine states where Chuck Collins had identified "target" senators who were still on the fence. On February 27, Responsible Wealth announced that it had amassed more than 400 signatures for its petition. But most of the people who signed remained very far in the background. William Gates was the principal advocate and the public face for the group. He wrote newspaper columns, held an on-line argument with Pete DuPont on Slate.com, debated the issue with Arizona Republican Senator Jon Kyl on CNN's *Crossfire,* appeared at the Capitol more than once for photo-ops, and testified against repeal before the Senate Finance Committee. But even Gates acknowledged that the tax needed mending: he urged an increase in the exemption to $3.5 million for individuals, $7 million for couples. And he suggested that adjustments in the rules might be necessary to help families who wanted to leave small businesses or farms to their children.

In his defense of the estate tax, Gates emphasized the risks that repeal posed for the nation's charities. When facing an estate tax, people often choose between leaving money to the federal government or to the charity of their choice. Gates and his group worried that charities would not do nearly so well if it cost nothing to leave the money to a family member instead. "The estate tax," the February newspaper ad said, "exerts a powerful and positive effect on charitable giving. Repeal would have a devastating impact on public charities."

Gates also tried to present the philosophical case in favor of the estate tax. Repeal, he claimed, was an attack on the American Dream. He invoked Theodore Roosevelt's idea that a levy on inheritances was needed to inhibit "large fortunes passed from generation to generation forming ever larger pools of money and accretions of power." The estate tax, he said, keeps us "closer" to the "ideal" of a nation which ensures "that all children start their lives on a level playing field." He also invoked the richest citizens' duty to repay the benefits provided by government: calling the tax an appropriate levy "on those who have so very fully enjoyed the benefit of the things this country provides," Gates emphasized that the ability to amass a great fortune turned on the good fortune of being born in the United States "rather than Ethiopia." To cap his arguments, he also insisted that accumulating wealth depends on having a bit of luck.

Ultimately, Gates and his allies had little impact on the 2001 congressional debate over whether to repeal the estate tax. They entered the fray late, with enormous fanfare and a great deal of publicity from the nation's major newspapers, but they were not a factor in the political arena. The NFIB labeled Gates's group Billionaires Against Real Families, or BARF. It also challenged those who signed Gates's ad to sign a contract pledging to bequeath their entire estates to the U.S. Treasury. No one signed.

When the president signed the tax bill on June 5, 2001, Responsible Wealth issued a press release vowing "The Battle Isn't Over Yet." Collins and Gates called the 2001 bill "primarily symbolic," and Gates emphasized the limits of the legislation, saying "we feel we won a partial victory in delaying full repeal." Certainly, the bill included prolonged phase-ins and repeal still needed to be made permanent. But calling it a "victory" for the opposition to repeal was a real stretch, since even during his campaign, Bush had proposed delaying repeal for eight years. Still, Gates and Collins did not give up. In 2003, they published a book defending the estate tax called *Wealth and Our Commonwealth: Why America Should Tax Accumulated Fortunes.* Their limited campaign goes on. William Gates plays bridge seriously, but apparently not congressional politics.

Gates and his colleagues accomplished one thing for sure by their 2001 ad campaign. They made one of America's few African American billionaires angry. Bob Johnson holds degrees from both the University of Illinois and Princeton. He works on the top floor of the headquarters of BET Holdings, Inc., the company that he founded and now runs as CEO. BET occupies a gated complex adjacent to the DC rail yards, about a 15-minute cab ride from Capitol Hill. To get there, you must head in the opposite direction from the granite office towers of K Street's lobbyists and the trade association headquarters scattered along Pennsylvania Avenue. Once you are buzzed through BET's electronic metal gates, you find yourself between a large television studio on the far side of the complex and the round glass eight-story tower that houses the main corporate offices. The tower looks completely out of place in its surroundings, a slightly run-down, African

American, working-class neighborhood. The lobby is glass-fronted with walls padded by a silver and gold material that looks like silk. Two televisions, with their sound off, play constantly. When we walk in they are showing a black minister dressed to the nines with a call-in number crawling across the bottom of the screen. He appears on just one of the many stations that Bob Johnson has developed over the years. You are still inside the beltway, but it sure doesn't feel that way.

Bob Johnson has also lived the American Dream. In 1979, when he was a 34-year-old lobbyist for the cable television industry, he invested $15,000 of his own money, along with $500,000 contributed by Telecommunications, Inc., to create Black Entertainment Television, the nation's first channel with programming targeted to African Americans. In 1991 he took BET Holdings public, making it the first company traded on the New York Stock Exchange to be controlled by an African American, and making Bob Johnson rich. He was then worth about $130 million. In November 2000, Viacom acquired BET for about $2.5 billion in stock, in the process transferring a reported $1.6 billion to Johnson. He became America's first African American billionaire. (Oprah Winfrey soon became the second.) Johnson insisted that BET remain headquartered in Washington, and he stayed on as BET chairman and CEO, reporting to the leaders of Viacom.

BET's executive suite is loaded with fine art thanks to Johnson, who is a renowned collector of African American art. Paintings and prints cover the walls, and the waiting room outside Johnson's office is loaded with statuary. Johnson himself is a winning character. His dress is casual: black pants, a black polo sweater buttoned to the top, and a grey blazer. He is relaxed and charming, with an easy-going grace that puts his guests immediately at ease. You feel as if you are sitting with the salesman he once was rather than the magnate he has become.

Discussion of the estate tax animates Johnson. Sitting at the head of his conference table overlooking the railroad tracks, Johnson is as firm in his opposition to the tax as anyone we have seen. His arguments could not be more different from those of Pat Soldano or Harold Apolinsky, but his passion is the same. Johnson attributes his opposition to the death tax's impact on African American wealth and black-owned businesses. "If you think about it," he says, "black people only started accumulating wealth in this country sometime after the 1960s, after the civil rights era. It began with home-ownership, which is a huge factor, and then eventually businesses started to grow up."

Johnson then turns philosophical, mixing his history of African Americans' difficulties building up wealth with his own experiences and attitude. "Once I'd found the way to accumulate the wealth, I started thinking about how I could retain it," he says. "The double taxation seemed inherently unfair" in light of blacks' troubled history in the United States. "African Americans, having faced state-sponsored—or if not state-sponsored then state-endorsed—discrimination have the toughest odds in getting capital, the toughest odds in getting access to more capital, the toughest odds for growing that capital. And then, when it comes to the estate tax, they're on the same level playing field with the people who faced none of those obstacles. That just seemed to me unfair." Johnson views a tax holiday for African Americans as an appropriate form of black reparations. "Now, I know it's difficult to come out and say as a matter of policy that African Americans ought to be treated differently by the tax law, but that's my personal feeling on it. I wouldn't have a problem if the law said the estate tax doesn't kick in for African Americans until 2050."

This businessman is particularly concerned about the potential effects of the estate tax on African American opportunities in the years ahead. "Nearly all black businesses came from black seed capital," he says. "If more blacks retain their wealth, the second generation will use that wealth to expand those businesses. If black businesses are sold to pay estate taxes, they will not be bought by blacks; they will be bought by whites." Johnson makes this last statement without even a hint of irony, apparently forgetting for the moment, or simply ignoring, the criticism he took from black commentators for selling BET to the white-owned Viacom.

Though previously aware of the repeal debate, and having begun to plan for passing his own wealth on to his two teenaged children, Bob Johnson says he did not actively engage in the death tax contest until he saw "the newspaper ad signed by Bill Gates, Sr., George Soros and the other wealthy Americans who called themselves Americans for Responsible Wealth." Their initiative made him mad. "No one called me up, and said, 'Hey, Bob, do you want to sign this letter?' There wasn't a single black person on the list. My feeling was you rich white people may want to pay this tax, but I don't want to, and I don't think it's fair."

Incensed, Johnson sent a letter to 60 or so African American friends and business associates. He informed them that he planned to use their names in a newspaper ad opposing the estate tax, and any person who didn't want to appear in the ad should contact him. He treated silence as consent. He told everyone he would pay, so they needn't send any money to participate. He got 49 signatures, and on April 4, 2001, he ran ads in the *New York Times, Washington Post,* and *USA Today.* When asked what this exercise cost him, he replies, "Let's say $200,000." Johnson was easily the wealthiest person on the list. He estimates the combined net worth of all the others who signed at somewhere between $150 and $300 million.

The ad eloquently stated Johnson's case against the estate tax. It began with the standard claim that the "Estate Tax is unfair double taxation since taxpayers are taxed twice—once when the money is earned and again when you die. The income taxes you pay, in some cases up to 40 percent, already redistribute wealth and provide for government services." It then made its particular pitch for African American interests, asserting that the "Estate Tax will cause many of the more than 1 million Black-owned family businesses to fail or be sold," leading "the entire Black community" to suffer. The ad continued:

> Unlike most White Americans, many African Americans who accumulated wealth did so facing race discrimination in education, employment, access to capital, and equal access to government resources. In many cases, race discrimination was supported by governmental policies and failure to enforce equal rights laws. It is unfair and unjust for the government through the Estate Tax to seize a portion of the estate of the individuals it failed to provide equal opportunity.
>
> The Estate Tax is particularly unfair to the first generation of the high net worth African Americans who have accumulated wealth only recently. These individuals may have family members and relatives who have not been as fortunate in accumulating assets who could directly benefit from their share of an estate as heir. Elimination of the Estate Tax would allow African Americans to pass the full fruits of their labor to the next generation and beyond. Elimination of the Estate Tax will help close the gap in this nation between African American families and White families. The net worth of an average African American family is $20,000 or 10 percent of the $200,000 net worth of the average White

family. Repealing the Estate Tax will permit wealth to grow in the Black community through investment in minority businesses that will stimulate the economic well-being of the Black community and allow African families to participate fully in the American Dream.

Finally, Johnson concluded with the standard argument that the complexities of the estate tax impede economic growth and waste resources.

Johnson's ad attracted immediate responses. The day after it appeared, former Representative and Republican Vice Presidential candidate Jack Kemp sent a memo to the entire Senate, enclosing the ad and describing it as "the single best and most succinct statement I have seen of why we all believe Congress should repeal this economically destructive tax, which is so harmful to the first generation of black entrepreneurs." That afternoon, in a Rose Garden speech to the U.S. Conference of Mayors, President Bush also invoked Robert Johnson and his claims about the estate tax's impact on African Americans. Bush said, "As Robert Johnson of Black Entertainment Television argues, the death tax and double taxation weighs [sic] heavily on minorities who are only beginning to accumulate wealth. The Senate needs to hear that message." Looking out for his entire tax package, the president went on, the "Senate needs to leave enough money in the proposed budget to not only reduce all marginal rates, but to eliminate the death tax, so that people who build up assets are able to transfer them from one generation to the next, regardless of a person's race."

Not everyone applauded Johnson's efforts, however. One African American commentator described Johnson's ad as "an outrageous insult to the common sense and sensibilities of the people whose interests are invoked: The 99.5% of the Black public that is not rich. Robert Johnson's gamesmanship is both shameless and breath-taking." He added, "Johnson's formula is the same-old trickle down Reagan dogma, with a cruel and ridiculous Reparations-scented twist."

Bob Johnson himself is uncertain whether his ad made any impact in Congress. He recalls reading an article "in one of those very liberal magazines, the *New Republic*, some place like that, where they said my ad had made a difference." He also remembers being told that President Bush mentioned him and the ad in the Rose Garden at some point, although Johnson says he didn't see or hear the president's speech. He mentions these tidbits almost as asides. If this is self-promotion, it is a very sophisticated form of the art.

Johnson believes that he had no particular impact on converting African Americans legislators to favor repeal—although as we've seen, some members of the Congressional Black Caucus did vote for repeal. As he says, "Whenever I talk to black politicians about this, they listen, and then they say, 'Sure Bob, we should do something, but you don't need to worry about it, you've got enough money. We're proud of you, but don't bother us on this.'"

Outside of Congress, Johnson does say he was approached by many groups seeking to enlist his support. "They wanted me to come to their meetings, join these coalitions," he says. "I didn't want to do all that. I think I did a few television interviews, maybe some newspaper stuff, not much." He was never asked to testify before Congress.

While he regards the death tax as "confiscatory" and supports privatizing Social Security in some way (George Bush in May 2001 named him to his Commission to Strengthen Social Security), Bob Johnson still considers himself a Democrat and is surprised that many others apparently do not. He was struck after running his pro-repeal ad that soon friends were coming up to him and saying, "Bob, I didn't know you were a Republican." One black commentator even called him "a Trojan Horse, an aggressive political operative of the Bush White House posing as a Democrat." Johnson, who raised more than half a million dollars for Bill Clinton's presidential campaigns, rolls his eyes at such claims and sits back in his chair, an easy smile playing across his lined face, his gesture suggesting how ridiculous an idea this is.

Other critics do not detect just a Republican streak in Bob Johnson's opposition to the estate tax—they see self-interest as well. David Plotz, writing for *Slate,* says that Bob Johnson "proves everyday that a black businessman can be—and should be—as ruthless, opportunistic and greedy as any white one." Despite the undeniable truth of Johnson's claims about the difficulties that African Americans face in accumulating wealth, it is impossible to know how much of this charming and charismatic man's antipathy to the estate tax is political and altruistic, and how much is concern for keeping his personal fortune intact. Whatever his motivation, Bob Johnson's ad did undermine the efforts of Bill Gates and his allies. By giving the battle of billionaires a racial twist, Johnson seemed to have neutralized Gates's and Collins's campaign to preserve the tax.

While notable for its ability to attract public attention, the billionaires' battle that unfolded in the months leading up to the passage of the 2001 bill was in many ways simply a microcosm of the broader, often one-sided debate that repeal forces had been winning slowly but surely for years. As Grover Norquist put it, a great deal of one's attitude toward the estate tax depends on one's attitude toward the rich. Gates, Soros, Buffet, and the other billionaires defending the tax were trying to reprise Teddy Roosevelt's argument that Americans need to prevent the creation of a permanent economic aristocracy. Yet Gates's son, the most ubiquitous image of great wealth in the United States today, is the product not of aristocracy but of entrepreneurial capitalism. This fact highlights how anti-repeal forces failed to match their rhetoric to the spirit of the times. Many Americans at the end of the 1990s applauded the rich and believed that they themselves would soon be joining their ranks. Bob Johnson's arguments about black wealth accumulation—both historically accurate and new to the debate—were quickly deployed by others to reinforce the repeal movement's Horatio Alger premise: in America's meritocratic society, great wealth is a reflection of hard work, not privilege. As long as this underlying instinct about how rich people become rich persisted, no group of billionaires could convince enough people, and certainly not enough politicians, that the danger of economic royalism in our democracy outweighed any benefit from eliminating the progressive taxation of inheritance in America.

Paint-by-Numbers Lawmaking

The president proposes; Congress disposes. A hackneyed truth, but it leaves a crucial question unanswered: How does Congress decide what to do in response to presidential proposals? The 2001 tax legislation confirms Bismarck's adage that no one should ever see how law or sausages are made. But we cannot avert our eyes here.

Since the late 1980s, Congress has played paint-by-numbers tax lawmaking. The game requires Congress to fit tax legislation into a fixed revenue target for the forthcoming budget period. The budget window used to be five years, but it was child's play simply to postpone large revenue losses until the sixth year. To inhibit such dodges, the budget period was extended in the 1990s to ten years. As it has turned out, however, this longer period only makes the feints and tricks more elaborate. Moreover, looking ahead ten years is not easy, even from the high perch of Capitol Hill. So the process of enacting changes to the tax code puts great pressure on the revenue estimates of the congressional scorekeeper, the Joint Committee on Taxation.

In 2001, the total ten-year revenue cost of President Bush's tax proposals was originally estimated to be $1.62 trillion (see table 1).

But this magic number was not fixed. House Republicans wanted to increase it, while Senate Democrats attempted to whittle it down. Early in 2001, the top Democrats in the Senate and House, Tom Daschle and Dick Gephardt, announced that they would support tax cuts—but only at a cost of $900 billion over the coming ten years. They arrived at their number by taking CBO's $5.6 trillion surplus estimate for the ten-year period, excluding the amounts attributable to Social Security and Medicare payroll taxes, and dividing the remainder into thirds: one-third for reducing the government's debt, one-third for additional spending, and one-third for tax cuts. Then, the amount available for tax cuts fell to about $750 billion because Daschle and Gephardt insisted on counting the interest costs of the

Table 1

Proposal	Total Cost* (in billions of dollars)
Reduce Individual Income Tax Rates	$500.7
Create New 10 Percent Bracket	310.6
Increase Child Tax Credits	192.7
Reduce the "Marriage Penalty"	111.8
Phase Out Estate and Gift Taxes	266.6
Subtotal	**$1,482.3**
Enhance Charitable Contributions	$56.0
Enhance Education Savings Accounts	5.6
Permanently Extend Research and Experimentation Credit	49.6
Extend for One Year Other Expiring Provisions	3.4
Other Tax Incentives	123.2
Total	**$1,620.2**

*Estimates are for total costs of the president's proposals, 2002–2111.
Source: Office of Management and Budget, February 2001.

tax changes. Any tax reductions would decrease expected government revenues, funds that otherwise would have been used to repay the government debt thereby creating an additional interest burden. Bush did not take this added interest into account in his $1.62 trillion figure. Daschle and Gephardt repeatedly pointed out that Bush's plan would exceed $2 trillion over the ten-year period including the extra interest expense. George Bush ignored this point, no doubt regarding it as carping.

The Democrats' $900 billion offer changed the debate substantially. The Democrats had conceded that there would be large tax cuts; the contest now would be about the shape and overall size of the package. Washington's smart money was on a number between the president's and the Democrats'. A good bet. A fifth-grader knows that $1.25 trillion, essentially the amount that, under Congress's scorekeeping rules, ultimately got signed into law, is halfway between $900 billion and $1.6 trillion.

In addition to the bill's size, the second number critical for the president's plan to succeed was 51, a majority of the Senate. Nothing could pass Congress with fewer than 51 Senate votes. And in a Senate evenly divided between Republicans and Democrats—as was the case for the first half of 2001, until Jim Jeffords's defection from the GOP—every senator's vote was important. Indeed, some Republicans feared the key number might actually be 60, the number of votes needed to break a Senate filibuster. But garnering 60 votes, which would require 10 Democrats plus all 50 Republicans, seemed beyond reach. Already three Republicans—John McCain of Arizona, Jim Jeffords of Vermont, and Lincoln Chafee of Rhode Island—had expressed concerns about the overall size of Bush's proposal. Only one Democrat, Zell Miller of Georgia, instantly embraced the president's plan.

To make sure that only 51 votes would be needed, the tax bill had to become a part of "budget reconciliation." Reconciliation occurs when the two houses of Congress "reconcile" their tax and spending bills to produce a budget. The time for Senate debate is limited, meaning that reconciliation bills can pass by 51 votes rather than the 60 that are needed to quell a filibuster. But it was questionable whether reconciliation, which had been intended and generally used to enact deficit-reduction measures, could also be used to pass a tax cut. It had happened before, at least in 1975 and 1996, but despite these precedents, it would be April before George Bush would know for sure whether the reconciliation process would be available for his 2001 tax cuts.

Like dances at weddings, the tax legislation minuet follows certain protocols. The Constitution grants the House of Representatives the prerogative to go first. So we begin there, even though the real action occurred in the Senate.

The House rules allow a united majority party to control both the substance and the timing of legislation. And Denny Hastert and his fellow House Republicans stood firmly behind George Bush's tax plan. Their gambit was to muster votes from Democrats, thereby fulfilling Bush's campaign pledge to have bipartisan dealings with Congress and signaling the Senate that the president's proposals enjoyed strong support in both parties. This quest for Democratic support explained Hastert's tactical decision to break the Bush plan into three pieces for House votes.

When tax legislation begins in the House, it is the Ways and Means Committee that steps onto the dance floor first. Bill Thomas became chairman of Ways and Means in January 2001 in part because the House Republican leaders thought he would be the best person to push the president's legislation through the committee and through Congress. Thomas wasted no time. He held his first committee hearing on Bush's tax plan on February 13, less than a week after the president sent it to Congress. The next day the committee's Republicans met to discuss the proposals, and on March 1 the full committee approved the first part of the president's plan: a cut in income tax rates costing $958 billion over ten years—nearly $150 billion more than the president had requested. The bill created a new lowest 12 percent tax bracket and dropped the top rate from 39.6 percent to 33 percent. The House passed it on March 8 by a vote of 230 to 198, garnering only 10 Democratic votes. Liberals regarded the tax cuts as too heavily skewed toward the wealthy, and conservatives complained that the vote was taken before the House had developed an overall budget. It was a good start, but Hastert wanted to get more Democrats on board.

In March the House moved on to consider the next installment of the president's plan, relief for married couples and families with children, but lawmakers were also working on the budget for the upcoming year. On March 28, the day before the House would vote on the second tax cut bill, it passed a budget resolution that called for at least Bush's proposed $1.62 trillion in tax reductions. Majority leader Dick Armey, along with some of his fellow House Republicans, had urged that the resolution explicitly permit an even larger tax cut than the president had requested. Some Republicans viewed this position simply as a ploy to push back the goalposts for the eventual negotiations with the Senate. But some of the House's fervent tax-cutters genuinely regarded Bush's proposals as too modest. And many members, including Jennifer Dunn, had become concerned that estate tax repeal, still awaiting House action, might be difficult to fit within the president's $1.62 trillion envelope. She had cause to worry.

Repeal advocates had suffered a major setback two days earlier when Lindy Paull, chief of staff for the Joint Committee on Taxation, released a memo to John Buckley, chief counsel for the Ways and Means Committee's Democrats, that substantially increased the JCT's official estimate of the costs of repeal. Paull told Buckley that abolishing the estate and gift tax beginning in 2002 would cost $662.2 billion during the ten-year budget period—a surprisingly large amount, since the total revenue expected from the tax during that period was only $409.7 billion. How could the cost of repeal exceed the revenues the tax was expected to raise? As Paull explained in the memo, "[T]he estimates for our proposal include significant revenue effects that result from a variety of income tax avoidance opportunities made possible by the repeal of the estate and gift tax."

The tax avoidance game that worried the JCT was actually quite simple. If wealth could be transferred tax-free, people could give assets to their children in lower income tax brackets, or to a relative abroad who is not subject to U.S. income tax, just before interest or dividends are paid. The low- or zero-bracket recipient would then collect the income and later return the asset, plus the accrued money, to the original high-bracket owner. Several tax attorneys had told the tax-writing committees and their staffs about this gambit and other techniques for saving income taxes. The Ways and Means Committee, for example, had heard testimony about these problems on March 22. And the threat to revenue collection was substantial: the JCT's new estimate predicted 50 cents or more of lost income taxes for every dollar lost directly from estate and gift tax repeal.

Repeal proponents were shocked by the size of the new JCT estimate. Adding insult to injury, the updated figure included an offset for substantial revenues from increased income taxes from assets transferred at death. Prior to 2001, people who inherited assets did not owe any capital gains taxes on gains that had accrued before the bequest. But the JCT was now assuming that estate tax repeal legislation would also include a "carryover basis" rule—a provision imposing capital gains taxes on the pre-inheritance gains when wealthy heirs sell inherited assets. This change had been included in the estate tax repeal legislation passed in 2000, which was vetoed by President Clinton, but it was not part of President Bush's plan.

So by March 28, the House had passed a budget resolution that had the potential to push the overall cost of tax cuts well above the president's request. This made Hastert's job of getting Democratic support and legislation amenable to the Senate a lot more difficult—while estate tax repeal was now looking like a much more expensive proposition. The coalitions seeking to kill the estate tax were not happy.

A day later, the House voted on the second installment of Bush's plan and produced an overwhelming victory for the president. By a margin of 282-144, with the support of 64 Democrats—nearly one-third of the total number in the House—representatives voted to lower taxes for families with children and for certain married couples. This bill would cost $399 billion over ten years. Once again, zealous House tax-cutters had taken the president's lead and upped the ante. President Bush had proposed resurrecting a deduction for married couples when both spouses work, which had been enacted under Ronald Reagan but taken away as part of his 1986 tax reform legislation. But conservative House Republicans insisted on cuts for married couples whether or not both spouses work—at a cost of $111 billion more than the president's plan. The House bill recouped some of this excess with more stingy child-credits than Bush wanted, but even so, it cost nearly $95 billion more than the president had proposed. So the first two bills passed by the House together cut taxes by about $240 billion more during the period from 2001 to 2011 than George Bush had urged.

Estate tax repeal was trailing behind, and the revenues available to fund it were being diverted to other causes. Bill Thomas told reporters that "the smorgasbord has more food out there than you're going to eat." But he underestimated his colleagues' appetite.

By March 29 the House had passed $1.37 trillion of tax cuts. To stick to the $1.62 trillion number, only $250 billion was left for everything else. The House had not yet enacted President Bush's proposed tax credits for corporate research and development expenditures or enhanced deductions for education and charitable gifts. These items were estimated to cost $111 billion more, which would leave less than $150 billion for estate tax repeal—less than a quarter of the $662.2 billion forecasted cost if the tax were repealed in 2002.

To make matters worse, other ideas were also competing for that money. Ways and Means Committee members Rob Portman, an Ohio Republican close to President Bush, and Ben Cardin, a Maryland Democrat, had introduced legislation increasing income tax incentives for retirement savings totaling $51.7 billion over ten years. On May 2 this bill, which was extremely popular within the Congress and highly prized by the insurance and securities industries, would pass the House by the overwhelming margin of 407 to 24. And the list went on. Bush's cuts in income tax rates made it imperative to provide relief from the alternative minimum tax; otherwise millions of middle-class taxpayers would soon have to pay its greater tax. And a variety of expiring income tax breaks were also waiting to be extended. Estate tax repeal was being squeezed from many sides, even in the House of Representatives, where it enjoyed great support.

On March 29, the day the House voted tax cuts for parents and married couples, the Ways and Means Committee voted 24 to 14 to repeal the estate tax—very slowly. Only one committee Democrat approved of the measure. His vote was no surprise: it was John Tanner of Tennessee, who had cosponsored an estate tax repeal bill with Jennifer Dunn. But it was significant because it marked the first time that year that any Democrat had voted in committee for a tax cut. One Republican, Amo Houghton of New York, voted against repeal (Houghton is a member of the Corning glass family, and some describe him as the wealthiest member of Congress). The committee bill dropped the top estate tax rate from 55 to 53 percent in 2002, 50 percent in 2003, and by one or two percentage points every year thereafter to a 39 percent rate in 2010. The tax would then be repealed in 2011. The committee bill also included a carryover basis provision, imposing new capital gains taxes when heirs sell inherited assets worth more than $1.3 million. But even with carryover basis, the slow decline in rates, and its long-delayed repeal, the JCT estimated the committee's repeal bill to cost $192.8 billion over ten years.

On a strict party-line vote, the committee defeated a proposal by New York's Charles Rangel, the ranking Democrat, to increase the estate tax exemption immediately from $650,000 to $2 million and to $2.5 million in 2010 ($4 million and $5 million, respectively, for married couples). Under the bill as passed, the exemption would rise only to $1 million in 2006 ($2 million for a married couple), as had already been scheduled under prior law.

Robert Matsui, a California Democrat on the committee, offered a bill to repeal the estate tax immediately, explaining that he was demonstrating the folly of enacting tax legislation to take effect a decade hence. This symbolic protest actually won the support of seven Democrats on the committee, but was defeated by a 31 to 7 vote. Republican Clay Shaw of Florida, explaining the unanimous Republican vote against the proposal, said that his party wanted "to be responsible" and "to have enough money left" for other items.

The committee's estate tax repeal bill passed the House on April 4 by a vote of 274 to 154. Fifty-eight Democrats voted for it, seven fewer than had supported repeal a year earlier, when they thought a Bill Clinton veto would make their votes a freebie. Still, more than a quarter of House Democrats had lined up behind repeal. The Democrats lost votes on virtually all fronts. They lost many of the usual southern and border-state moderates. They also lost four members of the Congressional Black Caucus, four

Hispanic Americans, and one Asian American. James Trafficant of Ohio—not yet sent to prison—voted yes, as did several other rust-belt conservatives from Illinois, Pennsylvania, and Michigan. Perhaps most surprising was the defection of 12 California representatives (of a total of 32 Californians). It is rare for the Democrats to lose more than a couple of Californians on any ideologically contested issue. The Democrats also lost three votes from Washington state—Frank Blethen territory—and one from Oregon. Only the big-city liberals held firm against repeal. On the other hand, three Republicans voted against the measure; none had in 2000. Amo Houghton said that "the Founding Fathers" would not have wanted to create a "leisure class." The JCT, which was still fiddling with its revenue estimates, reduced the ten-year cost by just over $7 billion to $185.6 billion.

The House bill was considerably less generous than either George Bush's proposal, which would have repealed the tax sooner, or the bill that Jennifer Dunn had introduced in January. Dunn would have reduced the top estate tax rate by 5 percentage points each year, from 55 percent in 2002 to 5 percent in 2010, before eliminating the tax completely. By keeping the top estate tax rate at a much higher 39 percent in 2010, the House bill greatly increased the risks that a future Congress might decide to keep the tax, especially if it needed the revenue—the tax would then be worth much more to the federal budget. And, unlike the House bill, neither the president's proposal nor Dunn's had increased capital gains taxes on bequests.

The slow reduction in estate taxes toward repeal in 2011, which Bill Thomas had deliberately fashioned to keep down the ten-year revenue cost, concealed the true price of estate tax repeal. When fully phased in, the House estate tax bill would cost four times the official JCT estimate.

The day the House passed estate tax repeal, the Senate took a key vote on its own budget resolution. Three Republicans—Jim Jeffords, Lincoln Chafee, and Pennsylvania's Arlen Specter—voted to shrink the ten-year cost of any tax cut by nearly $450 billion. Their defiance sent a clear signal that getting George Bush's tax cuts through the Senate would be considerably more difficult than in the House. Two days later, on April 6, the Senate formally adopted its budget. All 50 Republicans and 15 Democrats—including 4 Democratic members of the Senate Finance Committee—voted to make the overall tax cut $1.27 trillion. Of this amount, $85 billion would come in 2001, leaving $1.18 trillion for the years 2002 through 2011. The latter was $440 billion less than George Bush had proposed for the same period. The envelope was shrinking. And the House had already squeezed estate tax repeal down to fit other items into its substantially larger budget.

Louisiana's John Breaux, the Senate's Democratic dealmaker extraordinaire, was concerned that the budget resolution might be transformed into a futile exercise during the inevitable negotiations with the House over the final legislation. So while the Senate debated the resolution, Breaux corralled Majority Leader Trent Lott and demanded written assurance that Senate leaders would not raise the ten-year cost of tax cuts above $1.25 trillion in subsequent negotiations with the House. Breaux promised Lott that in return for this commitment, he would deliver the necessary Democratic votes. Lott agreed. A few hours later Breaux fulfilled his promise: the budget resolution passed with 15 Democratic votes, votes that Lott had been unable to secure just a few hours earlier.

The Senate's budget resolution ensured that tax cuts could be enacted through reconciliation so that only 51 votes would be required. West Virginia's Robert Byrd wanted to object. But he knew he would lose. No matter what the Senate parliamentarian ruled—and Byrd believed he would get a favorable ruling from this particular parliamentarian, Bob Dove, who would soon be fired by Trent Lott—the Senate can overrule the parliamentarian by a majority vote. Fifty Republicans were ready to vote against Byrd, and Vice President Dick Cheney stood ready to break a tie. Byrd's objection would fail. So he retreated to the usual senatorial refuge: he gave a speech. "Posterity," he said, "will judge us, in considerable measure, by whether we, in our time, continue to abuse the reconciliation process."

Abuse or not, the day's votes had assured George Bush a victory. The Senate had committed to cut taxes by more than three-quarters of the amount Bush had proposed. The president would not get his full loaf, but he would get considerably more than half. And much creative counting remained to be done. Bush might still get nearly everything he wanted. And he knew it. Bush sounded generous in his victory, saying "I applaud today's action and congratulate the Republicans and Democrats who helped make it happen." The president should have given himself the pat on the back.

On April 25, two days after Congress returned from its Easter recess, Bush invited Max Baucus, the Senate Finance Committee's ranking Democrat, to the White House to discuss the tax cut legislation. Baucus told the president that he supported a large tax reduction, one that is "fair and equitable to Montanans and rural America." A week later, on May 1, Bush and congressional leaders announced that they had agreed to a final budget plan including $1.25 trillion in tax cuts for the ten years 2002 to 2011, plus $100 billion in immediate, retroactive tax relief to stimulate the economy in 2001. The $1.35 trillion total was more than 80 percent of what George Bush had asked for. It was also what the Democrat John Breaux and his allies wanted: the ten-year total beginning in 2002 was Breaux's exactly, and the 2001 number only slightly greater than Breaux had proposed.

April had been a good month for the president. By May 9 and 10, the House and Senate were able to adopt these new numbers formally in a joint budget resolution. The magic number was settled. The House vote was 221 to 201 with 6 Democrats in favor; the Senate split 53 to 47. Republicans Lincoln Chafee of Rhode Island and Vermont's Jim Jeffords, then still a Republican and a member of the Senate Finance Committee, voted against the resolution. Only five Democrats supported the plan—ten fewer than had voted for the prior Senate resolution—but those ten switched their votes because of changes in spending, not because they disagreed with the tax cut number. Once again, John Breaux served as the broker to get the Democratic votes. He, Max Baucus, Bill Nelson of Nebraska, another Senate Finance Committee member, and Max Cleland and Zell Miller, both from Georgia, voted for the resolution. Miller had staunchly supported Bush's plan all along. The last vote cast was by Blanche Lincoln, a Democratic member of the Finance Committee from Arkansas, who wavered visibly before voting "no."

The *Wall Street Journal* described "the repeal of the inheritance tax" as the "most contentious tax issue in the budget resolution vote." The coalitions immediately got to work, both inside and outside the beltway. During the week before the vote, the NFIB had spent $145,000 on advertisements supporting repeal. Commercials ran in Arkansas (the home state of Blanche Lincoln), Georgia (Cleland and Miller), Louisiana (Breaux), Montana (Baucus), and Nebraska (Nelson). The NFIB spent its money wisely. On behalf of the opposition, William Gates, Sr., spoke at a Capitol Hill rally on May 10, spending only the cost of an airline ticket and a hotel. In response the NFIB issued a not-so-subtle press release: "It's one thing to say you don't want tax relief for yourself, but it's quite another to work to kill tax relief for those who don't have the same means to shelter their life savings and assets the way these billionaires do." The group then received an additional chance to dig at the "billionaires" when the antitax National Taxpayers Union Federation released a letter written by the Nobel Laureate economist Milton Friedman and signed by 277 other economists opposing the estate tax. The NFIB's president John Berthold issued another press release, claiming, "The economic community's widespread opposition to the tax trumps any support for the tax by a clique of cloistered billionaires and other limousine liberals."

On May 10, the day the $1.35 trillion budget resolution was announced, Senate Finance Committee Republicans and Democrats met to see what pieces would fit into the agreement. Chuck Grassley, the Finance Committee chairman, announced that his priorities were income tax rate reductions, estate tax repeal, relief from marriage penalties, and increased tax credits for children—also George Bush's priorities. His wish list mirrored the president's agenda, but he previously had said that "much of it was my agenda anyway." "He didn't steal it from me, but we ended up in the same place, only I was there two years before he was, or in some cases fifteen years." In any event, Bush and Grassley were singing from the same songbook.

The budget resolution gave the Finance Committee only until May 18—eight days—to report a bill to the Senate. For a committee evenly divided between Republicans and Democrats, this was "a tight deadline," as Max Baucus said. "Everybody's got a view," he added. "This is not easy." Under the reconciliation process, which was being used to foreclose a filibuster, it was not feasible for the Senate to consider the tax bill piecemeal as the House had done. Grassley had to fashion a single bill that would pass the Senate reasonably intact. Doing so would require help from some of his committee's Democrats. And, unlike in the House, where the rules essentially preclude any changes to a committee's tax bill, any measure that emerged from the Finance Committee might face an unlimited number of amendments on the Senate floor. Robert Torricelli, a New Jersey Democrat, described the squeeze on estate tax repeal as "a collision between the lowering of the marginal rates, providing for the child credit and the deductibility of college tuition, and the complete repeal of the estate tax." He told the *Wall Street Journal* that the estate tax rates could be lowered and the exemption raised, but "a repeal becomes very difficult." Grassley's committee had its work cut out for it.

On May 11, Charles Grassley and Max Baucus released their description of a bill to be considered by the Finance Committee on May 15. It included the key elements of George Bush's plan: (1) cuts in income tax rates, but with a top rate of 36 percent rather than the 33 percent that the president had proposed and the House had approved; (2) reductions in the marriage penalties; (3) an increase in child tax credits to $1,000; and (4) repeal of the estate tax in 2011. Under the Grassley-Baucus plan, by 2010, the estate tax exemption would have risen to $4 million and the top rate would be 40 percent. Their proposal would keep the gift tax at a top rate of 40 percent even after the estate tax was gone: a mechanism to lessen the cost of estate tax repeal by avoiding some of the income tax losses that the JCT had warned about. The plan also included the carryover basis provision for estates greater than $1.3 million.

On other matters, the Grassley-Baucus proposal included new tax breaks for education and retirement savings and some adjustments to the alternative minimum tax. They would also refund child tax credits to families who had no income liability, a feature demanded by Blanche Lincoln and Olympia Snowe, a Maine Republican who co-chaired the Senate's Centrist Coalition with John Breaux. Max Baucus echoed President Bush when he described this plan as "a tax bill that addresses the needs of working families." He added, "The country is in good economic shape. And now that we have a strong, well-balanced, bipartisan tax bill, I believe the economy will respond very well and continue its upward trend." Bush himself could not have said it better.

But neither the Republican nor the Democratic leadership was thrilled with the Grassley-Baucus proposal. And some influential Finance Committee members were publicly dissenting. Tom Daschle, the Democratic leader, continued to press for his $900 billion alternative, even though that train clearly was not leaving any station. Mississippi's Trent Lott, the Republican leader, along with Don Nickles of Oklahoma and Phil Gramm of Texas, tried to pressure Grassley to abandon his talks with Baucus and introduce a plan closer to the president's.

To fit their changes into the $1.35 trillion, ten-year envelope, Grassley and Baucus had resorted to making some of their tax cuts temporary. The alternative minimum tax changes, for example, were to last only until 2006, and a college tuition deduction, Senator Torricelli's pet idea, would expire after 2005. The top income tax rate would not start to fall until 2007, a year later than the president had envisioned. Estate tax repeal would be postponed until 2011, two years later than Bush wanted. The plan took more twists and turns than a country road.

Despite the grumblings, on May 15 the Senate Finance Committee voted 14-6, with the support of four Democrats—Max Baucus, John Breaux, Blanche Lincoln, and Robert Torricelli—in favor of legislation closely resembling the Grassley-Baucus plan. The estate tax changes were basically the same as Baucus and Grassley had proposed. The committee increased child credits and tuition deductions—meaning that the paint-by-numbers game required some new tricks. In a completely cynical ma-neuver, for example, 70 percent of corporate tax payments normally due on September 17 were postponed during 2001 and 2004 until October 1, the start of the federal government's new fiscal year. This two-week shift of government receipts allowed the committee to claim it was not using So-cial Security or Medicare funds to pay for tax cuts.

The Finance Committee also added a provision terminating the entire tax cut legislation on September 30, 2011, when the ten-year budget pe-riod covered under the Senate's budget resolution would expire. In other words, without further change, repeal of the estate tax would come into ef-fect on January 1, 2011 and expire nine months later, on September 30 of that year, when the tax would be resurrected. Margaret Milner Richardson, who had been IRS commissioner under Bill Clinton, quipped that this gimmick foreshadowed some lean years for funeral directors; relatives would keep loved ones on life support until the estate tax repeal was in place.

This "sunset" of the entire tax bill was necessary for the bill to escape a "Byrd Rule" objection on the Senate floor. The Byrd Rule allows any sen-ator to object to a provision deemed to be "extraneous" to budget recon-ciliation. A provision is extraneous if it "would decrease revenues during a fiscal year after the fiscal years covered by such reconciliation bill"—in this case after September 30, 2011. The rule is an attempt to inhibit some of the tricks by which lawmakers attempt to disguise the revenue costs of tax cuts by shunting them beyond the ten-year budget period. Once a senator raises a Byrd Rule point of order, it takes 60 votes to overrule. Thus, 60 votes would be necessary to keep the tax cuts beyond 2011, the same num-ber as required to defeat a Senate filibuster. It would be no easier to find 60 votes to waive the Byrd Rule than to pass the tax legislation outright. Some

Republicans thought they might avoid the Byrd Rule through a favorable ruling from the Senate parliamentarian. Indeed, some Democrats were convinced this prospect explained why Trent Lott had fired Bob Dove, the previous parliamentarian, earlier in 2001. But a favorable ruling was not in the cards. Thus, in the future, although the tax cuts enacted in 2001 may be extended by 51 votes, it will take 60 senators to make them permanent.

Some Washington insiders, including the NFIB and much of the leadership of both the Tax Relief Coalition and the Family Business Estate Tax Coalition, claim that they anticipated the sunset all along. Bob Packwood certainly expected it. Indeed, although the sunset did not appear in the legislation itself until the middle of May, a few Washington publications, including *Congressional Quarterly Weekly*, had predicted a sunset as early as March, just as the legislative process was getting underway. Whether coalition leaders warned their small business and farm members that estate tax repeal would be long delayed and then disappear is an important question. There is no evidence suggesting that these organizations polled their members on what they thought about alternatives to repeal. Armed with this knowledge, many small business owners and farmers might well have preferred the Democratic alternative of an immediate, substantial increase in the exemption and a significant rate reduction. David Pankonin, the Nebraska farm supplier who had briefly become a spokesman for reform some years earlier and remained a loyal NFIB member, was not for total repeal but reports that he was never asked what he thought of compromises. Apparently, in the countdown to the passage of the bill, decision-making in the coalition had become a top down affair.

The Finance Committee bill contained one additional estate tax wrinkle intended to keep its revenue costs down. Since 1924 the estate tax has contained a credit for state death taxes. This credit essentially shares estate tax revenues between the states and the federal government. The Finance Committee bill would immediately halve the states' credit and eliminate it entirely in 2005. In essence, the Finance Committee had financed part of its tax cut by taking money from state governments. As Bob Graham of Florida said, "We are raping the states." Graham voted against the bill in committee, but to no avail.

Chuck Grassley began the Senate debate on the bill with an emotional speech on Thursday, May 17. He began by commending President Bush for his leadership. He related over and over how he and his "friend Max

Baucus" had worked together since mid-January, meeting at least weekly to put a bill together. He emphasized the bipartisan vote in the Finance Committee (and took some credit for it when he stated that he had met often with individual members of the committee "in their offices—not in my office, in their offices"). Grassley then used a farmer's analogy, likening the process to planting corn and hoping that seeds would sprout. "Senator Baucus and I sowed that seed and that seed sprouted," he said. "I know now it sprouted; I didn't know then that it would sprout." And in the now common fashion, the Iowa senator described what the bill would do for certain Iowa families. The families he mentioned have never met Grassley. They were surprised to learn that he had spoken of them—accurately, they told us. Grassley closed by describing this as "a responsible bill," not a "risky" one. And once again, he thanked Max Baucus.

A week later the Finance Committee bill emerged from the Senate floor virtually intact, having faced down an onslaught of amendments. The reconciliation process limits the time for Senate debate to 20 hours, but the time for voting does not count. Thus the Senate—which likes to call itself the world's greatest deliberative body—debated amendment after amendment, for a minute or so each, before taking a vote. Someone called it a "vote-a-rama."

After a few close calls on certain amendments, it became clear that the Grassley-Baucus approach would hold. An amendment by Missouri's Jean Carnahan to cut the top income tax rate by only one percentage point in order to give larger cuts to lower-bracket families lost by a vote of 48 to 50. A substantially similar proposal offered by John McCain lost on a tie vote of 49 to 49 the same day, and failed again the next day on a 50 to 50 tie. Bob Graham's amendment to stop the "rape" of the states by phasing out the state estate tax credit at the same pace as the federal estate tax lost by 39 to 60. Amendments to increase the estate tax exemption instead of repealing the tax failed by similar votes. Another attempt to avoid total repeal—a proposal by Byron Dorgan, a North Dakota Democrat, to reduce the top estate tax rate to 45 percent and repeal the tax for qualifying family-owned businesses and farms—lost on a 43 to 56 vote. Neither the Tax Relief Coalition nor the Family Business Estate Tax Coalition supported any of these amendments.

After the amendment frenzy was exhausted, the Senate passed the tax cut legislation by a vote of 62 to 38 on May 23. All 50 Republicans voted for the bill. So did 12 Democrats: Finance Committee members Baucus,

Breaux, Lincoln, Nelson, and Torricelli; Georgia's Cleland and Miller, Jean Carnahan of Missouri, Dianne Feinstein of California, Tim Johnson of South Dakota (Daschle's home state), Herb Kohl of Wisconsin, and Mary Landrieu of Louisiana. Carnahan, Cleland, Johnson, Landrieu, and, at the time, Torricelli were all expecting to run for reelection in 2002 in hotly contested races, and thought they could not afford to vote against tax cuts. Ultimately Torricelli did not run. Carnahan and Cleland lost anyway.

The JCT estimated that the Senate version of estate tax repeal would cost $145.7 billion over the ten-year budget period. The Senate had thus cut $40 billion from the House version of repeal, and, based on the JCT's estimates, its estate tax repeal legislation was estimated to cost less than half the president's plan during the coming ten years. Repeal had passed both houses of Congress, but in a substantially diminished form (see table 2).

A week before the Senate passed its bill, on May 16, the House had voted by 230 to 197 to reaffirm its reduction of the top income tax rate to 33 percent. The House had needed to pass its own reconciliation measure to take to a House-Senate conference. But the Senate had shown great reluctance to drop the top rate below 36 percent. It was now necessary for the House and Senate to compromise their legislation into a single bill. It was May 24. The president wanted final passage before Memorial Day on May 28. Congress wanted to go home for the holiday and a recess. The next few days would not be easy.

Table 2

Proposal	President Bush	House	Senate
	Total Cost* (in billions of dollars)		
Reduce Individual Income Tax Rates	$560.2	$575.1	$404
Create New 10 Percent Bracket	317.1	383.2	438.7
Increase Child Tax Credits	210.7	175.9	194.7
Reduce the "Marriage Penalty"	102.7	223.3	60
Phase Out Estate and Gift Taxes	**305.9**	**185.6**	**145.7**
Deduct Education Expenses	6.1	–	33.5
Enhance Retirement Savings	–	51.7	40.3
Other Items	135.5	20.1	33.1
Total	**$1,638.2**	**$1,620.1**	**$1,350.0**

*Estimates are for total costs through 2011 from the Joint Committee on Taxation as of May 24, 2001, after the Senate passed its bill.

The Final Four

After nearly a decade of planning and campaigning by repeal advocates, the fate of the estate tax would ultimately come to rest with four men deliberating behind closed doors on Capitol Hill. The repeal movement had succeeded in bringing the issue to the fore and had then exerted all the political pressure it could muster. But in the end, those members of Congress most closely associated with the estate tax debate, such as Jennifer Dunn, would not be in the room. The coalitions, the lobbyists, and even the legislators would just have to await the outcome of what is, in essence, a secretive affair.

When the House and Senate pass differing versions of legislation, as they did with these tax cut bills, standard operating procedure calls for the appointment of a "conference committee" of representatives and senators to resolve the differences. The committee's report, containing final legislation, must then pass both houses of Congress intact before being sent to the president for his signature. Beyond these general guidelines, however, the process remains notably unregulated. The rules simply require that identical legislation be approved by a majority of the conference committee members from both the House and Senate. Typically, these committee members will include the ranking majority and minority lawmakers on the House and Senate committees responsible for the legislation—in this case, House Ways and Means and Senate Finance—and others. But the House and Senate need not send equal numbers. Nor must the conference committee deliberate in public or keep any record of its discussions.

Many observers and participants have criticized the conference process. A common complaint is that the committee's secrecy affords special pleaders too much opportunity to influence legislation. Conference committees are like "the third house of Congress or even the Supreme Court of legislation," Richard Cohen once wrote in the *National Journal*. "Imagine a shadowy arm of Congress composed of a handful of senior members who hold secret, late-night meetings to mull over key questions of federal policy," he says. "No rules govern their activities, and once they've made their decisions, their legislative handiwork is presented to rank-and-file lawmakers on a take-it-or-leave-it basis."

The conference committee for the 2001 tax legislation—a law containing hundreds of pages of amendments to the tax code—entered its conference with a very short timetable. The Senate had passed its $1.35 trillion tax bill on Wednesday, May 23. President Bush wanted Congress to send him legislation that he could sign by Memorial Day, the following Monday, before Congress disappeared for a week's recess. Bush claimed that the faltering economy demanded prompt action. If the Treasury was not ready to mail tax rebate checks during the summer, he would blame Congress for not getting legislation onto his desk soon enough. Congress commonly leaves town on the Thursday, or Friday at the latest, before a holiday. Not this Memorial Day weekend.

To complicate matters further, chaos had erupted that week in the Senate as rumors escalated that Vermont's Jim Jeffords would soon announce that he was leaving the Republican Party. Jeffords was apparently planning to become an Independent but vote with the Democrats. This defection would shift Senate control to the Democrats, making South Dakota's Tom Daschle the new majority leader and transferring to him the power to set the Senate's legislative agenda. Max Baucus would replace Chuck Grassley as chairman of the Finance Committee. Senate Republicans were in high dudgeon, blaming George Bush and his staff for Jeffords's defection. The Democrats, for their part, could think or talk of little else but how they would wield their new power. For President Bush, the immediate crucial question was what would happen to the tax cuts. Jeffords promised the president that he would not change parties until the tax legislation was approved by Congress, allowing Republicans to retain a majority on the conference committee. He then formally announced on Thursday, May 24, that he was leaving the Republican Party. Everyone knew he would not wait forever. His announcement escalated the pressure for Congress to finish the tax bill before its Memorial Day recess.

The Senate appointed nine conferees, five Republicans and four Democrats. The Republicans were Charles Grassley, of course, Don Nickles of Oklahoma, Texas's Phil Gramm, Orrin Hatch from Utah, and Alaska's Frank Murkowski. The Democrats selected Max Baucus and John Breaux,

Tom Daschle, and John Rockefeller IV of West Virginia. The House selected only three conferees: Republicans Bill Thomas and Majority Leader Dick Armey, and Charles Rangel, the Ways and Means Committee's ranking Democrat from New York. They were outnumbered, but Denny Hastert emphasized that the House was not simply going to "cave in" to the Senate. "We expect to be heard," Hastert said. "We know what compromise is."

It is an open secret about conference committees that everybody must get something. If the committee report is going to be sold as final legislation, everyone has to walk away claiming to be a winner. But stuffing every item coveted by every legislator crucial to passage into the Senate's $1.35 trillion budget constraint would not be easy.

Conferees typically all meet together to hash out the differences between House and Senate bills. But not this time. This conference committee met only once—to rubberstamp a final agreement fashioned by four of its members—Chuck Grassley, Max Baucus, John Breaux, and Bill Thomas. This foursome was evenly divided between Republicans and Democrats, but it had three senators and only one representative from the House. No House Democrats were present, because in a Republican-dominated House, no Democratic votes were needed to pass the final legislation. It was, to say the least, an unusual group of conferees.

We have already described in some detail Bill Thomas, the smart, aggressive, and acerbic Californian. He had been planning for the conference for months. He had sharpened the details of his position and had aggressively been recruiting allies even before the conference began. On Wednesday, May 16, the day the House passed its reconciliation tax bill lowering marginal income tax rates, Thomas met to discuss strategy with Republican leaders of the House and Senate. The meeting included Denny Hastert, Dick Armey, Tom DeLay, J. C. Watts, and Jim Nussle from the House as well as Chuck Grassley and Don Nickles from the Senate. During the next several days Thomas conferred several more times with Hastert and Armey on the House side, and with Trent Lott and Grassley from the Senate, to plot his course. He also spent considerable time on the Senate floor buttonholing lawmakers during the Senate's tax bill debates on Tuesday and Wednesday, May 22 and 23. On Tuesday evening, Thomas and Dick Armey met to discuss the upcoming conference with Senators Phil Gramm and Orrin Hatch. This time, the meeting also included Nick Calio and Mark

Weinberger from the Bush administration. The next morning Thomas, Calio, and Weinberger were together again at a breakfast meeting that Treasury Secretary Paul O'Neill hosted in his conference room for Thomas and Chuck Grassley. Later that day, while the Senate was concluding its voting on the tax bill, Senators Grassley, Baucus, Breaux, Gramm, and Hatch met with Hastert, Armey, Calio, and Weinberger in Thomas's Ways and Means Committee office right off the House floor to prepare further for the forthcoming conference.

After this whirlwind of debating, strategizing, and deal-making, Thomas was ready to put down an opening bid to start the conference process. On Wednesday night, after the Senate bill finally passed, he presented his initial Republican offer to a "pre-meeting" of the conference committee on the Senate side of the Capitol. This late-night meeting—the last before Baucus, Breaux, Grassley, and Thomas began meeting alone on Thursday—was attended by these four plus Phil Gramm and Dick Armey. As these conversations unfolded, it became unmistakable that what Bill Thomas really cared about was getting the top income tax rate as low as possible. He simply was not going to accept the Senate's 36 percent rate. He had come a long way from his roots as a union plumber's son.

But Thomas was potentially facing some tough competition. John Breaux, for example, had a lot at stake in the tax bill. Soon after George W. Bush knew he would become president, he had invited Breaux to Austin and offered him a cabinet post. Breaux declined, regarding his position in the evenly divided Senate as potentially much more powerful. The tax bill provided Breaux with his first opportunity since that conversation to exercise his power and vindicate that decision.

Breaux well deserves his reputation as the Senate's most accomplished deal-maker. His website trumpets Louisiana's largest newspaper, the New Orleans *Times-Picayune,* calling Breaux "a mainstream southern Democrat who has the skill to fashion legislative coalitions that draw extremes toward a bipartisan middle." Along with Maine's Republican Senator Olympia Snowe, Breaux co-chaired a "Centrist Coalition" of Senate Democrats and Republicans, a group that he helped found in 1994 to seek bipartisan solutions on a whole range of issues.

Breaux has been in politics virtually since he was old enough to vote. He got his political start at the side of Louisiana Governor Edwin Edwards. (Edwards was a powerful, flamboyant, nonsmoking, nondrinking four-term governor with a weakness for high-stakes gambling and attractive women, who in the year 2000 at age 73 was convicted of federal racketeering charges.) When he was first elected to the House in 1972, John Breaux at age 28 was Congress's youngest member. The Senate's reigning tennis champion, he is also charming and high-spirited. Louisiana Congressman Billy Tauzin says that Breaux fell asleep during his bar exam, having partied late the night before, and he showed up at the 2000 Democratic convention in Los Angeles in full Mardi Gras regalia. But do not underestimate John Breaux because of his Cajun drawl or his light-hearted manner. In the legislative rough-and-tumble, he is not to be trifled with.

Breaux's Democratic colleague on the conference committee, Max Baucus, matches neither Breaux's focus nor his skill as a legislator or negotiator. He is indefatigable but, truth be told, he would rather be running a marathon than sitting through marathon negotiations. Having come to the Senate in 1978, he had enjoyed few legislative accomplishments in two and a half decades. Like Chuck Grassley, Baucus comes from a farming family and remains proud of his rural roots. In 1995 and 1996, he walked the entire length of Montana. In 2000, along with his brother and a cousin, he rode his Harley from Montana to Sturgis, South Dakota, to attend an annual motorcycle rally. One day a month he experiences a "Day in the Life" of a Montana resident; in doing so, he has worked at Montana farms, ranches, schools, and on highway construction. Always attuned to the problems of small businesses and farmers, prior to 2001 Baucus had spent more of his time and energy on trade matters than on taxation.

In May 2001, Max Baucus was worried about his reelection bid the next year. Montana is a Republican state, carried by George Bush in 2000 by 25 percentage points. As decisions about the tax bill loomed, he was torn between actively participating in Democratic Senate politics and getting reelected. One Senate insider told a *National Journal* reporter in December 2000 that Max Baucus was "going to have to walk a tightrope between doing what's right for his party and doing what's right for his political life." Six months later, as the tax conference was getting underway, it was clear that Max Baucus's tightrope led right into George Bush's arms.

Chuck Grassley, who is often seen with his suit jacket slung over his shoulder and black leather briefcase in hand, looks more like a high school teacher approaching retirement than the Senate's only working farmer. Long before he came to head the Senate Finance Committee, Grassley had worked closely with Max Baucus on agriculture issues. Many in the Senate are more eloquent than Grassley, but none works harder. He pays careful attention to detail and speaks in a slow, deliberate, plain-spoken way, relying frequently on farming metaphors. As he himself says, "What you see is what you get, a person who has not forgotten his roots." He adds, "Maybe my style is a lack of style." But he doesn't lack for substance. Grassley is a "workhorse," in the words of John Breaux. "He'll schedule a hearing at 8 o'clock in the morning," Breaux says, "when most people in Louisiana are still drinking Bloody Marys." In fact, Grassley is a Baptist who doesn't drink alcohol no matter what the time of day. He does not even allow his staff to drink at work-related events, including Republican fundraisers.

When Grassley became chairman of the Senate Finance Committee in January 2001, he was determined to restore the committee's lost luster and power. He also wanted to improve its relationship with the House, particularly with the Ways and Means chairman. By May 23, as the conference began, he had done both. And as usual, Grassley was well prepared for the negotiations. He knew the final bill would have to hew closely to the measure that he and Max Baucus had worked out, which had just passed the Senate. Grassley had little room to move if he was to retain a Senate majority.

On Thursday, May 24, the conference meetings among Grassley, Baucus, Breaux, and Thomas began in earnest. These four met in Baucus's "hideaway" on the Senate side of the Capitol. Many senators have these so-called hideaway offices near the Senate floor, allowing them to stick close by when the Senate is in session and taking votes. These offices are also much more convenient than the Senate office buildings for members of the House. This day the four conferees would do their real work here.

Lindy Paull, chief of staff of the Joint Committee on Taxation, also participated in the meetings. The negotiators were trying to fit many moving pieces within the Senate's revenue constraint. As they shuffled the ideas for compromises around, the JCT scurried to produce revenue estimates of the many variations.

The Bush administration was represented by Andrew Card, Nick Calio, and Mark Weinberger—but they were not invited to join the meetings in Baucus's hideaway. Instead, they ensconced themselves in Vice President Cheney's Senate office, where they were readily available for consultation. Vice presidents rarely use this office, a large and ornate suite of rooms right off the Senate floor, but on occasions such as these it becomes handy.

Thursday was a crazy day. In the morning, Jim Jeffords formally announced that he was leaving the Republican Party, meaning that the Senate was about to be reorganized. The resulting commotion brought the meeting of the four negotiators to a temporary halt. After they had resumed, Chuck Grassley emerged from the meeting later in the day and told reporters that the process was "moving slow." He added, "We could be here all night." Complaining about the difficulty of fitting all the proposals into the Senate's budget constraint, Bill Thomas quipped, "$1 trillion, 350 billion stretched out over 10 years just doesn't get what it used to."

In the afternoon, Baucus and Breaux presented their "Democratic offer" to Grassley and Thomas, countering the Republican bid that Thomas had put forth the night before. It suggested a top income tax rate of 35 percent beginning in 2008, $185 billion in refundable child credits for 2001 to 2011, $72 billion in marriage penalty reductions for low- and moderate-income couples, $39.3 billion in enhanced pension savings incentives, $35.5 billion in income tax credits and deductions for education, and assorted other provisions. The estate tax changes proposed by the Democrats totaled $119.7 billion from 2002 to 2011—down $25 billion from the Senate bill. The exemption would rise slowly to $4 million ($8 million for a married couple) by 2010, when the top rate would be 45 percent. The state credit would be repealed in 2004. The gift tax would be retained and carryover basis would be added. More than three-quarters of the total revenue loss would come in the last three years, and less than 10 percent before 2006.

The Democrat's offer totaled $1.34 trillion over the period 2001–2011, leaving the Republicans $10 billion to play with and still fit into the Senate's $1.35 trillion window. Bill Thomas called the offer "totally unacceptable." That evening a somewhat larger group met to discuss ideas for a possible compromise, with the four negotiators joined by Republicans Dick Armey, Phil Gramm, and Don Nickles along with the president's three men, Andrew Card, Nick Calio, and Mark Weinberger.

On the morning of Friday, May 25, after getting a report on the progress—or lack thereof—in the negotiations, George Bush telephoned both Chuck Grassley and Bill Thomas to urge them to work out a compromise. The president again said he wanted them to get a bill passed before Congress left for the Memorial Day recess. The White House was beginning to worry that if the legislation were delayed, the whole thing might unravel.

At ten o'clock the four negotiators began a marathon session. At one moment during that Friday's meetings, Bill Thomas, a congressman shut up in a room with three senators, opened the door and handed a folded paper to reporters lurking outside Baucus's hideaway. "Help, I am being held hostage." He did manage to escape twice to meet with congressional Republican leaders, once on the House side in Dick Armey's office and once on the Senate side in Don Nickles's office.

Finally, at about eight that evening, the four negotiators reached an agreement. An hour later, the entire conference committee met for the first and only time. Everyone knew that their gathering was simply a formality to ratify officially and sign the agreement that Baucus, Breaux, Grassley, and Thomas had fashioned.

It takes a magnifying glass to see the differences between the conference agreement and the Senate bill, or even the Democrats' "totally unacceptable" Thursday offer. Phase-ins and phaseouts of the tax cuts had been adjusted, but the main components of the bill were about the same in size and form. The key to the final agreement was an additional nearly $70 billion that the four negotiators found to spread around by terminating the legislation on December 31, 2010, rather than—as the Senate had—on September 30, 2011, the end of the federal government's final fiscal year of the ten-year budget period. This extra money, labeled the "honey pot" by congressional insiders, sprinkled largesse here and there that allowed everyone to claim victory. Bill Thomas got slightly greater tax cuts for high-bracket taxpayers; Olympia Snowe and Blanche Lincoln got slightly more generous refundable child credits; and so on.

The final estate-tax repeal provisions were estimated to cost $138 billion over the ten years from 2002 to 2011, 45 percent of what the president had proposed. The tax was repealed only for people who die between January 1 and December 31, 2010. The top rate was reduced slowly and not terribly deeply, bottoming out at 45 percent in 2009. The exemption would rise to $3.5 million in 2009. The gift tax was retained with a $1 million lifetime exemption, and carryover basis was added, effective in 2010, for transfers in excess of $1.3 million. Thus, some people might inherit assets free of estate tax during the one-year repeal, but would owe capital gains taxes when they sell those assets. The $1.3 million exemption from the new capital gains tax is considerably lower than the final $3.5 million estate tax exemption. Table 3 illustrates the prin-

Table 3

Proposal	Total Cost* (in billions of dollars) President Bush	Final Legislation
Reduce Individual Income Tax Rates	$560.2	$453.6
Create New 10 Percent Bracket	317.1	421.3
Increase Child Tax Credits	210.7	171.8
Reduce the "Marriage Penalty"	102.7	63.3
Phase Out the Estate Tax	**305.9**	**138.0**
Deduct Education Expenses	6.1	29.4
Enhance Retirement Savings	–	49.6
Other Items	135.5	20.4
Total	**$1,638.2**	**$1,348.5**

*Estimates are for total costs of the president's proposals through 2011 and the final legislation through December 31, 2010, from the Joint Committee on Taxation, May 26, 2001.

cipal differences between the costs of the president's proposal and the final agreement.

One last hurdle remained. House rules normally delay a vote on a conference report for at least one day after it is filed in order to give those representatives (or, more likely, their staff) who actually want to read the legislation time to learn what it says. But no member of Congress was willing to stay in Washington until the Sunday of Memorial Day weekend. So the House Rules Committee passed a new rule eliminating the one-day waiting period. Majority Leader Dick Armey announced on Friday that the tax bill could be filed as late as midnight, and that lawmakers would have one hour to read the legislation before debate began. The report filled hundreds of pages, and it was not easy reading. It did not matter; the vote was wired.

The House passed the final version of the tax bill that Saturday morning by a vote of 240 to 154, with 28 Democrats, one Independent, and all House Republicans on board. The Senate followed suit that evening by a vote of 58 to 33, with the same 12 Democrats—nearly one-fourth—in favor as had voted for the Senate's original version. Republicans Lincoln Chafee and John McCain voted "no." Jim Jeffords voted "yes," fulfilling his agreement with the president to support the tax bill before leaving the GOP.

Charles Grassley called the bill a victory for bipartisanship. Not everyone agreed. Senate Democratic Leader Tom Daschle lamented that "once again working families get left behind." The incoming Democratic chairman of the Senate Budget Committee, Kent Conrad of North Dakota, who had fought the bill every step of the way, complained that the legislation would actually cost more than the $1.35 trillion official figure. "They've ripped off the last page of the calendar and are making believe 2011 doesn't exist," he said, referring to the last-minute change that terminated the legislation at the end of 2010, nine months before the end of the ten-year budget period. Conrad warned that the bill had "serious implications for the fiscal integrity of the budget." Charlie Rangel, the ranking Ways and Means Democrat, had been completely frozen out of all conference negotiations since the House Democratic votes were irrelevant to the passage of the bill. Not surprisingly, he also failed to see things Grassley's way. Rangel described the bill as "one big fraud on the American people," saying Republicans had packed "it with every kind of gimmick and sleight of hand I've ever seen."

Charles Grassley gave appropriate credit to George Bush, resorting, as he so often does, to farming metaphors. "George Bush planted the seeds of tax cuts as candidate Bush months ago," Grassley said. "With cultivation in Congress the seeding has thrived."

President Bush released a statement from Camp David, where he was spending his Memorial Day weekend. He hailed the legislation as a "landmark," saying that because of this bill, "American taxpayers will have more money in their pockets to save and invest and the economy will receive a much-needed shot in the arm." He added, "I commend the members of the House and Senate, Republican and Democrat alike, who made this happen. Tax relief is a centerpiece of our American agenda and I look forward to signing it into law." Andrew Card reminded people of the widespread skepticism in early 2001 that George Bush could bring the tax cuts "to reality," noting with satisfaction that now "he has."

In January 2001, Chuck Grassley had said he hoped to have a tax bill to the president by Labor Day. This had seemed a realistic target at the time. Ronald Reagan, who had enacted the last large tax reduction two decades earlier, signed his 1981 tax cut legislation on August 13, a foggy day at his California ranch. George W. Bush had outdone Reagan by months. The *Economist* magazine described the 2001 tax act as "a remarkable achievement for Mr. Bush," adding that the "largest tax cut since Ronald Reagan will have been passed in less than five months, far faster than the Gipper managed, despite the slimmest of congressional majorities and widespread public apathy." George Bush signed the legislation at a large White House ceremony on June 7 with much fanfare.

But the ink was hardly dry from Bush's signature before grousing over the bill's sunset began. Bill Thomas, quite properly, blamed the Senate for terminating the bill at the end of 2010. Along with Dick Armey, Phil Gramm, and Don Nickles, Thomas insisted vociferously that he would immediately introduce legislation to make the bill permanent. If you did not know better, you never would have suspected that all of them had signed the conference agreement. President Bush also began urging Congress to make the tax cuts permanent. But this was not to be, at least not any time soon. Tom Daschle and his Democrats now were in control of the Senate. By the time Republicans recaptured the Senate in the 2002 elections and retook power in 2003, George Bush had moved on to other tax-cutting priorities. And the big surpluses predicted in January 2001 were rapidly transforming into large deficits. Bush still called for making the 2001 law permanent, but his new priority was to eliminate individual income taxes on dividends. Congress did give him a substantial cut in the dividend tax that year, but it was another tax bill with a sunset. The Byrd Rule remained a barrier to getting permanent tax cuts through the Senate. Although Congress in 2003 speeded up some of the 2001 income tax cuts, it did not touch the 2010 sunset. The estate tax provisions remained unchanged.

In February 2004, President Bush's budget again called for making the 2001 tax changes permanent. But, he also made clear that repealing the estate tax was not his top priority. This time, extending income tax reductions, particularly child credits and marriage penalty relief that were scheduled to expire, took precedence. And the government's financial picture had continued to deteriorate. The administration was forecasting a $521 billion deficit for 2004 alone. That year Congress did nothing to the estate tax.

Unlike Ronald Reagan's 1981 tax cut, the public seemed little excited by the enactment of George Bush's most sought-after prize. With the exception of the $300 checks ($600 a couple) that most Americans would receive in 2001, many of the tax cuts were not scheduled to materialize for years, then only to disappear not long thereafter. Marshall Wittman of the Hudson Institute said he had never seen "such apathy" about a large tax reduction. He asked, "What if you passed a tax cut and no one cares?" Jim

Jeffords's defection from the Republican Party was news topic number one in the period following the final vote. Rather than trumpeting George Bush's remarkable legislative achievement, television's talking heads reported endlessly on the machinations over reorganizing the Senate. They pondered at excruciating length what Jeffords's change might mean for the Bush presidency.

Amidst all this attention on the former Republican, and on the president who had allowed him to go, no one predicted that Bush's tax triumph would be so easily repeated in 2003. For a guy who in Dirk Van Dongen's memorable phrase had just "made his bones" in Washington, George Bush received few accolades. With extraordinary skill, the president who had lost the popular vote secured his foremost legislative priority—a large and controversial tax cut—only five months after taking office. But his victory was bittersweet. It was bittersweet as well for those who had pushed so hard for so long to repeal the estate tax.

Winners, Losers, and Uncertainty

Shortly after the 2001 tax act was signed, Charles Grassley proclaimed that this tax bill "is a victory for Republicans, it is a victory for Democrats, and it is a victory for the president, but most of all, it is a victory for the American people." But not everyone won. And even for some "winners," victory rang quite hollow. For those who had worked long and hard for estate tax repeal, the result was ambiguous at best. Repeal was passed into law on paper, but with the actual elimination of the tax delayed by ten years, the reality remained very much in doubt.

To be sure, George W. Bush won. He won big. Soon he would begin claiming credit even for the $300 and $600 refund checks that the Treasury would send taxpayers between August and October 2001—refunds from a cut not included in the president's original proposals, but which Democrats had originated and insisted on. Chuck Grassley also won large. He demonstrated his skill, which many had doubted, in getting a massive, complex, and tendentious tax bill through the Finance Committee and the Senate, both of which were evenly divided between Republicans and Democrats. Grassley's victory was a paean to hard work, perseverance, and patience. Don Nickles, Phil Gramm, and other Senate conservatives who truly believed in the wisdom of the tax cuts—indeed, in the wisdom of virtually any tax cuts—also emerged victorious.

On the Democratic side, John Breaux surely won. He cemented and polished his already outsized reputation as a Senate dealmaker, as a man who everyone had to deal with. Max Baucus probably can also be counted a winner. In 2002 he secured the reelection he coveted to his Montana Senate seat. If he weakened his standing within his Democratic Party and lost sway with its Senate leaders in the process, that was a price he was willing to pay.

Over in the House, Denny Hastert, Dick Armey, Tom DeLay, and the rest of the GOP leadership also walked away winners. They completely controlled the action on their side of the capitol. They not only kept their Republican majority 100 percent united but, by dividing the bill into pieces, also picked up many Democratic votes along the way. By the end they had a number of Democrats on record supporting some of their top priorities, including estate tax repeal.

Bill Thomas also won. He controlled his committee, generally seen as the most powerful in the House. He showed he could work with the House leadership, and he forged a far better relationship with key senators than had his predecessor as Ways and Means chairman. Thomas won no friends among the Democrats on his committee, but he seemed to care little. He seemed confident he would never need them.

So who lost? Some losers are obvious. The completely ineffectual and ever more embittered House Democrats lost. Their leader, Dick Gephardt, failed to garner even one Republican vote against the bill. Nor was he able to keep all of his Democratic colleagues from supporting the president's proposal. Indeed, more than one-third of House Democrats voted for the measures to cut taxes for married couples and families with children, more than a quarter for estate tax repeal, and 28 supported the final legislation.

The Ways and Means Committee's ranking Democrat, Charlie Rangel, had tried to slow the bill's momentum, but without real success. Some Washington insiders credit Rangel with prompting and publicizing the JCT's large upward revision of the cost of estate tax repeal, just as the Ways and Means Committee was poised to take up the issue in March 2001. But Rangel's victories, if any, were small. He was completely excluded from the final conference committee negotiations. In essence, Rangel and his House Democratic colleagues had no say whatsoever about the contents of the legislation—no one needed to include them, since passage was assured without any of their votes. They did not even delay the bill; one can hardly imagine the legislation moving through Congress any faster.

Moreover, House Democrats did not position themselves well for the next election. They lost seats in the 2002 midterm election, a time when the party out of the White House has virtually always gained congressional seats. Soon after that election, Nancy Pelosi of California replaced Dick Gephardt as leader of the House Democrats as Gephardt embarked on an unsuccessful run for the Democrat's nomination for president. Only time would tell whether that reshuffle would help.

Likewise, the Senate Democratic leadership emerged as losers, having tried and failed to muster their troops to oppose the president's plan. Tom Daschle received a temporary boost when Jim Jeffords defected from the GOP just as the final touches were being put on the 2001 tax act, but the legislation struck the party a serious blow. John Breaux, not Daschle, appeared to be leading the Senate's Democrats. The Democrats' ineffective opposition in the Senate raised already pressing questions about both the party's leadership and its direction. The party was unable to develop any coherent and popular policy alternatives to the president's agenda.

Kent Conrad of North Dakota, the Democratic ranking member of the Senate Budget Committee and a member of the Finance Committee, worked hard to defeat or change the legislation, but to no avail. In January he had told Alan Greenspan that his endorsement of tax cuts would "unleash the deficit dogs" and "throw fiscal responsibility out the window." He had led the Democratic forces against estate tax repeal and argued frequently and passionately that the tax cut's size threatened the nation's financial solidity. Along with Maine's Republican Senator Olympia Snowe and others, Conrad tried to tie any tax reduction to the government's actual financial condition. This group of senators worried that the large budget surpluses that the CBO was forecasting in 2001 would never materialize. So they tried to insert a "trigger" mechanism in the legislation that would bring the tax cuts enacted for future years into effect only if the surpluses actually occurred—an idea that Federal Reserve Chairman Alan Greenspan had suggested in testimony before the Senate and that Treasury Secretary Paul O'Neill had quietly supported. During Senate consideration of the tax bill, Indiana Democrat Evan Bayh offered an amendment supported by Conrad and Snowe, as well as many of the Democrats who ultimately voted for the bill, to delay implementation of the tax cuts unless specified reductions in the government's debt—funded by surpluses—actually occurred. The amendment lost 49 to 50, despite the support of five Republicans. Six Democrats, including Max Baucus and John Breaux, voted "no." Ironically, the Byrd Rule operated here to require a 60-vote majority to pass the amendment, so it failed by more than its one-vote defeat suggests.

The failure of the trigger idea, which she had strongly supported and worked hard for, took some of the gloss off Olympia Snowe's considerable success in making the tax bill's child credits refundable to moderate-income families who owe no income tax. She was also instrumental in increasing the size of these credits. In the process, Snowe struck a small blow against the forces for estate tax repeal. She insisted that she would not support any conference agreement that failed to devote as many dollars over the ten-year period to child credits as to repeal of the estate tax.

Expanding our survey outside the beltway, the states lost big. The bill's estate tax provisions took a direct hit at the states. Under prior law, due to an important political compromise reached in the 1920s, an individual subject to a state-imposed estate tax could subtract up to a certain amount of the state tax from their federal tax liability. Thus, when the home state levied an estate tax no larger than the federal credit, as 38 states did, state estate taxes didn't really cost taxpayers anything. The 2001 bill, however, promptly started lowering and then repealed the state credit in 2005—years before the repeal of the federal estate tax. Twenty-eight states, mostly in the south and west, which had linked their estate tax to the federal credit would have no estate tax by 2005; their revenues simply shrank. Four more states are expected to eliminate their estate taxes by 2010. In the remaining 18 states and the District of Columbia, estate taxes are being retained, and in some, such as New York, people will end up having to pay higher estate taxes in the early years of the tax bill's odd phase-in schedule (because they could no longer subtract state payments) than under the law before the 2001 act. In essence, federal lawmakers, looking for ways to make their own budget numbers work, had grabbed money from state coffers without asking.

The states had shot themselves in the foot by not protesting until too late. In 2001 the National Governors Association and the National Conference of State Legislatures had decided not to oppose either the repeal of the estate tax or the proportional phaseout of the state credit, despite the revenue loss it implied. Why the silence? For one thing, taking a position on federal tax policy is always hard for state governments and the organizations that represent them in Washington. It is difficult to expect governors from different political parties to forge a unified position concerning federal tax legislation. Republican governors and legislators also wanted to support the new Republican president. And when George Bush came into office, the states, like the federal government, were still enjoying budget surpluses from the economic boom of the 1990s. Many were in the process of enacting their own tax cuts and did not regard the loss of death tax revenue as significant. Finally, as a political reality, the states knew that there was no point in urging retention of the federal estate tax simply to preserve their own revenues. That argument would not fly. Throughout most of the debate over the 2001 tax cuts, therefore, state governors and legislators remained silent.

The House bill would have repealed the state credit in sync with the phaseout of the federal estate tax. Thus, if the federal tax was reduced by 10 percent in a given year, the state credit would also be reduced by 10 percent. When senators Chuck Grassley and Max Baucus announced their tax cut plan on May 15, however, they proposed repealing the state credit much more rapidly than the federal estate tax. In effect, they planned to deprive the states of revenues to help fit more federal tax cuts within the Senate's $1.35 trillion limit. Shortly after they made their announcement, Russ Sullivan, a Senate Finance Committee staffer, told members of the National Conference of State Legislators that the money being taken from the states—nearly $150 billion over the ten-year period—was necessary to get the revenue cost of the tax bill down from $1.5 to $1.35 trillion. He also observed that the previous silence of state groups had helped make this money grab politically palatable.

State politicians and their representatives in Washington then hit the roof. From May 15 until the conference committee report was finalized on May 26, they attempted to scale back repeal of the state credit and restore the House approach. Governors made calls to numerous members of Congress. Florida Governor Jeb Bush, the president's brother, called the White House. Jeb was direct: "While I support the eventual repeal of the estate tax, shifting the burden merely allows Washington to spend more, while requiring us to spend less." A total of 37 governors, including 21 Republicans, signed a letter requesting equal treatment between the states and the federal government for estate tax changes. In the Senate, Bob Graham of Florida, whose state stood to lose more than 2.5 percent of its total revenue, took up the states' cause. All to no avail. The final law reduced the state tax credit by 25 percent in 2002, 50 percent in 2003, and 75 percent in 2004, before eliminating it entirely in 2005. The JCT's Chief of Staff Lindy Paull, who had been in the room during the final four-man negotiations that produced the conference report, observed that the state "credit was originally phased out gradually, but when the conference needed money, it was easy money." She added, "The states weren't watching it very carefully."

In 2003, Governors Paul Patton of Kentucky and Dirk Kempthorne of Idaho, chairmen of the National Governors Association, again wrote to Chuck Grassley, Max Baucus, Bill Thomas, and Charlie Rangel urging them to "ensure equal treatment between states and the federal government with regard to the estate tax changes" of the 2001 act. "Not only have the federal changes imposed difficult conformity choices on states," they added, "but they have also infringed on the authority and flexibility of the states to respond to the needs and priorities of our citizens." Nothing changed.

By the time Patton and Kempthorne wrote their letter, most states, like the federal government itself, were confronting serious deficits. A few, including Florida, are prohibited by their constitutions from increasing their own estate taxes to make up the lost revenues. Others are reluctant to raise taxes, but by January 2004 more than a dozen had enacted laws to stem their tax losses. The states had expected to lose some revenue from the 2001 act, but they lost a good bit more than they had anticipated. And the nationwide uniformity brought about by the credit has disintegrated, creating new interstate variations requiring costly estate planning and perhaps prompting some wealthy people to move. The states' complacency was costly.

In surveying who won and who lost from the 2001 act, the members of the coalitions pushing estate tax repeal are the most difficult group to assess. The coalitions' leaders won the repeal for which they had fought so long. They declared victory. But the 2001 legislation repeals the tax only for the year 2010, after which time the entire legislation terminates. Some of the act's provisions will no doubt be extended—the expansion of child credits and marriage penalty relief, for example. But permanent estate tax repeal is far from a sure bet. President Bush and the coalitions urged Congress to make the 2001 repeal permanent, but by the end of 2004 Congress had failed to act.

The coalitions and the president could easily have obtained an immediate, large increase in the estate tax exemption and more rapid rate reductions had they abandoned their efforts for outright abolition of the tax. But neither would accept anything less than repeal, no matter how distant or tenuous. In sticking to that position, they chose to accept the risk that repeal will be postponed or reversed. This risk rose substantially as the federal budget surpluses predicted in 2001 failed to materialize. The budget has since fallen into large deficits.

The coalitions' leaders, however, insisted on repeal in some form, and their political clout was important to the White House's larger plans. Bush and his team understood that they needed the fervency of the pro-repeal movement to keep up the momentum for passing the entire 2001 tax cut legislation. In an interview with a Washington journalist in the summer of 2001, not long after the president had signed the legislation, Karl Rove described how he viewed the role of these pro-repeal organizations:

> You look at the outside groups and you start seeing auto dealers and NFIB and so forth and they get something out of the rate cuts, but what they are really worried about is how am I going to pass this on to my kids, so this [repeal] was the raison d'être. If we had done reform rather than repeal, the energy would have gone out of a lot of the groups.

Rove then showed the journalist a list of members of the Tax Relief Coalition and said:

> Look at that list and it's almost everybody. I mean grocery store people, the auto dealers, you name it. Small business guys are sitting there saying, "How do I give this to my kid without paying $50,000 in insurance premiums." You know, I had a small business. I had a huge insurance policy on me that would allow me if I die, in essence, to pay the tax.

The interviewer then pointed out that some of Bush's own legislative advisors were warning that repeal would cost the federal government hundreds of billions of dollars more than reform. Rove's response tends to confirm the criticism that former Secretary of the Treasury Paul O'Neill made in Ron Suskind's 2004 bestseller, *The Price of Loyalty,* that political calculations outweighed long-term policy considerations in the Bush White House. Rove said:

> That's right [it would cost hundred of billions more]. But this was not a big deal . . . I knew where the President was all along and he was rock

solid. I mean he, you know . . . it was like okay, great. His attitude was why are we going to ask these guys out there to take the heat and get only fifty or sixty percent of the advantage. If they are going to get heat for repealing the death tax, they are going to get virtually the same heat for quote "reforming" the death tax, but they are not going to get the benefit of having gotten it done. And they will have alienated their allies and you know . . . it was an easy thing.

It was easy for President Bush to hold steadfast for repeal because the coalitions held fast. And Congress never forced George Bush or the coalitions to compromise. The mystery is why it was so easy for the coalitions to stick to their insistence on total elimination, when most of their members would have benefited from a large and more secure increase of the exemption.

One answer comes from the philosophers in the coalitions. Grover Norquist and his fellow tax-cut zealots wanted repeal as matter of principle, not tax relief as a matter of fiscal policy. Nor were they particularly concerned with the particular plight of small businesses or farmers. Norquist is adamant that he "would not cross the street" for anything less than repeal. Phil Gramm described the basic tenet, as he sees it, to the *Washington Post* in May 2001. "The last form of bigotry acceptable in this country," he said, "is bigotry to the successful." Norquist elaborated this point with considerably more flair—as is his way—when he likened favoring the estate tax to "the morality of the Holocaust" in an interview with Terry Gross of NPR's *Fresh Air*:

> NORQUIST: I think it speaks very much to the health of the nation that 70-plus percent of Americans want to abolish the death tax, because they see it as fundamentally unjust. The argument that some who play at the politics of hate and envy and class division will say, "Yes, well, that's only 2 percent," or, as people get richer, 5 percent in the near future of Americans likely to have to pay that tax. I mean, that's the morality of the Holocaust. "Well, it's only a small percentage," you know. "I mean, it's not you, it's somebody else." And in this country, people who may not make earning a lot of money the centerpiece of their lives, they may have other things to focus on, they just say it's not just. If you've paid taxes on your income once, the government should leave you alone. Shouldn't come back and try and tax you again.

GROSS: Excuse me. Excuse me one second. Did you just . . . compare the estate tax with the Holocaust?

NORQUIST: No, the morality that says it's OK to do something to a group because they're a small percentage of the population is the morality that says that the Holocaust is OK because they didn't target everybody, just a small percentage . . . And arguing that it's OK to loot some group . . . or kill some group because it's them and because it's a small number, that has no place in a democratic society that treats people equally . . . when South Africa divided people by race, that was wrong. When East Germany divided them by income and class, that was wrong. East Germany was not an improvement over South Africa.

GROSS: So you see taxes as being the way they are there is now terrible discrimination against the wealthy comparable to the kind of discrimination of, say, the Holocaust?

NORQUIST: Well, what you pick—you can use different rhetoric or different points for different purposes, and I would argue that those who say, "Don't let this bother you . . . The government is only doing it to a small percentage of the population." That is very wrong. And it's immoral. They should treat everybody the same. They shouldn't be shooting anyone, and they shouldn't be taking half of anybody's income or wealth when they die.

Gross then took a break; when she returned to the air she changed the subject.

As Norquist's inflammatory rhetoric makes clear, for many inside-the-beltway conservative operatives, estate tax repeal had little to do with sound tax or fiscal policy. Like Denny Hastert in the House, the political strategists in the coalitions saw that their best bet lay in framing the estate tax debate in total isolation from any other aspect of government funding—such as who would make up the shortfall in revenue if and when the tax was eliminated. This allowed the discussion to hew toward the abstract moral questions and away from the real world implications of repeal. It also served as a simple, succinct battle cry to unite the coalition members.

In addition to the strategists, the extremely wealthy were ready to make a bet for repeal, even if it is temporary and does not happen until 2010. They recognize full well that Congress may change the law before then. But increasing the exemption to $5 million or even $10 million won't make a lot of difference in the tax bills of the very wealthy families financing Pat Soldano's efforts or for a billionaire such as Bob Johnson. Nor would an increased exemption and lower rates allay the concerns of those with hundreds of millions in assets, people like Frank Blethen. The wealthier you are, the more the repeal gamble looks like a bet worth taking.

On the other hand, this gamble gets a lot riskier as you move down the wealth scale to mere millionaires or families with $10 to $20 million of wealth—the small business owners who make up the bulk of the NFIB, Chamber of Commerce, and the other trade associations of the coalitions, including the great majority of farmers. The benefits from a large increase in the estate tax exemption and a rate reduction are large for these folks. The costs of postponing the exemption are great and the sunset of repeal is a risky proposition. And while everyone waits to find out what will eventually happen to the 2001 repeal, the uncertainty is costly. Life insurance premiums to fund potential estate tax liabilities must continue to be paid. Costly estate planning cannot be stopped.

A brief look at estate tax data illustrates how the benefits of reform, compared to repeal, would have affected farmers and small businesses. The number of farmers actually subject to the estate tax is quite small and would be tiny if the exemption were $5 million. Of the 52,000 taxable estate tax returns filed in the year 2000 (with an exemption of $650,000), only 2,765, or 5.3 percent, had any farm assets. If the exemption that year had been $5 million, only 254 decedents with farm assets, or 0.5 percent, would have been taxable. In 2001, that number would have been 175. The number of small business owners affected is larger, but is still low relative to the entire estate tax base. Taxable estate tax returns filed in 2001 that included small business assets were 11.9 percent of the total (6186 of 51,841). And again, the vast majority of these small business owners would be free of the tax altogether with a $5 million exemption. In that case, only 1,663 estates containing small business assets would have been subject to the tax.

Exempting farms and small businesses completely from the tax would cost only a small fraction of the revenues forgone from full repeal. In fact, the bulk of wealth that is actually taxed—nearly two-thirds—is liquid portfolio wealth: publicly traded stocks, bonds, and other liquid assets. The vast majority of estates have more than enough liquid wealth to pay the tax. Farms and small businesses dominated the political story, but they are only a small part of the financial reality.

Kitty Kelly might infer from this anomaly that the farmers and small businesses were stalking horses for the billionaires and hundred-millionaires who, with their massive portfolio wealth, pulled strings from behind the scenes. We lack the smoking gun that would prove her right, but the question remains, why did the coalitions not splinter? Some large portion of the small business owners and farmers who make up pro-repeal membership organizations should, by all logic, have split ranks with the super-rich to free their members from the estate tax's burden sooner—and with security.

Coalition members and others offer a variety of answers. Clearly the QFOBI experience—a promised exemption for small business that failed to fulfill the promise—soured many groups on anything short of repeal. Compounding this skepticism about the reality and stability of proposals to increase the exemption was the widespread distrust of the Democrats pushing the idea. No one in the coalition was prepared to believe that an offer of estate tax relief by Charlie Rangel or Tom Daschle was sincere. Here today, gone tomorrow was the fear. The coalitions' closest allies in Congress—Jennifer Dunn, Jon Kyl, and Phil Gramm, to name a few—bolstered this fear by insisting that the coalitions should settle for nothing less than repeal.

Grover Norquist, of course, agrees. "You shouldn't be double taxed when you die; [that's] principle," he says. "Well, taxes shouldn't be quite so high when you die; that's special pleading." "The American people," he adds, just so you get it, "like principled arguments; they do not like special pleading arguments."

Some members of the coalitions do not believe repeal will be further postponed. Nor do they buy the argument that Congress will allow it to sunset. As they put it, "The good news is that Congress has ten years to make repeal permanent." They fail to add that Congress also has as many years to postpone or eliminate repeal. They believe that their political prowess will keep this from happening. Dan Blankenburg, who insists he knew all along that the bill would sunset, claims that "it was important to get the principle of repeal on the books." The coalitions' leaders are confident that now that they have achieved repeal legislation, even of this limited sort, they can "always get an exemption deal."

As we saw earlier, however, the leaders of the Washington groups did not make extensive efforts to poll their members on the alternatives to repeal. In this regard, recall that Dan Blankenburg was not only the chair of the Family Business Estate Tax Coalition and one of the top lobbyists for

NFIB. He was also the legislative director of the White House–inspired Tax Relief Coalition, which had pledged to support the president's agenda. Given this level of interpenetration between the large pro-repeal membership groups and the Bush White House, it is worth wondering whether the leadership of these organizations at some point became sufficiently coopted that the interests of their individual members, most of whom would have been spared the tax by exemption, were not their first priority.

Alternatively, some argue that the coalitions did not waver in backing the bill because repeal was the only action they could all agree on. David Rehr, president of the National Beer Wholesalers Association, told Ways and Means Democrat Bob Matsui, "If you're serious and want to get on board, offer to raise the exemption to $50 million." Rehr recalls that Matsui raised his eyebrows at that figure, which stood no chance of making it into law. But Rehr meant it; he says, "$8 million is not a serious number." Winning repeal, any kind of repeal, was a victory; anything less, a defeat. The overwhelming fear was that if the coalitions split apart at all, they would get nothing. Not all the organization heads agreed with this judgment or the strategy, but they kept their mouths shut.

Ultimately, it is difficult to believe that the small business owners or the farmers were clearly informed about the costs and benefits of the alternatives. Their Washington representatives were committed to abolishing the death tax. As the revenue dollars available for repeal shrank dramatically between George Bush's proposal in early February and the final legislation at the end of May 2001, the only way to sustain the momentum for the tax bill was to put on blinders, ask few questions, and push for repeal. As David Rehr puts it, "At some point this issue became a crusade and that made a big difference. Anytime you can switch from your average work environment where people go to their coalition meetings, take notes, report back, etc., and you shift to where people are thinking to themselves in the shower every morning, 'What are the five things I can do today to kill the death tax,' then you've got real momentum and it's hard for the opposition to stop." The question is whether this tactic, insisting on repeal and nothing less, will hold going forward. What will happen as the small business owners and farmers come to understand just what they got—and what they failed to get?

Lessons Learned and Missed

Stories Trump Science

There once was a newly elected Republican living in the White House. After a wave of scandals at the end of the previous administration, the American people hoped that this president would restore propriety and honesty to the executive branch. He had an ambitious domestic agenda, including a reduction in income taxes, and he had several advantages as he set out to get his priorities enacted into law. For one thing, the Republicans controlled both houses of Congress. For another, the federal budget was enjoying large surpluses, making proposals to reduce federal tax revenues widely popular. In these propitious circumstances, the president set out to enact major tax cut legislation that he hoped would include not just reductions in federal income taxes, but also a repeal of the tax on inheritances, the federal estate tax.

This is not the story of the George W. Bush administration. The new president was Calvin Coolidge. Vice President Coolidge had taken over as chief executive in 1923 upon the death of Warren Harding, in the wake of the Teapot Dome oil scandal, in which a member of Harding's cabinet was revealed to have been taking bribes. Coolidge restored the nation's confidence, returned a sense of stability and optimism to the White House, and in 1924 was elected to a new term in the White House. And under his administration, the estate tax was nearly repealed.

But only nearly. Repeal failed. Ironically, the forces fighting to preserve the estate tax in the 1990s fell into many of the same traps as did those fighting to abolish it in the 1920s. Why was the issue understood so differently 80 years earlier?

The 1925–26 repeal effort was founded on a Progressive-era belief in the ever-increasing power of social sciences such as economics, sociology, and political science to inform the public and rationalize political decision-making. John Dewey, the philosophical architect of Progressivism, was famous for his view that a program of political reform rooted in the scientific outlook would spread throughout society as people became more rational and less susceptible to superstition and moralism. Dewey thought that this scientific diffusion would both result from and reinforce democracy. He even went so far as to identify democracy with mass adherence to the scientific method. Through ongoing engagement with the political process, citizens would increasingly approach politics as scientists approach experimentation; democratic choice would happily converge with "scientific" knowledge.

Unlike the effort that would culminate in the 2001 tax cuts, the earlier push for repeal originated inside Washington. It was led by Coolidge's Treasury Secretary, Andrew Mellon. Mellon was a model of integrity—and a very rich man. He had built a fortune in finance and business, having founded numerous companies, including Gulf Oil. He was 65 in 1921 when he resigned from 60 directorships of banks and corporations to take the Treasury post at President Harding's request. His longtime lawyer, Philander Knox, had urged the new president to give Mellon the job, saying his client "is one of the few cases where his wealth is an accurate measure of his ability." When Coolidge moved into the White House, he decided to keep Mellon in his post.

Andrew Mellon opposed the federal estate tax as a matter of principle. He also had much to gain personally from its repeal, as one of the nation's wealthiest men. Indeed, by 1925, even after four years on a relatively low Treasury salary, Mellon paid $1,882,600.25 to the Treasury in income taxes. He was the nation's fourth-highest taxpayer that year, trailing only John D. Rockefeller and Henry and Edsel Ford; by comparison, Henry Heinz, president of the Heinz Food Company, paid $191,374. Bill McKechnie, the manager of Mellon's hometown Pittsburgh Pirates baseball team, paid $17.80. Mellon's son Paul wasn't kidding when he entitled his autobiography *Reflections in a Silver Spoon.*

Self-interest aside, however, Calvin Coolidge and Andrew Mellon both regarded taxing inheritances as the proper province of the states, not the federal government. Thus, notwithstanding Mellon's objections to the tax in any form, the debate in the 1920s became about which level of government should impose it, rather than an attack on the morality of the tax itself. Some state governors wanted the federal government to keep collecting estate taxes but to increase the federal credit for state death taxes. The *New York Times,* by contrast, agreed with Coolidge and Mellon that Washington should have no part in the estate tax, noting that with a large state tax credit, the estate tax would produce "negligible" revenue for the federal government. "The Treasury does not need the estate tax," the *Times* concluded in a January 1926 editorial urging its repeal.

Mellon believed also that the estate tax destroys private capital. Coolidge agreed, contending that the tax decreased incentives for people to work hard and lessened national productivity. Coolidge and Mellon also rejected the social justifications for taxing inheritance advanced by the Progressives; they saw no problems with large fortunes passing intact from one generation to another.

In Congress, repeal's most important advocate was Reed Smoot, chairman of the Senate Finance Committee. Smoot was one of Calvin Coolidge's most trusted allies in the Senate. In 1926, facing a competitive campaign for reelection in Utah, he won a close race thanks in no small part to Coolidge's support (and that of the Mormon Church). A few years later he became famous—or infamous—for the Smoot-Hawley Tariff Act of 1930, which greatly increased taxes on goods imported into the United States. Smoot was philosophically opposed to the very idea of taxes upon income or wealth, preferring to use consumption as the national tax base. In 1921, he had unsuccessfully pushed for a national sales tax. And by 1926, when estate tax repeal came onto the legislative agenda, he was ready for the fight.

By the time the Senate Finance Committee took up repeal of the estate tax in January 1926, the House of Representatives had already passed its own bill that would cut taxes by $336 million, considerably more than the $250 million that Mellon and Coolidge had recommended. But estate tax repeal was not included in the House bill. Both the chairman of the Ways and Means Committee, William Green, a moderate Republican from Iowa, and its ranking Democrat, John Nance Garner of Texas, strongly opposed estate tax repeal. Green and Garner each faced strong constituent pressures to repeal the tax, but neither budged. Green was concerned that if the federal tax were repealed, the states would follow suit, and large, tax-free inheritances would result. He also linked estate tax repeal to an offsetting tax increase by demanding that revenues lost from estate tax repeal be made up by increased income taxes, a change that he rejected simply because he regarded the estate tax as much better than the income tax. Green argued that the estate tax was simpler, did not destroy business initiative or incentives, and simply burdened heirs who enjoyed their wealth but had done nothing to create it. Garner took a more moderate stance, wanting to reduce the estate tax but not repeal it.

Ultimately, with only three dissenting votes, the Ways and Means Committee halved the top estate tax rate (on estates greater than $10 million, or $100 million in 2004 dollars) from 40 to 20 percent. The committee also dramatically increased the credit for state death taxes from 25 to 80 percent of the federal take. Even this compromise went further than Green would have liked. In November 1925, the House passed the committee's bill.

Nearly two months later, on the eve of reporting its version of the 1926 tax legislation, the Senate Finance Committee was still embroiled in debate over what to do with the estate tax. Contrary to press reports predicting that the senators would adopt the House bill, Smoot's committee voted to repeal the estate tax. Smoot achieved this result by trading Republican support for lower income tax rates on middle-income people for Democratic votes for estate tax repeal. Sounds like 2001. So the cost of the bill continued climbing, reaching $362 million in the final Senate Finance Committee version.

Progressive senators attempted unsuccessfully to restore the estate tax when the debate moved to the Senate floor in late January. President Coolidge himself had sowed confusion about the solidity of his commitment to estate tax repeal by endorsing the House bill "in principle" in his 1926 State of the Union Address. On January 20, the *New York Times* reported the president's concerns that the Senate Finance Committee's bill might not be "prudent." Three days later, Coolidge recanted and reiterated his support for estate tax repeal, so long as the Treasury could still pay off the public debt without those revenues.

As always, the House and Senate conference committee met in secret and left no record of its debates. It was no secret, however, that the sticking point was repeal of the estate tax. Senator Smoot stuck firmly to his position favoring repeal; Representative Green was adamantly opposed. The leaders of the House and Senate tax-writing committees were at loggerheads. At one point the House conferees stormed out of the session. But the conference reached agreement on February 19, 1926. The final bill generally followed the House approach, cutting estate tax rates and increasing the state credit, but it also increased the exemption to $100,000 ($1 million in current dollars) and included some retroactive relief for 1925. The legislation reduced federal revenues by $381 million in 1926 and $343 million in 1927, due mostly to income tax cuts.

During the battle for repeal in 1925 and 1926, small business representatives, such as the U.S. Chamber of Commerce, supported repeal, as they would again in 2001. They were joined in this effort by the governors of 32 states. The American Farm Bureau, however, opposed repeal, emphasizing that taxes in America should be "levied in proportion to taxpaying ability" and arguing that no one tax alone could accomplish that mission. Farmers paid little in estate taxes, and the American Farm Bureau asserted that "to abandon this tax" would increase farmers' "relative tax burden."

The nation's two leading tax economists, who frequently disagreed over issues of tax policy, Thomas Sewall Adams of Yale University, who had long served as Treasury's top tax advisor, and Edwin A. Seligman of Columbia University, also favored retaining the federal estate tax. Adams said that "a large estate or inheritance represents to the typical beneficiary—in material part or degree—something akin to unearned wealth," adding, "I merely insist that if we must tax, it is better to tax him who merely receives than him who earns." Urging Congress to retain the estate tax and use its revenues to reduce income or other taxes, Seligman described Mellon's contention that an estate tax "destroys capital"—that it will "kill the goose that lays the golden eggs"—as "erroneous."

The 1926 legislation was widely regarded as a triumph of "scientific taxation." The *New York Times* heralded the law as reflecting "scientific methods of taxation, economically just and distributing the burden fairly upon the basis of ability to pay." W. M. Kiplinger, who a few years earlier had founded the nation's first personal finance magazine, described the 1926 act as "the most scientific tax law yet enacted." Indeed, it "was expected to be," given that the legislation was the "product of thousands of minds— the minds of corporation officers, of trade association heads, of bankers, of lawyers, of accountants." His description of their activities rings familiar. "They wrote sections of the bill, placed these drafts in the hands of the committees or their representatives in Congress, furnished these representatives with technical arguments for certain amendments, and organized support within Congress. No previous tax law has had the same high degree of study outside Congress as this one."

Viewing beltway politics as a laboratory of scientific endeavor seems quaintly naïve today, utterly deaf to the tones of political reality. In 1929, for example, Dewey maintained that it is primitive to think of crime as having moral causes. He thought that Americans would eventually get over this "prescientific" view of "evil," he said, just as surely as they had gotten over the once prevalent idea that diseases have moral causes. Dewey presumably would have been shocked at what Walter Berns described as the morality of anger in defending the revival of capital punishment in the late 1970s.

In politics, trying to replace morality with science is foolhardy. Michael Dukakis demonstrated this dramatically in his 1988 bid for the presidency. A defining moment occurred when Bernard Shaw, moderating a presidential debate, asked what Dukakis would want done with someone who raped his wife. Dukakis replied with a policy wonk's lecture on effective deterrence. This was widely acknowledged to be a major political blunder. It exemplified his disastrous insistence, in the face of George H. W. Bush's donning of Ronald Reagan's moralistic legacy, that "this election is about competence, not ideology." John Kerry made a similar claim, to the same effect, in 2004.

Like Kerry, Dukakis, and Dewey before them, the opponents of estate tax repeal failed to grasp that in politics, science is never enough. By expecting science to sway political opinion, the repeal opponents let the ball get away from them. While the Democrats snoozed, their opponents transformed one major tax policy—the levy on inheritances—from a radical fringe reform to an apparently populist demand to repeal an "immoral" tax.

Perhaps the single best example of modern-day "scientific" opposition to repeal is a weighty array of conference papers collected in *Rethinking Estate and Gift Taxation,* published by Brookings and edited by two economists, Bill Gale of Brookings and Joel Slemrod from the University of Michigan. Billed as a nonpartisan volume, the papers generally debunk the standard economic assertions of repeal advocates with sophisticated statistical treatments of a variety of issues, including the estate tax's impact on savings, inequality, and charitable giving. The editors' overview essay echoes the conclusions of Thomas Adams and Edwin Seligman from the 1920s in concluding that the "supposed negatives of the estate tax—its effects on savings, compliance costs, and small businesses—lack definitive supporting evidence and in some cases seem grossly overstated." At last look, this 515-page tome ranked 656,071 on Amazon's sales list. No member of Congress claims to have read it.

Publications from the more activist anti-repeal think tanks, such as the Center on Budget and Policy Priorities, weighed much less but were similarly premised on the conviction that giving people more accurate information would do the trick. Here are a few representative titles: "Estate Tax Cuts Would Benefit Wealthiest Americans: Targeted Changes Could Help Family Businesses and Farms"; "Eliminating the Estate Tax: A Costly Benefit for the Wealthiest Americans"; and "Estate Tax Repeal and the Top Income Tax Rate Cut: A State-by-State Look at Who Would Benefit." As we have detailed, think tanks favoring repeal produced plenty of economic analyses to the contrary, arguing that ending the estate tax would increase economic growth and benefit the entire nation.

The notion that the best defense is a statistically well-supported argument grounded in social science informed much of the 2001 political resistance to repeal. Unlike their predecessors in 1926, who also made moral arguments about the unfairness of inherited wealth and America not being a society based on pedigree, the opponents of repeal at century's end stuck to the facts. They explained patiently that most people would not pay the tax, that repeal would benefit only the richest 2 percent, that the estate tax was not really double taxation once you understand the step-up-in-basis rules, and so on. Like John Dewey, the groups working against repeal in the most recent battle assumed that if people could only be enlightened about the scientific realities, their hearts and minds would follow.

The trouble is that macroeconomic predictions about the effects of a policy change are notoriously controversial and suspect. In the political process, economic predictions today routinely serve to justify and even mask ideological contests. You tell us who is predicting the effects of a particular tax law change and we will know what they are going to say. Tax policy has become the domain of politics and ideology rather than hard facts and scientific proof. Jack Kemp in the 1990s, for example, was somehow able to overcome the vagueness of his Tax Reform Commission's recommendations for eliminating the income tax to make the bold claim that the proposal would double U.S. GDP from $6 to $12 trillion in a decade. But this statement was more an expression of an unwavering faith than a reflection of any consensus among economists.

In essence, anyone predicting the economic consequences of tax changes is claiming to know the unknown. This is not because there are no answers. Rather, it reflects the reality that the economy is so complex that you can find an economist to defend or impeach almost any claim about taxes. If tax cuts are sold as leading to economic growth, which then fails to materialize, there is always an alternative explanation: The cuts weren't big enough. The Federal Reserve raised interest rates, offsetting the benefits. Congress failed to cut spending. On the other side, it will be said that in the past, periods with tax increases or high tax rates were periods of substantial economic growth. Or that the real problem is the deficit, made worse by the tax cuts. Or that unemployment should be addressed more directly. In the absence of one definitive answer, answers proliferate. Proponents of a given change can always find economists ready to testify about the economic benefits that will result.

What was remarkable about the repeal campaign was that the forces arrayed against the estate tax managed to confound the one principle that comes closest to being a truth about taxation. To the extent that there is a consensus on tax policy, it holds that the central trade-off is between economic efficiency and equity. A progressive tax system based on people's ability to pay, such as the U.S. income tax or estate tax, necessarily sacrifices some economic efficiency. In the 1970s, the Brookings economist Arthur Okun described this phenomenon as a "leaky bucket"—when you tax capital income or wealth, or impose progressive rates to satisfy the public's insistence that taxes be fair, some of the economic growth that might otherwise occur leaks out of the system. The most notable modern-day effort to halt the leaks occurred in the United Kingdom in the 1980s, when Prime Minister Margaret Thatcher replaced local property taxes with a flat, per capita levy, euphemistically termed a "community charge." This change was extremely unpopular with the British people and proved a disastrous political mistake for Thatcher.

No one is calling for a poll tax in the United States today. The economists and politicians who want to lessen the leaks instead advocate eliminating taxes on wealth and investment income. These proposals would replace the income tax with a flat tax on consumption or wages and, of course, eliminate the estate tax. The rub, however, is that we do not know with any degree of confidence just how large the leaks from any of these taxes are. Economists and politicians on the right claim that, when we tax wealth or income from wealth, the leaks are very large; those on the left insist that they are quite small. It is not surprising, therefore, that in the estate tax debate, the Heritage Foundation, the Republican Joint Economic Committee of Congress, and other economists produced numerous studies claiming severe adverse economic consequences of the tax, while their opponents produced replies claiming that these studies were grossly overstated.

Equity and efficiency thus usually hang on opposite sides of the scales of tax justice. But beginning in the 1990s, those fighting to repeal the estate tax managed to capture both the fairness and economic benefit arguments. Some of their fairness arguments derived from questionable premises. For example, despite considerable evidence that much inherited wealth escapes income taxation, repealers claimed that the death tax created unfair "double taxation." But finding double taxation is child's play; double and even triple taxation are everywhere. Our salaries are taxed by the wage tax to finance Social Security, another wage tax to finance Medicare, by both state and federal income taxes, and again by sales taxes when we spend whatever is left. The right question is whether particular tax burdens are too high. The estate tax is the federal government's only tax on wealth. By 2001, it may have reached too many people and had top rates that were too high. But by focusing on its potential for "double" taxation, those favoring repeal created a claim of fundamental unfairness—a claim that pointed toward repeal rather than restructuring.

Beyond the double tax claim, the rhetoric of death—the endlessly repeated image of the tax collector and the undertaker hovering together around the death bed—helped. But what put death tax repeal over the top were the stories: Chester Thigpen and his tree farm, David Pankonin and his farm supply business, Tina Brown's premature and painful demise—an amalgamation of tear jerkers and model citizens who fulfilled the American Dream through their efforts and ingenuity. With these people and many others like them, the repealers had the fairness angle covered. They had gained the high moral ground.

Nor was the efficiency rationale difficult to muster: as we have seen, macroeconomic arguments about public policy often reflect creativity and ideology more than hard facts. This is especially true in the area of taxation, which is so little understood by most Americans. Senator Daniel Patrick Moynihan once described those who actually understood the Internal Revenue Code as a "clerisy," a highly specialized group with knowledge that, if it wasn't actually secret, it might as well be, given its complexity. Most people tend to agree with him. Most citizens would simply like to send the IRS a smaller check (or no check at all) every April. They may be able to recite a few broad liberal or conservative principles from political ads or newspaper coverage; but beyond that, Americans know and think little about tax policy.

In the face of malleable economic "facts" and a generally low level of information about tax policy among the American public, the pro-repeal forces found a lethal combination: alternative "scientific" studies combined with philosophical arguments about basic fairness, and compelling, real-life narratives. Those defending the estate tax countered with only dry economics and their "top 2 percent" refrain. Absent contrary moral arguments or compelling personal stories, their scientific rationality had little allure for the public or their representatives in Washington.

Nor do the repeal opponents seem to have learned from their failure. In 2003 the Center on Budget and Policy Priorities was still publishing "Permanent Repeal of the Estate Tax Would Be Costly, Yet Would Benefit Only a Few Very Large Estates," "Estate Tax Affects Very Few Family Businesses," and so on. The Republican-controlled Joint Economic Committee, by contrast, published a rejoinder that not only claimed significant economic benefits from repeal but also used the "American Dream" rhetoric with supporting stories of how the tax threatens small businesses. Congresswoman Rosa DeLauro—in charge of the political message for the House Democratic leadership—continues to explain the 2001 defeat by saying that they failed to get their message out. She does not seem to consider that they might have had an inadequate message.

But if rational argument is not the cornerstone of political decision-making, then what better explains the process? In this regard, contrast John Dewey's faith in the democratic power of "scientific" argument with the psychologist Jerome Bruner's account of how people think. Bruner contends that a narrative mode of comprehending reality runs alongside our rational scientific capacities and is never displaced by them. The narrative mode is relentlessly particular, concerned with people and their stories. It lacks the top-down character of scientific theorizing. It attracts people by stimulating their empathy. A narrative is something you relate to, rather than something you are persuaded by. A good narrative includes a moral with heroes and villains—especially when it is intended to move people to action. "A good story and a well-formed argument," Bruner insists, "are different natural kinds." This is why a compelling narrative so often trumps a well-supported argument. Winning political movements embrace compelling stories that people can relate to, that people can feel part of.

Successful political activists have always understood the power of compelling narratives. In constructing an effective political story you must make people associate your preferred course of action with their preexisting dispositions, their ideological commitments, and their view of how the world works. Lee Atwater famously demonstrated this skill in masterminding Ronald Reagan's stories about welfare queens shopping in Cadillacs and George H. W. Bush's notorious Willie Horton ads eight years later. The scientific opposition replied, "How many women on welfare go shopping in Cadillacs?" "What proportion of paroled inmates commit murder?" But to no avail. Atwater knew that once you are arguing the numbers, he has already won the most important battle.

Those working to repeal the estate tax acted on this understanding from the beginning. They knew that compelling stories revolve around captivating characters—both heroic figures who evoke empathy and villains who breed outrage. Repeal advocates portrayed themselves with care. Jim Martin, the wizened Ted Turner look-alike passing around his reusable Ben Franklin award, exudes the aura of someone selflessly fighting for a cause he believes in deeply and from which he, personally, stands to gain nothing. And Martin's 60 Plus Association works on behalf of an interest group that everyone hopes to join: the deserving elderly who simply want to sustain themselves in retirement and pass something on to their families. Harold Apolinsky, the "Southern Paul Revere," is another apparently selfless advocate—taking evident delight in championing a cause that he insists will put estate planners like himself out of business. Frank Blethen is a political liberal who has embarked on a quest to save small-town newspapers from being gobbled up by avaricious monsters such as Gannett and Knight-Ridder. Who would not call him a man with a noble cause? Bob Johnson of BET personifies the American Dream. He wants to repeal the estate tax, he claims, to keep wealth in the African American community. He is willing to risk ostracism from his politically correct Democratic friends for such an important cause.

The architects of repeal also picked poster-child characters who were merely rich rather than super-rich. Maybe they had read their history books. A century ago, Max Weber pointed out that the Protestant ethic helps underpin capitalism because it legitimates the accumulation of wealth by appealing to values that are widely endorsed in Protestant cultures: asceticism, thrift, and hard work. For Weber, Benjamin Franklin—the author of "a penny-saved-is-a-penny-earned," and the namesake for Jim Martin's award—epitomized the merger of capitalist economics and Protestant morality. Repeal advocates' stories invoked this powerful ethic. The statistical responses of their opponents simply did not gain any moral or political traction.

Small business owners, family farmers, first-generation entrepreneurs—the hard-working folks who comprise the grasstops in local communities—all seem to combine accessible success with virtue. The wan smile on Chester Thigpen's weathered face lends credence to his Everyman image; being African American ices the cake. The $400,000 estate tax bill that forced John Kearney to raid his son's college tuition fund to meet his small business's payroll drives this message home: people who pay the estate tax face pressures on the family budget that every middle-class family can understand. They do the right thing by their employees at great personal cost. Bill Beach's recycled family-farm horror stories describe disasters that would move anyone.

Even when the stories of truly wealthy people came to the fore, they were carefully humanized. Harold Apolinsky's angry account of how Alabama developer John Harbert had to deal with the estate tax's implications when given six months to live is one example. Pat Soldano's wrenching story of the Brown family's double dose of fatal cancer—compounded for years by heartless IRS estate tax auditors—is another. Death is the great leveler. Everyone knows they could be struck down tomorrow. By calling the tax the "death tax" and placing the undertaker and the tax collector side-by-side, the coalitions made the IRS look like the avaricious beneficiary of personal tragedy. Even the travails of the very wealthy took on a universal hue.

Contrast these figures with William Gates, Sr., the most visible opponent of repeal. Gates does not come across as inauthentic or insincere. Yet the father of the world's richest man, who in his retirement now spreads his son's largesse around the world, could scarcely be described as a sympathetic figure to whom ordinary Americans can relate. Repeal proponents had no difficulty labeling him a "limousine liberal," most obviously because he has no estate tax problem, and everyone knows it. His son already has the dough. Bill Gates's sidekick, Chuck Collins, is an earnest person, but he has no moving personal story. As a full-time activist for redistributive causes, he is not likely to appeal to anyone outside of the traditional political left. The other billionaires who took up the anti-repeal cause—Steven Rockefeller, George Soros, and Warren Buffett—may be household names, but their commitment was perfunctory. And they are, in any case, too elitist to garner much empathy from the public.

Surprisingly, the opponents of repeal never tried to shift the rhetoric away from the hard-working business owners and farmers to those who benefit most from inherited wealth—the rich children who are born on third base yet behave as though they have hit triples. Most have little or no interest in running their father's or mother's businesses. Had the anti-repeal forces wheeled out arresting examples of prodigal children, the American public might have responded. Andrew Carnegie, whom many considered a traitor to his class when he pushed for a death tax in 1889, contended that "of all the forms of taxation," a progressive tax on transfers at death "seems the wisest." He believed that at least 50 percent "of the millionaire's hoard" should go to finance government. Moreover, this self-made man thought that his fellow millionaires who wanted to leave "great fortunes to their children" did not recognize the dangerous implications of such inheritances. "If this is done from affection, is it not misguided affection?" he asked. "Observation," he said, "teaches that, generally speaking, it is not well for the children that they should be so burdened." He advocated only moderate inheritances; more was a "curse." The parent, he said, "who leaves his son enormous wealth generally deadens the talents and energies of the son, and tempts him to lead a less useful and less worthy life than he otherwise would."

What Andrew Carnegie observed a century ago is surely a timeless phenomenon. The late-twentieth-century opponents to estate tax repeal could easily have produced poster children of their own to accompany their reams of statistics. Yet, they failed to make the moral case Carnegie had advanced, let alone to embellish it with compelling contemporary characters—a serious mistake given what the other side was doing. Only real human stories showing the distasteful face of tax-free inheritance might have contested the stories making the human case for repeal. And only with some emotional persuasion could they have given the numbers and statistics a shot at scientific persuasion.

The anti-repealers need not have mimicked Lee Atwater by running ads featuring Patricia Hearst or Michael Skakel, asking why such criminals should get a tax break on wealth they never lifted a finger to earn. The slogan "Bush favors tax breaks for rich murderers" would have been too much.

Instead, the kind of people who feature in the HBO documentary "Born Rich" might have become symbols for the anti-repeal forces. For example, Luke Weil, the heir to the Autotote gaming fortune, has been described in the *Arizona Republic* as a "loathsome creature." He gloats about being so rich that Brown University would not throw him out even though he attended only eight "academic commitments" during his four years there, including both classes and exams. After receiving his Brown degree, Mr. Weil accepted employment with the investment firm Bear Stearns. Weil describes himself as a "precocious" drug user, who first tried LSD in the summer after sixth grade. He adds that he has racked up bar tabs worth thousands of dollars at a night club in the Hamptons. "These things happen," he explains. His take on marriage and romance? "The need for a prenup was drilled into my head since I was 5 years old," he says, adding that he would never marry an "ungrateful bitch," a "gold-digger" who refused to sign. Weil is clear about his attitude toward the little people. "If someone rubs you the wrong way, say a kid from some shitty little town in Connecticut, I can just say 'fuck you,' I'm from New York; I can buy your family, piss off."

Paris Hilton or Nicole Ritchie, heirs to the Hilton Hotel fortune and the pop icon Lionel Ritchie, respectively, might also have served the purpose. The *New York Times* called the two social belles "ditsy," "ignorant," and "pampered" when their series "The Simple Life" debuted on Fox television. Ms. Ritchie had been charged with heroin possession in California, and a pornographic tryst of Ms. Hilton and her former boyfriend had traversed the Internet, both while the heiresses' show was being filmed. In the first episode, Paris Hilton, Conrad Hilton's great-granddaughter, asks an Arkansas family, "What is Wal-Mart?" "Is it, like, where they sell wall stuff?" A reporter for the *New York Post* told Don Imus that she had never seen anyone "so rich, so dumb, so vacuous." Watching the debut show, she said, almost made her a "communist."

Jamie Johnson, who created and directed "Born Rich," is himself an heir to the Johnson & Johnson fortune, which his great-grandfather founded. The film begins with Johnson contemplating his upcoming twenty-first birthday party, which looks to be out of the Great Gatsby movie. That night he will "inherit more money than most people can spend or earn in a lifetime." Johnson wonders aloud whether his life can get any better. "We live in a country that everyone wants to believe is a meritocracy," he says. "We want to believe everyone earns what they have. I guess if it makes you feel better, keep telling yourself that." At the show's end, Jamie Johnson says that his great-grandfather accomplished the American Dream. "I live outside the American Dream," he says.

Think of the fun someone could have choreographing ads featuring such recipients of inherited wealth to put the repeal forces on the defensive. The point could have been made even more vividly had the anti-repealers proposed substituting a tax on inheritances for the estate tax. An inheritance tax is a tax on living heirs with its exemption level and rates determined by the amounts of bequests received. With an inheritance tax, it is easy to adjust the tax for family circumstances, for example, to delay the imposition of tax until a small business or farm is sold outside the family. Taxing people who receive bequests would put the burden on those who actually get the wealth and better align tax rates with ability to pay. Taxing recipients of wealth might also avoid the charge of "double" taxation leveled at the estate tax. And, as we have suggested, many of the people being taxed could far more easily be made to look like the Luke Weils and Paris Hiltons of this world than the David Pankonins and Chester Thigpens. Consider also the rhetorical advantage of a "windfall" tax over a "death" tax.

No one opposed to estate tax repeal ever tried any initiative of this kind, so we will never know what success they might have had. They at least could have given the anti-repeal side a competing narrative—one with quite a different moral. Ne'er-do-well recipients of inherited wealth are unsympathetic characters because they violate the very values of thrift and hard work invoked by repeal advocates. But all the issue-defining characters appeared in favor of repeal.

The lack of counter-stories and human dramas placed the Democratic leadership at a major strategic disadvantage. They had ceded the terrain on which the battle was to be fought—a concession that more often than not in politics determines the outcome. They were left trying to split enough groups from the repeal coalitions to displace repeal with a large estate tax reduction. An increase in the estate tax exemption to $4 million or even $5 million and halving the estate tax rates had come to define "victory." One problem with this effort to split the coalitions was that the repeal coalition members themselves had become part of the repeal story. They too had become righteous characters pursuing a noble quest. This bond held the Family Business Estate Tax Coalition and the Tax Relief Coalition together in the face of divisive forces. When we asked coalition members why the other side had been unable to split the farmers by excluding farms from the tax, or to entice some small business owners with a substantial increase in the exemption, they nearly always invoked their moral commitment to repeal.

To make matters worse, the anti-repeal forces actually helped the repeal movement claim the moral victory. The defenders of the estate tax sang a constant refrain, telling people "you won't pay this tax, only other people will, so it is in your interest to keep it." This self-interest chorus allowed the repeal coalitions to tell their members that their cause was righteous, not selfish. Ironically, this infusion of moral absolutism made it more difficult—once the legislative debate came down to a trade-off between postponed and sunsetted total repeal versus an immediate exemption increase and rate reduction—for the coalition members to converge on a compromise that might better have served the interests of most of their constituents. Splitting the difference about financial interests is one thing, compromising on moral issues another altogether. (Of course, it was also much easier to make the coalitions swallow a sunset clause because until at least March 2001, few in the rank-and-file of the repeal movement had the slightest inkling of a looming sunset clause. Many did not learn of it until after George Bush had signed the 2001 legislation. As things turned out, repeal forces could not have known how this episode might have ended.)

Repeal opponents were so far behind the curve that they did not advance any serious moral arguments in favor of an estate tax until two years after repeal had been enacted. Aside from a brief mention of moral issues in William Gates's February 2001 ad, they relied almost exclusively on appeals to statistics and self-interest. In their 2003 book *Wealth and our Commonwealth,* Gates and Collins began to offer arguments appealing to equality of opportunity. But they have yet to come up with any memorable stories that will grab anyone on a visceral level. People are not merely persuaded by stories; they identify with them. Only then do the stories' morals become compelling.

In addition to memorable characters and a moral, a good story also has a satisfying ending. We have described how those working for repeal first managed to get the issue onto the congressional agenda long before their opponents took the threat seriously, and then how they built momentum for its enactment. Gathering momentum was hard work. People from outside the beltway had to be motivated to meet with members of Congress, to participate in estate tax summits, to run ads and editorials supporting repeal, and to identify and contact wavering and vulnerable representatives at critical moments. Focusing on repeal rather than reform provided what, at the time at least, seemed like an unambiguous destination. From the standpoint of the repeal movement's motivating story, it supplied a clearly defined goal. Moreover, if repeal were ever abandoned as the goal, coalition members feared that they could not easily agree on a new one. For some, an increased exemption had the greatest appeal, for others lower rates. A team finds it easier to move downfield when they know their goal than when they stumble around guessing in the fog.

Pursing death tax repeal in a narrative rather than a scientific vein had the great advantage of short-circuiting complexity. Everyone knows that experts disagree on economic matters. No one is surprised when liberals and conservatives wheel out experts to present arguments and statistics to sustain their side's positions and to impeach their opponents. Today in the political arena we rarely see ideologically opposed economists agreeing about the facts as Thomas Adams and Edwin Seligman did in the 1920s. We all know how the liberal Paul Krugman or the conservative Milton Friedman will come out on an issue, however impressively each may argue his case. When there is science on both sides and it conflicts, all the math, to borrow George Bush's felicitous phrase, becomes "fuzzy."

Since the public is in no position to adjudicate disagreements among economists, it is a tall task to persuade people to support or oppose tax changes on the basis of a scientific argument. If economic debates are transformed into a storytelling endeavor, the target audience moves into a comfortable zone where the storyteller simply has to provide an issue they can relate to and values they embrace—not economic arguments they must struggle to understand. So Frank Luntz's instruction to candidates to avoid any reference to numbers when talking about taxes is right on the mark. People feel moved by the accounts of Chester Thigpen or John Kearney and outraged at the travails of Tina Brown's family, whatever the statistics. People trust their reactions to such stories, even if the stories are not representative or, as in the case of Chester Thigpen, actually misleading. And when, as here, the people telling the stories are people whom the legislators know well—their grasstops constituents—the storytellers unleash a powerful political force.

Not surprisingly, this version of the political process is not the political scientists' view of how legislation is enacted. After all, the scientific mode defines their enterprise. They are good at science; it shapes their reality. They "bewail the particularity," as Bruner puts it, of those who operate in the narrative mode. What is surprising, however, is how little the Democratic political leadership seems to understand the political power of storytelling so long after Ronald Reagan turned it into an art form. George W. Bush pushed his proposals with his "tax families" at his side. Democrats seem still to be living in John Dewey's fantasy world where science alone will move people to political action. As James Carville lamented to Tim Russert on "Meet the Press" shortly after the 2004 election, "[The Republicans] produce a narrative; we produce a litany."

Most Democrats we spoke to agreed that they were asleep at the switch with respect to the estate tax. But few seem to understand that their problems go well beyond mere inattention. Rather, the Democrats' failure goes to the very core of their approach to convincing the American public that they are right about two of the most fundamental questions in any system of government: how and why the country should tax its citizens.

Money, Money, Money

Repeal advocates had many advantages in 2001. They had changed the terms of the debate from self-interest to basic fairness. They had woven a compelling narrative, invoking the American Dream, to make their case. In the White House they had a committed president who, unlike Calvin Coolidge, never blinked in his commitment to repeal. On Capitol Hill they also had an effective advocate: the elegant and eloquent Jennifer Dunn, a soccer mom's soccer mom, a business woman's business woman. They enjoyed complete Republican control of the House of Representatives and had gained willing Democratic collaborators such as John Breaux and Max Baucus in the evenly divided Senate. They had marshaled the most powerful Washington lobbies—the NFIB and the other members of the Tax Relief Coalition—to their side, as well as grasstops constituents to plead their personal cases to legislators who were friends. They had the conservative tax-cutting philosophers such as Grover Norquist, Dick Armey, and Phil Gramm in their corner. Having been hard at work for nearly a decade, they were well organized and committed to their cause. And they had one last thing that their opponents lacked. They had money, money, money.

The most obvious link between money and repeal came from the ultrawealthy. They stood to gain the most from full repeal, and they got what they wanted. Pat Soldano's extremely rich supporters—the Gallo, Mars, Brown, and other fortunate families financing her estate tax lobbying work—saw legislation enacted with broad bipartisan support from which they and their ilk derived most of the benefits. Despite the complaints from the farmers and small businesses, multimillionaire and billionaire portfolio wealth forms the great bulk of taxable estates. The numbers tell it all: three members of the Mars family, for example, have $10.4 billion each in net worth; Ernest Gallo has $290 million, according to the 2003 *Forbes* list of the 400 wealthiest Americans. Others have even more; *Forbes* reports that five Waltons, four from Blanche Lincoln's Arkansas, have $20.5 billion each.

Moreover, in the contest between repeal and reform, the interests of the ultrarich, who stood to gain little from an increase of $5 million or even $10 million in the exemption, prevailed over those of the merely rich, for whom an extra few million dollars was the whole ball game. Of course, this talk of "prevailing" depends on the gamble that full repeal will become permanent. But taking the gamble looks better and better the richer you get: an increased exemption gets you little, whereas delayed repeal at least gives you a shot at something very substantial indeed. In that sense, money won, big money won big, bigger money won bigger, and the biggest money won the most.

And they certainly helped finance their victory. Big-money families bankrolled Soldano's Policy and Taxation Group, as well as her tireless efforts to put together the Family Business Estate Tax Coalition and keep it together—eyes focused on the prize of full repeal—down the stretch. They also paid for her DC lobbying: a week every month in Washington plus, no doubt, behind-the-scenes support for the coalition. They helped fund the work of the renowned lobbying firm Patton Boggs, paying $40,000 each year from 1997 to 2000 through Soldano's group. And then there were the other attorneys and lobbyists we met and were told about, who attended coalition meetings but would not reveal their clients' names. Though the ultrarich wanted very much to promote the cause, they were mindful that success depended on repeal's retaining its populist hue, so they stayed in the background. All this money from the ultrarich supporters was crucial to funding the repeal effort. Given the billions of dollars at stake for these wealthy families, this was a tiny investment that will pay an enormous dividend if repeal becomes permanent.

This said, the flow of cash did not affect the legislative result in the way that people who fret over money's role in politics usually complain of. Campaign contributions, soft money, spending limits for political candidates, and the like have become controversial issues, but they mattered relatively little in the estate tax fight. For one thing, no one we spoke to in the Bush administration, on the Hill, or among lobbyists, interest groups, or journalists thought that estate tax repeal had been a major issue for contributors. The most frequently repeated view was that campaign contributors are overrated when it comes to getting legislation passed. Washington insiders consider lobbying and interest groups far more important. Even when well-heeled contributors influence politicians' votes, their sway has more to do with milieu than with money.

About a hundred members of Congress are multimillionaires, people who move in wealthy circles. As one pollster commented, members of Congress may indeed be telling the truth when they return from fundraisers saying, "Everyone I talked to wants repeal." But they have a slanted perspective. Whom they talk to and what they hear greatly exaggerates the intensity of public opinion on the issue.

In some congressional districts, the mere presence of powerful constituents may shape a legislator's vote on a particular issue, rendering campaign contributions redundant. In Hawaii, Neil Abercrombie was acutely aware of the interests of the Campbell estate, and he supported a special provision in the repeal bill to give them more time to pay their estate taxes at a lower rate. Yet since 1993 they have given a mere $15,650 to his campaigns, a pittance during a decade of semiannual campaigns and a drop in the bucket for the Campbells. Arkansas has several large companies owned by wealthy families, including the Waltons, the Tysons, and the Stevens, all of whom are widely believed to have a massive influence on state politics. As one legislative aide remarked, "You need to take care of those constituents." When families have such large assets at stake, in 2001 "taking care" of them meant voting for repeal. Another Hill staffer was candid about these families' influence: "You can't run for the Senate in Arkansas if the Waltons oppose you, and for them the estate tax was non-negotiable." Finding a smoking gun linking Arkansas Senator Blanche Lincoln's support for repeal to particular wealthy families is, in the nature of the case, impossible. Yet insiders do not doubt that a link exists.

Money mattered more fundamentally in shifting the tectonic plates underlying American tax debates. This reconstruction of the politics of tax policy has been a long-term affair. With the 2001 legislation, the likes of Richard Mellon Scaife, Edwin Noble, Joseph Coors, and Charles Koch realized a significant return on their three decades of investments in activist, conservative think tanks. They have spawned teams of smart, energetic researcher-activists for whom the supply-side hostility to all taxes on capital is second nature. The activities of people like Bill Beach and his subordinates at Heritage supply legitimacy and ideological ammunition to the lobbyists and interest groups—such as the participants in Grover Norquist's Wednesday meetings—who work relentlessly, day in and day out, to keep up the tax-cutting pressure on the Hill.

In bringing the conservative tax-cutting agenda from the margins to the mainstream, the new think tanks have also transformed the limits of ac-

ceptable conduct. Researchers from Heritage routinely engage in more ex-
plicit political activism than any of the activities that got the American Enterprise Institute into so much trouble during Barry Goldwater's presidential campaign. Indeed, Heritage founder Paul Weyrich has proudly flaunted
his access to, and influence over, both George W. Bush's administration and
congressional Republicans. To inoculate themselves from any potential vulnerability due to accusations of partisanship, these activists have preempted
would-be critics by attacking the purported neutrality of the "policy wonk"
think tanks such as Brookings and the Urban Institute. With a wide margin for political maneuvers, Bill Beach's Working Group for Death Tax Repeal was intimately involved in virtually every aspect of the repeal campaign, for all practical purposes placing Heritage's considerable resources at
the repeal coalition's disposal.

It is unsurprising, then, that Heritage started receiving contributions
from Harold Apolinsky's American Family Business Institute as early as
1995. That year Apolinsky apparently raised $100,000 to fund Bill Beach,
an investment that bore fruit a year later when Beach's study, "The Case for
Repealing the Estate Tax," proved so influential in gaining early Republican support for repeal. About a quarter of this amount came from John
Harbert, the affluent Alabama developer who, given six months to live, had
been stunned to learn that his estate would be taxed at a 55 percent rate
that would devastate his business. In fact, Harbert and several other Apolinsky clients ultimately contributed much of the $250,000 that Heritage
spent on estate tax repeal from the mid-1990s through 1999. The balance
came from the foundation's own assets, augmented by Heritage's direct mail
fundraising campaigns that explicitly referred to the "death tax" in making
their pitch.

Impressive as the early activities of the conservative think tanks were,
they did not have a monopoly on "research" geared to supporting estate tax
repeal. Wealthy individuals were also giving money to other conservative
economists and to accounting firms in the mid- to late-1990s to fund research on the economic impact of the estate tax. Studies that produced the
right results were disseminated; those that were unhelpful were shelved.

Unable to match this funding, the far less affluent forces on the politi-
cal left were reduced to playing not very effective catch-up. Bob McIntyre's
Citizens for Tax Justice is essentially a one-man show, and Gary Bass's
OMB Watch is not much bigger. Even the most impressive liberal think

tank, Bob Greenstein's Center on Budget and Policy Priorities, has an operating budget that is less than a third of Heritage's. That Heritage could devote one full-time researcher and a half-time one to estate repeal in the critical late 1990s period, when the liberal think tanks were doing virtually nothing, underscores how important money is in shaping the terms of political debate. Democrats may finally be getting the message. In 2003 Bill Clinton's former chief-of-staff John Podesta started a Democratic alternative to Heritage, the Center for American Progress. Like Paul Weyrich and Edwin Feulner 30 years before him, Podesta seems to have grasped that unless substantial resources are devoted to developing, incubating, and marketing alternative winning ideas, the terrain that has been lost is not going be regained. But there is a lot of ground to make up.

Money and the wealthy families that possess it also made a difference in the repeal effort because of the unusual position in which many family-owned newspapers found themselves in relation to this particular tax controversy. Frank Blethen of the *Seattle Times* was certainly the newspaper owner who took the lead advocating repeal. But many smaller family-owned newspapers in local markets had large stakes in the outcome as well. Representatives of the Newspaper Association of America and others repeatedly assured us that the normal firewalls between editorial policy and news reporting remained in place on the estate tax controversy. But, despite their insistence, one would have to be gullible indeed to believe that the owner's interest in the outcome did not attenuate the press's watchdog role. The Newspaper Association of America and the National Newspaper Association routinely distributed information and materials favoring repeal to their member publishers. Even if the firewall was retained with respect to the editorial and reporting pages, it stretches credulity to believe that the editorial writing itself was not affected by financial interest. And newspaper owners are often in a much stronger position to influence their legislators than others with less powerful voices. Blethen's own website, for example, contains editorials from the *Seattle Times, Press Enterprise,* and the *San Jose Mercury News,* all voicing disapproval with the burden that the estate tax places on family-owned newspapers.

In addition, there were ads put together by Blethen himself—to be downloaded from his website and run for free in key constituencies—which he claims have run in more than 75 local newspapers. One ad asks people to contact their members of Congress and urge estate tax repeal because Americans, communities, experts, businesses, and voters all "say it's bad." The implicit financial commitment represented by this advertising space was surely substantial and unmatched on the other side. This is to say nothing of ads that appeared in *Roll Call* and *The Hill* prior to the 2001 vote, which were clearly aimed at members of Congress.

Money was also vital in replacing the eccentric collection of early repeal advocates—people such as Jim Martin and Harold Apolinsky—with a cohesive coalition of organized professionals who could be counted on to get the job done down the stretch. At first blush the coalition got by on remarkable little money, with the member associations paying $500 in annual dues to the Family Business Estate Tax Coalition, and the coalition spending only $40,000 annually. But this doesn't count whatever was spent directly by the coalition members on behalf of repeal. In any event, the coalition was ingenious at making its money go a long way. Its members took advantage of e-mail and the Internet to communicate and disseminate information. They were also skillful at convincing grasstops constituents in important districts to pay for their own trips to Washington to testify or meet with representatives—perhaps rewarding them with a photo-op with a high government official. When it really mattered, groups such as Jim Martin's 60 Plus would foot the bill to fly in someone like Chester Thigpen, the African American tree farmer from Mississippi, to give congressional committees personal testimony about the cruel oppression of the death tax.

The coalition also made effective use of existing infrastructures at the NFIB, NAM, the AFB, the National Cattlemen's Beef Association, and various chambers of commerce to lobby on their behalf, communicate with members, and publicize their cause. This coordination was made easier by the substantial overlap between the membership of the Family Business Estate Tax coalition and these other groups. Many trade associations, including, for example, the Food Marketing Institute and the National Beer Wholesalers Association, were also members of Americans Against Unfair Family Taxation. And in early 2001, groups like the NFIB, NAM, and the U.S. Chamber of Commerce also joined the Tax Relief Coalition to lobby for President Bush's entire tax package. All this activity and the sheer hours on the job represented a huge financial aid package to the repeal movement. But these were invisible expenditures that would never be aggregated into a simple lump sum like campaign contributions, and they would never show up in any budget or press release.

The various interconnected pro-repeal coalitions, composed primarily of associations of small businesses, each focused on different but related tasks. Small business was better suited to working House members; farmer groups such as the American Farm Bureau concentrated on senators. By almost all accounts, the coalitions were well run, highly coordinated, and maintained an excellent working relationship among all the groups involved. In all these ways the FBETC leaders made inventive use of the resources at their disposal—the type of resources not available to the other side.

And all along, the wealthy families like Pat Soldano's clients and contributors hovered in the background with their checkbooks. Just how much they contributed will surely never be known. Certainly these wealthy families funded a good deal of the polling and research on the repeal side—whether directly targeted research by lobbyists or more indirectly targeted work by academics, think tanks, and groups such as Luntz Research, Americans Against Unfair Family Taxation, McLaughlin and Associates, and the NFIB. Repeal advocates were exceedingly reluctant to discuss the funding sources that went into killing the estate tax, but someone certainly paid for it. The polling alone cost hundreds of thousands of dollars, if not millions. One poll on the other side by Greenberg Research cost OMB Watch $80,000. OMB Watch did not even conduct a focus group before the poll, as they normally would have, because they lacked sufficient resources.

Luntz and others were quite open about their links to Soldano, whose contracts were likely footing many of their bills. Her Center for the Study of Taxation commissioned, for example, Luntz's 2001 poll showing that a majority of gay and lesbian Americans supported a law that would repeal the tax and his 2003 poll revealing the declining importance of the "death tax" nomenclature. As another example, the 60 Plus Association sponsored a survey which suggested that a majority of the public considered the "death tax" unfair, conducted by "the polling company," an outfit run by Kellyanne Conway, whom the *National Journal* has called "one of Washington's most influential conservatives aged 40 or younger." Much of the additional polling on the repeal side was funded in similar ways.

In any event, there was a constant supply of money. Its availability was vital at critical junctures. No less important was the lack of equivalent spending on the other side. Harold Apolinsky was surprised that the repeal effort cost much less than he originally anticipated, but in political competition, expenditures are relative to what the opposition is shelling out.

Organized labor spent little or nothing. Neither did the philanthropic community. The life insurance industry spent a bit more, but never wholeheartedly joined the cause. The wealthy families and groups supporting the repeal movement may have spent small amounts measured against the billions of estate taxes at stake, but their contributions were massive compared to the paltry sums on the other side. They more than neutralized the competition.

The opposition to repeal simply didn't have the cash to mount a fight. One explanation for the success of estate tax repeal sees it simply as a story about concentrated benefits and diffuse costs. The small numbers of wealthy Americans who stood to benefit from the bulk of the $138 billion in estate tax savings by 2010 (and a further $700 billion during the subsequent decade if the repeal were extended) had immense amounts at stake. By contrast, the costs of making up this foregone revenue would be diffused so widely over more than 150 million taxpayers that the average voter would scarcely notice the difference—let alone connect any increased taxes to this repeal and change his vote because of it.

But this story is incomplete. No doubt public opinion on the estate tax reflected low levels of intensity in part because its repeal would have little noticeable impact on the overwhelming majority of those being polled. But not everyone faced diffuse costs from repeal. As we have noted, it would deliver large blows to two well-defined groups: the life insurance industry and the nonprofit sector. Major life insurance companies in the estate-planning business were looking at millions of dollars in lost revenues. And when the fight turned to making repeal permanent, the stakes rose even further: some of these might go out of business if repeal is not allowed to sunset. As for the nonprofits, estimates vary about how large an impact repeal will have on charitable giving, but the consensus, if not the unanimous verdict, is that the impact will be very large for many charities such as universities and hospitals. The people in charge of these institutions certainly fear repeal.

So why did the life insurance companies and nonprofits not do more to fight repeal? Both these groups have well-organized, well-funded, and well-connected lobbyists in Washington. Ordinarily they would swing into action when their members' interests were so manifestly threatened.

Once again, the trail leads us back to money. The life insurance industry certainly doesn't lack for cash. The Association of Advanced Life Un-

derwriting did manage to form the ASSETS coalition to lobby against repeal, spending about $2 million to hire former Republican Senator Alan
Simpson to lead the effort and for a public relations firm to craft its campaign. But this was the big exception. The insurance industry was unwill-
ing to spend anything like the resources necessary to mount a viable opposition to the repeal campaign. Many organizations such as the American
Council of Life Insurers repeatedly declined anti-repeal funding requests
from OMB Watch and Responsible Wealth.

Wealthy, largely Republican, executives with personal interests in repeal
controlled the purse strings. The insurance industry is about as Republican
as it is possible for an industry to be. Opposing this kind of tax cut just goes
against the grain for these people. Moreover, the executives of major insurance companies are typically multimillionaires themselves. They receive
seven-figure annual salaries, colossal retirement benefits, and golden para-
chutes to ease their fall if retirement comes earlier than planned. The chairmen of insurance companies that would be hardest hit by repeal—such as
Jon Boscia of Lincoln National Corporation (who earned $4 million in
2002) and David Stonecipher of Jefferson-Pilot Corporation ($3.2 million
in 2002)—had much to gain financially from repeal. Wouldn't these personal interests temper any impulse to fight repeal?

The nonprofit sector is less ideologically homogeneous than the insurance industry, but highly dependent on the good will of wealthy Americans. The major donors to and board members of the nonprofits with the
most at stake—museums, symphonies, universities, and hospitals—are
wealthy individuals who themselves would benefit from estate tax repeal.
As the contretemps at the Council on Foundations' 2001 estate tax "retreat"
revealed, nonprofits seek funds from a broad array of donors, many of
whom would not be enamored with an organization that took a stand
against repeal or was known to be working against it behind the scenes.
And, as we were told repeatedly, there are no secrets in Washington.

There was, of course, a handful of wealthy Americans—Bill Gates, Sr.,
George Soros, Steven Rockefeller, Warren Buffet, and others—who came
out against repeal. But compare *Forbes*'s listing of the nation's wealthiest
400 people in 2001 with the 123 names on Chuck Collins's anti-repeal
"Call to Preserve the Estate Tax" petition, which appeared in the *New York
Times* in February that year. Only nine names overlap. There are many exceedingly wealthy Americans out there that nonprofits need to avoid alien-

ating. As Congressman Neil Abercrombie said to us, "People keep saying that the estate tax is only paid by the top 2 percent. There are over a hundred million taxpayers in America. When you think about it, 2 percent of that is a lot of people."

Opponents of estate tax repeal, such as Gary Bass of OMB Watch and Chuck Collins of Responsible Wealth, complained repeatedly about their low budgets and fundraising nightmares. "The other side has endless resources, so we will always lose if we get into a war of ads," says Bass. "We have no money. I can't emphasize enough how little our resources are. We can't fly people in. It costs money to develop a website." Although William Gates and a few others paid for the "Much Ado about the Very Few" ad and made some donations to Brookings to study the impact of the tax on the federal budget and charitable giving, such contributions came way too late in the debate and paled by comparison with the money spent by pro-repeal forces. The billionaires may have signed the ad, but they didn't put their money where their mouth was. William Gates, George Soros, or Warren Buffett could have solved Bass's and Collins's fundraising troubles by cutting a single check. That they did not do so indicates that their support was rather tepid. A billionaire who wants to get rid of the estate tax to save his kids from writing a huge check to the IRS is likely to care a lot more about the issue, and spend a lot more on it, than a billionaire whose main concern is the potential damage of repeal to his favorite charitable organization.

Opponents of repeal have stepped up their efforts to solicit funds in recent years, but at the same time repeal advocates have been spending even more money to push to make repeal permanent. For example, Americans for Job Security, a Virginia-based interest group with an antitax agenda, spent an estimated $1 million in the 2002 election cycle, targeting moderate Democratic senators who opposed permanent repeal, including Tim Johnson in South Dakota, Jean Carnahan in Missouri (who lost that race), Tom Harkin in Iowa, and Blanche Lincoln in Arkansas. In Minnesota, the group attacked incumbent Senator Paul Wellstone in a series of ads so negative that they even prompted Republican challenger Norm Coleman to request that the group stop running them. One 60-second radio spot depicted an enraged couple confronting the prospect of paying the estate tax after inheriting a farm from one of their parents:

WIFE: Senator Wellstone just voted to keep the death tax.
HUSBAND: Paul Wellstone actually voted to tax people because they died?
WIFE: What's going to happen?
HUSBAND: We're going to have to sell the farm.
WIFE: No, Lloyd, we're going to call Paul Wellstone and tell him our folks paid their fair share. And to keep his money-grubbing hands off our farm.

Americans for Job Security did not stop there. In 2002, the group flew a plane over the Minnesota State Fair each day with a banner that read, "Wellstone . . . quit taxing the dead." Paul Wellstone himself died in a plane crash before the election.

Money in politics is always a hot topic—but nearly all the discussions focus on campaign contributions. In Washington, massive legislative energy went into opposing or supporting the ban on soft money contributions that was eventually imposed by the McCain-Feingold bill in 2002 and upheld by the Supreme Court in 2003. More dramatic proposals constantly emanate from the chattering classes inside and outside the academy. In his 2003 book *The Two Percent Solution,* Matthew Miller advocates the idea of "patriot dollars" proposed by law professors Bruce Ackerman and Ian Ayres—publicly funded contributions that individuals could give to candidates anonymously, along the lines of the secret ballot. He also lauds Jonathan Rauch's idea of public financing for candidates who agree not to accept private money, combined with instant disclosure of all private contributions. He contends that such reforms would create "a more democratic market of political ideas."

Maybe so. But our study of estate tax repeal makes us wonder about the impact of campaign finance reform on the laws that actually are enacted in Washington, D.C. Changing the campaign finance system would have had little effect on the story we have related here. Campaign contributions were not utterly irrelevant to the debate over the estate tax, to be sure. The Gallo family contributed over $1 million to political candidates of both parties in the decade leading up to the 2001 tax cuts. The National Federation of Independent Business, the leader of the repeal coalition, spent $2.8 million, and Americans for Fair Taxation contributed another $2 million to candidates in the 2000 election cycle. Contributors give for a reason, and they expect something in return. These groups care about other issues too, but estate tax repeal was widely broadcast as one of their top priorities.

But while the totals here are substantial, the contributions to individual campaigns are small when measured against the vast amounts needed to mount a successful bid for Congress. In the 2000 election cycle, the average winner in a House race spent just over $840,000; the average loser spent over $307,000; and the most expensive single campaign cost almost $7 million. In the Senate, the average winner spent over $7.2 million; the average loser spent over $3.8 million; and the most expensive campaign cost over $63 million.

A single campaign goes through this much cash, but the contributions from individuals and groups concerned about the estate tax were distributed among scores of politicians. Some of this giving is heavily lopsided: the NFIB, for example, gives almost all of its money to Republicans. But it has become routine for major corporations and political action committees to contribute to leading politicians of both parties, as well as to all influential politicians on committees where they have interests at stake. After the Enron scandal broke, one commentator wryly noted that Enron had "contributed to so many politicians that those who hadn't received any had a general suspicion of unimportance hanging over them." In 2002, it was reported that more than half of the House of Representatives and 91 senators had received Arthur Andersen cash since 1989. During the same period, 71 senators and 186 House members (43 percent) reported taking contributions from Enron. When the races are so costly and the largesse spread so far and wide, the amounts that repeal coalitions were willing to spend would usually add just drops to each individual campaign's bucket.

From this perspective it is perhaps less surprising that the Campbell estate's gift to Neil Abercrombie's 2000 campaign was tiny; that the Gallo family gave a mere $1,000 to Max Baucus, the ranking member of the Senate Finance Committee; or that Jennifer Dunn got $4,000 from the National Cattlemen's Beef Association, $9,000 from the Food Marketing Institute, $4,000 from the National Federation of Independent Business, and $6,000 from the National Beer Wholesaler's Association. Compare these contributions from coalition members to the more than $1.7 million she received for that election.

This diffusion of fairly small amounts over large numbers of candidates partly explains why, in interview after interview, lawmakers from both political parties insisted that their position on estate tax repeal did not have much to do with campaign contributions. According to the liberal Massachusetts Democrat Barney Frank, who opposed repeal, contributions were simply "not a big factor in the estate tax debate." Neil Abercrombie acknowledged getting money from groups who supported his position on repeal, but he insisted, "This issue was not brought up to me by contributors." Doug Lathrop, the legislative aide for Jennifer Dunn, insisted that she would have been fighting for repeal "whether or not she got a cent from anyone." They all believed that other factors, such as the involvement of the grasstops constituents, mattered more than campaign contributions. Many lobbyists echoed the view that campaign contributions might be important to getting politicians elected, but they are greatly overrated when it comes to getting legislation enacted, or halting it.

Thus, while money was an essential ingredient of the repeal movement's success, campaign contributions were a comparatively small part of this story. Money had its greatest impact on estate tax repeal by facilitating activities that lie at the core of what the First Amendment protects: research and publishing, political organizing, and the propagation and dissemination of opinion. The investments in conservative think tanks spanning more than three decades, the funding for research and polling, the relentless pressure from the mutually reinforcing patchwork of antitax coalitions and interest groups, the money spent by Soldano's families on her Center for the Study of Taxation and her tireless lobbying advocacy with wavering politicians, the newspaper editorials and advertising for which Frank Blethen was responsible—these ways for money to influence the political process would all still be there even if private campaign contributions were totally disallowed. And the Constitution will allow constraints on none of these activities.

Money also had less tangible indirect effects: the inescapable influence of wealthy constituents on politicians, the wealthy milieu in which so many of America's politicians travel, and the conflicts of financial interest that tempered the enthusiasm of those who might have fought hardest against repeal. It is often said that the antidote to one-sided speech in American politics is more speech to the contrary. But effective political speech often requires money. Because there was so little of it on the other side, the pro-repeal forces found themselves pushing against an open door to a degree that astonished even them. Unless this financial gap closes, and equivalently funded forces begin to emerge and sustain themselves, the power and effectiveness of the antitax movement in the United States is unlikely to wane any time soon. Controlling campaign finance will not stop money from working its way in Washington. Water flows around a rock.

Morals of the Mysteries

Our tale began with three mysteries: Why did such broad, diverse swaths of Congress and the voting public converge to oppose a tax that only a tiny slice of the wealthiest Americans actually pay? How did the organized repeal coalitions withstand the dual pressures from their own conflicting interests and the outside forces that sought to tear them asunder? Finally, why didn't the inclusion of death tax repeal in President Bush's already mammoth 2001 tax cut legislation spur more opposition—and why was the opposition that did materialize so stunningly ineffective? The preceding pages have unraveled the threads of these mysteries to reveal numerous political twists and turns, many oddities of personality and circumstance, effective leadership, the lack of it on the other side, and sheer good luck binding the seams of repeal. But repeal was not just a historical accident. Beneath the contingencies of fact and circumstance lie enduring morals about the power of principle—and perhaps also the dangers of compromise.

What moved the public to support repeal? Most frequently, the people we spoke with attributed the unexpected public support for repeal to misinformation and semantics. Many more Americans believe that they or their children will pay the estate tax than is actually the case. It could be a simple lack of understanding; it could be irrational exuberance about how much wealth they will accumulate. In any event, many Americans worry needlessly about the tax. We also often heard that the "death tax" language reinforces the misunderstanding. Everyone understands death. How many people know what is a taxable estate? The death tax label added moral momentum to the case for repeal, turning the taxman into a pimp for the grim reaper. We lost count of how frequently we were told what a brilliant stroke it was to rename the tax—not to mention the number of people who took credit for the idea.

But our exploration of public opinion revealed that support for repeal remains strong even when people learn the truth about who actually pays, and that the "death tax" label has had diminishing impact over time. The folk wisdom in Washington, which attributes the widespread support for repeal to the gap between belief, rhetoric, and reality, misses the real story.

In fact, it was the low intensity of public opinion about tax questions in general, and the estate tax in particular, that made the tax vulnerable to repeal. The pro-repeal forces recognized this and took brilliant advantage of it. They understood that tax debates are not won by giving the public more information. The trick is giving them the right kind of information from your point of view, shaping the lens through which they come to see the issue at hand. If you know that the estate tax generally ranks rather low among Americans' priorities, and, when it appears on their radar at all, it is the subject of misunderstanding and misapprehension, what do you do?

If you were a repeal advocate in the mid- to late-1990s, your smartest bet would be to elicit confirmations of the existing negativity in public opinion about the estate tax but also make the issue look more important than it actually was. And that is precisely what the repeal forces did: they ran dozens of polls that simply asked whether it is fair to tax people's estates when they die. The message was short and sweet; by portraying repeal as a stand-alone issue (to tax, or not to tax), the pollsters avoided the risk of provoking debates about issues that Americans care about more. Repeal advocates then widely publicized the negative responses, creating the picture of a populist groundswell of support for repeal.

Faced with these facts, the repeal opponents lost the opportunity to change the focus. They might have run comparable numbers of well-publicized polls that compared repeal to other choices about what to do with taxpayer dollars. If you were a smart anti-repeal pollster, how would you respond? You would arm yourself with public spending issues that people really care about, and show where estate tax repeal falls on the list of priorities. If Americans had considered that estate tax repeal might leave fewer dollars available for prescription drug benefits for the elderly, say— or for more broad-based tax cuts—the tepid opposition to the estate tax might have been revealed. And both the media and politicians in Washington would have perceived the stakes of repeal far differently. As it was, however, the silence from the anti-repeal forces was so deafening that even independent pollsters began to follow the pro-repeal tack. They, too, mostly polled the estate tax as a stand-alone issue. However unwittingly, they helped to reinforce the pro-repealers' lock on the running room of public opinion.

The "death tax" label succeeded for much the same reason as the pro-repeal polls. Both tactics shifted the debate away from the facts (since the misinformation played to the repealers' advantage anyway) and economic policy (since the public well knows that articulate experts can be lined up to argue any side of a tax policy issue, any day of the week). Instead, the talk of "death" and stand-alone repeal focused the lens on a more general morality. Frank Luntz shows a profound grasp of how to take advantage of people's cognitive limitations when he advises candidates never to mention numbers when discussing tax issues, but instead to present them as moral questions. Most people have no idea how to resolve complex fiscal policy debates. But having an opinion on a moral question, where experts are not thought to exist in a democracy, is another matter altogether. And while the repeal forces made a moral case on one side, their opponents left it unanswered. They argued about the math of who pays and how much, without joining the fight over questions of morality, fairness, and democratic values.

Clever tactical use of lenses also informed the ways in which the pro-repeal forces hitched their moral argument to the American ethic of hard work and thrift. Because the estate tax can be viewed as affecting two different taxpayers—the donor of accumulated wealth and the recipient of inherited wealth—its democratic implications can be portrayed in two very different ways. The pro-repeal forces understood that when the focus is kept on the donor (and on the working rich rather than billionaires), the estate tax seems like an immoral levy. Hence the endlessly recycled claims that the tax penalizes work, that it amounts to double taxation, and that it rewards those who waste money rather than save it. The family farmers, the small business owners, the Chester Thigpens, all embody the work ethic. They exemplify American virtue. The argument for repeal became an argument about how these virtuous Americans were being unjustly penalized by the death tax.

On the other hand, if the focus were to shift to the heirs who acquire their wealth through a lucky twist of genetic fate, estate tax repeal begins to seem much more consistent with aristocracy than democracy. As we have suggested, the opposition might have fought the repealers on their own terms by proposing that a tax on inheritances be substituted for the estate tax and then asking the public whether they really wanted to give the Paris Hiltons and Luke Weils a tax break. If they had shifted the focus to the recipients of vast fortunes and the windfalls they get without lifting a finger, then a tension between the repealers' arguments and the work ethic would have become manifest. The moral argument would have been joined, and the anti-repealers would have forced a debate about equality of opportunity and the American dream. This was the debate that took place in 1926, and it was followed by 75 years of taxing estates. Instead, however, repeal opponents disputed the facts. They shouted into the wind about numbers and argued about how representative the Chester Thigpens actually were. In so doing, they ceded the moral terrain to the repealers.

Still, though, the emergence of so much unanticipated Democratic support for repeal on Capitol Hill remains a nagging mystery. In a democracy such as ours, where vast inequalities of income and wealth coexist with universal suffrage, shouldn't the poor be able to soak the rich? James Madison famously warned that "there is, perhaps, no legislative act in which greater opportunity and temptation are given to a predominant party to trample on the rules of justice. Every shilling which they overburden the inferior number is a shilling saved to their own pockets." Couldn't Democratic legislators have found a sure vote-winner by rallying their constituents against what they could portray as an aristocratic tax break?

But politicians' incentives do not derive so directly from the electoral map. Politicians are subject to many pressures other than public opinion, and if mass preferences are not intense on a particular subject, a canny legislator will often do better to respond to organized interest groups, lobbyists, grasstops constituents, and coalitions, whose members have intense preferences and the wherewithal to help or hinder a political career. In many of our interviews we heard a recurring refrain that no one in Congress was ever in danger of losing a seat for supporting repeal. But the same was not true about opposing it. In many congressional districts and states, politicians had good reasons to please key individuals, families, owners of small businesses, and other groups favoring repeal; indeed, many risked punishing retribution if they fought against repeal.

In addition, Democrats also face a far different electoral base from the dated picture that many commentators hold. The Democratic constituency is increasingly professional, rather than blue collar. In fact, since 1994, the average per capita income has actually been higher in Democratic congressional districts than in Republican ones. This fact is starkly at odds with the conventional view of the typical Democratic constituency as a cross between a city slum and an Appalachian hollow. The grasstops in Democratic constituencies are wealthy. The party's financial base includes Hollywood celebrities and successful trial lawyers, not to mention the inhabitants of luxurious Malibu estates. Why would anyone expect the politicians whose careers depend on these voters to go to the wall to keep the estate tax? Party leaders might be committed to the tax for a mixture of policy, ideological, and historical reasons, but no one should expect them to feel much heat from their constituents in support of estate taxes.

On the Senate side, self-interest and the milieu in which senators travel also played a role. In the summer of 2004, the *New York Times* identified four Democratic senators whom John Kerry was reportedly considering to be his vice presidential running mate. Like Senator Kerry himself, all four were millionaires, with the poorest, Bill Nelson of Florida, said to have a net worth between $1.8 and $7 million. On both sides of the aisle, the Senate is a club of millionaires who fully understand and feel the potential burdens of the estate tax.

The conventional picture of politicians as mere transmission belts for aggregating public opinion into legislation also misses the vital importance of political entrepreneurship in getting things done on Capitol Hill. It takes work and skill to get enough cosponsors to make the House leadership put a piece of legislation into its top ten priorities—a step that enhances a measure's chances of becoming law. Christopher Cox could not move his repeal bill past this threshold, but Jennifer Dunn did. She convinced Dick Armey, Tom DeLay, and the rest of the Republican House leadership that she could bring along enough Democrats from both Ways and Means and the backbenches (including liberals such as Neil Abercrombie and members of the Congressional Black Caucus such as Albert Wynn) to give repeal a good chance of surviving a conference committee with the more liberal Senate.

When repeal did make it to the Senate, the years of relentless commitment from Senator Jon Kyl dating back to the mid-1990s, and the links he had forged with others, were essential ingredients for success. So, too, was the commitment from the Bush White House and the work of its Tax Relief Coalition. These institutional forces were far more consequential than public opinion, which gave repeal proponents all the running room they needed.

The second mystery, concerning how the repeal coalition held together in the face of so many centrifugal pressures, also deepened as we learned more of the story. Democrats produced a constant stream of offers to lure wavering groups: repealers could have won exemptions for farmers, special treatment for family-owned businesses, lower tax rates, and an increase in the tax threshold that would have immunized the overwhelming majority of coalition members from the estate tax entirely. Many of these proposals would have taken effect right away without the uncertainties that the slow phase-in sunset clause has given repeal.

While fending off the Democratic offers, the coalition had to reconcile the natural conflicts of interest among its wealthier and less wealthy members. In the heat of legislative battle on Capitol Hill, repeal was traded off against a change in the income tax rules that took away the ability to pass wealth free of capital gains taxes. This change was particularly galling to farmers, family-owned newspapers, small supermarket chains, and other small businesses that have highly appreciated assets and little cash. By contrast, this trade—and foregoing targeted exceptions and an increased threshold for the tax—was much more palatable to the wealthiest supporters of repeal, who had the most to gain from gambling on the whole enchilada. And some of the coalition members and their advisers remembered that in the 1970s a similar carryover basis provision was enacted but was repealed before it took effect (on the ground that it was too complex). Nevertheless, it is no surprise that some of the most tense coalition meetings involved finding ways to keep the lower ranks on board for total repeal despite the costly trade-offs.

Ironically, as we have shown, it was precisely the merely rich—the small business owners, farmers, and grasstops constituents—who did most of the work for repeal. Ultimately, they would see little or no immediate benefits from the 2001 law, and they may well have done much better under the

Democrats' proposals. Certainly in the short term, the reform alternatives were a much better deal for them than what was eventually achieved. The 2001 legislation has repeal phasing in slowly, while state estate tax credits are lost early on—a double downer that for some actually pushed total estate tax rates higher before they started to go down. Moreover, all the chips are wagered on new legislation to extend the repeal beyond 2010. Given the uncertainties about repeal's timing and permanence, the "victorious" coalition members must continue to spend money on estate-planning life insurance. And on fighting the repeal battle. The whole wager looks worse in retrospect as the government's financial condition has deteriorated since the 2001 act was signed.

Social scientists have long known of the inherent instability of political coalitions based on nothing more than shared economic interests. To take the simplest case, think of three people voting on how to divide a dollar. Whatever the initial vote, there is always a potential majority for change. This at least partially explains why tax policy changes so frequently, why new tax legislation is enacted almost every year. When we look at groups like the Family Business Estate Tax Coalition, what needs explanation is not only why it stayed together, but why it stayed together in pursuit of an objective that was less than optimal for most of its members.

So why did the repeal strategy triumph? For one thing, ever since the Republican takeover of the House in 1994, the Democrats' power to deliver on their various compromise proposals has been far from certain. The majority Republican leadership has vice-like control of the legislative agenda in the House, and, in a closely divided Senate, any specific estate tax reforms tailored to win over repealers' hearts were vulnerable to individual senators' freelancing. Had the Clinton White House thrown its weight behind a compromise that substantially increased the exemption at any time before the 2000 election, moderate Republicans and conservative Democrats might have pushed it through—as they did with welfare reform in 1996. But, other than its support for the failed QFOBI legislation, Clinton's administration showed no interest in estate tax reform. After President Bush took office in January 2001, he and his Tax Relief Coalition took over the management of the tax cut on Capitol Hill. By the time that repeal's sunset became clear, later in the spring, family farms and small business interests were in no position to dictate terms to the administration or Capitol Hill.

The path of exemptions and exceptions also seemed much less attractive after the debacle of QFOBI—the estate tax relief measure that provided so little real relief. This legislation had convinced many coalition members that incrementalism was likely a dead end. The lesson they took from QFOBI was the importance of maintaining a unified front for repeal. As the coalition discussed and debated potential exceptions and exemptions, they saw that if they abandoned their commitment to full repeal, they would likely not find common ground for any alternative. Splintering would be inevitable.

Leadership was also part of the answer. The repeal pioneers' passionate commitment in the early years created a unified sense of mission that sustained the coalitions down the stretch. To the end, Dirk Van Dongen and the rest of the leadership of the Tax Relief Coalition never wavered. The effective leadership on the Hill from Congresswoman Dunn and Senator Kyl was as important to repeal's success as it was unmatched by opposing leadership on the Democratic side. Consistently out-thought and out-maneuvered, Democratic leaders were a dollar short and a day late.

And, as we have emphasized, resources were also vital. Pat Soldano's wealthy families and others ensured that the coalitions had whatever they needed to do their work, and the other side packed no countervailing economic or organizational punch. The insurance industry, the nonprofits, and organized labor all had their reasons for keeping out of the fray, but their abstention deprived the opposition of any well-funded interest groups who might have hived off potential dissenters within the coalition.

Ultimately, however, the mysterious survival of this coalition turns on the same force as the mysterious public and congressional support for the cause: the moral arguments for repeal. From the early work of Harold Apolinsky and Jim Martin, through Frank Blethen's efforts at the *Seattle Times* and the formation and growth of the Family Business Estate Tax Coalition, the key players considered themselves on a mission to abolish an injustice. Political activists like these are seldom motivated solely by their economic interests. If they were, they would rarely judge it worth their while to participate in politics at all. Rather, a huge part of the coalition members' motivation was their sense that the estate tax is an immoral tax, an unfair tax. They saw themselves as contributing to the public good by getting rid of it. This righteous sense of purpose got them to go to meetings, to work the phones, to line up grasstops constituents, and to do all the other things that made the coalition so effective.

This raises the question, did the coalition actually win in 2001? If you oppose a tax on the grounds that it is wrong and should not exist at all, a sunset clause that might bring the tax back in the future must seem profoundly unsatisfying. However, as many of the moral crusaders told us, any of the compromises that might have secured permanent legislation were simply unacceptable. A moral argument that a tax is wrong does not permit distinctions among farmers, small businesses, and large businesses. Nor do they think it justifies special treatment to people who have less than three, or even five, million dollars. The same moral commitments that held the group together made it difficult for them to compromise. Indeed, even after the 2001 bill—sunset and all—became law, coalition members were still resisting Democratic overtures to compromise with an increased exemption and lower rates. Why? They regarded it as morally indefensible.

Our third mystery concerns the weakness and ineptitude of the opposition to death tax repeal, both on and off Capitol Hill. Our inspection has revealed the lack of interest group opposition to be less perplexing than is often supposed. Groups on the traditional left such as organized labor, who might once have been counted on to resist inroads into America's system of progressive taxation, are fighting for their very survival. For them, spending time and resources defending the estate tax is an unwelcome distraction. The liberal think tanks and activist groups are massively outgunned: as of yet, there is simply no liberal match for groups such as the Heritage Foundation and Grover Norquist's Americans for Tax Reform. And when the liberal groups did speak up against repeal, they failed to respond to the moral case that their opponents had fashioned, and that Heritage and CATO, in particular, had articulated and disseminated so well.

Conventional analysis would attribute the lack of opposition simply to the mismatched benefits and burdens of estate tax repeal. The big beneficiaries, Pat Soldano's clients and their ilk, are small in number but they have a great deal at stake. It is therefore worth their while to commit time and money to the fight. The costs of repeal, on the other hand, are widely dispersed. Even hundreds of billions of dollars in lost revenues each decade will not appreciably increase the burden for any individual taxpayer—particularly when that revenue is not earmarked for specific spending anyway, and repeal is not linked to any offsetting tax increases or correspond-ing cut in benefits or services. This imbalance is one reason why liberal Democrats on the Hill find it so difficult to mobilize groups like organized labor around tax questions.

By the late 1990s repeal forces had gained so much momentum that it was too late for the opponents to counter by dedicating estate tax revenues to funding a specific popular expenditure, such as Medicare or Social Se-curity. Taxes earmarked for particular spending programs are always more popular than those that simply fund general government expenditures. By dedicating these tax revenues to specific spending, the opposition might have pointed to those people whose benefits would have been lost from re-peal. But once repealers had mustered a majority of the House in favor of eliminating the tax altogether, this strategy was foreclosed.

Nevertheless, the conventional story is only partly accurate. In fact, as we have discussed, powerful organized lobbies stand to lose significantly from repeal—particularly in the insurance industry and among philan-thropic institutions. But these groups got started too late and, stymied by the mixed incentives of wealthy executives and charitable boards and donors, they failed to develop convincing arguments for retaining the tax. Rallying people against a moral argument requires a serious moral counterargument. No one believes that the purpose of the estate tax is to promote philanthropy. And the insurance industry's convoluted and dis-ingenuous arguments about retaining the tax to ensure predictability underscored that their real motivation—to keep selling estate-planning life insurance—was unspeakable.

As for Capitol Hill, much of our story about the lack of effective op-position from the Democratic leadership centered on blunders and missed opportunities: a failure to see the repeal movement's forward march until it was too late and an inability to deflect their opponents and compete for public opinion. But there were larger forces at work here as well, forces that go back to the formation of the Democratic Leadership Council (DLC) fol-lowing Walter Mondale's devastating 49-state loss to Ronald Reagan in 1984—forces that may over time portend even greater difficulties for pro-gressive taxation in America.

A coalition of southern Democrats and northern neoliberals formed the DLC in an effort to forestall electoral oblivion by refocusing the party away from traditional stalwart constituencies among labor, minorities, and anti-establishment progressives and toward Reagan Democrats and other swing voters. Accordingly, DLC New Democrats such as Gary Hart, Paul Tsongas, and Michael Dukakis sought to steal the Republicans' thunder by advocating fiscal conservatism and anticommunism. The hope was that a Republican-lite agenda would make inroads into what Kevin Phillips had identified in 1969 as the emerging Republican majority, which by the mid-1980s had officially emerged. They knew that the left wing of the Democratic electoral base had nowhere else to go.

Arkansas Governor Bill Clinton became DLC chair in 1990 on his way to the presidency. Clinton is often credited with transforming the DLC tactical impulse into an electoral strategy. "Triangulation" is the label associated with his approach; as his Labor Secretary Robert Reich defines it, "finding positions equidistant between the Democrat and Republican." The tactic of proposing a large part of what opponents advocate is intended to eat into their support while holding onto your own political base. Clinton's 1996 welfare reform is frequently cited as a classic of this genre, though his policies on a multitude of issues were cut from the same cloth. Bill Clinton might have turned triangulation into an art form, but this technique is not the sole province of the Democrats. George W. Bush's efforts prior to the 2004 election to enact a prescription drug benefit in Medicare costing hundreds of billions of dollars—the kind of spending Republicans had long lamented—offers a prime instance on the Republican side. During the 2001 tax legislation, Max Baucus, with his own reelection in mind, and John Breaux were the Democrats' principal triangulators.

Compromise to move toward your own goals, your long-term commitments, is one thing; but abandoning principle in the interest of winning is something else altogether. This is why there is a world of difference between triangulation and Grover Norquist's calculating pragmatism. Norquist never considers compromises that threaten his strategic goals. Triangulation may be an effective tactic in isolation, but it becomes a disastrous long-term strategy whenever it is manifestly opportunistic—devoid of any clear moral purpose. Indeed, pursued for its own sake, triangulation undermines your strategic objectives if it does not displace them entirely. Once your opponents understand your game, they can drag you along toward their goal simply by moving the posts. Newt Gingrich understood this well, and that was how he managed to shift the terrain of American politics so decisively to the right after the Republican takeover in 1994.

Robert Reich puts the difficulty for the Democrats this way: "The so-called center has continued to shift to the right because conservative Republicans stay put while Democrats keep meeting them halfway." Garry Wills is even more harsh in his assessment of Bill Clinton's legacy:

The legacy should include partial responsibility for the disabling of the Democratic Party. There were things to be said against the Democratic Leadership Council and the "triangulation" scheme of Dick Morris, by which Clinton would take positions to the right of most congressional Democrats and to the left of the Republican Party. But Clinton, as a Southerner, knew that the party had to expand its base back into sources of support eroded by the New Right. This was a defensible (in fact a shrewd) strategy as Clinton originally shaped it. He could have made it a tactical adjunct to important strategic goals. But after the scandals, all his maneuvering looked desperate—a swerving away from blows, a flurried scrambling to find solid footing. His very success made Democrats think their only path to success was to concede, cajole, and pander. . . . Clinton bequeathed to his party not a clear call to high goals but an omnidirectional proneness to pusillanimity and collapse.

Nowhere have the strategic consequences of triangulation become more starkly evident than with the Bush tax cuts. George W. Bush came into office in January 2001 with less electoral legitimacy or political mandate than any president in modern history. Yet he was able to produce history's largest tax cut in record time. Democratic leaders such as Tom Daschle raised the white flag early on in 2001 by making it clear that they would count it a victory if the reductions could be held to $900 billion over ten years (which did not happen). Ralph Nader had a point when he argued in 2003 that "so right-wing is the DLC, mounted imperiously on [the Democrats'] sagging party, that even opposing Bush's tax cuts for the wealthy . . . is considered ultraliberal and contrary to winning campaigns." In less than a decade, the Democratic leadership's position on the estate tax had become almost unrecognizable: the same people who had previously advocated lowering the exemption to $200,000 in order to fund Medicare enhancements were now endorsing an increase in that tax threshold to as much as $5 million to forestall outright repeal.

The death tax repeal forces did not succumb to triangulation. They simply refused to put reform on the table. "Our strategy was to start from full

repeal," a Republican Senate aide said, "and then negotiate down to full repeal." To be sure, they had the advantages of a legislative majority and a
galvanized base of support fervently committed to the cause. But the repeal
forces occupied this commanding position because they had drawn a line
in the sand based on principle. The Democratic triangulators, by contrast,
had through their long series of compromises and reform proposals signaled
that their commitment was to tactics over substance. Fatally, they failed to
make the moral case against repeal. Until they manage to fashion a system
of principles and defend them on the grounds that they are right, the Democrats seem destined to play catch-up in a contest where their adversaries
pick the route, set the rules, and define the terms of debate. And, in the
arena of tax policy, estate tax repeal is not the only item on the Republicans' agenda. Even larger fights lie ahead.

Another Storm Gathering

It is tempting to view repeal of the estate tax in 2001 as an isolated political event—a perfect storm. A well-organized, totally focused group had gathered into political coalitions to fight for repeal. Its most effective and visible members were small business owners and farmers—productive, industrious, successful Americans who had aroused the sympathy of members of Congress and the American people, priming public opinion to encourage repeal of the "death tax." By January 2001, the winds were headed in their direction. A president committed to their cause sat in the White House. Projected surpluses seemingly gave the federal government plenty of money to spare, and a large tax reduction had become a popular prescription for an ailing economy. Republicans completely controlled the House, and they secured aid in the Senate from a handful of Democrats anxious to compromise. The congressional Democratic opposition was stunningly ineffectual. Outside Congress, some well-financed, politically powerful groups stood to lose a lot from repeal, but they stayed on the sidelines, rendering the resistance disorganized and underfunded. Repeal had leadership, luck, and perfect timing on its side.

Yet it would be a mistake to attribute the success of the repeal movement merely to the skilled navigation of several lucky winds. Rather, the outcome of this contest over the taxation of inherited wealth marks a larger shift in our nation's politics. Repeal of the estate tax was not an anomalous event, nor was it just about one piece of the Internal Revenue Code. This death tax effort has been a critical piece of an attack on the very idea of progressive taxation in America. Progressive taxation requires that those who have more should contribute a larger share of their resources to support the government, so that it can enforce the laws, build the roads, defend and secure the nation, and sustain numerous other programs for the benefit of its citizens. This particular struggle both reflects and contributes to a much broader change in the political landscape of the United States today: the growth and increasing success of an antitax movement that has been attacking the foundations of progressive taxation.

Progressivity is not an inevitable aspect of our nation's tax law. It was achieved through a massive, 60-year political struggle from the Civil War until the beginning of World War I. But from the passage of the Sixteenth Amendment in 1913 until very late in the twentieth century, the idea of progressive taxation based on ability to pay seemed as stable and fundamental to American policy as "no taxation without representation." The 2001 enactment of estate tax repeal is the first instance since World War I where a significant progressive tax on income or wealth has been excised altogether.

A tax on large inherited estates is the most steeply progressive tax in the United States, for it affects only the wealthiest people and doesn't apply at all to the vast majority of citizens. About half of all estate tax revenue is collected from the largest 10 percent of taxable estates, those valued at more than $5 million (the wealthiest 0.1 percent of the population). And the largest 1 percent of taxable estates—fortunes exceeding $20 million each—have generally paid more than one-fifth of total estate taxes. For nearly a century this tax has been a mainstay of our government's financial system, held in place by the nation's vision of a society based on equality of opportunity rather than inherited wealth. And although it raises only a relatively small percentage of the total federal revenue, it still contributes a good deal of money: indeed, repeal is expected to cost $700 billion in the decade after it comes into effect.

Enacting repeal ratifies the much broader success of a conservative Republican wing that has been attacking progressive taxation and pushing its antitax agenda over the past three decades. This antitax movement first took hold in the new generation of conservative think tanks, including the American Enterprise Institute, CATO, and Heritage, which emerged in the 1970s. But it was not until the presidential election of Ronald Reagan in 1980 that the idea of substantially reducing the size of the federal government acquired real momentum. The arrival of Grover Norquist and other conservative activists in Washington in the 1980s added fuel to the fire, as did the Republican congressional revolution led by Newt Gingrich in 1994. Finally, the antitax revolution became the main game in town when George W. Bush became president in 2001.

To be sure, neither the fight over the estate tax nor the larger debate about progressive taxation is anywhere close to being over. The fat lady never sings in tax politics. Every year Congress amends the tax code in one way or another, and large-scale reform is always being talked about. No victories are final, no defeats irreversible. At the beginning of the twenty-first century, the tax cutters had the political stars aligned in their favor and they made great strides. But, over time, a dramatic shift has occurred. The baseline from which all tax debate now starts has been moved to a place considered unimaginable as recently as the mid-1990s. For those seeking to transform the structure of taxation in America, this is only the beginning. Other storms are gathering.

Looking back, the most remarkable feature of repeal was what a long shot it was at the start. As we have reported, the abolition movement began in the early 1990s with an unlikely band of political outsiders: Pat Soldano from Orange County, California; Frank Blethen from Seattle, Washington; and Harold Apolinsky from Birmingham, Alabama. Washington wisdom regarded repeal as a pipe dream. It did not even make the wish list of Newt Gingrich's 1994 "Contract with America"; an increased exemption was the most that document was willing to urge. As late as 1998, Washington's expert lobbyists still sought only a larger exemption for small businesses and farmers—the QFOBI legislation. But the forces for repeal had been gathering momentum throughout the country, rallying grasstops business owners to the cause and picking up congressional allies one by one.

Against all odds, the early coalition moved the unthinkable into the realm of the possible. And once the prospects for repeal became imminent, the Washington insiders took over. It is hard to pinpoint precisely when this shift occurred. Perhaps when George W. Bush was inaugurated. Or maybe a month later, when Dirk Van Dongen and his Tax Relief Coalition replaced the FBETC as the key group pushing for the 2001 legislation. Certainly by the time the final four negotiators came together in late May to divide up the 2001 tax cuts. The outside forces were not replaced; they were coopted, or, as they prefer to say, assimilated. The repeal pioneers now had powerful allies in the halls of power, who had moved their cause to the center of the political action.

But they paid a price. Estate tax repeal had become simply one piece—an extremely important piece, to be sure—in the larger Republican antitax movement. Bringing repeal and the broader antitax agenda together energized the antitax wing of the party by marrying a strong, single-issue coalition to the larger movement. Their fight against the "death tax" has substantially enhanced the clout of those who see the federal government as inherently wasteful and Americans as overtaxed.

But the choice to spend political capital and energy on repeal was not always self-evident. In fact, Grover Norquist and the economists from AEI expressed some concern that the death tax repeal movement would draw energy and momentum away from the larger antitax struggle. The economists preferred cuts in corporate and capital gains taxes, which they were sure would provide greater stimulus in terms of economic growth. But they need not have worried. Ever the pragmatist, Norquist saw that the estate tax had become one of those points of vulnerability in the Tax Code that he is constantly seeking. He believes in floating possibilities endlessly— even wildly unrealistic ones—searching for those that can gain political traction. Most antitax activists agree with Grover that you must go with the pieces of the larger agenda that catch political fire, biding your time for more. Estate tax repeal caught fire in 2001. In the end, Norquist's pragmatism paid off.

Fellowship with the broader Republican movement to cut taxes on wealth and capital income helped broaden the estate tax coalitions, insulating them against potential competitors within the GOP and mollifying with the promise of future tax relief those whom repeal moved to the back of the line. Thus, although the core coalition was composed principally of small business owners and farmers, they made common cause with the large multinational corporations that were their natural competitors in 2001 for the available tax-cut dollars. Shareholders may have preferred corporate tax relief, but when Bush stuck firm on deferring their demands, the companies' highly paid executives were not too distressed. They could expect to receive a nice bonus by ridding themselves and their families of the potentially large personal burdens of the estate tax. In addition, there was the promise that corporate support for repeal in 2001 could yield corporate tax breaks down the road—and it did.

As the activist Republican tax cutters look to take more territory, their challenge will be to re-create political conditions of the sort that produced estate tax repeal. Their goal is clear. The next target is the income tax. Indeed, much of the policy aristocracy of the Republican Party has long considered the income tax enemy number one. When Ronald Reagan made tax reform his top legislative priority in his second term, many observers were surprised that he chose to restructure the income tax rather than to try to replace it. Public opinion had already signaled that the path might be clear. From 1945 until 1972, the American people viewed the income tax as the fairest tax in the nation. But increasing complexity and the widespread marketing of tax shelters was making the income tax seem opaque and unfair. By 1976, Jimmy Carter was running for president, calling the income tax "a disgrace to the human race." Since 1980, polls reveal the income tax ranking last among the American public in terms of fairness. And for more than two decades since, it has been the main target for Republican antitax advocates.

By the early 1990s, it had become clear that the grand bipartisan compromise underlying Ronald Reagan's 1986 income tax reform, which had promised—but failed to deliver—a broad-based, low-rate, fairer and simpler income tax, had come unraveled. Bill Clinton's 1993 increase in income tax rates finally convinced many leaders of the Republican Party that the income tax must be "pulled out by its roots," as former Ways and Means Chairman Bill Archer always put it. Archer and other GOP leaders have urged substituting some form of tax on what people spend for the income tax, which is levied on what people earn and own.

Inherent in the antagonism toward the income tax is a broader attack on progressive taxation. In accepting the Republican vice presidential nomination in 1992, Dan Quayle left no doubt that, while the assault on the income tax could be cloaked in the desire to simplify Americans' tax lives and spur economic growth, the ultimate target was progressive taxation. His audience of Republican convention-goers burst into thunderous applause when he asked, "Why should the best people be punished?"

The next presidential campaign in 1996 brought the income tax under a threat not seen since 1913: the field was crowded with candidates calling for outright repeal of the levy. Steve Forbes, the dynastic heir to a fortune and a magazine bearing his name, entered the race to promote replacing the income tax with the "flat tax," a single-rate tax on consumption disguised to look like an income tax. Individuals would pay taxes only on their wages, not on interest, dividends, capital gains, or wealth. This flat-tax idea was also embraced by the presidential candidate Senator Arlen Specter of Pennsylvania and by House Majority Leader Dick Armey of Texas. Richard Lugar, Indiana's senior senator and another Republican aspirant to the White House in 1996, wanted to replace the income tax with a national sales tax collected by the states. A commission led by Jack Kemp, who would become Bob Dole's running mate in 1996, made no specific recommendations—but it set out principles for tax reform that could be met only by a flat-rate consumption tax. Television's John McLaughlin predicted the demise of the income tax as approaching "metaphysical certainty."

The rub, however, is that this top-down challenge to the income tax has not yet achieved traction with the public. Even though voters told exit pollers that they favored the "flat tax" more than its messengers, Dan Quayle's "best people" decided that it was more important to eliminate the estate tax than the income tax—or at least that they were more likely to succeed by taking on this much smaller target. The income tax accounts for about half of all federal revenues, compared to the estate tax's 1 or 2 percent. And getting rid of the income tax requires consensus on what should replace it, something that so far has been lacking.

Eliminating taxes on capital or capital income is a tricky business. The 2001 cuts in the top income tax rates could be sold only in combination with enhanced tax credits for children and other popular tax cuts for middle-income families, such as reductions in the marriage penalty. As always, however, Grover Norquist has a plan—one that can be enacted in stages: abolish estate taxes and the alternative minimum tax, eliminate all taxes on capital gains and individual taxes on dividends, provide "infinitely expandable" tax-free savings plans, and allow businesses to deduct immediately their purchases of capital assets. "You do those things," he says, "then put a single rate on it and you now have Dick Armey's flat tax." He's right. And since 2001, George Bush has obtained major cuts in capital gains and dividend taxes, proposed a major expansion of tax-free savings accounts and substantially increased business write-offs of equipment, taking several steps toward Norquist's goal.

This is why John Cassidy, writing for *The New Yorker* shortly after Bush announced in his August 2004 acceptance speech at the Republican convention that tax reform would be a priority in a second term, could say, "Bush's tax cuts weren't just bigger than Reagan's, they were more strategic." Unsurprisingly, Cassidy turned to Grover Norquist to explain the strategy. "[P]eople get the vibes," Norquist said. "They understand what we're trying to accomplish. Do you think it was an accident that the first three tax cuts moved toward expensing business expenditures, toward universal IRAs, toward getting rid of the capital gains tax, toward getting rid of the double taxation of dividend income, toward getting rid of the death tax? No. It is consistent with a vision." That vision would shift the nation's tax burden away from taxing wealth and capital income. As Cassidy concludes, "[L]abor would end up shouldering practically the entire burden of financing the federal government." The editorialists for the *New York Times* concur, claiming that Bush's call for an "ownership society" can mean only one thing: "a shift in the tax burden on to wages and salaries—or, put more simply, a wage tax." Larry Lindsey, who had been George Bush's principal economic adviser during Bush's first presidential campaign and during the first years of his presidency, offered a similar idea in the *Wall Street Journal.* He wants to move the nation to a "cash-flow tax" that would allow deductions for businesses' purchases of capital goods and for individuals' savings.

But there are pitfalls along the path. While it is tempting to believe that the nation of the Boston Tea Party will embrace any tax cut, the general public is neither as passive nor as powerless as one might think. Corporate taxation offers an illustration. With the onset of recession in 2001, economists of all political persuasions knew that a cut in corporate taxes would provide more economic bang-for-the-tax-cut-buck than a long-delayed repeal of the estate tax. But they faced public resistance to reductions in corporate tax rates. Indeed, corporate tax relief induces considerable class-based opposition of the sort that did not emerge for the estate tax. Americans may applaud and even identify with wealthy individuals, but they feel very differently about large corporations. Why do Americans get angry about giving tax relief to the companies that created Mickey Mouse and Wonder Bread, while supporting proposals to let Jamie Johnson and Ally Hilfiger inherit grand fortunes tax free?

One answer is that, no matter how well financed, connected, or organized, large corporations have not yet found any effective narrative for attacking corporate taxes. Even when people work for large corporations or own shares of stock in them, no empathetic link binds them to large firms. As a result, corporations have had to achieve tax reductions largely through self-help, by crafting tax shelters or relocating corporate headquarters to places like Bermuda. Even when Congress enters the corporate tax cut game, simply reducing rates remains politically risky: it usually fashions complex new provisions that reduce the corporate burden in ways that defy public comprehension, for example by increasing deductions for equipment purchases or liberalizing the tax treatment of income earned abroad.

By contrast, the repeal coalitions successfully transformed the estate tax into a tax on death, which every taxpayer faces. But although everyone dies, not everyone who dies pays the estate tax. So repeal advocates also invoked the American Dream, the virtue of creating and passing along a successful family business. The estate tax became a villain, the taxman stood between each American and his dream.

Going forward, however, estate tax repealers may face stiff competition from those who care more about other tax cuts. The repeal enacted in 2001 is provisional and temporary, but so were the income tax rate cuts that Bush cared most about. Capital gains and dividend tax cuts enacted in 2003 are also scheduled to expire. Since the 2001 legislation, George Bush has repeatedly called for making the estate tax repeal permanent. But he also has asked for other tax cuts. In 2003, he wanted to eliminate income taxes on dividends. In 2004, he urged additional income tax relief for savings. Bush's tax cut ideas have accumulated. In the 2004 State of the Union speech, his description of the "unfinished business" included the increased child tax credits, marriage penalty reductions, and income tax rate cuts, as well as death tax repeal. He also praised the reductions in taxes on capital gains and stock dividends, proposed refundable tax credits for lower-income Americans who purchase health insurance, and 100 percent tax deductions for premium payments on certain types of health insurance. The list goes on and on.

Meanwhile, out in the country, starting in Texas, an even more radical movement for restructuring the nation's tax system has been quietly building force. With an audacity exceeding the switch to the "death tax" label, the prophets of this cause herald a "fair tax plan." They propose replacing virtually the entire federal tax structure—the corporate and individual income taxes, the payroll taxes that finance Social Security and Medicare, and whatever is left of the estate tax, if anything—with a national sales tax. Americans for Fair Taxation (AFT) kicked off its campaign in a press conference in Houston, Texas, on January 7, 1998. The group immediately announced a $30 million multimedia advertising campaign. Its leading strategist was Dennis Calabrese, a former chief of staff and principal campaign advisor for House Majority Leader Dick Armey. One of its major funders was Jack Trotter, a wealthy Houston investor, who is a close family friend and campaign contributor to Bill Archer, then chairman of House Ways and Means. Another big AFT donor was Leo Linbeck, a construction magnate who has been friends with Archer since their days in elementary school together. Linbeck said then that he expected the fair-tax campaign to take years and to cost $90 million.

AFT's leaders insist that they can make up the revenue lost from all the taxes they would replace with a 23 percent sales tax rate. But many analysts regard this claim as wildly unrealistic—a low-ball tax rate, chosen to build public support. Who wouldn't rather have a 23 percent sales tax than both a 15.3 percent payroll tax and an income tax at rates ranging from 10 to 35 percent? Brookings economist Bill Gale, along with other disbelievers, has pointed out that a rate at least ten percentage points higher would be needed to avoid a huge revenue shortfall and very large deficits. AFT's response? They claim their plan would spur massive economic growth, so not to worry.

Tom Wright, self-described Texas "oil field trash" who in July 2003 was named executive director for AFT, explained in a 1998 *Washington Post* op-ed that the "key to understanding" AFT's sales tax proposal is that it is "revenue neutral." This means "[n]ot raising taxes, not lowering, not redistributing." He added that the "last time people like Mr. Gale decided they were smarter than our founding fathers, we got the 16th Amendment and the income tax." AFT urges repealing that amendment to make the income tax unconstitutional. And if the tax produces too little revenue to fund current expenditure, so what? This will just create new incentives to slash government's size.

What about progressivity? The liberal tax policy operative Bob McIntyre, for example, accuses AFT of redistributing the tax burden away from the rich—not a difficult claim to make, since even the wealthiest Americans would pay only 23 percent on goods and services they purchase and nothing on their wealth or income. Wright responded in the *Houston Chronicle* that McIntyre's "calculations are confusing, where a sales tax would only simplify." He also repeated the claim that "AFT's proposal (and every other sales tax proposal) is revenue neutral."

By the time of the AFT announcement in 1998, the group reported that it had already spent $2 million analyzing the economic effects of its plan through a linked "charitable" research organization, the National Tax Research Committee. The list of economists who have worked for the organization includes numerous well-known academics from leading universities. It also features Heritage's Bill Beach and Steve Moore from the CATO Institute. The AFT website contains many papers by experts heralding the economic and simplification benefits of the proposal.

Don Sipple, who had been a media adviser to Bob Dole's presidential campaign, produced television advertisements for AFT, and Fred Steeper, a Republican pollster from Michigan, analyzed their results. Richard Wirthlin, Ronald Reagan's pollster, also did some surveys. Since 1998, AFT has also been aggressively building activist and grassroots support. In addition to claiming a simpler and fairer tax system, AFT tries to rally the public to its side by promising to get rid of the IRS entirely and let the states collect the sales tax for the federal government. Americans love to hate the IRS. In his presidential campaign, Steve Forbes always had prompted his greatest applause when he told his audiences that his tax plan "would turn the I.R.S. into R.I.P."

By early 2004, AFT had chapters in all 50 states. They were drawing people and raising money by holding meetings, providing speakers, hosting dinners and other social receptions, distributing information locally, and coordinating letter-writing campaigns. The group already had an e-mail list of tens, if not hundreds, of thousands of volunteers. AFT does not hesitate to ask them regularly for money: $800 for an op-ed, $150 for radio shows, $700 for a television spot. The AFT website lists many organizations we know well from the estate tax movement, including both NFIB and NAM, as well as the Tax Foundation, Citizens for Sound Economy (now headed by Dick Armey), and, of course, Grover Norquist's Americans for Tax Reform.

In 2004, the "fair tax" campaign stands about where the estate tax repeal movement was in the mid-1990s. A Georgia congressman, John Linder, a member of the House Republican Steering Committee and next in line to chair the House Rules Committee, has been the key House sponsor of the Fair Tax bill since he first introduced it in 1999. That bill, which claims "to promote freedom, fairness and economic opportunity," has been accumulating Republican cosponsors ever since. As of January, 2004, 42 representatives had signed on as cosponsors, including Majority Leader

Tom DeLay. A similar bill was introduced in the Senate on July 30, 2003, with bipartisan cosponsorship from two other Georgians: Republican Saxby Chambliss and Democrat Zell Miller.

Linder hopes to do for the "fair tax" what Jennifer Dunn did against the death tax. He explains that the House cosponsors have been multiplying because members "have been hearing about it from their constituents." As he says, "Their desire to get rid of the intrusive and burdensome IRS can be a tremendous motivating force for public policy." In 2004 John Linder also offered the Fair Tax plan as a way to strengthen George Bush's re-election campaign. "Take the focus off Iraq and attack the Internal Revenue Service," he advised. "I think [Bush] would have a huge increase in turnout."

In August 2004, the Drudge Report suggested that the "fair tax" movement might have picked up another powerful ally, citing "Hill sources" as saying that House Speaker Denny Hastert would push for replacing the nation's current tax system with a national sales tax. Hastert himself says, "People ask me if I'm really calling for the elimination of the IRS and I say I think that's a great thing to do for future generations of Americans." In his book, *Speaker: Lessons from Forty Years in Coaching and Politics*, Hastert seems to hedge a bit, suggesting that the tax system would be improved by "adopting a VAT, sales tax, or some other alternative."

In the Senate, the AFT bill lost one of its original cosponsors in 2004, due to Zell Miller's retirement. But other strong AFT advocates were hoping to replace him. The public spokesman for AFT when Miller first introduced the Senate bill was Herman Cain, a highly successful African American businessman who rose from a hamburger cook to become regional vice president of Burger King and then chairman and CEO of the struggling Godfather's Pizza chain of restaurants. Within a year after Cain took charge, Godfather's had turned a profit. Cain, a staunchly conservative Republican who is a powerful public speaker, served for two years as a predecessor to Denise Fugo as chairman of the National Restaurant Association. He also advised the presidential campaigns of Steve Forbes and Jack Kemp. When Cain announced he would seek Miller's Senate seat, early in 2004, the "fair tax" was a key plank in his campaign. Cain lost in the July Republican primary to a conservative Congressman, Johnny Isakson, who was elected to the Senate, but Cain insists he mustered much grassroots support for the "fair tax."

South Carolina's Jim DeMint had better luck, defeating former governor David Beasley for the Republican Senate nomination. DeMint, who owned a market research firm in Greenville, South Carolina, before being elected to the House in 1998, was a House cosponsor of the "fair tax." But when his Democratic opponent Inez Tannenbaum accused him of supporting a 23 percent sales tax "on everything from milk to mortgage payments," DeMint backed and filled. He claimed that he supported the legislation only to give impetus to the effort to reform the nation's tax system, and then somehow asserted—without any regard for the facts—that "a revenue-neutral 9 percent is more like it." "With the end of income tax payroll deductions and the IRS, it's a change worth pursuing," he added. DeMint was elected to the Senate.

Liberal think tanks and Democrats within Congress dismiss the "fairtax" crowd as dreamers. The liberals are sure that this nation will never stand for replacing the progressive income tax with a flat-rate sales tax. Serenely confident, AFT's opponents do little or nothing to prepare for a fight. Elimination of the income tax is not realistic; it cannot happen. Until George Bush was elected president, and even after, they were equally sure the estate tax wasn't going anywhere either. Have they learned nothing?

Make no mistake. Estate tax repeal, along with the "fair tax" movement and its cousin the "flat tax" campaign—both of which would replace the income tax—are key pieces of a three-decade effort to fundamentally restructure our nation's tax system by eliminating all taxes on wealth and income from wealth. At the inception of the twenty-first century, the great battle over distributive tax justice that culminated early in the twentieth century has been renewed. Bill Frenzel, the moderate Minnesota Republican who retired from the House in 1991 and now hangs his hat at Brookings, observes that Democrats still believe the progressivity consensus that prevailed 70 years ago holds firm today. They seem blissfully unaware that opponents of progressive taxation are on the move.

And if progressive taxes and progressive tax rates are purged from the tax system, the amount of taxes the government can raise becomes limited. Low- and moderate-income people simply cannot afford to pay enough in taxes to finance the government's current expenditures, whether the dollars go to homeland security, national defense, Social Security, Medicare, Medicaid, or elsewhere. Of course, advocates of proposals like the "fair tax" understand that eliminating the progressive elements of our nation's tax system would be a highly effective way to "starve the beast" of the federal government. For antitax activists such as Grover Norquist, that is indeed the goal. Remember how fond he is of saying, "I don't want to kill the government, I just want to get it down to a size where I can drown it in a bathtub."

In the early 1990s, the movement to repeal the estate tax was like a tropical depression thousands of miles away in the Atlantic Ocean—something that even the most vigilant weatherman would hardly have noticed. In 2001 it hit Washington, D.C., with hurricane force. In 2004, the broader movement to eliminate the income tax has already become a tropical storm and is nearer to land than was the estate tax a decade earlier. We cannot now know how or when this gale will hit Washington, or if it does hit, what the result will actually be. Much, as we have seen, depends on the conditions. But if the estate tax repeal story has any lessons at all to offer, surely it should signal to the opposition that they ignore the early signs of such storms at their own risk—and the risk of the very principles of tax justice they seek to protect. The other side has learned well that aiming high, carrying on relentlessly despite setbacks, and building momentum inside the beltway and throughout the country can lead to great payoffs.

We offer no specific predictions here. As Mark Twain reputedly remarked, "The art of prophecy is very difficult—especially with respect to the future."

Epilogue

2004 was a quiet year in the effort to make estate tax repeal permanent. Congress was preoccupied with other tax issues: legislation to replace a tax subsidy for exports, which had been held illegal by the World Trade Organization and which turned into a $140 billion feeding frenzy for large corporations. Congress also managed to extend child credits and marriage penalty relief enacted in 2001. The estate tax sat quietly on the back burner.

Until the November election, the little news that did surface was disappointing to repeal forces. Our story here carried us through the repeal movement's success in 2001, but by 2004 those banking on repeal's endurance had new reasons to worry. The estate tax remained in the limbo fashioned by the 2001 legislation—a long-delayed repeal scheduled to self-destruct the year after it finally happens. When George W. Bush took office in January of 2001, the Congressional Budget Office estimated that federal budget surpluses would total $5.6 trillion in the ten years ahead. The government's financial future looked bright, and there seemed plenty of room to cut taxes. So the Bush administration did exactly that—in 2001, 2002, 2003, and 2004.

The reality that set in was stunningly different. The federal deficit in 2003 exceeded $400 billion, and in January 2004 the Bush administration announced the shortfall for the coming year would be at least as big, even without including any expenditures for the Iraq war after September of that year. CBO was then predicting deficits of $2.7 trillion over the next decade, even assuming that none of the 2001–2003 tax cuts were made permanent. But private forecasters such as the Concord Coalition, Decision Economics, and Goldman Sachs insisted that total deficits of $5 to $5.5 trillion were a more realistic projection. The Bush tax cuts had been accompanied by massive increases in spending—even nonmilitary domestic spending. This baby was not going to drown in a bathtub anytime soon.

Ron Suskind's book about George Bush's first treasury secretary, Paul O'Neill, *The Price of Loyalty,* reports Vice President Dick Cheney asserting, in November 2002, that "Reagan proved deficits don't matter." Ronald Reagan, of course, proved no such thing; he didn't even try to. Reagan signed two large tax increase laws in the years following his big tax cut. By 2004 deficits had started to matter, and matter a lot in some offices on Capitol Hill.

The Senate, which had always been less steady for repeal than the House, was showing considerable concern about the burgeoning federal deficits. A majority of senators in 2004 tried to reinstate "paygo" spending rules, like those of the 1990s, which would require any spending increases or tax reductions—including permanent estate tax repeal—to be paid for either with offsetting tax increases or spending cuts. Identifying those people who would have to pay for repeal this way would have substantially lowered the odds for making repeal permanent. The House blocked this effort. Equally troubling to the pro-repeal forces, some of their staunchest supporters in the Senate were wavering. What they were speaking now had been unthinkable in 2001.

The *Washington Post* reported that Jon Kyl was searching for a compromise that would increase the exemption and lower rates. Immediately after this story was printed, Kyl denied any such thing. When Don Nickles, who like Kyl had been a stalwart for repeal in 2001, went public with such a compromise proposal, however, the pro-repeal coalitions were genuinely shaken. A group identified as Americans for Job Security bought a full-page ad in *Roll Call* with pictures of John Kerry and Don Nickles side-by-side below a headline asking, "Which Senator would allow a hard working small business owner to pass on more to their children?" The ad continued, "If you guessed Nickles, you guessed wrong," and, after professing great surprise that liberal Democrats had voted for a higher exemption than Nickles was now proposing, urged people to call Senator Nickles and tell him to "kill the death tax permanently." When Nickles announced that he would not run for reelection in 2004, the pro-repeal forces barely shrugged.

They were a bit more concerned, however, when their staunchest ally in the House, Jennifer Dunn, announced that she would retire from Congress at the end of 2004. But the House remained safely in Republican hands after the 2004 election, and it retained a solid majority in favor of repeal. In 2003, the House had voted for permanent repeal. With repeal on the books, losing Dunn now was hardly disastrous. Anyway, the real problem had been on the Senate side.

In the run-up to the November 2004 election, the American electorate focused far more closely on news from Iraq, the general state of the economy, and gay marriage than on the rising or declining fortunes of the estate tax. But the election results brought the repealers some good news. George W. Bush was reelected. Republicans also increased their majorities in both the House and Senate. House Republicans gained a handful of seats, and, more importantly, the Republicans enjoyed a 55-45 edge in 2005 in the Senate. Of the nine new senators elected in 2004, seven favored permanent repeal of the estate tax, a gain of three votes over the preceding Congress. The Senate was edging very close to 60 votes for repeal.

With the legitimacy of his presidency now secure, the president left no doubt that he would begin spending his political capital and that "tax reform" would be one of his main priorities. What he meant by tax reform remained to be seen. But George Bush had spoken so frequently of making his tax cuts permanent that the pro-repeal lobby took heart. Large and continuing deficits remained a problem, and a Senate victory no slam-dunk, but the electoral stars could hardly have aligned any better for the pro-repeal forces.

Yet in some ways it is more illuminating to consider how the antitax forces would have responded to the defeat that did not come in 2004. Listen, one more time, to Grover Norquist—whose eye is always keenly focused on the big picture. Several months before the 2004 election, he summed up the stakes very differently than many Democrats, Republicans, or pundits. Recognizing that a second Bush administration would obviously help entrench his antitax, anti–big government agenda, he insisted that a Kerry victory would be only a minor setback for the conservative crusade, now in its fourth decade. Norquist was sure that the Democrats could not win control of Congress, severely limiting a Kerry administration's options to legislate. "We can stop him from getting anybody on the Supreme Court, we won't let him raise taxes. No part of the Republican coalition would be damaged or destroyed by a Kerry victory."

Overconfident? Not as it turned out. But, even if John Kerry had won, Norquist's is the kind of confidence, grounded in righteous certitude and strategic vision, that keeps political movements going—through setbacks and against the odds, as well as when they enjoy success.

What will happen; what does our future hold? There are many scenarios, both for the estate tax itself and for Norquist's broader attack on progressive taxation and his agenda of whittling down the size of the federal government. Perhaps the deficits will ultimately make repeal an ephemera— a temporary victory that never takes root. Or, contrariwise, perhaps the deficits themselves will be our future: Congress may find itself incapable of either resisting tax cuts or cutting spending—with frightening long-term financial consequences. We could become Japan of the 1990s. Then again, there is the scenario where Norquist and his compatriots actually succeed in creating a permanent tax rebellion, which starves the government, including the New Deal and Great Society programs like Social Security and Medicare, for revenue. In that case, we might really become two Americas: one quite well-to-do, the other impoverished. We could become Brazil.

Make no mistake, the antitax forces are working tirelessly to dismantle America's system of progressive taxation. They are patient. They are serious. They are determined. They know that what they want cannot be accomplished at a fell swoop. Hence their strategy: death by a thousand cuts. What strategy is there on the other side?

60 Plus Association   Senior citizen advocacy group run by estate tax repeal advocate Jim Martin. Worked actively to promote repeal in early days of pro-repeal efforts and subsequently.

501(c)(3) Organization   A tax-exempt non-profit organization eligible for deductible charitable contributions that fits certain criteria set forth in the tax code. To maintain tax-exempt status, 501(c)(3) organizations may not engage in lobbying activity.

AALU   Association of Advanced Life Underwriting. Trade association whose members sell insurance to wealthy clients. An anti–estate tax repeal insurance lobby group.

ACCF   American Council for Capital Formation. Organization funded by businesses and business groups principally in support of corporate and capital gains tax cuts. Founded by lobbyist Charls Walker.

AEI   American Enterprise Institute. Conservative think tank founded in 1943 as an alternative to the Brookings Institution. Supported publication of materials that advocated estate tax repeal.

AFB   American Farm Bureau. Advocacy group that pushes for legislation favorable to farmers. A member of the FBETC and an active supporter of estate tax repeal.

American Business Is Local Enterprise   Group that Senator Robert Packwood formed in 1996 for the purpose of fighting for estate tax repeal. Senator Packwood refused to identify the group's members.

American Council of Life Insurers   380-member organization composed of life insurance vendors. Opposed estate tax repeal but did not actively lobby against it.

American Family Business Institute   Group associated with estate tax repeal advocate Harold Apolinsky's early anti–estate tax efforts.

American Family-Owned Business Act of 1995   Bill introduced by Senators Robert Dole and David Pryor that would have created a special $1.5 million estate tax exemption for family businesses and farms and would also have taxed amounts over that figure at half the normal estate tax rates, thereby creating a maximum 27.5 percent rate.

Americans Against Unfair Family Taxation   Pro-estate tax repeal coalition composed of advocacy groups such as the Food Marketing Institute and the National Beer Wholesalers Association. Conducted a number of polls on estate tax issues.

Americans for a Fair Estate Tax   Coalition organized by OMB Watch in 2001 to advocate for estate tax reform over repeal. Composed of various labor, child welfare, civil rights, and other liberal groups including Independent Sector, MoveOn.org, the AFL-CIO, and the Children's Defense Fund.

American Vintners Association   Association that advocates in support of wineries; subsequently renamed the National Association of Wineries / WineAmerica. Also a member of the FBETC.

Assistant Secretary of the Treasury for Tax Policy   Senior advisor to the Secretary of the U.S. Treasury Department; in charge of analyzing, developing, and implementing tax policy. Oversees the tax policy offices at the Treasury Department.

Associated General Contractors   Organization promoting the interests of construction contractors. Member of the TRC.

ATR   Americans for Tax Reform. Grover Norquist's antitax group and an advocate of estate tax repeal.

BET Holdings   Black Entertainment Television Holdings. Company originally owned by Robert Johnson, billionaire businessman and vocal estate tax repeal advocate.

Black Caucus   Group consisting of African American members of the U.S. Congress, which advocates legislation considered important to African American constituencies. Formally the "Congressional Black Caucus."

Black Caucus Minority Business Task Force   A group promoting legislation pertaining to minority-owned business. Led by estate tax repeal supporter Representative Albert Wynn (D-MD).

Black Chamber of Commerce   Nonprofit organization dedicated to economic development in African American communities. Supported estate tax repeal.

Bradley Foundation   Conservative foundation associated with the fortune of late-nineteenth-century Milwaukee philanthropists Lynde and Harry Bradley. A major source of support for conservative think tanks.

Brookings Institution   Important research-oriented liberal think tank founded in 1916. Produced large quantity of scholarly work in opposition to estate tax repeal.

BRT   Business Roundtable. Association of CEOs from 150 top U.S. companies. Initially lobbied the administration of President George W. Bush for corporate tax cuts, but later joined the TRC.

budget reconciliation Process by which both Houses of the U.S. Congress merge, or "reconcile" their tax and spending bills. This process is governed by a specific set of procedural rules, the most important being that no fillibuster is possible and, therefore, that 51 senate votes can secure passage.

budget resolution Motion that passes in a House of the U.S. Congress that provides parameters for the coming year's federal budget.

Byrd Rule Senate rule that allows any U.S. senator to object to legislative provisions deemed "extraneous" to the budget reconciliation process. A provision is extraneous if it "would decrease revenues during a fiscal year after the fiscal years covered by such reconciliation bill." Once a senator raises a point of order under the Byrd Rule, 60 votes are required to overrule such an objection.

carryover basis A tax provision that will produce capital gains taxes on pre-inheritance gains when wealthy heirs sell inherited assets.

CATO Institute Think tank founded in 1977 to promote libertarian ideals in the national political debate. Advocated estate tax repeal.

CBO Congressional Budget Office. Congressional office responsible for providing nonpartisan data and economic analysis for Congress to use in creating the federal budget.

Center for Responsive Politics Nonprofit research group that tracks the role of money in politics.

Center for Tax Justice A liberal research and advocacy organization for tax issues "to give ordinary people a greater voice in the development of tax laws," led by Robert S. McIntyre. Published reports opposing estate tax repeal.

Center for the Study of Taxation A nonprofit organization founded on April 21, 1992, by repeal advocate Patricia Soldano and a group of concerned families to study the effects of the estate tax on the economy and family-owned businesses.

Center on Budget and Policy Priorities Small liberal think tank formed in 1981 to analyze the federal budget process and its effect on low-income Americans. Published significant body of anti–estate tax repeal research.

Charls Walker and Associates Lobbying group associated with renowned corporate lobbyist Charls Walker. Initially lobbied President George W. Bush to include corporate tax breaks in the 2001 tax cut bill. Group eventually abandoned its efforts to do so when the business community united behind the president's 2001 proposals.

conference committee A joint congressional committee composed of members from both the U.S. House of Representatives and the U.S. Senate. Responsible for melding bills passed in different versions by both houses.

Congressional Record Official record of Congressional proceedings. Published daily when Congress is in session.

Contract with America   Campaign document outlining the agenda of the Republicans in the U.S. House for 1994. Proposed raising the estate tax exemption.

Council of Economic Advisors   Board of three economists, appointed by the president to provide him with economic analysis and advice on the development and implementation of economic policy.

Council on Foundations   Nonprofit umbrella organization of over 2,000 foundations. Did not take a position on estate tax repeal despite its concerns about the negative effects that the tax might have on charitable giving.

CSE   Citizens for a Sound Economy. A well-funded conservative Republican group that advocates tax cuts. Former House Majority Leader Dick Armey assumed its chairmanship in 2002.

Cymric Family Office Services   Patricia Soldano's wealth management company. Provides services such as tax plans and family offices for wealthy families.

deathtax.com   Pro–estate tax repeal website started by repeal advocate and *Seattle Times* publisher Frank Blethen. Includes pro-repeal advertisements and articles as well as "horror stories" about families hurt by the estate tax.

Death Tax Elimination Act   House bill cosponsored by Representatives Jennifer Dunn and John Tanner and introduced in 1999 proposing repeal of the estate tax. Also known as HR 8.

Death Tax Summit   Annual pro–estate tax repeal meeting aimed at bringing repeal advocates together to strategize and to lobby members of Congress.

deduction   An amount taxpayers subtract from their gross income or adjusted gross income to calculate the amount of taxable income.

Democratic Leadership Council   Nonprofit organization composed of Democratic politicians seeking to promote the "New Democrat" agenda, a set of moderate-liberal policy goals. Associated with the presidency of Bill Clinton.

Earned Income Tax Credit   Refundable tax credit for low-income working individuals and families. The amount of credit is determined by family size and earnings. May result in government checks to families if the amount of credit exceeds the amount of taxes owed.

Education Savings Account   Savings account that individuals can set up to pay educational expenses of a designated beneficiary. Funds in the account may grow tax-free until distributed.

estate tax   Tax imposed on transfer of property at the time of the donor's death. Also known as the death tax.

Estate Tax Elimination Act   U.S. Senate bill, sponsored by Senator Jon Kyl and introduced in 1999, that proposed repeal of the estate tax. Also known as S. 1128.

estate tax exemption   Amount of a taxpayer's income that is exempt from the estate tax. Amount was $650,000 in 2001; scheduled to rise to $1 million. Following the passage of estate tax repeal, amount is scheduled to rise each year until the tax is phased out.

exclusion   An item taxpayers are permitted to exclude when they calculate gross income for tax purposes.

exemption   An amount taxpayers are permitted to deduct from their adjusted gross income. Along with the standard deduction, the figure is used to determine the threshold below which no tax will be due.

exploratory committee   Group that a potential candidate for a political office may establish to gauge his or her chance of electoral success.

FBETC   Family Business Estate Tax Coalition. Main pro–estate tax repeal group. Established in 1995 and composed of over a hundred member organizations representing more than six million individuals. Member organizations included the National Federation of Independent Business, the National Association of Manufacturers, and the Food Marketing Institute.

FMI   Food Marketing Institute. Grocery retailer and wholesaler industry group and FBETC member.

gift tax   Tax imposed on property that a donor gives voluntarily. Because it applies to gifts of property that are conferred on donees before the donor's death, the gift tax is linked to the estate tax.

Grassley-Baucus Bill   1997 estate tax reform proposal. Provided an estate tax exemption for the first $1.5 million of family-business assets and a further exemption for half of the next $8.5 million of property.

Greenberg Research   Democratic organization that conducted polls to assess public opinion on the estate tax.

Heritage Foundation   Large conservative think tank founded in the early 1970s. Published significant amount of material in support of estate tax repeal.

Hispanic Chamber of Commerce   Organization supporting Hispanic-owned businesses and advocating legislation to encourage their growth. Favored estate tax repeal.

House GOP Conference   Group consisting of all Republicans in the U.S. House. Serves as the organizational forum for selecting Republican House leaders for each Congressional session. Meets weekly to discuss party policy and pending legislative issues.

House-Senate conference   A joint meeting between representatives from the U.S. House and the Senate that resolves differences between House and Senate bills.

Independent Sector   Association of over a million charitable, educational, religious, health, and social welfare nonprofit organizations. Eventually came out against estate tax repeal. Joined the Americans for a Fair Estate Tax Coalition, but never played a strong advocacy role.

Insurance Agents and Brokers of America   Organization of insurance agencies (not companies) and FBETC member. Actively promoted estate tax repeal at the congressional-district level.

International Foodservice Distributors Association   Organization of food distributors and member of the TRC Management Committee.

joint budget resolution   Legislative motion that provides parameters for the coming year's federal budget passed by both houses of the U.S. Congress.

Joint Economic Committee   Congressional committee, composed of members of both the U.S. House and Senate, that acts as an advisory panel in economic matters, reviewing economic conditions and recommending economic policies. Estate tax repeal proponent Jennifer Dunn served on this committee, which, in 1998 and subsequently, issued an anti–estate tax report entitled "The Economics of the Estate Tax."

Joint Tax Committee   Congressional committee, composed of members from both the U.S. House and Senate, provides staff responsible for various aspects of the tax legislative process, including estimating revenue effects of pending legislation. Committee also assists the congressional tax-making committees in preparing and revising drafts of tax bills and oversees the process by which the House and Senate reach agreement on bill provisions.

Kill the Death Tax Coalition   Estate tax repeal advocate Jim Martin's early effort to organize groups against the estate tax. Formed in 1993 and expanded throughout the decade, the coalition comprised, among others, various small business organizations, including Concerned Women for America, Women for Tax Reform, and the African American Group Project 21.

Luntz Research   Conservative consulting firm headed by Frank Luntz that worked on estate tax repeal for Patricia Soldano. Also represents the NFIB, the U.S. Chamber of Commerce, and the National Association of Manufacturers.

luxury car tax   A tax on the sale of cars priced above a certain level. No longer assessed in the United States.

Mandate for Leadership   List of ten legislative priorities set by the 1994 Republican leadership of the U.S. House. Included an increase in the estate tax exemption, but not estate tax repeal.

marriage penalty   Feature of the U.S. tax code that imposes a higher marginal tax rate on a married couple than both members of the couple would pay as single persons.

McLaughlin and Associates   Polling organization that conducted surveys of attitudes about the estate tax issue for wealthy supporters of estate tax repeal.

NAA   Newspaper Association of America. Organization of family-owned newspapers and an early FBETC member. Created ads and other publicity materials for FBETC.

NAM   National Association of Manufacturers. Organization representing approximately 14,000 businesses, two-thirds of which are small or mid-sized. Active FBETC member and early leader of the TRC.

National Beer Wholesalers Association   Organization of beer wholesalers. Member of Americans Against Unfair Family Taxation and FBETC.

National Farmers' Union   Association, consisting of 300,000 small farmers, that eventually opposed estate tax repeal at the urging of UFE.

National Newspaper Association   Organization of newspapers that publicized materials in favor of estate tax repeal.

National Restaurant Association   Organization composed of restaurant owners. Active participant, under Denise Marie Fugo's leadership, in the TRC. TRC Management Committee member.

NAW   National Association of Wholesale-Distributors. Small business lobbying association headed by Dirk Van Dongen. One of four groups leading TRC effort. Member of TRC Management Committee.

NCBA   National Cattlemen's Beef Association. Trade association for cattle farmers. Early pro-repeal group and FBETC member. Nicknamed the "Don Quixote of tax reform" by the media, the NCBA was particularly important in promoting estate tax repeal in the U.S. Senate.

NFIB   National Federation of Independent Business. Association of 600,000 small businesses and a leader of the FBETC. Also a TRC leader and member of TRC Management Committee. Considered the most powerful business lobbying organization in Washington.

Office of Tax Policy   Office of the U.S. Treasury charged with formulating and implementing federal tax policy. Supervised by the Assistant Secretary for Tax Policy.

Olin Foundation   Conservative foundation that disburses the fortune of early-twentieth-century philanthropist John Olin. Major supporter of conservative think tanks.

OMB   Office of Management and Budget. White House office in charge of overseeing the White House's role in the federal budget process.

OMB Watch   Small liberal think tank concerned with fiscal policy issues important to nonprofit organizations. Actively opposed to estate tax repeal and helped organize the Americans for a Fair Estate Tax coalition.

PAC contributions   Donations made to political campaigns by the political action committees of companies, labor unions, and other organizations. Now subject to strict giving limits under federal campaign finance laws.

paint-by-numbers lawmaking   Process by which members of the U.S. Congress, in conformity with statutory requirements, tailor tax legislation to meet a fixed revenue target for the requisite federal budget period.

partnership   An association of one or more persons created for the purposes of owning and running a business. Partnerships themselves are not taxed; taxes are imposed only on partnership members.

Patton Boggs   Prominent Washington lobbying firm that acquainted Patricia Soldano with the processes of political influence at the federal level.

payroll tax   Tax imposed on employees and employers based on the amount of wages. Social Security taxes are an important example.

phase-in   Slow implementation of new federal policy. Describes, for example, the method by which estate tax repeal takes effect under the 2001 estate tax repeal legislation.

Philanthropy Roundtable   Conservative association of nonprofit organizations. Founded in the late 1970s in response to alleged leftist leanings of America's philanthropic community.

Pioneers   Honorific title for supporters who raised over $100,000 for George W. Bush's 2000 presidential campaign.

Policy and Taxation Group   A lobbying organization founded on August 14, 1996, by Patricia Soldano, dedicated to repeal of the estate tax.

Project 21   African American organization and member of the Kill the Death Tax Coalition.

proprietorship   A business in which an individual owns all assets and liabilities in his or her personal capacity.

QFOBI   Qualified Family-Owned Business Interests. Complex estate tax reform provision incorporated into 1997 tax legislation. Provided an exemption for the first $1.3 million of a business's assets.

ranking member   Most senior member of the minority party on a House or Senate committee.

Republican National Committee   National leadership committee of the Republican Party.

research and experimentation credit   Tax credit for companies that engage in certain kinds of research.

Responsible Wealth   UFE project formed to combat estate tax repeal. Led by anti-repeal activist Chuck Collins.

RJC   Republican Jewish Coalition. Organization headed by St. Louis billionaire Sam Fox that conducts fundraising efforts for Republican political candidates. TRC member.

Scaife Foundation   Conservative foundation associated with prominent conservative activist Richard Mellon Scaife. Provides significant financial support to conservative think tanks such as the Heritage Foundation.

S corporation   A corporation in which individual shareholders pay taxes, but the corporation itself does not.

Senate Finance Committee   Committee of the U.S. Senate responsible for bills pertaining to trade and taxes.

Small Business Committee   Committee of the U.S House of Representatives that recommends legislation pertaining to small businesses.

soft money   Money contributed to political parties to get around the federal caps on financial contributions to particular political candidates.

state tax credit   Provision that allows owners of estates to subtract from their federal estate tax bill death taxes they pay at the state level up to a given amount. Allows states to collect death taxes equal in size to the maximum allowable credit.

step-up in basis   Tax law provision that allows the revaluing at death of inherited assets at their fair market value for the purpose of assessing capital gains tax liability, resulting in forgiveness of capital gains taxes.

sunset   A statutory provision designed to lapse after a set period of time unless formally renewed. The estate tax repeal provision will expire (or "sunset") after ten years unless Congress renews it at that point.

tax credit   An amount taxpayers can subtract from their total tax liability. Differs from a tax deduction, an amount taxpayers can subtract from their gross or adjusted gross income.

Taxpayer Relief Act of 1997   First of the tax cuts enacted during Bill Clinton's presidency. Included QFOBI.

TRC   Tax Relief Coalition. Business coalition formed to support President George W. Bush's proposed 2001 tax plan. Led by Dirk Van Dongen and NAW, the U.S. Chamber of Commerce, NFIB, and NAM.

TRC Management Committee   Eleven-member committee at the head of the TRC.

triangulation   A political strategy of taking aspects of two opposing positions and combining these parts to craft a third position. Usually implies a position somewhere between the Democratic and Republican alternatives. Associated with the Clinton presidency.

United for a Fair Economy   Small Boston-based liberal advocacy group that fought against estate tax repeal. Parent organization of Responsible Wealth.

United Seniors   Nonprofit organization that promotes conservative policies in support of senior citizens. Worked actively for estate tax repeal as a member of the Working Group for Death Tax Repeal.

Urban Institute   Founded in 1968, the largest Washington think tank. Research oriented and liberally inclined. Published some scholarly papers that voiced anti–estate tax repeal views.

U.S. Chamber of Commerce   Business group representing over three million American businesses. TRC leader and TRC Management Committee member.

Ways and Means Committee   Committee of the U.S. House responsible for crafting all tax, trade, and much health care legislation.

Wednesday meetings   Weekly meetings in Washington, D.C., where nearly a hundred conservative lobbyists, politicians, and opinion-leaders meet to exchange information and plan legislative strategy. Hosted by Grover Norquist.

Working Group for Death Tax Repeal   Pro–estate tax repeal coalition formed by Bill Beach of the Heritage Foundation in 1996. Composed of 20–25 groups including think tanks such as CATO and AEI and lobbying organizations such as the 60 Plus Association and NFIB.

BIBLIOGRAPHIC ESSAY

Many interviews informed the authors of the book. These are not specifically cited herein. The following essays, by chapter, give citations for other materials referenced by the authors or quoted in the book. Unless otherwise indicated, all Internet sources were available as of August 2003.

CHAPTER 1: A POLITICAL MYSTERY

For an overview of the estate tax and who was taxed by it before the 2001 tax legislation passed, see Joint Committee on Taxation, "JCT Describes Present Law, Proposals on Estate, Gift Taxation," *Tax Notes Today* (March 15, 2001) and Barry W. Johnson and Jacob M. Mikow, "Federal Estate Tax Returns, 1998–2000" at http://www.irs.gov/pub/irs-soi/00esart.pdf (April 14, 2004). For historical background information on the estate tax, see Barry W. Johnson and Martha Britton Eller, "Federal Taxation of Inheritance and Wealth Transfers," at http://www.irs.gov/pub/irs-soi/inhwlttr.pdf (April 14, 2004). For numbers about the distribution of wealth in America, see, for example, Wojciech Kopczuk and Emmanuel Saez, "Top Wealth Shares in the United States, 1916–2000: Evidence from Estate Tax Returns," National Bureau of Economic Research Working Paper No. W10399, March 2004, and sources cited for chapter 9.

CHAPTER 2: GENESIS OF THE REPEAL COALITION

For background on Soldano's family office business, see http://www.cymricfamily office.com/aboutus.html. On the story of the Brown family for whom she works, see Pat Soldano, "Death Taxes Should Take from the Wealthy; but How Much? The Story of Tina and Pat Brown" (September 2001), at http://www.naa.org/ artpage.cfm?AID=2904&SID=1039. For more information on Soldano's Center for the Study of Taxation founded in 1992, see http://www.center4studytax.com/ and LJH Global Investments, http://www.ljh.com/forums_1995.htm. Soldano's efforts were bankrolled by many prominent families including the Mars family and the Gallos. For background on the political involvement of the Gallo family, see George Lardner, "A Little Bit for Everyone in HR 11409," *Washington Post*, October 7, 1978; James Endrst, "Frontline Traces Donations to Candidates," *Hartford Courant*, January 29, 1996; Rich Jaroslovsky, "Washington Wire: A Special

Weekly Report from the *Wall Street Journal's* Capital Bureau," *New York Times,* July 25, 1986; Albert Crenshaw, "Tax Break Expiring; Loophole Benefits Bequests from the Rich," *Washington Post,* October 1, 1989; Frank Prial, "Wine Talk," *New York Times,* April 14, 1993. The Gallos have contributed to both Republican and Democratic national committees, and politicians of both political persuasions in California (they reside in Modesto). The Gallo Winery and the Mars family also contributed tens of thousands of dollars to Soldano's groups since the late 1990s. See Jonathan Weisman, "Linking Tax to Death May Have Brought Its Doom," *USA Today* (May 20, 2001). Data on the lobbying income for Soldano's Policy and Taxation Group in 1997 and 1998, its lobbying expenditures in 1999 and 2000, and contributions to it from Patton Boggs came from a search of the Center for Responsive Politics website at http://www.opensecrets.org. For more information on Patton Boggs and its legendary lobbying prowess, see http://www.pattonboggs .com, "Profiles in Power: The 100 Most Influential Lawyers in America," *National Law Journal* (June 12, 2002); "The Lobbyist," 60 Minutes transcript (August 22, 1999), at http://www.pblaw.com/Articles/articles/60_minutes.html; Kate Ackley, "The K Street Divide: Big 4 Leads the Way," at http://www.pblaw.com/aboutus/ articles/big4.html; and Influence Inc. 2000: Top Lobbying Firms: Patton Boggs LLP, at http://www.opensecrets.org/pubs/lobby00/toplobby02.asp. On the work that Patton Boggs has done on the estate tax issue, see Jonathan Weisman, "Estate Tax Compromise Sought," *Washington Post,* June 18, 2003, p. E1, at http:// www.washingtonpost.com/ac2/wp-dyn/A7142-2003Jun17?language=printer; and Christina Nuckols, "Lobby for Rich Pushing to End Virginia's Estate Tax," *Virginian Pilot,* January 12, 2003, at http://www.hamptonroads.com/pilotonline/ news/nw0112rich.html.

For background on Harold Apolinsky, see his profile at http://www.sirote .com/sirote.asp?section=attorneys&page=index%2Easp&action=indiv&id=112, and his testimony before the House Ways and Means Committee, "Hearing on Reducing the Estate Tax Burden" (January 28, 1998), at http://waysandmeans .house.gov/legacy/fullcomm/105cong/1-28-98/1-28apol.htm. Also see Ethan Wallison, "One-Man Gang Wages War against Death Tax," *Roll Call* (April 3, 2000) and Bob Thompson, "Sharing the Wealth?" *Washington Post Magazine,* April 13, 2003, p. W8. For general information on Jim Martin and the 60 Plus Association, see http://www.60plus.org and http://www.60plus.org/about-bio.asp; Stephen Goode, "Martin Sounds Death Knell for 'Death Tax,'" *Insight* (December 14, 1998); John Gizzi, "Launching George W. in Politics," *Human Events* (January 1, 1999), at http://www.60plus.org/news.asp?docID=286; John McCaslin, "Dubya and Buddha," *Washington Times,* July 13, 2001, p. A9; Andrea Billups, "Bush Pal around for Long Haul," *Washington Times,* August 11, 2001, at http://www .washtimes.com/national/20010811-10060702.htm, and http://www.60plus.org/ news.asp?docID=245.

The Family Business Estate Tax Coalition, formed in 1995, was led by the National Federation of Independent Business (http://www.nfib.org), the National

Cattlemen's Beef Association (http://hill.beef.org/estatetax/), the National Association of Manufacturers (http://www.nam.org), the American Farm Bureau (http://www.fb.org), the Food Marketing Institute (http://www.fmi.org), and the National Association of Manufacturers (http://www.nam.org).

CHAPTER 3: SQUALL OR SEA CHANGE?

In the election of November 8, 1994, Republicans regained control of both houses of Congress for the first time since the Eisenhower administration in 1953–54. For a more detailed description of this event and its effect on the political landscape, see Dan Balz, "A Historic Republican Triumph: GOP Captures Congress; Party Controls Both Houses for First Time Since 50s," *Washington Post*, November 9, 1994, p. A1; Richard Berke, "The 1994 Elections: The Overview; GOP Wins Control of Senate and Makes Big Gains in House," *New York Times*, November 9, 1994, p. A1; and R. W. Apple, "The 1994 Elections: News Analysis; A Vote against Clinton," *New York Times*, November 9, 1994, p. A1.

A number of conservative legislators and activists were particularly instrumental in leading the Republican insurgency and reshaping the political agenda. Biographical information on Newt Gingrich can be found at "A Newt Chronology" at http://www.pbs.org/wgbh/pages/frontline/newt/newtchron.html and his profile at http://www.aei.org/scholars/scholarID.20,filter./scholar.asp. For background on the Republican House Majority Leader Dick Armey, see http://premierespeakers.com/2708/index.cfm. Additional information on Grover Norquist of Americans for Tax Reform can be found at http://www.atr.org/aboutatr/ggnbio.html. For a summary of Norquist's political activities, see Robert Dreyfuss, "Grover Norquist: 'Field Marshal' of the Bush Plan," *The Nation* (April 26, 2001), at http://www.thenation.com/doc.mhtml?i=20010514&s=dreyfuss, and Susan Page, "Norquist's Power High, Profile Low," *USA Today*, June 1, 2001, at http://www.usatoday.com/news/washington/2001-06-01-grover.htm; John Maggs, "Grover at the Gate," *National Journal* 35 (October 11, 2003): 3100–3107; and Nina J. Easton, *Gang of Five: Leaders at the Center of the Conservative Crusade* (New York: Simon & Shuster, 2000), 135–176. For more information on former Congressman Bill Frenzel's political career, see http://www.brook.edu/scholars/BFRENZEL.HTM; Dale Russakoff, "For Frenzel, an End to House Arrest," *Washington Post* (November 1, 1990), p. A21; and "Three Major Losses," *Washington Post* (November 15, 1990), p. A24.

One of the ten bills that was part of the 1994 "Contract with America" was the Job Creation and Wage Enhancement Act, which called for an increase in the estate tax unified credit amount (from $600,000 to $700,000 in 1996, $725,000 in 1997, and $750,000 in 1998; after 1998 this would be adjusted for inflation). This bill was introduced as HR 9 by Congressmen Bill Archer (R-TX) on January 4, 1995, and passed the House on March 3, 1995, but without the estate tax provision. Information on the bill was acquired though a search of http://thomas

.loc.gov. A full text of the "Contract with America" can be found at http://www.townhall.com/documents/contract.html.

CHAPTER 4: AN OPPORTUNITY MISSED

Internet sources for this chapter were available as of January 2004. The Qualified Family-Owned Business Exemption (QFOBE) was created in 1997. It responded to pressure from the business and farm communities by creating the Qualified Family-Owned Business Exclusion to allow family-owned business a higher ($1,300,000) exclusion. It was modified into the Qualified Family Owned Business Interests (QFOBI) deduction in 1998. Information on the early estate tax reform legislation can be obtained from a search of http://thomas.loc.gov. For background on early efforts at estate tax law changes, see Edward Cowan, "Defining an Estate Tax Limit," *New York Times,* July 6, 1981, p. D1; Jan Rosen, "Tax Watch; Family Business in a Legal Tangle," *New York Times,* October 2, 1989, p. D2; Thomas Watterson, "Family-Owned Businesses Cashing in on a Break," *Boston Globe,* December 10, 1990, p. 20; Watterson, "Family-Owned Firms Could Get a Break from Congress," *Boston Globe,* April 30, 1990, p. 17; Albert Crenshaw, "Tax Proposals for the Heart and Soul," *Washington Post,* June 27, 1993, p. H1; Jim DeSimone, "Small Business Owners Send Concerns to Clinton," *Orlando Sentinel,* March 29, 1995, p. B1; Gary Klott, "Small Business," *Orlando Sentinel,* June 25, 1995, p. H2; Klott, "Small Business Targeted for Many Tax Breaks," *Chicago Tribune,* June 27, 1995, p. 5; "Digest," *Washington Post,* July 29, 1995, p. F1; and Frank Seffinger, "Plan Gives Tax Relief on Transfer of Family Firms," *Rocky Mountain News,* August 23, 1995, p. 52A. Also see Statement of Senator Murray on the American Family Business Preservation Act, *Congressional Record* vol. 141, no. 2 (January 5, 1995), and Statement of Senator Dole, "Targeting Estate Tax Relief to Family Owned Businesses," *Congressional Record* 141, no. 94 (June 9, 1995).

On July 28, 1995, Senators Robert Dole and David Pryor introduced S.B. 1086, the American Family Owned Business Act, to exclude from the gross estate specified portions of the value of qualified family-owned business interests. See Statements on Introduced Bills and Joint Resolutions, *Congressional Record* 141 (July 28, 1995) for the list of supporting groups. On March 19, 1997, Senator Charles Grassley (R-IA) introduced S.B. 479, the Estate Tax Relief for the American Family Act of 1997, to provide for an annual incremental increase, from the then-current $192,800 credit to a credit of $1 million by the year 2002. It had 21 cosponsors and was referred to the Senate Finance Committee. For Senator Lott's comments, see "Lott Would Slay Estate Tax 'Monster,'" *Tax Notes Today* (March 20, 1997). For Bob Packwood's repeal prediction, see Ben Wildavsky, "NFIB Soft on Repeal of Estate Tax?" *National Journal* (March 15, 1997). On April 24, 1997, Senator Don Nickles (R-OK) introduced S.B. 650 to reduce estate taxes to a 20% rate on estates over $1 million and a 30% rate on those over $10 million.

On August 5, 1997, the Taxpayer Relief Act (P.L. 105–34), which was introduced on June 24, 1997, as HR 2014, was signed into law to increase gradually the unified credit amount to $1 million by 2006. It created the Qualified Family-Owned Business Exemption (QFOBE), giving such businesses a $1,300,000 exclusion. The QFOBE was created in 1997 and modified into the Qualified Family Owned Business Interests (QFOBI) deduction in 1998, found in §2057 of the Internal Revenue Code. This provision was modified by the IRS Restructuring and Reform Act of 1998, which became P.L. 105–206 on July 22, 1998. The 1998 legislation limited the exception for family-owned businesses to 15 partners or fewer, though this was increased to 45 in 2001. For Grassley's comments on the "technical improvements" being made with QFOBI, see "Grassley Bill Would Cut Estate Tax Rates," *Tax Notes Today* (April 1, 1997).

The specific provisions of QFOBI can be found in Internal Revenue Code sections 2033A and 2057. For background on QFOBI, see "Estate Tax Relief for Family-Owned Businesses" (February 2000), at http://www.ntca.org/leg_reg/taxes/estate.html; Shannon O'Brien, "Estate Tax Treatment of Family Owned Businesses: The Evolution of Internal Revenue Code Section 2057," *University of Missouri, Kansas City, Law Review* 6 (1999): 495–518; Jerry Kasner, "After the Estate Tax Family Business Deduction, What Next?" *Tax Notes* 88 (September 18, 2000): 1503; R. Lee Grant, "Comment: Analysis of the Recapture Tax for Qualified Family-Owned Business Interest Deductions," *Ohio Northern University Law Review* 26, no. 289 (2000); and "Issues, Interests, and Advocates," *Legal Times* (February 3, 1997), p. S30. For one effort to explain how QFOBI applies by Smith and Zuccarini P.S., a firm of estate-planning lawyers, see http://www.smithzuccarini.com/Qualifying%20for%20the%20QFOBE%20Deduction.PDF. For arguments about the need for further reform after the enactment of QFOBI, see "Keeping the Family Business in the Family Can Be Tough When You've Got an Uncle Named Sam," *Spokesman-Review* (November 16, 1997); William Beach, Heritage Foundation, "A Scorecard on Death Tax Reform" (June 25, 1998), at http://www.heritage.org/Research/Taxes; and William Beach, "Time to Repeal Federal Death Taxes: The Nightmare of the American Dream" (April 4, 2001), at http://www.heritage.org/Research/Taxes/.

For some information on the early efforts of the coalition, see T. R. Goldman, "Budget Plan Means Lobby Spree," *Legal Times* (May 19, 1997), p. 1, and Lori Nitschke, "Eager to Hack at Estate Tax, Foes Welcome New Allies," *CQ Weekly* (September 11, 1999). The poll described in the text was conducted by Luntz Research Company, August, 1998.

Some background information on Bob Packwood and his role in the estate tax debate can be found in "Rushing away from Taxes," *New York Times,* December 22, 1996, Sect. 1, p. 30; Alissa Rubin, "Packwood Joins Group Battling Estate Taxes," *Rocky Mountain News,* March 27, 1997, p. 6B; Jim Barnett, "The Afterlife of Bob Packwood," *Seattle Times,* October 5, 1997, p. B5; David Segal, "Lawmakers Strive to Reduce Estate Tax," *Washington Post,* July 28, 1997, p. A8; and Bob Thompson, "Sharing the Wealth?" *Washington Post Magazine,* April 13, 2003, p. W8.

CHAPTER 5: AN ADVOCATE FOR THE WORKING RICH

For general information on the life of Congresswoman Dunn and her career in politics, see http://www.house.gov/dunn/bio.htm. For more on Dunn's political career and her consideration for cabinet positions by the Bush administration, see Alex Freyer, "Will Murray Meet Her Match?" *Seattle Times,* February 25, 2003. For the way Dunn conceives of the estate tax issue, see the May 28, 1999, editorial she wrote on the "death tax" that appeared in *Insight* magazine at http://www.house.gov/dunn/oped/dtaxop.htm, and her article "Why We Need Permanent Repeal of the Death Tax" in the March/April 2004 issue of *Tax Features,* published by the Tax Foundation, which is also quoted in the text.

On Dunn's ability to "speak eloquent suburban," see Joni Balter, "Dunn's No-Go Decision Leaves GOP Scrambling," *Seattle Times,* April 17, 2003. On Dunn as a "translator to women," see "The GOP: Is the Day of the Hothead Over?" *Business Week,* September 8, 1997. On Dunn's ability to avoid "being defined by 'women's issues,'" see "This Woman's Place Is in the House," *Washington Times,* July 13, 1998. On Dunn's older son being named Reagan for the former president, see Freyer, "Will Murray Meet Her Match?" On Microsoft's support for Dunn, see Ken Silverstein, "The Microsoft Network," *Mother Jones* (January/February 1998). On Dunn being one of Gingrich's "chief lieutenants," see "Not Quite a Dunn Deal," *Seattle Post Intelligencer,* April 27, 1997. On Bill Archer's view that we should "pull the income tax out by its roots and throw it away so it can never grow back," see his April 15, 1997, floor statement on the Taxpayer Protection Act, at http://www.epic.org/privacy/databases/irs/archer_statement_497.html.

Ideological ratings for Jennifer Dunn are from the *National Journal* (in 1999, Dunn voted more conservatively than 84% of House members on economic issues, 56% more conservatively on social issues, and 55% more conservatively on foreign policy; in 2000, Dunn voted more conservatively than 76% of House members on economics issues, 52% on social issues, and 78% on foreign policy), the American Conservative Union (90% for life, 92% in 2002, 88% in 2001, 88% in 2000, 80% in 1999, 96% in 1998, 92% in 1997, 100% in 1996, 80% in 1995, 86% in 1994, and 91% in 1993), and the Americans for Democratic Action (5% in 2002, 0% in 2000, 10% in 1999, 0% in 1998, 0% in 1997, 0% in 1996, 5% in 1995, 5% in 1994, 5% in 1993). Dunn's ratings from business groups come from the U.S. Chamber of Commerce (99% cumulative, 100% in 2002, 95% in 2001, 95% in 2000, 96% in 1999, 100% in 1998, 100% in 1997). For Dunn's record on the environment, see ratings from the League of Conservation Voters (18% in 107th Congress, 7% in 106th, 21% in 105th, 12% in 104th, 11% in 103rd) and Patrick McMahon, "Some See Environment as GOP Weakness," *USA Today,* July 23, 2002.

Information on the various bills introduced and their cosponsors can be found on the congressional website at http://thomas.loc.gov. The following is a brief summary of the most important bills: On July 23, 1993, Representative Christopher Cox (R-CA) introduced HR 2717, the Family Heritage Preservation Act (to repeal the federal estate and gift taxes and the tax on generation-skipping transfers), the first major estate tax repeal legislation. It gained 29 cosponsors by 1994, 102 cosponsors by 1996, and 204 cosponsors by 1998, including the entire GOP leadership. Cox reintroduced the legislation on February 1, 1995 (HR 784), March 3, 1997 (HR 902), and January 6, 1999 (HR 86). Dunn did not become a cosponsor of the Cox bill until March 20, 1997. The bill was referred to the Ways and Means Committee and finally taken up in 1998. For a brief biography of Cox, see http://cox.house.gov/html/bio.cfm.

On March 27, 1995, Senator Jon Kyl (R-AZ) introduced S.B. 628, the Family Heritage Preservation Act, to repeal the federal estate and gift taxes and the tax on generation-skipping transfers (nine cosponsors). The Senate Finance Committee held hearings on the bill in June of the same year. In August 1995, Jennifer Dunn (R-WA) began working to create a bipartisan coalition of Republicans and Blue Dog Democrats to push for an exemption for family-owned businesses. After the enactment of QFOBI on March 14, 1998, Dunn introduced HR 3879, the Estate and Gift Tax Rate Reduction Act of 1998, to amend the Internal Revenue Code of 1986 by phasing out the estate and gift taxes over a ten-year period. It attracted 133 cosponsors and was referred to the House Ways and Means Committee. On January 19, 1999, Senator Kyl again introduced S.B. 56, the Family Heritage Preservation Act, to repeal the federal estate tax (26 cosponsors).

On February 25, 1999, Representative Dunn (R-WA) first introduced HR 8, the Death Tax Elimination Act, which would gradually phase out the estate tax over a ten-year period. It eventually received 244 cosponsors. This marked a change in language from "estate tax" to "death tax" (from the first law introduced by Dunn in May 1998). On May 26, 1999, Senator Kyl introduced S.B. 1128, the Estate Tax Elimination Act of 1999, a bill cosponsored by Senator Bob Kerrey (D-NB), which would amend the Internal Revenue Code of 1986 to repeal the federal estate and gift taxes and the tax on generation-skipping transfers, provide for a carryover basis at death and establish a partial capital gains exclusion for inherited assets. It had 30 cosponsors and was referred to the Senate Finance Committee. A similar bill, cosponsored by Kyl and John Breaux (D-LA), was introduced on February 7, 2001, to repeal the tax but preserve a step-up in basis of certain property acquired from a decedent.

CHAPTER 6: STORIES FROM THE GRASSTOPS

The stories of the difficulties faced by family farms and businesses due to the estate tax are from William Beach, the Heritage Foundation, "Death Tax Devastation: Horror Stories from Middle Class America," at http://www.deathtax

.com/deathtax/beachpro.html. The account of John Kearney's experience with the estate tax is partially derived from David Cay Johnston, "Despite Benefits, Democrats' Estate Tax Plan Gets Little Notice," *New York Times,* July 13, 2000, p. C1. The account of David Pankonin's experience with the estate tax is partially derived from David Pankonin, "Will Uncle Sam Inherit the Family Business?" *Wall Street Journal,* November 28, 1995.

CHAPTER 7: CHANGING THE FACE FOR REPEAL

Remarks made by Chester Thigpen are from his February 1, 1995, statement before the House Ways and Means Committee. The story of Chester Thigpen has been endlessly recycled by repeal advocates; see James Martin, "Dying Should Not be a Taxable Event," *Vital Speeches of the Day* 65, no. 24 (October 1, 1999), at http://www.60plus.org/vitalspeeches.asp?docID=349; Martin, "The Death Tax Is Killing the Family," *Washington Times,* May 22, 1997, p. A19; Martin, "Death and Taxes," *Washington Times,* May 22, 1997; Martin, "Senior Voice," *60 Plus Newsletter* (April 1998); Martin, *Insight* 14, no. 46 (December 14, 1998); Martin, "Death Tax Watch," *Washington Times,* February 21, 2001, p. A17; William Beach, "Death Tax Devastation: Horror Stories from Middle-Class America," at http://www.deathtax.com/deathtax/beachpro.html; "What Chester Thigpen Spent a Lifetime Working for, the Federal Government Wants to Take Away," National Center for Public Policy Research (May 1996), at http://www.nationalcenter.org/thigpen.html; Edmund Peterson, "Estate Tax Bite Threatens Black Business," *Insight* (July 29, 1996); Project 21 Chairman Edmund Peterson's Statement on Repeal of the Estate Tax (March 3, 1997), at http://www.project21.org/p21estatetax397.html; Lawrence Goodrich, "A Taxing Fight over How to Save Family Farms," *Christian Science Monitor,* March 5, 1997, p. 4; Statement of Douglas Stinson in his testimony before the House Ways and Means Committee on January 28, 1998, at http://waysandmeans.house.gov/legacy/fullcomm/105cong/1-28-98/1-28stin.htm; Statement of Dr. A. G. "Skeet" Burris before the House Subcommittee on Forests and Forest Health on September 14, 2000; Joint Economic Committee Study, "The Economics of the Estate Tax" (December 1998), at http://www.house.gov/jec/fiscal/tx-grwth/estattax/estattax.htm; Joshua Green, "Meet Mr. Death," *American Prospect,* 12, issue 9 (May 21, 2001), at http://www.prospect.org/print/V12/9/green-j.html; and Bob Thompson, "Sharing the Wealth?" *Washington Post,* April 13, 2003, at http://www.taxpolicycenter.org/news/share_wealth.cfm. For photos of Chester Thigpen, see "Outstanding Tree Farmers 1995, Chester and Rosette Thigpen," at http://www.treefarmsystem.org/gallery/1995farmer.cfm   and   http://www.usda.gov/oc/photo/99cs1535.htm.

On Frank Blethen and his commitment to racial justice and diversity, see Blethen's keynote address to the Society of Professional Journalists National Convention on October 5, 2001, entitled "2001: A News Odyssey, Part II," at http://www.maynardije.org/columns/guests/011010_blethen/011010_blethen2/. Also see the *Seattle Times* website at http://www.seattletimescompany.com/working/ diversity.htm and http://www.seattletimescompany.com/communication/pr.1999 .htm. On the risk that the estate tax poses to minority-owned newspapers, see Martin, "Dying Should Not be a Taxable Event," and Frank Blethen's Opening Remarks entitled "Only in Variety is There Freedom," at a symposium on the independent family newspaper in America at the University of Illinois at Urbana-Champaign (November 8, 2002). For the problem that the tax creates for minority businesses in general, see Joseph H. Astrachan and Craig E. Aronoff, "A Report on the Impact of the Federal Estate Tax: A Study of Two Industry Groups," Family Enterprise Center of the Coles School of Business, Kennesaw State College (July 24, 1995). For additional stories of the harm done to minority businesses by the tax, see Jennifer Dunn, "Op-Ed on the Death Tax," *Insight* (May 28, 1999), at http://www.house.gov/dunn/oped/dtaxop.htm, and the editorial by Black Chamber of Commerce President Harry Alford, "Blacks Should Help in Doing Away with the Death Tax," at http://www.nationalbcc.org/issues/default.asp?id=1319. See also Project 21 News, "Study Shows Estate Tax Will Kill Many Black-Owned Family-Run Businesses; Great-Grandson of Slaves Says Estate Tax Would Breakup Family Farm and Harm Environment" (May 11, 1996), at http://www .nationalcenter.org/estatetax.htm; and Syd Gernstein, "Death Taxes Are Killing Black Businesses," (July 2000), at http://www.nationalcenter.org/NPA301.html. For general information about Project 21, the national leadership network of conservative African Americans, see "Project 21: A History," at http://www.national center.org/P21History.html.

Background information on Alexis Scott-Reeves and the *Atlanta Daily World* was compiled from "Modern Journalists: Alexis-Scott Reeves," at http://www.pbs .org/blackpress/modern_journalist/reeves.html; Yusuf Davis, "Film Documentary Honors *Daily World*," *Atlanta Journal Constitution*, June 9, 1998; Joel Hall, "Atlanta Daily World Has Long, Illustrious History," *Atlanta Daily World*, August 2, 2002, at http://www.zwire.com/site/news.cfm?newsid=4937794&BRD=1077& PAG461&dept_id=498597&rfi=6; M. Alexis Scott, "ADW: News and History Since 1928," *Atlanta Daily World* November 4, 1999, at http://www.zwire.com/ site/news.cfm?newsid=16075&BRD=1077&PAG461&dept_id=237841&rfi=6; Alfred Charles, "Covering Atlanta's World Since 1928: Newspaper Continues Delivering News to the African American Community," *Atlanta Journal Constitution*, May 25, 2003; Jim Auchmutey, Catherine Fox, and Lyle Harris, "Walking Tour," *Atlanta Journal Constitution*, July 2, 1996; Gary Pomerantz, "Journalist Takes Helm of 'Family Legacy' the *Daily World*," *Atlanta Journal Constitution*, August 15, 1997; "Struggling for a Voice: Women Reporters in the South" (March 19, 2002), athttp://www.emory.edu/COLLEGE/JOURNALISM/events_womenwriters.shtml; "Atlanta's King's 'Sweet Auburn' Recovering after Years of Decline" (January 17,

1998), at http://www.cnn.com/US/9801/17/kings.sweet.auburn/; "William Alexander Scott II," at http://www.blackpressusa.com/history/GOG_Article.asp?News ID=2052; Cynthia Tucker, "William Scott III: A Life That Was Well-Lived," *Atlanta Journal Constitution,* March 11, 1992; "Atlanta Daily World," at http://www.fatherryan.org/BlackPress/html/atl.htm; "Atlanta Life Insurance Company Names Alexis Scott-Reeves as New Board Member," at http://www.atlantalife.com/NewsRelease/NewsRelease5.html; and Amy Hirth, "A Predestined Career Takes *Daily World*'s Reeves to the Top," at http://www.mindspring.com/~sartor/gradyhs/south0299_reeves.html. Also see the website of the *Atlanta Daily World* at http://www.zwire.com/site/news.cfm?brd=1077.

For Scott-Reeves's involvement in the estate tax issue, see Samantha Sommer, "Estate Tax Repeal Finds Allies in Black Leaders," *Atlanta Journal Constitution,* April 4, 2001; Jeff Dickerson, "Repeal Would Make Sense," *Atlanta Journal Constitution,* June 6, 2000; and Mark Sherman, "Repeal of the Estate Tax May Be Well on Its Way," *Atlanta Journal Constitution,* April 23, 2000. Also see Family Business Horror Story #8, William Beach, "Death Tax Devastation: Horror Stories from Middle-Class America," at http://www.deathtax.com/deathtax/beachpro.html.

Background information on Alejandro Aguirre and his newspaper *Diario Las Americas* was compiled from Florida Arts Council Bios at http://www.florida-arts.org/about/FloridaArtsCouncilBios.htm; Benigno Aguirre, "Ethnic Newspapers and Politics: *Diario Las Americas* and the Watergate Affair," *Ethnic Groups* 2 (1979): 155–65; "Good for You," *Stuart News/Port St. Lucie News,* August 3, 1997 and December 16, 2001; "Newspaper Publisher to Discuss Communism," *Sun Sentinel,* April 21, 2002; Joseph Mann, "Spanish Daily Set to Debut," *Sun Sentinel,* October 6, 2000; Deborah Circelli, "Panel to Examine State Energy's Future," *Palm Beach Post,* September 10, 2000; Marguerite Plunkett, "Pennysaver Plans Spanish Edition," *Palm Beach Post,* June 18, 1999; Scott Gold, "Bush Picks Nominees for College Boards," *Sun Sentinel,* February 25, 1999; John Craddock, "State Has Many Women, Minorities, Eligible for Council," *St. Petersburg Times,* April 21, 1991; Letta Tayler, "In Cuba Private Libraries Draw Threats," *Newsday,* June 9, 2002; and William Rodriguez, "Travel Restrictions a Necessary Measure against Castro's Cuba," *Tampa Tribune,* April 25, 2002. Also see the *Diario*'s website at http://www.diariolasamericas.com/DPortada.htm.

For a list of members of Congress who supported repeal, see the roll call vote at http://clerkweb.house.gov/cgi-bin/vote.exe?year=2001&rollnumber=84. For the statement of Sanford Bishop on the House floor on June 6, 2002, see http://www.house.gov/bishop/deatax.html. For press releases from the office of Congressman Wynn on this issue, see "Bush's Tax Plan: Robin Hood for the Rich?" (February 8, 2001), at http://www.wynn.house.gov/issues2.cfm?id=3143; "Why Small Businesses Are Critical to Our Community's Growth," at http://www.wynn.house.gov/display2.cfm?id=3162&type=Issues; "Wynn Says 99% Is Enough! Calls Republican Bill Excessive and Reckless" (June 6, 2002), http://www

.wynn.house.gov/issues2.cfm?id=3095. Also see Karen Hosler, "Estate Tax Bill Passes House," *Baltimore Sun,* June 10, 2000, p. 1A, and Hosler, "House Upholds Estate Tax Veto," *Baltimore Sun,* September 8, 2000, p. 1A.

For a list of minority groups supporting the death tax repeal, see "Death Tax Newsletter," issue 12 (July 28, 2000), at http://www.deathtax.com/deathtax/news0700.html. For information on the National Black Chamber of Commerce, see http://www.nationalbcc.org/issues/default.asp?id=1299, and for background on the Hispanic Chamber of Commerce, see http://www.ushcc.com. For details on the press conference held by minority business groups, see "Business Groups Call for an End to the 'Death Tax' Press Conference" (May 26, 1999), at http://www.nationalbcc.org/issues/default.asp?id=1313, and "Business Groups Call for Congress to End the Death Tax: Leaders Cite Perils to Minority and Family-Owned Businesses from Tax That Collects Little Revenue" (May 26, 1999), at http://www.nationalbcc.org/issues/default.asp?id=1313. For unofficial transcripts of West Wing episodes 48 ("Ways and Means") and 49 ("On the Day Before") that dealt with estate tax repeal, see http://www.angelfire.com/me4/emily6/westwing transcripts.html. On the relative wealth of Whites and African Americans, see Thomas M. Shapiro, *The Hidden Cost of Being African American: How Wealth Perpetuates Inequality* (Oxford: Oxford University Press, 2004).

On the effect of the death tax on women, see Travis Research Associates, "Survey of the Impact of the Federal Estate Tax on NAWBO Member Businesses," prepared for the Center for the Study of Taxation (February 23, 2000); John Hughes, "More Women Facing 'Death Taxes,'" *Olympian,* March 26, 2000; Nancy Pfotenhauer, "Independent Women's Forum Special Report—Women and the Death Tax: Saving for the Next Generation" (April 2002). For more on the involvement of minorities and women on this issue, see Joint Economic Committee Study, "The Economics of the Estate Tax" (December 1998); the statement of Pat Soldano in her testimony before the House Ways and Means Committee on April 13, 2000, at http://waysandmeans.house.gov/legacy/fullcomm/106cong/4-13-00/4-13sold.htm; and the statement of Amy Moritz Ridenour, President of the National Center for Public Policy Research at the Tax Day Rally in Washington, D.C., on April 15, 1992, http://www.nationalcenter.org/TaxDayAMR497.html.

For the Policy and Taxation Group's report on the 2004 poll and focus group survey of Hispanic business owners, see http://www.policyandtaxationgroup.com/ (last visited September 17, 2004). An article on Leslie Sanchez's IMPACTO Group, LLC can be found at http://www.scienceblog.com/community/older/archives/K/2/pub2690.html (last visited September 17, 2004).

Regarding the support of gays and lesbians for repeal of the tax, see Pat Soldano, "The Death Tax IS a Gay Issue" (July 21, 2001), at www.libertyeducationforum.org/lefcontents/readingroom/deathtax.pdf, and Luntz Research Companies Memorandum, "The Death Tax and Gay and Lesbian Americans" (April 24, 2001), at http://www.center4studytax.com/pub.htm#gaysurvey.

For more information on the concerns of minorities in passing an inheritance on to future generations, see Adrienne S. Harris, "Saluting the Past, Shaping the Future: The Future of Black-Owned Family Business," *Black Enterprise* (August 1995) and Cheryl D. Broussard, *The Black Woman's Guide to Financial Independence* (New York: Penguin Books, 1996), 151. For statistics on the racial wealth gap, see Melvin Oliver and Thomas Shapiro, *Black Wealth/White Wealth: A New Perspective on Racial Inequality* (New York: Routledge, 1995), and Robert Kuttner, "Sharing America's Wealth: The Necessary Role of Government in Broadening the Middle Class," *American Prospect* 14, no. 5 (May 2003). For a description of the 2000 meeting in Wisconsin with representatives of the presidential candidates, see Corissa Jansen, "What Do Candidates Offer Black Voters? People from 4 Parties Touch on Issues of Concern," *Milwaukee Journal Sentinel*, October 29, 2000.

On the effect of the estate tax on the environment, see Jonathan Adler, "The Anti-Environment Tax: Why the 'Death Tax' Is Deadly for Endangered Species," *Forest Landowner* (November/December, 1999) and NFIB, "Death Tax Kills Conservation Efforts" (June 3, 2002), at http://www.nfib.com/cgi-bin/NFIB.dll/public/advocacy/newsReleaseDisplay.jsp?BV_Session.

CHAPTER 8: TALKING THE TALK

The quotes on taxes from Abraham Lincoln and the definitions of the principles of "justice" and "virtue" are from Stephen Weisman, *The Great Tax Wars* (New York: Simon and Schuster, 2002), 6, 18. The description of politics comes from Ambrose Bierce, *The Devil's Dictionary*, at http://www.online-literature.com/bierce/devilsdictionary/16/.

Information on HR 4848, the Long-Term Care Family Security Act of 1992 (decreasing the unified credit amount to finance health care) introduced by Representative Henry Waxman (D-CA) and Richard Gephardt (D-MO), as well as HR 886 / S 696, the Medicare Prescription Drug Coverage Act (funding a prescription drug benefit with revenue from the estate tax) introduced by Representative Barney Frank (D-MA) and Senator Wellstone (D-MN) can be found through a search of http://thomas.loc.gov. For the suggestion by OMB Watch that revenue from the estate tax could be used to fund Head Start and child care programs, see "Estate Tax and Government Revenue" (February 8, 2001), at http://www.ombwatch.org/article/articleview/400/1/116/.

For information on the role of Jim Martin and the death tax rhetoric, see James Martin, "Dying Should Not Be a Taxable Event," *Vital Speeches of the Day*, Vol. 65, no. 24 (October 1, 1999), at http://www.60plus.org/vitalspeeches.asp?docID=349 and Joshua Green, "Meet Mr. Death," *The American Prospect*, vol. 12, issue 9 (May 21, 2001), http://www.prospect.org/print/V12/9/green-j.html. Also see the *Seattle Times* website at http://www.deathtax.com. On no one being able to take credit for the death tax label, see Representative Christopher Cox, "Estate-Tax Article Falls Short on Facts," *USA Today*, June 1, 2001, at http://cox.house.gov/press/coverage/2001/usatoday0601deathtax.htm. The use of the term can be found in Louis

Eisenstein, "The Rise and Decline of the Estate Tax," *Tax Law Review,* 11 (1956): 223; "Federal Tax Policy for Economic Growth and Stability," *Joint Committee on the Economic Report,* 84th Cong., 1st Sess. (Joint Committee Print, 1955); and Hearing before the Subcommittee on Tax Policy for Economic Growth and Stability, 84th Cong., 1st Sess. (1955). Also see Lee Anne Fennell, "Death, Taxes, and Cognition," *North Carolina Law Review* 81, no. 567 (2003).

Background on pollster Frank Luntz was compiled from the following sources: a biography of Frank Luntz found at http://www.clientplus.com/fintimes/t_leaders/tl_display.cfm?tl_ID=158 and http://www.luntz.com/frank.htm/. Also see "Editorial: Hypocrisy," *Daily Pennsylvanian,* April 21, 1995; "Column: Rosemary's Time," *Daily Pennsylvanian,* March 24, 1995; "Column: Can You Teach Too Well?" *Daily Pennsylvanian,* February 24, 1994; Daniel Gingiss, "DP Poll Examines Students' Sex Lives," *Daily Pennsylvanian,* February 14, 1994; Jeremy Zweig, "Graduation: Luntz Fighting to Keep Am Civ Course," *Daily Pennsylvanian,* May 14, 1993; Daniel Gingiss, "Long Hours Pay Off as U. Students Finish Poll," *Daily Pennsylvanian,* April 5, 1993; Kimberly May, "Luntz Named Harvard Fellow," *Daily Pennsylvanian,* February 2, 1993; "Frank Luntz Practices What He Teaches with Perot," *Daily Pennsylvanian,* June 4, 1992; Kenneth Baer, "Lecturer to Poll for Buchanan," *Daily Pennsylvanian,* January 14, 1992; Drew Zoller, "NEC Prevents Am Civ Class from Running in UA Elections," *Daily Pennsylvanian,* March 25, 1991; John Jurgensen, "Frankly Speaking; West Hartford Native Frank Luntz Knows What's What, and Makes His Living Telling It to Who's Who," *Hartford Courant,* May 5, 2003, p. H1; Lloyd Grove, "The Reliable Source," *Washington Post,* April 10, 2003; Nicholas Lemann, "The Word Lab; The Mad Science behind What the Candidates Say," *New Yorker,* October 16, 2000, p. 100; Ed Henry, "Heard on the Hill," *Roll Call* (April 8, 1999; October 12, 2000; July 12, 2001; November 19, 2001; February 11, 2002); Amy Keller, "Shop Talk," *Roll Call* (September 28, 1999; May 29, 2000; February 8, 2001); Keller, "The Message is the Medium So You Better Get to Know These 20 Top Republican Campaign Consulting Firms," *Roll Call* (August 12, 1996); Stuart Rothenberg, "Why Even Fellow Republicans Love to Hate Frank Luntz," *Roll Call* (July 31, 1995); Ben Sheffner, "The Republican Guard," *Roll Call* (December 5, 1994); Erica Niedowski, "Luntz' Personal Interest in Puerto Rico Raises Concern over His Objectivity," *The Hill* (September 10, 1997); Jennifer Senior, "Lott Courts GOP Pollster Luntz for GOP Message," *The Hill* (November 27, 1996); Sandy Hume and A. B. Stoddard, "Boehner, Luntz in Faceoff over GOP Message," *The Hill* (July 24, 1996); Sandy Hume, "GOP Pollster Takes Flak for Picking Clinton," *The Hill* (January 31, 1996); Doug Obey, "Memo Watch," *The Hill* (March 22, 1995); Marcia Gelbart, "New GOP Spirit Inspired Contract," *The Hill* (March 1, 1995); and James Toedtman, "Trying to Keep 'Death Tax' Alive," *Newsday,* April 13, 2002. Quotations from Luntz's editorial are from Frank Luntz, "Guest Column: 'R.I.P.' Democracy," *Daily Pennsylvanian,* September 24, 1992.

For Chairman Archer's undertaker/IRS combination, see Jerry Gray, "The

Budget Deal: The Overview; Bills to Balance the Budget and Cut Taxes Pass Senate," *New York Times,* August 1, 1997. For Speaker Newt Gingrich's IRS/undertaker combination, see "Gingrich Announcement of Tax Bill Passage," *Tax Notes Today* (September 29, 1998). For Congressman J. C. Watts's combination, see Russ Flanagan, "Making the Death Tax Repeal Permanent," *New Jersey Herald,* October 21, 2002, and "Making the Death Tax Repeal Permanent" slideshow at http://www.house.gov/herger/images/deathtax.ppt (March 15, 2004). For Senator Grassley's comparison, see "Senate Begins Debate on Tax Relief Reconciliation Act," *Tax Notes Today* (June 15, 2001). A review of the *Congressional Record,* accessed at http://www.gpoaccess.gov/index.html, reveals the numerous concurrences of the death tax and the American Dream in Congressional rhetoric.

Advice on how language can be used to the advantage of Republicans in general, and in the case of the estate tax repeal in particular, can be found in the books and pamphlets by Frank Luntz including *Tax Less, Spend Less, Do More; Language of the 21st Century* (Arlington, Va.: Luntz Research Companies, 1987); *Conservatively Speaking: How to Use the Language of the 21st Century to Win the Hearts and Minds of the American People* (Los Angeles: Center for the Study of Popular Culture, 1997). The polling evidence cited comes from Luntz Research Companies Memorandum, "Americans Talk Taxes" (January 27, 2003), http://www.center4studytax.com/Summary.pdf.

Quotes from Theodore Roosevelt come from his 1910 campaign speech, "The New Nationalism," the text of which can be found at http://teachingamericanhistory.org/library/index.asp?document=501 and a 1910 speech at the University of Paris, "Citizenship in a Republic: The Man in the Arena," the text of which can be found at http://www2.austincc.edu/dskramer/In%20the%20Arena-%20TR.pdf.

CHAPTER 9: EXPLOITING THE THINK TANK GAP

On the role of think tanks in general, see Donald Abelson and Evert A. Lindquist, "Think Tanks in North America," in R. Kent Weaver and James G. McGann, ed., *Think Tanks and Civil Societies: Catalysts for Ideas and Action* (London: Transaction, 2000); Dan Morgan, "Think Tanks: Corporations' Quiet Weapon Nonprofits' Studies, Lobbying Advance Big Business Causes," *Washington Post,* January 29, 2000; Ralph G. Neas, "A Special Report" (Washington, D.C.: People for the American Way, 2003); David Ricci, *The Transformation of American Politics: The New Washington and the Rise of Think Tanks* (New Haven: Yale University Press, 1993); Andrew Rich, *Think Tanks and Public Policy: The Politics of Expertise* (Cambridge and New York: Cambridge University Press, forthcoming); Andrew Rich and R. Kent Weaver, "Think Tanks in the National Media," *Harvard International Journal of Press/Politics* 5, no. 4 (2000): 81–102; Andrew Rich and R. Kent Weaver, "Advocates and Analysts: Think Tanks and the Politicization of Expertise in Washington," in *Group Politics,* ed. Allan Cigler and Burdett Lommis (Washington, D.C.: CQ Press, 1999); R. Kent Weaver, "The Changing World of Think Tanks,"

Political Science and Politics 22, no. 3 (1989): 563–79; Weaver, *Ending Welfare as We Know It* (Washington, D.C.: Brookings Institution Press, 2000); Weaver, "Data on Think Tank Operating Budgets," unpublished dataset (2003); and R. Kent Weaver and James G. McGann, "Think Tanks and Civil Societies in a Time of Change," in *Think Tanks and Civil Societies: Catalysts for Ideas and Action*, ed. R. Kent Weaver and James G. McGann (London: Transaction, 2000). On the number of think tanks, see Weaver and McGann, *Think Tanks and Civil Societies*; for the rankings of think tanks in terms of influence and credibility, see Richard Morin and Claudia Deane, "The Ideas Industry; A Car-Driven Plan to Get the Poor to Work," *Washington Post*, August 3, 1999, p. A13.

On the left, the Brookings Institution and the Urban Institute remain the major think tanks. For information on the Brookings Institution, see "Brookings Institution History: Part III. The Depression: Voice of Opposition," at www .brookings.edu; "Brookings Institution History: Part VII. New Agendas," at www .brookings.edu; Donald T. Critchlow, *The Brookings Institution 1916–1952* (DeKalb: Northern Illinois University Press, 1985). For Brookings work on the estate tax, see William Gale, James Hines, and Joel Slemrod, eds., *Rethinking Estate and Gift Taxation* (Washington, D.C.: Brookings Institution Press, 2001); "Rethinking the Estate and Gift Tax," Policy brief/Paper by William Gale and Joel Slemrod (March, 2001); and "Rhetoric and Economics in the Estate Tax Debate," *National Tax Journal* 54 no. 3 (September 2001) 579–612. For information on the Urban Institute, see www.urban.org.

On the rise of conservatism and right-leaning think tanks, see Sidney Blumenthal, *The Rise of the Counter-Establishment: From Conservative Ideology to Political Power* (New York: Perennial Library, 1986); David Brock, *Blinded by the Right: The Conscience of an Ex-Conservative* (New York: Crown, 2002); David Callahan, National Committee for Responsive Philanthropy, "$1 Billion for Ideas: Conservative Think Tanks in the 1990s" (March 1999); Claudia Deane, "On the Right, Think Tanks Awash in Cash," *Washington Post*, April 27, 1999, p. A15; Godfrey Hodgson, *The World Turned Right Side Up: A History of the Conservative Ascendancy in America* (Boston: Houghton Mifflin, 1996); John Judis, "Business and the Rise of K Street," in *The Paradox of American Democracy* (London: Routledge, 2001), at http://www.thirdworldtraveler.com/Democracy_America/ Rise_K_Street_POAD.html; Nicholas Lemann, "The Republicans: A Government Waits in Wings," *Washington Post*, May 27, 1980, p. A1; Dana Milbank and Ellen Nakashima, "Bush Team Has 'Right' Credentials, Conservative Picks Seen Eclipsing Even Reagan's," *Washington Post*, March 25, 2001, p. A1; Bob Morgan, "Conservatives: A Well-Financed Network," *Washington Post*, January 4, 1981, p. A1; National Committee for Responsive Philanthropy Special Report, "Burgeoning Conservative Think Tanks" (Spring 1991); Margaret Shapiro, "Mandate II," *Washington Post*, November 22, 1984, p. G1; and Robin Toner, "Conservatives Savor Their Role as Insiders at the White House," *New York Times*, March 19, 2001, Sect. 1, p. 1.

For information on the American Enterprise Institute (AEI), see www.aei.org.

Also see Ann Devroy, "Cheneys to Join Conservative Think Tank," *Washington Post,* December 31, 1992, p. C1; and Dana Milbank, "White House Hopes Gas Up a Think Tank For Center-Right AEI, Bush Means Business White House Transition," *Washington Post,* December 8, 2000, p. C1.

For information on the CATO Institute, see www.cato.org; Richard Morin, "Free Radical Libertarian—and Contrarian—Ed Crane Has Run the CATO Institute for 25 Years. His Way," *Washington Post,* May 9, 2002, p. C1; and Spencer Rich, "In the Think of Things, CATO Institute Fitting In after 20 Years," *Washington Post,* May 2, 1997, p. C1.

For background on the Heritage Foundation, see http://www.heritage.org/Support/about.cfm and http://www.mediatransparency.org/recipients/heritage_foundation.htm. Heritage's publications on the estate tax issue include William Beach, "Now Is the Time to Permanently Repeal Federal Death Taxes" (June 2003); Beach, "The Death Tax Must Die" (March 1, 2001); Beach, "Time to Repeal Federal Death Taxes: The Nightmare of the American Dream" (April 4, 2001); Beach, "Time to Eliminate the Costly Death Tax" (June 2000); Beach, "A Scorecard on Death Tax Reform" (June 25, 1998); and Beach, "Policy Backgrounder: The Case for Repealing the Estate Tax," *Policy Backgrounder* (August, 21, 1996). For more information on Beach, see http://www.heritage.org/About/Staff/WilliamBeach.cfm. Also see Daniel Mitchell, "The Truth about Tax Rates and the Politics of Class Warfare" (March 5, 2001).

For additional information on the Heritage Foundation, see Sidney Blumenthal, "Heritage Led by a True Believer," *Washington Post,* September 24, 1985, p. A10; Brock, *Blinded by the Right*; David Broder, "Thanks to Two Think Tanks," *Washington Post,* May 8, 2002, p. A21; Edwin Feulner, "The Heritage Foundation," in *Think Tanks and Civil Societies: Catalysts for Ideas and Action,* ed. R. Kent Weaver and James G. McGann; David Hoffman, "Reagan's Crusaders Fail to Find the Grail," *Washington Post,* July 4, 1982, p. A1; Howie Kurtz, "Meese Helps Group to Raise Funds," *Washington Post,* January 20, 1982, p. A2; Phil McCombs, "Building a Heritage in the War of Ideas," *Washington Post,* October 3, 1983, p. B1; Joanne Omang, "The Heritage Report: Getting the Government Right with Reagan," *Washington Post,* November 16, 1980, p. A6; David Remnick, "The Lions of Libertarianism," *Washington Post,* July 30, 1985, p. E1; Spencer Rich, "The Heritage Foundation's Solid Footing Conservatively Speaking, Think Tank Is Robust at 25," *Washington Post,* December 11, 1997, p. C01; and Kathy Sawyer, "Heritage Foundation Gives Reagan Passing Grade," *Washington Post,* November 22, 1981, p. A11.

For information on Joseph Coors, see Associated Press, "Brewery Magnate, Joseph Coors, Dies at 85" (March 17, 2003), at http://us.cnn.com/2003/US/Central/03/17/obit.joseph.coors.ap/; Edwin Feulner, "Coors, R.I.P.," (March 18, 2003), at http://www.nationalreview.com/comment/comment-feulner031803.asp; and Harold Jackson, "Joseph Coors: The Man Who Bought the White House for Ronald Reagan," *The Guardian,* March 19, 2003, p. 27, at http://www

.guardian.co.uk/usa/story/0,12271,916936,00.html. See also the biography of Edwin Feulner from the Heritage Foundation website, at http://www.heritage .org/About/Staff/EdwinFeulner.cfm. For information on Edward Noble, see http://www.mediatransparency.org/funders/noble_foundation.htm. The information on Richard Mellon Scaife was compiled from Karen Rothmyer, "Citizen Scaife," *Columbia Journalism Review* (July/August 1981), at http://www.cjr.org/ year/81/4/scaife.asp; Edward Spannaus, "Richard Mellon Scaife: Who Is He Really?" *Executive Intelligence Review* (March 21, 1997), at http://members.tripod .com/~american_almanac/scaife.htm; Karen Rothmyer, "The Man behind the Mask," *Salon* (April 7, 1998), at http://www.salon.com/news/1998/04/07news .html; Brooks Jackson, "Who Is Richard Mellon Scaife?" (April 27, 1998), at http://www.cnn.com/ALLPOLITICS/1998/04/27/scaife.profile/; "Key Player: Richard Mellon Scaife," *Washington Post,* October 2, 1998, p. A1, at http:// www.washingtonpost.com/wp-srv/politics/special/clinton/players/scaife.htm. Robert Kaiser, "An Enigmatic Heir's Paradoxical World," *Washington Post,* May 3, 1999, p. A1; Robert Kaiser and Ira Chinoy, "How Scaife's Money Powered a Movement," *Washington Post,* May 2, 1999, p. A1; Kaiser and Chinoy, "Scaife: Funding Father of the Right," *Washington Post,* May 2, 1999, p. A1, at http://www .washingtonpost.com/wp-srv/politics/special/clinton/stories/scaifemain050299 .htm; Kaiser, "Money, Family Name Shaped Scaife," *Washington Post,* May 3, 1999, p. A1, http://www.washingtonpost.com/wp-srv/politics/special/clinton/stories/scaife main050399.htm; and "Scaife Foundations," http://www.mediatransparency.org/ funders/scaife_foundations.htm.

For information on Paul Weyrich, see http://www.newsmax.com/pundits/bios/ Weyrichbio.shtml, http://www.mediatransparency.org/people/weyrich.htm, http:// www.wisdomquotes.com/000186.html, http://www.christianitytoday.com/ct/9ta/ 9ta044.html, and http://my.ohio.voyager.net/~dionisio/queer/Origins/Weyrich .html.

For information on the Center on Budget and Policy Priorities (CBPP), see www.cbpp.org and Spencer Rich, "Robert Greenstein: Legislative Impact by the Numbers," *Washington Post,* September 8, 1986. The CBPP's reports on the estate tax issue include Joel Friedman and Andrew Lee, "Permanent Repeal of the Estate Tax Would Be Costly, yet Would Benefit Only a Few, Very Large Estates" (June 17, 2003); Jon Springer, "Fact Sheet: Estate Tax Should be Reformed, Not Repealed" (June 17, 2003); Springer, "Fact Sheet: Estate Tax Affects Very Few Family Businesses" (June 17, 2003); Springer, "Fact Sheet: Repealing the Estate Tax Would Reduce Charitable Giving" (June 17, 2003); Friedman and Lee, "Permanent Repeal of the Estate Tax Would Be Costly, yet Would Benefit Only a Few, Very Large Estates" (revised June 3, 2002); Joel Friedman, "The Kyl Amendment to Lock in Permanent Repeal of the Estate Tax" (February 5, 2002); Iris Lav, "Estate Tax Repeal and the Top Income Tax Rate Cut: A State-by-State Look at Who Would Benefit" (May 14, 2001); Lav, "If Estate Tax Is Repealed, Repeal of Gift Tax Would Not Be Far Behind" (May 3, 2001); Friedman, "Lower-Cost Estate Tax

Repeal Reflects Slow Phase-In" (revised April 4, 2001); Iris Lav and Joel Friedman, "Can Capital Gains Carry-Over Basis Replace the Estate Tax?" (March 15, 2001); Isaac Shapiro, Iris Lav, and James Sly, "4,500 Very Large Estates Would Receive as Much in Annual Tax Reductions under Bush Plan as 140 Million Americans" (February 26, 2001); Lav and Friedman, "Estate Tax Repeal: A Costly Windfall for the Wealthiest Americans" (revised February 6, 2001); Elizabeth C. McNichol, Iris J. Lav, and Daniel Tenny, "Repeal of the Federal Estate Tax Would Cost State Governments Billions in Revenue" (December 12, 2000); Iris Lav and James Sly, "Estate Tax Repeal: A Windfall for the Wealthiest Americans" (August 30, 2000); Lav, "The Estate Tax, 'Double Taxation,' and Carry-Over Basis" (July 7, 2000); Lav, "Eliminating the Estate Tax: A Costly Benefit for the Wealthiest Americans" (revised July 20, 1999); and Lav, "Estate Tax Cuts Would Benefit Wealthiest Americans: Targeted Changes Could Help Family Businesses and Farms" (April 1997).

Many other think tanks worked actively on the issue. Much of the information on the think tanks in this chapter and their work on the estate tax issue comes from printed material published by the think tanks themselves. For information on the American Council for Capital Formation, see www.accf.org. Also see Jeffrey Birnbaum and Alan Murray, *Showdown at Gucci Gulch: Lawmakers, Lobbyists, and the Unlikely Triumph of Tax Reform* (New York: Vintage, 1988). Reports by the ACCF on the estate tax issue include "Comparison of Estate Tax Plans" (2001); Douglas Holtz-Eakin and Donald Marples, "Estate Taxes, Labor Supply, and Economic Efficiency" (2001); Allen Sinai "Macroeconomic and Revenue Effects of the Elimination of the Estate Tax" (2001); Douglas Holtz-Eakin, "The Death Tax: Impact on Investment, Employment and Entrepreneurs," American Council for Capital Formation Special Report (August 1999); and Mark Bloomfield, "Repeal of the Death Tax: Impact on US Economic Growth" (February 16, 2000).

For information on Americans for Tax Reform, see www.atr.org and Mike Allen, "Conservative Group Presses White House for Deeper Tax Cuts," *Washington Post,* July 8, 2001.

For information on Citizens for a Sound Economy, see www.cse.org.

For information on Citizens for Tax Justice, see http://www.ctj.org/html/ctjdesc.htm. For background on Bob McIntyre, see Peter Jennings and Todd Brewster, "In Search of America" (2002), pp. 67–69, 86, at http://www.ctj.org/pdf/pj.pdf. On the estate tax issue, see Citizens for Tax Justice, "Final Version of Bush Tax Plan Keeps High-End Tax Cuts, Adds to Long-Term Cost" (May 26, 2001). For information on the Family Research Council, see www.frc.org and Judy Sarasohn, "Special Interests: Litigator to Lead Family Research Council," *Washington Post,* September 21, 2000.

For information on the National Center for Policy Analysis, see www.ncpa.org. Its publications on the estate tax issue include Bruce Bartlett, "The Case for Abolishing Death Taxes," National Center for Policy Analysis Backgrounder (June 1997), at http://www.ncpa.org/bg/bg142a.html; Bartlett, "Estate Tax History Versus Myth" (July 2000); Bartlett, "Estate Tax Hurts Small Businesses" (Fall 2000);

Bartlett, "Estate Tax Shows Sticking to Principles Works" (June 2000); and Bartlett, "Estate Tax Burden Falls on the Less Wealthy" (June 2000). For information on the National Priorities Project, see www.nationalpriorities.org.

For information on OMB Watch, see www.ombwatch.org and Felicity Barringer, "Keeping Track of Budgeteers," *Washington Post,* December 21, 1984.

For information on the Tax Foundation, see www.taxfoundation.org; John M. Berry, "Tax Foundation Has an Unusual Way to Weigh the Burden," *Washington Post,* April 25, 1996; and Albert Crenshaw, "Research Group Buys Troubled Tax Foundation," *Washington Post,* October 9, 1989. The Tax Foundation's publications on the estate tax issue include Patrick Fleenor and J. D. Foster, "An Analysis of the Disincentive Effects of the Estate Tax on Entrepreneurship" (Washington, D.C.: Tax Foundation, 1994); Patrick Fleenor, "A History and Overview of Estate Taxes in the United States" (Washington, D.C.: Tax Foundation, 1994); Fleenor, "A History and Overview of Estate Taxes in the United States" (January 1994); and J. D. Foster, "Is the Estate Tax a Revenue Loser?" (December 1999).

For information on United for a Fair Economy, see www.ufenet.org and www.responsiblewealth.org. Their publications on the issue include "Good News: Five Senators Switch Votes, Now Oppose Early Repeal of Estate Tax" (2003); "A Call to Preserve the Estate Tax" (2003); "Estate Tax Repeal Opponents: 'The Battle Isn't Over Yet'" (2001); and "Bill Gates, Sr., Marian Wright Edelman, Senator Conrad and Others Rally to Preserve Estate Tax" (2001).

The work of some academics was also influential in the estate tax debate. On the pro-repeal side, see the work of Professor Edward McCaffery, "Grave Robbers: The Moral Case against the Death Tax," *Policy Analysis* no. 353 (October 4, 1999), at http://www.cato.org/pubs/pas/pa353.pdf, and his testimony before the Senate Finance Committee at a June 7, 1995, hearing on a possible increase in the estate tax exemption, at http://www.taxanalysts.com/www/readingsintaxpolicy.nsf/0/E31A65D09875EC7C85256810006E489F?OpenDocument. On the anti-repeal side, see the work of Neil Harl, "Repeal of Federal Estate Tax: A Good Idea or a Mistake?" (2001), at http://www.exnet.iastate.edu/agdm/articles/harl/HarlApr01.htm, and his testimony before the Senate Committee on Agriculture regarding estate and gift tax reform on February 26, 1997, at http://agriculture.senate.gov/Hearings/Hearings_1997/harl.htm. Also see Jonathan Blattmacher and Mitchell Gans, "Wealth Transfer Tax Repeal: Some Thoughts on Policy and Planning," *Tax Notes Today* (January 15, 2001).

On demographic changes and the intergenerational transfer of wealth, see Robert Avery and Michael Rendall, "Estimating the Size and Distribution of the Baby Boomers' Prospective Inheritances," American Statistical Association, *Proceedings of the Social Statistics Section* (1993): 11–19; John Havens and Paul Schervish, "Millionaires and the Millennium: New Estimates of the Forthcoming Wealth Transfer and the Prospects for a Golden Age of Philanthropy," Boston College Social Welfare Research Institute Report (October 19, 1999), at www.bc.edu/bc_org/avp/gsas/swri/swri_features_wealth_transfer_report.htm; John Havens and Paul Schervish, "Why the $41 Trillion Wealth Transfer Estimate Is Still Valid: A Review of Challenges and Questions," *The Journal of Gift Planning* 7, no. 1 (January 2003): 11–15, 47–50; Neal Karlen, "And the Meek Shall Inherit Nothing," *New York Times,* July 29, 1999, pp. B1–B10; and Susan Lang, "Baby Boom Generation Will Inherit $10 Trillion," *Cornell Chronicle,* December 16, 1993, at http://ic.shu.edu.tw/htpu/nir/search/gopher/gopher3.htm.

On basic trends in wealth holding over the past several decades, see Michael Davern and Patricia Fisher, *Household Net Worth and Asset Ownership: 1995,* U.S. Bureau of the Census, Current Population Reports, Household Economic Studies (Washington, D.C.: U.S. Government Printing Office, 2001); T. J. Eller and Wallace Fraser, *Asset Ownership of Households: 1993,* U.S. Bureau of the Census, Current Population Reports (Washington, D.C.: U.S. Government Printing Office, 1995); Maury Gittleman and Edward Wolff, "Racial Wealth Disparities: Is the Gap Closing?" Jerome Levy Economics Institute, Working Paper No. 311, Bard College (2000); Shawna Orzechowski and Peter Sepielli, *Net Worth and Asset Ownership of Households: 1998–2000,* U.S. Bureau of the Census, Current Population Reports, Household Economic Studies (Washington, D.C.: U.S. Government Printing Office, 2003); Ronald Straight, "Wealth: Asset-Accumulation Differences by Race—SCF Data, 1995 and 1998," *American Economic Review* 92, no. 2 (May 2002): 330–34; United States Census Bureau, "Overview of the Survey of Income and Program Participation," at http://www.bls.census.gov/sipp/overview.html; Edward Wolff, "Recent Trends in Wealth Ownership," Jerome Levy Economics Institute, Working Paper No. 300, Bard College (2000); and Wolff, "Inheritances and Wealth Inequality," *American Economic Review* 92, no. 2 (May 2002): 260–64.

CHAPTER 10: DISORGANIZED DEMOCRATS

Details on the Gephardt-Waxman bill can be found through a search of http://thomas.loc.gov/. For conservative reaction to the bill, see "Tax Cut Dollars and Dogmas," *The Phyllis Schlafly Report* 34, no. 9 (April 2001) at http://www.eagleforum.org/psr/2001/apr01/psrapr01.shtml. On other previous attempts to change estate tax law, see Debra Rahmin Silberstein, "A History of the Estate Tax—A Source of Revenue or Vehicle for Wealth Redistribution," *Brandeis Graduate Journal* 1, issue 1 at http://www.brandeis.edu/gradjournal.

For background on Larry Summers, see "Lawrence H. Summers Biography," at http://www.president.harvard.edu/biography/; "Lawrence Summers, Treasury Secretary," at http://www.washingtonpost.com/wpsrv/politics/govt/admin/summers.htm#TOP; and Bruce Bartlett, "Forgotten Estate Tax Homework," *Washington Times,* April 30, 1997, at http://www.ncpa.org/pi/taxes/may97b.html. On Summers's remarks on the estate tax, the hostile reaction to them, and his subsequent apology, see Clay Chandler, "Treasury Official Slams Estate Tax Rollback Effort," *Washington Post,* April 22, 1997, p. C1; Chandler, "Treasury Official Apologizes for Calling Tax Foes 'Selfish,'" *Washington Post,* April 24, 1997, p. A14; "GOP Rages at Remark on 'Selfish' Tax Break," *Washington Times,* April 23, 1997; "Passing Assets to One's Children Is Not a 'Selfish' Act," *Washington Times,* April 27, 1997; Sheldon Richman, "Cutting Taxes *Is* Selfish," *Freedom Daily* (August 1997), at http://www.fff.org/freedom/0897c.asp; Patrick Buchanan, "Death, Taxes, and Larry Summers" (1997), at http://www.cs.umanitoba.ca/~jacobs/jacobs/articles/death_tax.html; and "Administration Official Feels Heat for Estate Tax Remarks," at http://www.aiada.org/publications/this_week_in_washington/1997/this_week_in_washington0425.cfm. On criticism of Summers over the estate tax issue after his nomination as Treasury secretary, see "GOP Criticizes Clinton Choice for Treasury" (May 13, 1999), at http://www.evote.com/index.asp?Page=/news_section/1999-05/05131999LarrySummers.asp; Deborah McGregor, "Summers Faces 'Estate' Tax Test," *Financial Times,* May 14, 1999, p. 6; and "Summers Confirmed as Treasury Chief," *The Nation,* July 2, 1999. On Summers's belief that Democrats who supported estate tax repeal in 2000 were exercising a "free vote," see Owen Ullmann, "Both Sides of House to Repeal Estate Tax," *USA Today,* June 9, 2000, p. 10A.

In 1997, American Enterprise Institute scholar Norman Ornstein warned Democratic lawmakers about resisting reform of estate tax in response to demographic shifts and changing economic circumstances that will result in a larger number of people falling into the estate tax bracket. See Ornstein, "Boomers Beware: The Estate Tax Is Now Not Just for the Rich" (April 23, 1997), at http://www.aei.org/include/news_print.asp?newsID=7655. See also his "Estate Tax's End Might Squeeze Charitable Aid," *USA Today,* February 1, 2001, at http://www.aei.org/include/news_print.asp?newsID=12402, and "The 'Death Tax' Should Be Reformed—Not Eliminated," *Roll Call* (June 20, 2002), http://www.aei.org/include/news_print.asp?newsID=15625. For general background on Ornstein, see http://www.aei.org/scholars/scholarID.48,filter./scholar.asp.

For more information on Democratic support for repeal, see Glenn Kessler and Eric Pianin, "Tax Cuts Gaining, in Pieces; Breaking up Bill Wins Democrats," *Washington Post,* July 9, 2000, p. A1. Legislation calling for repeal of the estate tax repeatedly passed with strong bipartisan support. On June 9, 2000, HR 8, the Death Tax Elimination Act, passed the House 279-136, with the support of 213 Republicans, 65 Democrats, and 1 Independent. On July 14, 2000, HR 1836, the Death Tax Elimination Act of 2000, passed the Senate 59-39, with the support of 50 Republicans and 9 Democrats. The following Democrats voted for HR 8 in 2000: Abercrombie, Andrews, Baca, Baird, Barcia, Berkley, Berry, Bishop, Blagojevich, Boswell, Boucher, Boyd, Capps, Clayton, Clement, Condit, Costello, Cramer, Delahunt, Deutsch, Dooley, Eshoo, Etheridge, Farr, Forbes, Ford, Gordon, Hall, Holt, Hooley, Inslee, Jefferson, John, Lampson, Lantos, Lipinski, Lofgren, Lucas, Maloney, Martinez, McCarthy, McIntyre, McNulty, Mink, Mollohan, Moore, Moran, Pascrell, Peterson, Phelps, Rahall, Roemer, Sanchez,

Sandlin, Shows, Sisisky, Skelton, Tanner, Tauscher, Thompson, Traficant, Udall, Velazquez, Wise, and Wynn. That bill was vetoed by President Clinton. On the failed override attempt, see "House Republicans Fail to Override Clinton Estate Tax Veto" (September 7, 2000), at http://www.cnn.com/2000/ALLPOLITICS/stories/09/07/estate.tax/.

On April 4, 2001, HR 8, the Death Tax Elimination Act of 2001, passed the House 274-154, with the support of 215 Republicans, 58 Democrats, and 1 Independent. On May 16, 2001, HR 1836, the Economic Growth and Tax Relief Reconciliation Act, passed the House 230-197, with the support of 216 Republicans, 13 Democrats, and 1 Independent. On May 23, 2001, HR 1836, the Economic Growth and Tax Relief Reconciliation Act of 2001, passed the Senate 62-38, with the support of 50 Republicans and 12 Democrats. That bill was signed into law by President Bush on June 7, 2001. The following Democrats voted for HR1836 in 2001: Abercrombie, Bishop, Clement, Condit, Cramer, Gordon, Hall, John, Lucas, Maloney, McIntyre, Shows, and Traficant. Thus the following Democrats switched sides: Andrews, Baca, Baird, Barcia, Berkley, Berry, Blagojevich, Boswell, Boucher, Boyd, Capps, Clayton, Costello, Delahunt, Deutsch, Dooley, Eshoo, Etheridge, Farr, Forbes, Ford, Holt, Hooley, Inslee, Jefferson, Lampson, Lantos, Lipinski, Lofgren, Martinez, McCarthy, McNulty, Mink, Mollohan, Moore, Moran, Pascrell, Peterson, Phelps, Rahall, Roemer, Sanchez, Sandlin, Sisisky, Skelton, Tanner, Tauscher, Thompson, Udall, Velazquez, Wise, and Wynn.

The Democratic alternative proposed by Earl Pomeroy in the House on June 6, 2001, would have raised the exemption to $3 million effective January 1, 2003, permanently exempting 99.7% of all estates. It failed by a vote of 231 to 197; rejection of this amendment had the support of 18 Democrats. See Carl Hulse, "House Backs Permanent End to Estate Tax," *New York Times,* June 7, 2002, p. A16. This leaves in place the phased-in increases in the unified credit exemption of $1 million in 2002–3, $1.5 million in 2004–5, $2 million in 2006–8, and $3.5 million in 2009, when assets are taxed at rates of 18%–50% to complete abolition by 2009, but with the possibility of a revived estate tax with the 2000 threshold of $625,000 in 2010 if permanence fails.

On June 6, 2002, HR 2143, the Permanent Death Tax Repeal Act, passed the House 256-171, with the support of 214 Republicans, 41 Democrats, and 1 Independent. On June 12, 2002, the Senate Amendment 3833 to HR 8, to permanently repeal the estate tax failed in the Senate 54-44, with the support of 45 Republicans and 9 Democrats. See Carl Hulse, "Effort to Repeal Estate Tax Ends in Senate Defeat," *New York Times,* June 13, 2002, pp. A1, A34.

CHAPTER 11: PUSHING AGAINST AN OPEN DOOR

For a brief description of the problems confronting potential opposition forces, see Larry Elkin, "Estate Tax Debate Pits Reform against Repeal" (April 2001), at http://www.elkin.com/estate_tax_debate_pits_reform_against_repeal.htm.

Data on the decline in union membership from 1948–2001 is from the *Union Sourcebook 1947–1983* and the U.S. Bureau of Labor Statistics at http://www .laborresearch.org/charts.php?id=29. On the revenue shortfall of groups like the AFL-CIO's, see Hal Leyshon, "AFL-CIO Stays the Course," *Labor Notes* (January, 2002), at http://www.labornotes.org/archives/2002/0102/0102a.html. On the AFL-CIO's redirection of resources from lobbying to organizing, see its resolution "Building a Larger, Stronger Movement of America's Workers," presented at its 2001 convention, found at http://www.aflcio.org/aboutaflcio/about/convention /2001/resolutions/upload/res_1.pdf. Also see Alison Grant, "Retooling Organized Labor," *Plain Dealer,* March 21, 2003, at http://www.pennfedbmwe.org/news /3.21.03.htm; and Donna Goodison, "Jobs Cut, but Unions Seek Growth: Unions Lobbying Less, Organizing More," *Boston Herald,* April 24, 2003, at http://www .bostonherald.com/business/herald_hundred/hhlabr04242003.htm. The data on lobbying expenditures and campaign contributions during 1997–2000 of labor in general and the AFL-CIO in particular was obtained through a search of http://www.opensecrets.org and a review of http://www.opensecrets.org /pubs/lobby98/. Statistics comparing the lobbying expenditures of other interest groups and the business and union sectors from 1997–2000 also can be found at http://www.opensecrets.org/lobbyists/index.asp. Also see the Center for Responsive Politics report, "Influence Inc.: Lobbyists Spending in Washington" (November 1998), a summary of which can be found at http://www .opensecrets.org/pubs/lobby98/.

For background on the current state of organized labor, see Bruce Nissen, *Which Direction for Organized Labor?* (Detroit: Wayne State University Press, 1999); Paul Buhle, *Taking Care of Business* (New York: Monthly Review Press, 1999); Robert Zieger and Gilbert Gall, *American Workers, American Unions: The Twentieth Century,* 3rd ed. (Baltimore: Johns Hopkins University Press, 2002); and Nelson Lichtenstein, *State of the Union: A Century of American Labor* (Princeton: Princeton University Press, 2003). Labor groups, such as the AFL-CIO and the American Federation of State, County, and Municipal Employees (AFCSME), did express opposition to repeal through various letters and press releases but did not actively lobby against it. For background information on the AFL-CIO, see http://www.aflcio.org/aboutaflcio/about/thisis/index.cfm. For information on the activities of the AFSCME on the estate tax, see http://www.afscme.org/publications/ leader/2001/01020109.htm, and for a sample letter sent from AFSCME to Congress on this issue, see http://www.afscme.org/action/1030617.htm.

For a general description of trends in charitable giving, see the Council on Foundations, "Estate and Gift Tax Repeal: Information Brief," at http:// capwiz.com/cof/issues/alert/?alertid=12; Donors Forum of Chicago, "The Estate Tax and Charitable Giving" (April 2001), at http://donorsforum.org/forms_pdf/ 04estate.pdf; Bruce Bartlett, "Estate Tax Repeal Won't Affect Giving Much," National Center for Policy Analysis commentary (June 26, 2000), at http:// www.ncpa.org/oped/bartlett.html; Independent Sector, "Estate Tax and Charitable Bequests," http://www.independentsector.org/programs/gr/estatetax.html; "About the Estate Tax," http://www.ncrp.org/final%20fact%20sheet.doc; and John Springer, "Repealing the Estate Tax Would Reduce Charitable Giving" (June 17, 2003), at http://www.cbpp.org/6–17–03tax-fact3.htm. For information on charitable bequests made by estates in 2000, see "National Estate Information," at http://www.givingforum.org/pdfs/ei99national.pdf. The Congressional Budget Office in July 2004 estimated that increasing the estate tax exemption to $3.5 million would reduce charitable giving by less than 3 percent while repealing the tax would reduce donations to charity by 6 to 12 percent (Congressional Budget Office, "The Estate Tax and Charitable Giving," July 2004).

For analyses of the effect of estate tax repeal on charitable giving, see David Joulfain, "Estate Taxes and Charitable Bequests by the Wealthy," *National Tax Journal*, 53 (2000): 743; Eugene Tempel and Patrick Rooney, "Repeal of the Estate Tax: Its Impact on Philanthropy" (November 1, 2000), at http://www.philanthropy .iupui.edu/EstateTax.htm; Paul Schervish, "Philanthropy Can Thrive without Estate Tax," *Chronicle of Philanthropy* (January 11, 2001), at http://www.deathtax .com/deathtax/schervish.html; Norman Ornstein, "Estate Tax's End Might Squeeze Charitable Aid," *USA Today*, February 1, 2001, at http://www.aei.org/ ra/raorns010201.htm; Council on Foundations, "Estate and Gift Tax Repeal: Information Brief," at http://capwiz.com/cof/issues/alert/?alertid=12; Donors Forum of Chicago, "The Estate Tax and Charitable Giving" (April 2001), at http://donorsforum.org/forms_pdf/04estate.pdf; Frank Minton, "Reform, Don't Abolish Estate Tax," *Seattle Post-Intelligencer*, March 20, 2001; Independent Sector, "Estate Tax and Charitable Bequests," at http://www.independentsector .org/programs/gr/estatetax.html; Jon Bakija and William Gale, "Effects of Estate Tax Reform on Charitable Giving," Brookings Institution (June 2003), at http:// www.brookings.edu/dybdocroot/views/articles/gale/20030617.pdf; Glenn Kessler and Dan Morgan, "Some Want to Keep the 'Death Tax' Alive," *Washington Post*, February 18, 2001, p. A8; John Springer, "Repealing the Estate Tax Would Reduce Charitable Giving" (June 17, 2003), at http://www.cbpp.org/6-17-03tax-fact3 .htm; and Bruce Bartlett, "Estate Tax Repeal Won't Affect Giving Much," National Center for Policy Analysis commentary (June 26, 2000), at http://www.ncpa .org/oped/bartlett.html.

On Independent Sector's eventual decision to come out in opposition to repeal, see http://www.independentsector.org/about/about-is.htm and http://www .independentsector.org/programs/gr/estatetax.html for more on its role in the estate tax debate. The Council on Foundations, however, decided to remain neutral; see http://www.cof.org/index.cfm?containerID=18&menuContainerID=0&crumb =2&navID=41. For background information on the more conservative Philanthropy Roundtable, see http://www.philanthropyroundtable.org/history.html.

For information on the impact of estate tax repeal on the insurance industry, see Arthur D. Postal, "Congressional Action Adds Full Estate Tax Repeal to Life's Uncertainties" *Insurance Chronicle* 12, no. 23 (June 4, 2001): 1; and Sue Kirchhoff, "Tough to Plan on Estate Tax Changes Bring Turmoil to Insurers," *Boston Globe,* July 13, 2001, p. C1.

For more information on the companies that will be hardest hit by repeal, see "Full Estate Tax Repeal a Bummer," *Insurance Accounting* 11, no. 45 (November 20, 2000): 12. These companies include the Lincoln National Corporation (a profile of which can be found at http://biz.yahoo.com/p/l/lnc.html), Manulife Financial Corporation (see http://www.manulife.com/corporate/corporate2.nsf/Public/Homepage and http://biz.yahoo.com/p/M/MFC.html), and the Jefferson-Pilot Corporation (see http://www.jefferson-pilot.com/ and http://biz.yahoo.com/p/J/JP.html).

Various interest groups representing the insurance industry were divided on the issue of estate tax repeal. For information on the Independent Insurance Agents and Brokers of America, which supported repeal, see http://www.independent agent.com/. For background on the American Council of Life Insurers (ACLI), which opposed repeal but did not lobby against it, see http://www.acli.org/ACLI/About%20ALCI%20nonmember/Membership/default.htm. And for information on the Association of Advanced Life Underwriters (AALU) and the National Association of Financial Advisors (NAIFA), which supported the reform effort, see http://www.aalu.org/frameset.cfm?portal=172 and http://www.naifa .org/about.html, respectively. For a statement of the AALU position on the issue, see "Estate Tax Legislation," http://www.aalu.org/content.cfm?pageid=430. On the Republican response to the AALU's position, see Steven Brostoff, "GOP Rebukes AALU for Estate Tax Remarks," *National Underwriter* (February 14, 2000). Insurance groups that supported permanent reform based their arguments on its potential to facilitate estate planning through enhanced predictability. For a history of changes and modifications in estate tax law, see John Luckey, "A History of Federal Estate, Gift, and Generation-Skipping Taxes," *CRS Report for Congress* (August 9, 2001).

The two organized coalitions that did oppose repeal were Americans for a Fair Estate Tax, organized by the liberal advocacy group OMB Watch and Responsible Wealth, organized by Chuck Collins and William Gates, Sr. For information on the former group, see http://www.ombwatch.org/estatetax/. Members of the AFET coalition included Alliance for Children and Families, Alliance for Justice, American Arts Alliance, American Association of University Women, AFL-CIO, American Federation of State, County, and Municipal Employees, Americans for Democratic Action, Association of Art Museum Directors, Campaign for America's Future, Center on Budget and Policy Priorities, Child Welfare League of America, Children's Defense Fund, Citizens for Tax Justice, Coalition on Human Needs, Communications Workers of America (CWA), Evangelical Lutheran Church in America, Lutheran Office for Governmental Affairs, Friends of the Earth, Independent Sector, Institute for America's Future, Leadership Conference on Civil Rights, League of Women Voters, Minnesota Council of Nonprofits, MoveOn.org, National Committee to Preserve Social Security and Medicare, National Committee for Responsive Philanthropy, National Council of Nonprofit Associations, National Priorities Project, National Women's Law Center, NET-WORK, a National Catholic Social Justice Lobby, OMB Watch, Open Society Institute: D.C. Office, People for the American Way, Religious Action Center of Reform Judaism, Responsible Wealth, Taxpayers for Common Sense, United Church of Christ Justice and Witness Ministries, United for a Fair Economy, and US Action.

For information on Responsible Wealth, which was founded in 1997 as a project of United for a Fair Economy (http://www.faireconomy.org), see www.responsiblewealth.org. The group published a "Call to Preserve the Estate Tax Petition," which appeared in a February 2001 edition of the the *New York Times* and can be viewed at http://www.responsiblewealth.org/press/2001/estate_tax_call_pr.html. A list of the legislators targeted by Responsible Wealth can be found at http://www.responsiblewealth.org/estatetax/latest_news.html. Among other things, Responsible Wealth was successful in getting the National Farmers Union to back their cause. For information on the opposition of the NFU to repeal, see "Bill Gates, Sr., Joins the National Farmers Union to Demand Reform of the Estate Tax, Not Repeal" (March 2, 2003), at http://www.responsiblewealth.org/press/2003/Gates_NFU.html, and Jerry Hagstrom, "Bill Gates, Sr., Brings Estate Tax Crusade to Farmers' Union," *Congress Daily* (March 3, 2003), at http://www.ufenet.org/press/ufenews/2003/Gates_NFU_Congress_Daily.html. For more information on Responsible Wealth's arguments for keeping the estate tax, see William Gates, Sr., and Chuck Collins, *Wealth and Our Commonwealth: Why America Should Tax Accumulated Fortunes* (Boston: Beacon, 2003).

CHAPTER 12: THE RUNNING ROOM OF PUBLIC OPINION

Most of the public opinion data on the estate tax utilized in this chapter was derived from national polls conducted by major polling organizations, both independent and partisan. Many of these polls were found in the archives of polling on tax-related issues on the *National Journal* website, http://nationaljournal.com/members/polltrack/2003/issues/03taxes.htm. Our search of public opinion data on the issue included the following "nonpartisan" polls: ABC News/*Washington Post* Poll conducted December 12–15, 2002 (released December 18); Bloomberg Poll conducted February 27–March 2, 2001; CBS News/*New York Times* Polls conducted March 8–12, 2001 (released March 14) and November 20–24, 2002; Fox News/Opinion Dynamics Poll conducted January 14–15, 2003 (released January 16); Gallup Polls, sponsored by CNN and *USA Today,* conducted May 6–7, 1997, January 13–16, 2000, June 22–25, 2000, and February 19–21, 2001; CNN/Gallup/*USA Today* Poll conducted November 8–10, 2002; Gonzales/Arscott Research and Communications Poll conducted February 20–23, 2001; NBC News/*Wall Street Journal* Polls conducted by Peter Hart (D) and Robert Teeter (R) June 19–23, 1997, July 24–26, 1999 (released July 28), March 1–4, 2001 (released March 8), April 21–23, 2001 (released April 27), and December 7–9, 2002; NBC News Poll conducted by Hart and Teeter July 25–27, 1998 (released July 30); Pew Research Center for the People and the Press Polls conducted August 1997 and August 24–September 10, 2000 (released September 14); Rasmussen Research Portrait of America Poll conducted July 18, 2000; Wirthlin Worldwide Poll conducted August 6–9, 1999 (contained in the *Wirthlin Report* 9, no. 7 [September 1999]); Women Impacting Public Policy (WIPP) Poll conducted October 2001; and Zogby International Polls conducted February 2–4, 1998, August 21–23, 1999, June 6–8, 2000, October 4–6, 2000 (released October 8), October 7–13, 2000, and November 29–December 7, 2000 (released December 18). Nonpartisan poll data also came from a March 5–15, 2001, survey found in Keith Lantz, A. Lee Gurley, and Kenneth Linna, "Popular Support for the Elimination of the Estate Tax in the United States," *Tax Notes Today* 99 (May 26, 2003): 1263, and a February 5–March 17, 2003, survey by National Public Radio/Kaiser Family Foundation/Kennedy School of Government, "National Survey of Americans' Views on Taxes" (April 2003), at http://www.npr.org/news/specials/polls/taxes 2003/20030415_taxes_survey.pdf.

Polling data on the estate tax issue from Republican-leaning organizations included the following: Americans Against Unfair Family Taxation Polls conducted June 15, 1999, June 26–27, 1999 (by McLaughlin and Associates, released June 29), and January 13, 2000 (by McLaughlin and Associates); The Center for the Study of Taxation National Poll: Focus Group on Tax Reform and Instant Responses conducted in 1998; Luntz Research Companies Polls, including their August 1998 National Survey on Taxes and Social Security, their November 1998 Post-election Survey, an April 24, 2001, memorandum on the "The Death Tax & Gay and Lesbian Americans" at http://www.policyandtaxationgroup.com/pdf/ GAYANDLESBIANSURVEY.pdf, a June 2002 statewide survey of registered voters in Virginia (released July 1, 2003), and their January 16–21, 2003, memorandum "Americans Talk Taxes" (released January 27, 2003) found at http://www .policyandtaxationgroup.com/Summary.pdf; Market Strategies Poll conducted September 7, 1999, for the Republican National Committee; McLaughlin and Associates Poll conducted January 26–27, 2001; and the Polling Company Poll conducted in January 2000 for the 60 Plus Association.

Polling from Democratic-leaning organizations included the following: Emily's List Poll conducted December 7–14, 1999 (released January 6, 2000); Greenberg Quinlan Rosner Research Polls conducted June 11–13, 2001 (released June 19, 2001), and May 6–9, 2002 (released June 11, 2002, for OMB Watch); and Penn Schoen Berland Poll conducted February 15–21, 2001 (for the Democratic Leadership Council/Blueprint, released March 6, 2001).

For polling data demonstrating the unrealistically optimistic expectations of future wealth held by many Americans, see Bruce Bartlett, "Wealth, Mobility, Inheritance and the Estate Tax," National Center for Policy Analysis, *Policy Report* no. 235 (July 2000). Despite public awareness of the widening wealth gap as evidenced by the results of a 1993 *Time*/CNN/Yankelovich Partners poll, the data indicate declining support for government efforts to reduce the divide between rich and poor. See the 1997 survey by the Democratic Leadership Council and Jacob M. Schlesinger and Nicholas Kulish, "As Paper Millionaires Multiply, Estate Tax Takes a Public Beating, the Long Economic Boom Eases Many Misgivings about Inherited Wealth," *Wall Street Journal,* July 13, 2000, pp. A1, A8. Such results echo the responses given by those surveyed in Jennifer Hochschild, *Facing Up to the American Dream: Race, Class, and the Soul of the Nation* (Princeton: Princeton University Press, 1995). They also reinforce the arguments of Max Weber and Frank Parkin that the formal egalitarianism of the market distorts people's beliefs about their place in the income distribution and their possibility of becoming wealthy. See H. H. Gerth and C. Wright Mills, eds., *From Max Weber: Essays in Sociology* (New York: Routledge, 1997), 183–84; and Frank Parkin, *Class, Inequality, and Political Order* (New York: Praeger, 1971), 160–64. This evidence runs contrary to the predictions of a popular backlash to the growing concentration of wealth by Kevin Phillips in *The Politics of Rich and Poor* (New York: Random House, 1990). President Reagan's statement, "What I want to see above all is that this country remains a country where someone can always get rich," came from a June 28, 1983, news conference on the nation's economy, a transcript of which can be found at http://www.reagan.utexas.edu/resource/speeches/1983/62883f.htm. On the analogy of this issue to the Tories' failure to get political traction by running against Labour on an anti-Euro platform, see Graham Jones, "Now Blair Expected to Push for Euro" (June 7, 2001), at http://www.cnn.com/2001/WORLD/europe /UK/ 06/06/euro.whatnext/index.html/. On the analogy to the contradictory polling on the abortion issue, see "Poll: Abortion Is Murder but up to the Mother" (June 18, 2000), at http://www.newsmax.com/articles/?a=2000/6/18/192044.

For data on voter priorities and their intensity of preference on the estate tax issue, see NBC News Polls from June 1997, June 1998, July 1999, and March 2001; Pew Research Center Poll from September 2000; Penn Research Poll from February 2001 with analysis by Mark Penn, "What Americans Really Think about Bush's Tax Cut," at http://www.ndol.org/blueprint/spring2001/penn.html; CBS News/*New York Times* Polls from March 2001 and November 2002 with analysis by Dick Meyer, "Death (Tax) Takes a Holiday" (March 14, 2001), at http:// www.cbsnews.com/stories/2001/03/14/politics/main278884.shtml; Greenberg Research Poll from May 2002 with analysis by OMB Watch, "Public Attitudes on the Estate Tax" (June 11, 2002), at http://www.ombwatch.org/article/articleview/ 811/1/125/; ABC News/*Washington Post* Poll from December 2002; Luntz Research Poll from January 2003; Fox News/Opinion Dynamics Poll from January 2003; and the February-March 2003 National Survey of Americans' Views on Taxes. Also see Wendy Simmons, "Public Has Mixed Feelings about Tax Cuts," Poll Analyses, Gallup News Service (January 24, 2001), and David Rosenbaum, "Polls on Tax Cuts Find Voters' Messages Mixed," *New York Times,* July 19, 1999, p. A11.

On the effect of the "death tax" language on public opinion, see the Greenberg

Research Poll from 2002 and the Luntz Research Poll from 2003. This issue is also discussed in Jonathan Weisman, "Linking Tax to Death May Have Brought about Its Doom," *USA Today,* May 20, 2001, at http://www.usatoday.com/news/washdc/2001-05-21-estate.htm; Norman Ornstein, "Estate Tax's End Might Squeeze Charitable Aid," *USA Today,* February 1, 2001, at http://www.aei.org/ra/raorns010201.htm; and Joshua Green, "Meet Mr. Death," *American Prospect* 12, issue 9 (May 21, 2001), at http://www.prospect.org/print/V12/9/green-j.html.

Polls demonstrate that beliefs about the effect of the estate tax on the economy do not figure much into public opinion on repeal. See the Americans Against Unfair Family Taxation Poll from 1998, and Lantz, Gurley, and Linna, "Popular Support for the Elimination of the Estate Tax in the United States." Studies showing the allegedly deleterious economic effects of the estate tax include Bruce Bartlett, "Wealth, Mobility, Inheritance and the Estate Tax" and "Why Death Taxes Should Be Abolished," *Policy Backgrounder* no. 150 (August 18, 1999); Center for the Study of Taxation, "Federal Estate and Gift Taxes: Are They Worth the Cost?" (Costa Mesa, Calif.: Center for the Study of Taxation, 1996); Richard E. Wagner, "Federal Transfer Taxation: A Study in Social Cost" (Washington, D.C.: Institute for Research on the Economics of Taxation, 1993); Travis Research Associates, "Survey of the Impact of the Federal Estate Tax on Family Business Employment Levels in Upstate New York" (Albany: Public Policy Institute of New York State, 1999); Travis Research Associates, "Survey of the Impact of the Federal Estate Tax on NAWBO Member Businesses" (February 23, 2000), at http://www.policyandtaxationgroup.com/html/pdf/ImpactOnNAWBO.pdf; National Association of Manufacturers, "An Everyday Burden to American Business: Federal Estate and Gift Taxes" (Costa Mesa, Calif.: Center for the Study of Taxation, 1998); Douglas Holtz-Eakin, "The Death Tax: Impact on Investment, Employment and Entrepreneurs," *Tax Notes Today* (August 2, 1999); and Mark Bloomfield, "Repeal of the Death Tax: Impact on U.S. Economic Growth," Testimony before the Maryland General Assembly on Behalf of the American Council for Capital Formation (February 16, 2000), at http://www.accf.org/Feb00AnnapTest.htm.

Studies contesting these claims include Charles Davenport and Jay Soled, "Enlivening the Death-Tax Death-Talk," *Tax Notes* (July 26, 1999): 591–631; Iris Lav and James Sly, "Estate Tax Repeal: A Windfall for the Wealthiest Americans," Center on Budget and Policy Priorities (June 2, 2000); and William Gale, James Hines, and Joel Slemrod, eds., *Rethinking Estate and Gift Taxation* (Washington, D.C.: Brookings Institution Press, 2001). Edward McCaffery, unlike others who had focused on the economic arguments against it, made a case for repeal on moral grounds. See, e.g., "Grave Robbers: The Moral Case against the Death Tax," *Policy Analysis,* CATO Institute, no. 353 (October 4, 1999). Subsequent polling on the issue discussed next shows that widespread popular support for repeal could be attributed only to beliefs about the tax's unfairness rather than worries about its economic ramifications.

Polls repeatedly demonstrate a majority of the public backing repeal of the estate tax, with support for repeal across income groups and political parties. See the Center for the Study of Taxation Poll from 1998; Zogby International Polls from February 1998, June 2000, October 2000, and December 2000; Pew Research Center Polls from September 1998 and August 2000; Americans Against Unfair Family Taxation Poll from July 1999; Market Strategies Poll from September 1999; Emily's List Poll from December 1999; Polling Company Poll from January 2000; Gallup Poll from July 2000; Rasmussen Research Poll from July 2000; McLaughlin and Associates Polls from November 2000 and January 2001; Bloomberg Poll from February 2001; CBS News/ *New York Times* Poll from March 2001; *Tax Notes* March 2001 survey; Luntz Research Polls from April 2001 and January 2003; Greenberg Research Polls from July 2001 and May 2002; Women Impacting Public Policy Poll from October 2001; Fox News/Opinion Dynamics Poll from January 2003; and the February–March 2003 National Survey of Americans' Views on Taxes.

Polls reflect that most voters oppose the estate tax because of their belief in its unfairness. For early polling evidence on this point demonstrating support for Reagan's increase in the exclusion, see McCaffery, "Grave Robbers: The Moral Case against the Death Tax," p. 14. Additional polls illustrating voters' beliefs in the unfairness of the estate tax include those conducted by the National Federation of Independent Business (July 1995), Luntz Research (August 1998, April 2001, and January 2003), Americans Against Unfair Family Taxation (July 1999 and January 2000), Zogby International (August 1999 and November 1999), McLaughlin and Associates (November 2000, January 2001, and May 2001), *Tax Notes* survey (March 2001), and the National Survey of Americans' Views on Taxes. For more on the principled rather than self-interested support for repeal, see McLaughlin and Associates National Media Release, "National Poll: Estate Tax, Public Opposition to 'Death Tax' Even Stronger than Last Year" (February 8, 2001), at http://www.mclaughlinonline.com/newspoll/np2001/010208natl.htm; Remarks by Senator Kyl, *Congressional Record* (May 25, 2001), p. S5678–79; Luntz Research Companies Memorandum, "The Death Tax and Gay and Lesbian Americans" (April 24, 2001), at http://www.center4studytax.com/pub.htm#gaysurvey; Jonathan Weisman, "Linking Tax to Death May Have Brought about Its Doom"; and Simmons, "Public Has Mixed Feelings about Tax Cuts."

Much of the argument about the unfairness of the estate tax has revolved around the claim that it amounts to double taxation. See the July 1999 and July 2000 polls by Americans Against Unfair Family Taxation and the November 2000 and January 2001 polls by McLaughlin and Associates. The claim of double taxation is premised on the assumption that the assets in an estate have already been taxed once under the income tax, which is frequently not true.

People consistently oppose estate tax increases despite the fact that very few would be affected. See CBS News, "Poll: Split Signals on Taxes" (March 13, 2001), at http://www.cbsnews.com/stories/2001/03/13/politics/main278532.shtml. In reality, only the wealthiest of Americans are subject to the tax. See Jane G. Gravelle and Steven Maguire, "Estate and Gift Taxes: Economic Issues," *Congressional Research Service*, Report RL30600 (April 9, 2001), p. 7; Dick Meyer, "Death (Tax) Takes a Holiday" (March 14, 2001), at http://www.cbsnews.com/stories/2001/03/14/politics/main278884.shtml; Schlesinger and Kulish, "As Paper Millionaires Multiply, Estate Tax Takes a Public Beating," pp. A1, A8; Joshua Green, "Meet Mr. Death"; and Weisman, "Linking Tax to Death May Have Brought about Its Doom."

Polls repeatedly indicate public misperceptions about who pays the tax. See the 1999 Americans Against Unfair Family Taxation Poll; the May 2002 Greenberg Research Poll; the 2003 Survey of Americans' Views on Taxes; as well as Lantz, Gurley, and Linna, "Popular Support for the Elimination of the Estate Tax in the United States"; and Simmons, "Public Has Mixed Feelings about Tax Cuts."

On surveys about the effect of the tax on family businesses, see Joseph H. Astrachan and Craig E. Aronoff, "A Report on the Impact of the Federal Estate Tax: A Study of Two Industry Groups," Family Enterprise Center of the Coles School of Business, Kennesaw State College, Kennesaw, Georgia, (July 24, 1995), as cited in William W. Beach, "The Case for Repealing the Estate Tax," *Why America Needs a Tax Cut* (Washington, D.C.: Heritage Foundation), chapter 6, at http://www.heritage.org/taxcut/chapt6.html; Joseph Astrachan and Roger Tutterow, "The Effect of Estate Taxes on Family Business, Survey Results," *Family Business Review* 9 (Fall 1996): 303–14, as cited in Gale, Hines, and Slemrod, eds., *Rethinking Estate and Gift Taxation*, p. 46; Joint Economic Committee of the U.S. Congress, 1998, "The Economics of the Estate Tax: A Joint Economic Committee Study," pp. 23–25, as cited in Donald C. Clampitt and Jerry W. Terry, "National Taxpayers Union Foundation Issue Brief 137" (May 21, 2001), at www.ntu.org/main/press.php?PressID=407; Travis Research Associates, "Survey of the Impact of the Federal Estate Tax on Family Business Employment Levels in Upstate New York" (June 22, 1999), at http://www.policyandtaxationgroup.com/polls.htm#travis; Travis Research Associates, "Survey of the Impact of the Federal Estate Tax on NAWBO Member Businesses," prepared for the Center for the Study of Taxation (February 23, 2000), at http://www.center4studytax.com/myths.htm#travis; Travis Research Associates, Federal Estate Tax Impact Survey (Costa Mesa, Calif.: Center for the Study of Taxation, 1995) as cited in Bartlett, "Wealth, Mobility, Inheritance and the Estate Tax"; and The Polling Company, "Post-Election Survey Results—Groundbreaking Data on the Effects of the Death Tax" (November 27, 2000), at http://www.center4studytax.com/pub.htm#pollco. On misinformation regarding effects on family farms and businesses, see David Cay Johnston, "Focus on Farms Masks Estate Tax Confusion," *New York Times*, April 8, 2001; and Gale, Hines, and Slemrod, eds., *Rethinking Estate and Gift Taxation*, p. 46–47.

On the people's view of repeal after being given more information, see the July 2000 Gallup Poll, the May 2002 Greenberg Research Poll, as well as OMB Watch "Public Attitudes on the Estate Tax," and Simmons, "Public Has Mixed Feelings about Tax Cuts." On the question of repeal versus reform, see the July 1999 poll by Americans Against Unfair Family Taxation, the February 2001 Penn Poll, the February 2001 Gallup Poll, and the May 2002 Greenberg Research Poll.

On views of state residents regarding estate taxes, see National Taxpayer's Union, "Voters Opted to Trim Taxes at Ballot Box, Election Results Show" (November 8, 2000), at http://www.ntu.org/news_room/press_releases /pr_110800 .php3, regarding abolition of such taxes in Montana and South Dakota; the 2001 McLaughlin and Associates Poll of likely voters in Iowa, Louisiana, Montana, and New Mexico; the February 2001 Gonzales/Arscott Research and Communications Poll of Voters in Maryland; the November 1999 Zogby Poll of voters in·California; and the 2002 Luntz Research Poll of voters in Virginia.

On the increasing support for estate tax repeal over time see the 1998 and 2000 Zogby International Polls, the 1998 and 2000 Pew Research Polls, the 1998 and 2001 Luntz Research Polls, the 1999 and 2000 Americans Against Unfair Family Taxation Polls, the 2000 and 2001 McLaughlin and Associates Poll, the Greenberg Research survey from May 6–8, 2002, and the NBC News/ *Wall Street Journal* surveys from August 1999 and January 2001.

On the increasing momentum of the repeal forces, see Steven Greenhouse, "Soaking the Rich Isn't What It Used to Be," *New York Times,* July 16, 2000, at http://www.nytimes.com/library/review/071600estate-tax.html; Glenn Kessler and Dan Morgan, "Some Want to Keep the 'Death Tax' Alive," *Washington Post,* February 18, 2001, p. A8, McLaughlin and Associates National Media Release, "National Poll: Estate Tax, Public Opposition to 'Death Tax' Even Stronger than Last Year"; and Weisman, "Linking Tax to Death May Have Brought about Its Doom." On the inability of liberals to move public opinion on the issue even though people tend to support the Democratic position when fully informed, see Joshua Green, "Meet Mr. Death."

On public opinion more generally, see John R. Zaller, *The Nature and Origins of Mass Opinion* (Cambridge: Cambridge University Press, 1992), and Mark Smith, *American Business and Political Power: Public Opinion, Elections, and Democracy* (Chicago: University of Chicago Press, 2000). On public attitudes regarding the American tax system, see Robert Blendon, Stephen Pelletier, Marcus Rosenbaum, and Mollyann Brodie, "Tax Uncertainty: A Divided America's Unformed View of the Federal Tax System," *Brookings Review* 21, no. 3 (Summer 2003): 28–31.

CHAPTER 13: THE MISSING LINK

On the Association of Advanced Life Underwriters' (AALU) worry about a Republican president in the White House, see Gerald Sherman, Stuart Lewis, and Deborah Beers, AALU Bulletin, "The Presidential Campaign and the Estate Tax," *Washington Report* (January 21, 2000). A response letter was sent by Congresswoman Jennifer Dunn and Senator Paul Coverdell on February 4, 2000 to David Stertzer, the Executive Vice President of AALU. For more on this exchange, see

Steven Brostoff, "GOP Rebukes AALU for Estate Tax Remarks," *National Underwriter* (February 14, 2000).

For criticism of Bush's record as governor of Texas during the 2000 campaign, see Citizens for Tax Justice, "Texas Governor George W. Bush's Record on Taxes," (March 3, 2000). On the Bush 2000 campaign more generally, see Richard Berke, "By Staying Away, Bush Is the Talk of New Hampshire," *New York Times,* May 3, 1999, p. A9; Online News Hour, "Kicking Off the Campaign," (June 14, 1999), at http://www.pbs.org/newshour/bb/media/jan-june99/bush_6–14.html; Berke, "Bush Announces a Record Haul, and Foes Make Money an Issue," *New York Times,* July 1, 1999, p. A1; Lynne Duke, "Politics; A Reluctant Bow to Giuliani, with Arrows," *Washington Post,* August 12, 1999, p. A04; Berke, "Bush Takes Campaign Door to Door on Eve of Straw Poll," *New York Times,* August 14, 1999, p. A25; Thomas Edsall and Will Woodward, "Rivals May Get Thrashed Trying to Trip Bush," *Washington Post,* August 14, 1999, p. A04; Dan Balz and David Broder, "Bush Wins Iowa Poll," *Washington Post,* August 15, 1999, p. A01; David Broder, "Rivals Turn Attack on Victorious Bush," *Washington Post,* August 16, 1999, p. A01; Sara Miles, "Message: I Care (More than They Do)," *New York Times,* November 17, 1999, p. H7; Online News Hour Transcript, "Snapshot: George W. Bush" (November 19, 1999), at www.pbs.org/newshour; Alan Elsner, "Bush to Propose Tax Cuts in Speech Wednesday," *Reuters* (November 29, 1999); Alison Mitchell, "Bush Showcases Democrats to Bolster Bipartisan Image," *New York Times,* (April 26, 2000), p. A18; Ralph Hallow, "Bush's Campaign Tent Unites Diverse Factions; Even Whispers of Discord Disappear," *Washington Times,* June 9, 2000, p. A1; Walter Issacson and George W. Bush, "My Heritage Is Part of Who I Am," *Time Magazine,* August 7, 2000, p. 55; Frank Bruni, "The 2000 Campaign: The Texas Governor; Bush, in a Broad Attack on Gore, Paints Him as the Candidate of Big Government," *New York Times,* September 17, 2000, p. 22; and "In Speech, Bush Says It's Time for Leader Who Will Do the People's Business," *New York Times,* October 28, 2000, p. A10.

For discussion of Bush's tax cut plan, see Matthew Miller, "Duplicity Mars Debate over Estate Taxes," *Dallas Morning News,* July 28, 1999; David Yepsen, "Bush Attacks Barriers to Agricultural Trade; Farmers Are a Priority, He Promises," *Des Moines Register,* September 2, 1999; Frank Bruni and Richard Stevenson, "Bush Tax Cuts Are Assailed as Too Little or Too Much," *New York Times,* December 2, 1999, p. A2; Karen Tumulty, James Carney, and John Dickerson, "Saying One Thing, Doing Another; Bush on Taxes," *Time Magazine,* February 21, 2000, p. 30; and Edward Robinson, "Pocketbook Issues; The 2000 Election Brings Some of Small Business's Biggest Issues to the Forefront," *Time Magazine,* May 8, 2000, p. B28. For a more detailed description of the elements of Bush's proposal, see Eric Pianin, "Bush to Offer $483 Billion Tax-Cut Plan," *Washington Post,* December 1, 1999, p. A1; Richard Stevenson, "Bush to Propose Broad Tax Cut in Iowa Speech," *New York Times,* December 1, 1999, p. A1; and Richard Stevenson, "Dueling Plans on Taxes and Social Security," *New York Times,* January 12, 2000, p. A20.

On the Dole-Kemp estate tax proposal, see Barry Johnson and Martha Eller,

"Federal Taxation of Inheritance and Wealth Transfers," p. 21, at http://www.irs .gov/pub/irs-soi/inhwlttr.pdf. On John McCain's plan, see "Excerpts From Republican Candidates' Debate in Michigan," *New York Times,* January 11, 2000. On the details of Al Gore's proposal, see "Gore's Estate-Tax Plan Seeks to Assist Middle Class, Derail Repeal by GOP," *Wall Street Journal,* June 22, 2000. On Gore's criticism of Bush's proposal, see Alison Mitchell, "Bush Showcases Democrats to Bolster Bipartisan Image," *New York Times,* April 26, 2000.

On the evolution of George W. Bush's position on the estate tax issue, see the Office of Tax Policy Research Campaign Promises 2000 website at http:// www.otpr.org/campaign2000.html (entries for July 15, 1999; December 1, 1999; January 22, 2000; January 24, 2000; August 3, 2000; and October 17, 2000). Specifically, see "Statement by Governor George W. Bush on Agricultural Issues in Iowa" (July 15, 1999), George W. Bush Presidential Exploratory Committee, Inc., website at http://www.georgewbush.com/; George W. Bush speech, "A Tax Cut with a Purpose," delivered in Des Moines, Iowa (December 1, 1999), at http:// www.georgebush.com/News/speeches/120100_purpose.html; CNN: Evans, Novak, Hunt & Shields Transcript, "Gov. George W. Bush Discusses Campaign 2000" (January 22, 2000), at http://www.cnn.com/TRANSCRIPTS/0001/22/ en.00.html; Jonathan Alter and Howard Fineman, "The Front-Runner Speaks," *Newsweek,* January 24, 2000, at http://newsweek.com/nw-srv/printed/us/na/ a35619-2000jan16.htm; "Governor George W. Bush—Acceptance Speech, Philadelphia Pennsylvania" (August 3, 2000), at http://www.4president.org/speeches/ bushcheney2000convention.htm; and "The Third Gore-Bush Presidential Debate Transcript" (October 17, 2000), at http://www.debates.org/pages/trans2000c .html.

For information on the debates among Republican candidates, see Richard Berke, "The Republican Debate: The Overview," *New York Times,* December 3, 1999, p. A1; Berke, "Republican Candidates Gather for Courteous Debate," *New York Times,* December 7, 1999, p. A20; and Berke, "In a Fierce Debate, Bush Promises to Cut Taxes, Calling to Mind His Father," *New York Times,* January 7, 2000, p. A15. For information on the Bush-Gore debates, see "Transcript of Debate between Vice President Gore and Governor Bush," *New York Times,* October 4, 2000 p. A30; Editorial, "The First Presidential Debate," *New York Times,* October 4, 2000, p. A34; Richard Stevenson, "Sorting it Out: Tax Cuts and Spending," *New York Times,* October 6, 2000, p. A26; "Exam Time at the Debates," *New York Times,* October 8, 2000, p. 14; "The 2000 Campaign; Second Presidential Debate between Gov. Bush and Vice President Gore," *New York Times,* October 12, 2000, p. A22; "Exchanges between the Candidates in the Third Presidential Debate," *New York Times,* October 18, 2000, p. A26; Richard Stevenson, "Doing the Math behind Candidates' Debate Claims," *New York Times,* October 19, 2000, p. A28; and "The Final Presidential Debate," *New York Times,* October 18, 2000, p. A30.

For information on the members of Bush's economic team, see Richard Berke and Rick Lyman, "Training for a Presidential Race," *New York Times*, March 15, 1999; Richard Stevenson and Frank Bruni, "Bush Challenges the Orthodoxy but Is Still a Devout Conservative," *New York Times*, October 8, 1999, p. A1; and Robert Dodge, "Bush Learning His Economics from Experts," *Dallas Morning News*, June 28, 1999, p. 1D. For background on Larry Lindsey, see George Hager, "Gloom and Doom on the Campaign Trail; Bush Adviser Hopes to Convince Voters That It's Still the Economy, Stupid," *Washington Post*, June 8, 1999, p. E1; "Lindsay Wants Hot Dog Stand Economics in the White House," *Financial Times*, July 15, 1999, p. 3; and Richard Stevenson, "At Bush's Ear, a Supply-Sider with a Heart," *New York Times*, December 12, 1999. On Jennifer Dunn's support of Bush, see the List of "Pioneers" released by George W. Bush for President Campaign at http://www.commoncause.org/campaign2000/state.htm. Dick Cheney's comment is reported in Ron Suskind, *The Price of Loyalty* (New York: Simon and Shuster, 2004).

CHAPTER 14: BUILDING A STRONG OFFENSE

On the surplus predictions of the Congressional Budget Office, see CBO Testimony, Statement of Barry Anderson before the Committee on the Budget, United States Senate, "The Budget and Economic Outlook: Fiscal Years 2002–2011" (January 31, 2001) at http://www.cbo.gov/showdoc.cfm?index=2728&sequence =0; "CBO Surplus Projections Fuel Both Sides of Tax Cut Debate," *Tax Notes Today* (February 1, 2001); "Blue Dog Coalition Release on CBO Budget Projections," *Tax Notes Today* (February 1, 2001); "Gephardt Release on CBO Projections," *Tax Notes Today* (February 1, 2001); and "Thomas Reaction to CBO Surplus Numbers," *Tax Notes Today* (February 1, 2001). For information on Alan Greenspan's testimony, see "Greenspan Testimony at Senate Budget Committee Hearing on the Economy," *Tax Notes Today* (January 26, 2001); "Greenspan Endorses Tax Cuts, Social Security Privatization," *Tax Notes Today* (January 26, 2001); "Thomas Statement on Greenspan's Comments on Economy, Tax Relief," *Tax Notes Today* (January 26, 2001); "Grassley Statement at Senate Budget Committee Hearing on Economy," *Tax Notes Today* (January 26, 2001); "Blue Dog Coalition Release on Greenspan's Budget Approach," *Tax Notes Today* (January 26, 2001); and "Greenspan Mum on Taxes, but Says Plenty on Budget," *Tax Notes Today* (March 5, 2001).

For information on Speaker of the House Dennis Hastert, see Biography of House Speaker J. Dennis Hastert, at http://www.house.gov/hastert/bio.shtml; Katharine Q. Seelye, "The 106th Congress: The House; Hastert Is Sworn in as 51st Speaker and Puts Forth a Conciliatory Tone," *New York Times*, January 7, 1999 ("pool of bitterness"); Mark Leibovich, "Speak No Drivel; Dennis Hastert May Have Ended up in the Driver's Seat, but He Still Won't Blow His Own Horn," *Washington Post*, July 29, 2002, p. C1; "Back From the Brink: After Nearly Leaving, Watts Makes Run at Being Bush's Top Ally," *Roll Call* (January 8, 2001); and

Jonathan Franzen, "The Listener; How Did a Former Wrestling Coach End up Running the House of Representatives?" *New Yorker,* October 6, 2003.

For the quote by Thomas Brackett Reed, see *Congressional Record* (April 22, 1880): 2661.

For information on Ways and Means Chairman Bill Thomas, see Biography of U.S. Representative Bill Thomas, at http://billthomas.house.gov/Bio.asp; Richard Simon, "Californian Thomas Gets House Ways and Means Chairmanship," *Los Angeles Times,* January 5, 2001, p. A15 ("occasional fits of temper"); Juliet Eilperin, "GOP Leaders Make a Choice of Necessity; Many Confident Thomas Can Best Shepherd Bush's Agenda through Ways and Means Panel," *Washington Post,* January 6, 2001, p. A5 ("spirited policy wonk"); Robert Novak, "A Test of Wills over 'Death' Tax," *Chicago Sun Times,* February 15, 2001, p. 31 ("listening to all the arguments"); and Sheryl Gay Stolberg, "Lawmaker Apologizes for Poor Judgment," *New York Times,* July 24, 2003, p. A15 ("one of the most revered and reviled members of the House").

Bush assembled a capable team within his administration to secure the passage of his tax cut bill. For background information on Karl Rove, see Robert Bryce, "The Man behind the Candidate," *Austin Chronicle,* March 18, 1994, pp. 23, 28–30, 32–33; Bryce, "The Fab Four: Meet the People Maneuvering behind the Scenes to Put George W. Bush in the White House," *Salon* (June 16, 1999), at http://www.salon.com/news/feature/1999/06/16/advisors/index1.html; Jessica Reaves, "Person of the Week: Karl Rove," *Time Magazine,* November 7, 2002; "Bush's Chief Strategist," at http://abcnews.go.com/sections/politics/DailyNews/rove_profile001228.html.

For information on Assistant to the President for Legislative Affairs Nick Calio, see Juliet Eilperin, "Bush Team Veteran Returns to the Court; Calio to Sell President's Agenda on the Hill," *Washington Post,* January 31, 2001, p. A19; Kerry Kantin, "GOPers Say Calio Has Overcome 'Growing Pains,'" *The Hill* (March 20, 2002); Jake Thompson, "Tax Cut OK'd; It's the Biggest in Two Decades," *Omaha World Herald,* May 27, 2001; Albert Eisele, "The Jeffords Blame Game," *The Hill* (May 30, 2001); Peter H. Stone and Louis Jacobson, "A K-Streeter Returns to the White House," *National Journal* (January 20, 2001); John Breshnahan, "Friendly Fire for Bush's Lobbyist," *Roll Call* (June 4, 2001).

For background information on Mark Weinberger, assistant secretary to the Treasury for Tax Policy, see "Ernst and Young Names Mark A. Weinberger Director of National Tax Department," *Business Wire* (June 7, 2000); "Executive Changes," *American Banker* (June 12, 2000): 3; "President Clinton Names Mark A. Weinberger as a Member of the Social Security Advisory Board," *PR Newswire* (October 4, 2000); "New Assets," *National Law Journal* (October 23, 2000): B6; "Corporate Lobbyist Bush's Pick for Tax Post; Weinberger Won Breaks for Companies," *Baltimore Sun,* February 6, 2001, p. 1C; "Tax Report," *Wall Street Journal,* March 7, 2001, p. A1; "W&M Approves $193 Billion Estate Tax Repeal with Anti-avoidance Provisions," *Tax Notes Today* (March 30, 2001); "Treasury's Weinberger Preaches Bush Tax Cut," *Tax Notes Today* (April 4, 2001); Jonathan Weisman, "Lawmakers Look for Best Ways to Trim Bush's Tax Cut," *USA Today,* April 30, 2001, p. 4A; Greg Hitt and Mark Weinberger, "Treasury Official's Meetings with Firms Underscore a Gray Area in Ethics Rules," *Wall Street Journal,* May 23, 2001; "Treasury Responds to Blethen Death Tax Repeal Team," *Tax Notes Today* (August 2, 2001); Sydney Freedberg, "Now He's the One Making the Tax Rules," *St. Petersburg Times,* March 17, 2002, p. 1A; "The Clients," *St. Petersburg Times,* March 17, 2002, p. 18A; Department of the Treasury Office of Public Affairs, "O'Neill Announces Weinberger Plans to Leave Treasury" (March 26, 2002), at http://www.ustreas.gov/press/releases/po2036.htm; "National Briefing Washington: Tax Official to Leave Post," *New York Times,* March 27, 2002, p. A18; Ameet Sachdev, "Scandals Taxing for Audit Firms' Lawyers," *Chicago Tribune,* November 24, 2002; and Ameet Sacdev, "Ernst & Young to Pay IRS over Tax Shelters," *Chicago Tribune,* July 3, 2003. Also see Hearing before the Committee on Finance of the United States Senate, 107th Congress, First Session on the Nominations of Mark A. Weinberger to Be Assistant Secretary of the Treasury for Tax Policy, and John Duncan to Be Assistant Secretary of the Treasury for Legislative Affairs, February 28, 2001, Senate Hearing 107–22 (Washington, D.C.: U.S. Government Printing Office, 2001).

For information on White House Chief of Staff Andrew Card, see "Andrew H. Card Jr., Chief of Staff," at http://www.opensecrets.org/bush/cabinet/cabinet .card.asp; Claire Moore, "Quiet and Loyal Leader," *ABC News,* at http:// abcnews.go.com/sections/politics/DailyNews/card_profile.html; "Andrew Card, Chief of Staff," *ABC News,* at http://www.abcnews.go.com/sections/politics/ DailyNews/bush_advisers_card.html; "President's Chief of Staff Andrew Card," at http://www.usembassy.de/usa/etexts/gov/biograph/card.htm; "Card Won't Deal Gasoline Tax Hand," *Tax Notes Today* (April 22, 1992); "House Lawmakers Haggle over Health Care Jurisdictional Issues," *Tax Notes Today* (July 22, 1994); CNN Chat Transcript, "Andrew Card on the 2000 GOP Convention" (July 30, 2000), at http://www.cnn.cm/COMMUNITY/transcripts/2000/7/30/card/; *Fox News Sunday,* Transcript (December 17, 2000); Associated Press, "Bush Gets Tax Cut Advice," (December 18, 2000), at http://quest.cjonline.com/stories/121800/ gen_1218007461.shtml; Robert Novak, "Death Tax Doubts," *Washington Post,* February 15, 2001; Bob Schieffer, "Andrew Card, White House Chief of Staff, Discusses Jim Jeffords and the Presidential Tax Cut," *Face the Nation,* Transcript (May 28, 2001), at www.cbsnews.com/stories/2001/05/28/ftn/main2931615 .shtml?cmp=ill-searchstories; Curt Anderson, "Tax Deal Includes Rebate by Mid-Summer," *Chicago Sun-Times,* May 27, 2001; Susan Milligan and Sue Kirchhoff, "Senators Vote to Slash Bush Tax Cut By $448B," *Boston Globe,* April 5, 2001; "New Location, Same Old Tax Cut Debate," *Tax Notes,* February 15, 2001; and "Business Gives Bush Tax Plan a Break," *Orlando Sentinel Tribune,* March 4, 2001, p. A14.

For information on the activities and speeches of George W. Bush regarding his tax plan once in office, see "President George W. Bush's Inaugural Address" (January 20, 2001), at http://www.whitehouse.gov/news/inaugural-address.html; Office of the Press Secretary, "Remarks by the President at Meeting with Republican and Senate Leaders" (January 30, 2001), at http://www.whitehouse.gov/news/releases/20010130-2.html; Office of the Press Secretary, "Remarks by the President at Republican Congressional Retreat" (February 2, 2001), at http://www.whitehouse.gov/news/releases/20010202.html; Jonathan Weisman, "Bush Could Divide Bill for Tax Cuts," *USA Today*, February 14, 2001; Judy Keen and Jonathan Weisman, "GOP Readies Tax-Cut Promotional Blitz," *USA Today*, February 19, 2001, p. 5A; Office of the Press Secretary, "Address of the President to the Joint Session of Congress" (February 27, 2001), at http://www.whitehouse.gov/news/releases/2001/02/20010228.html; Office of the Press Secretary, "Remarks by the President at Nebraska Welcome" (February 28, 2001), at http://www.whitehouse.gov/news/releases/2001/02/20010228-4.html; Office of the Press Secretary, "Remarks by the President during Leadership Forum" (February 28, 2001), at http://www.whitehouse.gov/news/releases/2001/02/20010228-5.html; Office of the Press Secretary, "Remarks by the President at North Dakota Welcome Event, North Dakota State University Bison Arena, Fargo, North Dakota" (March 8, 2001), at http://www.whitehouse.gov/news/releases/2001/03/20010308-22.html; Office of the Press Secretary, "President's Tax Relief Plan Gives Greatest Relief to Lowest Income Taxpayers" (March 8, 2001), at http://www.whitehouse.gov/news/releases/2001/03/20010309-5.html; Office of the Press Secretary, "Statement by the Press Secretary" (March 8, 2001), at http://www.whitehouse.gov/news/releases/2001/03/20010308-14.html; Jonathan Weisman and Judy Keen, "Bush Prepares for Fight in Senate," *USA Today*, March 9, 2001, p. 4A; Office of the Press Secretary, "Remarks by the President during Meeting with Small Business Owners" (March 16, 2001), at http://www.whitehouse.gov/news/releases/2001/03/20010316-3.html; Office of the Press Secretary, "Radio Address to the Nation" (March 17, 2001), at http://www.whitehouse.gov/news/releases/2001/03/20010317.html; Office of the Press Secretary, "Remarks by the President to the Hispanic Chamber of Commerce" (March 19, 2001), at http://www.whitehouse.gov/news/releases/2001/03/20010319-8.html; Office of the Press Secretary, "Remarks by the President and the First Lady to Women Business Leaders" (March 20, 2001), at http://www.whitehouse.gov/news/releases/2001/03/20010320-2.html; Office of the Press Secretary, "Remarks by the President to the National Newspaper Association 40th Annual Government Affairs Conference" (March 22, 2001), at http://www.whitehouse.gov/news/releases/2001/03/20010322-1.html; Office of the Press Secretary, "Remarks by the President to the Greater Portland Chambers of Commerce Meeting" (March 23, 2001), at http://www.whitehouse.gov/news/releases/2001/03/20010323.html; Office of the Press Secretary, "Remarks by the President in Billings, Montana Welcome Event" (March 26, 2001), at http://www.whitehouse.gov/news/releases/2001/03/20010327.html; Office of the Press Secretary, "Remarks by the

President in Kansas City, Missouri" (March 26, 2001), at http://www.whitehouse
.gov/news/releases/2001/03/20010326-6.html; Jonathan Weisman and Mimi
Hall, "Bush Aide Suggests Tax Shift; Estate Tax Repeal Levy Might Be Delayed,"
USA Today, March 27, 2001, p. 1A; Office of the Press Secretary, "Remarks by
the President to Southwest Michigan First Coalition/Kalamazoo Chamber of
Commerce Joint Event on the Economy" (March 27, 2001), at http://
www.whitehouse.gov/news/releases/2001/03/20010327-5.html; Donald Lam-
bro, "White House Denies Delay in Repealing Estate Tax," *Washington Times,*
March 28, 2001, p. A6; Office of the Press Secretary, "Remarks by the President
in Meeting with House and Senate Leaders" (March 28, 2001), at http://
www.whitehouse.gov/news/releases/2001/03/20010328-4.html; Office of the
Press Secretary, "Remarks by the President to the National Restaurant Association" (April 2, 2001), at http://www.whitehouse.gov/news/releases/2001/04/
20010402-7.html; Office of the Press Secretary, "Statement by the President"
(April 4, 2001), at http://www.whitehouse.gov/news/releases/2001/04/20010404
-11.html; Office of the Press Secretary, "Remarks by the President to the U.S.
Conference of Mayors National Summit on Investment in the New American
City" (April 5, 2001), at http://www.whitehouse.gov/news/releases/2001/04/
20010405-4.html; Office of the Press Secretary, "Remarks by the President at Horatio Alger Awards" (April 6, 2001), at http://www.whitehouse.gov/news/
releases/2001/04/20010418-4.html; Office of the Press Secretary, "Remarks by
the President at Tim Hutchinson for Senate Reception" (April 25, 2001), at
http://www.whitehouse.gov/news/releases/2001/04/20010426-8.html; Office of
the Press Secretary, "Remarks by the President in New Orleans, Louisiana Welcome" (April 25, 2001), at http://www.whitehouse.gov/news/releases/2001/
04/20010426-6.html; Office of the Press Secretary, "Statement by the President
on Tax Agreement" (May 1, 2001), at http://www.whitehouse.gov/news/
releases/2001/04/20010501-9.html; Patti Mohr, "O'Neill Confident Tax Cut to
Be Passed Intact by June 1," *Tax Notes* (May 8, 2001); Office of the Press Secretary, "Remarks by the President in Ceremony Honoring the Small Business Person of the Year" (May 8, 2001), at http://www.whitehouse.gov/news/
releases/2001/04/20010508-3.html; Office of the Press Secretary, "Remarks by
the President after Passage of the Tax Cut Plan" (May 26, 2001), at
http://www.whitehouse.gov/news/releases/2001/04/20010529-4.html; Jonathan
Weisman, "Bush's Tax-Cut Hardball Seems to Have Paid Off," *USA Today,* May
29, 2001, p. 8A; Office of the Press Secretary, "Remarks by the President in
Tax Relief Celebration" (June 4, 2001), at http://www.whitehouse.gov/
news/releases/2001/04/20010605-1.html; Office of the Press Secretary, "Remarks by the President in Tax Cut Bill Signing Ceremony" (June 7, 2001), at
http://www.whitehouse.gov/news/releases/2001/06/20010607.html; and Office
of the Press Secretary, "President Speaks at Tax Celebration Event in Iowa
(June 8, 2001), at http://www.whitehouse.gov/news/releases/2001/04/20010608-2
.html.

CHAPTER 15: THE BIRTH OF A NEW COALITION

On the Rose Garden ceremony launching his tax plan once he became the president, see "Bush to Unveil Tax Cut Plan Today," *Bulletin's Frontrunner* (February 8, 2001) and James Toedtman, "Tax-Cut Stampede Begins; Interest Groups Line up for Relief in $1.6 trillion Bush Proposal," *Newsday*, February 12, 2001. With reason, the Bush Administration was concerned with losing big business support as evidenced by the following: Dan Morgan, "Business Backs Bush Tax Cut; under Pressure, Groups Agree to Defer Push for Wider Relief," *Washington Post*, March 4, 2001; and Jack Faris, "Small Business Tax Cut Benefits," *Washington Times*, March 4, 2001. Bush put together a team to initiate contacts with the corporate world, including Vice President Dick Cheney, Senior Adviser Karl Rove, White House Chief of Staff Andrew Card, Treasury Secretary Paul O'Neill, Commerce Secretary Don Evans, and Chief Economic Adviser Larry Lindsay. For more information on members of the team and the team's role, see Thomas B. Edsall and Dana Milbank, "White House's Roving Eye for Politics; President's Most Powerful Adviser May Also Be the Most Connected," *Washington Post*, March 10, 2003; and Richard W. Stevenson, "Quiet on the Lobbying Front; Sudden Halt to Coalition's Bid for Corporate Tax Breaks," *New York Times*, February 23, 2001. For a brief biography of Secretary Donald L. Evans, see http://www.commerce.gov/bios/evans_bio.html (September 27, 2003).

For more information on Charls Walker, see "Bush to Unveil Tax Cut Plan Today"; James Toedtman, "Tax-Cut Stampede Begins; Interest Groups Line up for Relief in $1.6 Trillion Bush Proposal," *Newsday*, February 12, 2001; Morgan, "Business Backs Bush Tax Cut"; Jill Abramson, "The Nation; Lobbyists Waitin' on the Levy for Their Ship to Come In," *New York Times*, March 4, 2001; and Marc Lacey and Richard W. Stevenson, "To Blunt Criticism, Bush Reunites Working Families Backing His Tax Cut," *New York Times*, February 8, 2001. On Walker's methods, see Jill Abramson, "The Business of Persuasion Thrives in Nation's Capital," *New York Times*, September 29, 1998. On Walker's long relationship with George W. Bush, see Richard A. Oppel, Jr., and Jim Yardley, "The 2000 Campaign: The Texas Governor; Bush Calls Himself Reformer; the Record Shows the Label may be a Stretch," *New York Times* (March 20, 2000). On Walker's formation of a new business coalition before meeting with the president on February 7, 2001, see Stevenson, "Quiet on the Lobbying Front." Finally, see Morgan, "Business Backs Bush Tax Cut"; and Abramson, "The Nation; Lobbyists Waitin' on the Levy for Their Ship to Come In," for information on Walker abandoning his attempt to include tax cuts for big business in Bush's plan.

For general information on the American Council for Capital Formation, see their website at http://www.accf.org. See the November–December 2000 ACCF newsletter for the announcement of ACCF high-ranking members entering the Bush administration, at http://www.accf.org/NovDec00.htm (September 27, 2003).

Simultaneously, the Business Roundtable was introducing a pro–big business tax proposal. See Lacey and Stevenson, "To Blunt Criticism, Bush Reunited Working Families Backing His Tax Cut." For more general information, see the BRT website at http://www.brtable.org.

On Bush's February 7, 2001, luncheon with key business leaders, see Lacey and Stevenson, "To Blunt Criticism, Bush Reunites Working Families Backing His Tax Cut"; Tom Hamburger and Jim VandeHei, "The Bush Tax Plan: Generous GOP Donors Discuss the Details over Closed-Door White House Lunch," *Wall Street Journal,* February 8, 2001; and Jill Abramson "The Nation; Lobbyists Waitin' on the Levy for Their Ship to Come In."

On Bush's other activities on February 7, 2001, see Lacey and Stevenson, "To Blunt Criticism, Bush Reunited Working Families Backing His Tax Cut" and "Bush to Unveil Tax Cut Plan Today," *Bullentin's Frontrunner* (February 8, 2001), which also include Representative Dunn's description of Bush's backbone. On Bush's first press conference as president, see Stevenson, "Quiet on the Lobbying Front." On Bush's first Rose Garden Ceremony, see "Bush to Unveil Tax Cut Plan Today."

General information on Dirk Van Dongen can be found in Jeffrey Birnbaum, "The Man in the Middle," *Fortune Small Business,* April 1, 2002; Louis Jacobson, "The Roundtable's Turnaround," *National Journal,* June 28, 2003; and the National Association of Wholesale-Distributors (NAW) website. For more information on the NAW, see its website at http://www.naw.org. On the White House recruitment of Dirk Van Dongen, see Alison Mitchell, "Interest Groups Are Gearing Up for High-Stakes Tax Cut Fight," *New York Times,* February 24, 2001. On Van Dongen being a Bush "Pioneer," his relationship with Nick Calio, and Grover Norquist's thoughts on Van Dongen, see Birnbaum, "The Man in the Middle." Labor Secretary Chao announced Bush's nickname for Van Dongen at a speech given to the NAW; see "Labor Secretary Provides Upbeat Outlook at NAWD Session," *National Journal's Congress Daily* (January 29, 2003). Bush himself referred to Dirkus as his "good buddy" at a Rose Garden speech. "Remarks by President George W. Bush re: the Economy and His Economic Proposals," *Federal News Service* (April 15, 2003).

On Bush's Indian Treaty Room meeting with various business advocate groups on February 23, 2001, see Mitchell, "Interest Groups Are Gearing Up for High-Stakes Tax Cut Fight," at http://clinton3.nara.gov/WH/Tours/OEOB/html/Indian_Treaty.html (September 12, 2003); "National Restaurant Association Leaders Personally Meet with President Bush to Endorse Tax Cut Plan," at http://www.restaurant.org/pressroom/print/index/cfm?ID=165 (February 23, 2001; September 27, 2003); and "NRA: Bush Seems to Be Restaurant-Friendly Prez," at http://www.sfsn.com/SW/news/01-0607/news5.html (June/July 2001; September 27, 2003). For information on Citizens for a Sound Economy (CSE), a conservative organization also represented at the Indian Treaty Room meeting, see its website at http://www.cse.org.

For information on Denise Marie Fugo, chairperson of the National Restaurant Association and owner of Sammy's in Cleveland, Ohio, see Susan Houston, "A National Trend," *News and Observer,* February 28, 2001; "National Restaurant Association Urges Congress to Override Clinton Veto of Death Tax," *U.S. Newswire* (September 8, 2000); "National Restaurant Association Applauds Senate for Burying the Death Tax," *U.S. Newswire* (July 14, 2000); "National Restaurant Association Asks Senate to Follow House in Relinquishing the Death Tax," *U.S. Newswire* (July 12, 2000); R&I Special Report, "Bellwethers," at http://www.rimag.com/012/sr.htm (June 15, 2000); "Denise Marie Fugo Elected National Restaurant Association Chairman of the Board," *U.S. Newswire* (May 21, 2000); Angela Townsend, "Fine-Dining Pioneer Sammy's Closes Flats Restaurant, Will Cater," *Plain Dealer,* April 30, 2000; "Top Local Businesswomen to Be Saluted," *Plain Dealer,* May 7, 1996; and Mary Strassmeyer, "Ball Glitter Is Facet of Celebrating Orchestra," *Plain Dealer,* September 19, 1993. For more information about Sammy's itself, see http://www.milioni.com/risto/america/dati/70.HTM (September 27, 2003). On Fugo's view of the death tax, see "National Restaurant Association Asks Senate to Follow House in Relinquishing the Death Tax," *U.S. Newswire* (July 12, 2000).

For general information about the National Restaurant Association, see its website at http://www.restaurant.org.

On the number of members in the U.S. Chamber of Commerce, see its website at http://www.uschamber.com/about/default (September 16, 2003). On the number of members in the National Federation of Independent Business, see its website at http://www.nfib.com. To view the USCC's stance on the estate tax and learn more about its ability to round up grassroots support through Grassroots Action Information Network, see http://www.uschamber.com/press/releases/2001/april/01-59.htm (September 1, 2003), http://www.uschamber.com/government/issues/econtax/estategift.htm (September 16, 2003), and http://www.uschamber.com/chambers/action/default (March 29, 2004); and "U.S. Chamber of Commerce Release Urging Swift Action on Tax Cuts," *Tax Notes* (March 7, 2001). A brief description of the organization's history, including President Taft's call for a "central organization" for chambers of commerce in 1911, can be found at http://www.uschamber.comabout/history/default (September 16, 2003). For a directory of USCC members, see http://www.uschamber.com/chambers/chamber_directory.asp (March 16, 2004).

For information on the National Association of Manufacturers, including its mission statement, leadership, membership description, and policy agenda, see its website at http://www.nam.org. On NAM's leadership within the TRC, see Mike Baroody (of NAM), "NAM Official Hails Formation of Tax Relief Coalition," *Tax Notes* (March 7, 2001); Tax Relief Coalition News Conference, *Congressional Schedules* (March 6, 2001); and "Business Gives Bush Tax Plan a Break; Trade Associations and Corporations Backed off Their Agendas in Hope of Accommodation Later," *Orlando Sentinel Tribune,* March 4, 2001.

On the BRT joining the TRC, see Dan Morgan, "Business Backs Bush Tax Cut;

Under Pressure, Groups Agree to Defer Push for Wider Relief," *Washington Post,* March 4, 2001.

To view TRC's March 6 open letter to Congress with its then 175-membership list attached, see "Tax Relief Coalition Letter to Congress," *Tax Notes* (March 7, 2001).

For more information on the Republican Jewish Coalition, see its website at http://www.rjchq.org. On the RJC's chairman and Republican fund-raiser extraordinaire, Sam Fox, see the RJC website; "Fox to Chair 2003 United Way Campaign," at http://www.bizjournals.com/stlouis/stories/2003 (October 13, 2003); Katharine Q. Seelye, "Big Donors Unfazed by Prospect of Soft Money Limits," *New York Times,* March 24, 2001; Don Van Natta, Jr., "The Nation: The Donors Rule, but in Name Only," *New York Times,* August 6, 2000; Jo Mannies, "Clayton Man, a Top Adviser to Bush, Leads List of Missouri Political Donors; for 'Good Government,' He's Given $300,000 to GOP in the Past Year," *St. Louis Post-Dispatch,* May 21, 2000. Regarding RJC's Ashcroft television advertisements, see Jo Mannies, "Top GOP Donor Wages Campaign to Win Jewish Support for Ashcroft," *St. Louis Post-Dispatch* (January 21, 2001) and http://www.usajewish .com/scripts/usaj/paper/Article.asp?ArticleID=1058. On Sam Fox's presence at the February 7, 2001, luncheon with President Bush, see Tom Hamburger and Jim VandeHei, "The Bush Tax Plan." On the RJC March 1, 2001, meeting at the White House, see http://www.jewishsightseeing.com/usa/wash_dc/capitol_building/sd3 -9alan_greenspan.htm (September 27, 2003). For more information about the RJC forum, which attracted all six Republican Presidential hopefuls for the first debate, see http://archive.salon.com/news/feature/1999/12/03/jews (September 27, 2003). On Ari Fleischer joining the RJC Board, see "Ari Fleisher Joins Republican Jewish Coalition Board of Directors," *RJC Newsletter* (September 10, 2003). On RJC members who serve as ambassadors, see Jeremy Feiler, "Phila. Lawyer Nominated as Ambassador," *Philadelphia Business Journal,* June 20, 2001, and http://www.usembassay.it/mission/amb/amb-bio-en.htm (Mel Sembler's biography; October 7, 2003).

Regarding Kirk Blalock's move from the White House to the lobbying world, see Peter H. Stone, "Bush Aides Take the K Street Exit," *National Journal,* May 24, 2003.

For more information on the TRC generally, its grassroots activities, and member support, see http://www.taxreliefcoalition.org. A copy of the TRC May 19 letter sent to "target" senators may be viewed at http://www.taxreliefcoalition.org/ docs/2003-05-22/Ltr_to_Sens_Yes_on_Sen_Final_%20Passage_05_19.pdf (which gives information regarding its membership and the TRC Management Committee at that time; March 29, 2004).

CHAPTER 16: BILLIONAIRES BATTLE

For information on United for a Fair Economy, see their website at http:// www.faireconomy.org, and for information on Responsible Wealth, see their website at http://www.responsiblewealth.org. Background information on Bill Gates, Sr., can be found in Dan Ackman, "Papa Gates On Death and Taxes," *Forbes Magazine,* January 20, 2003, at http://www.forbes.com/finance/2003/01/20/cx_da_0120gates.html; Amy Reiter, "Gates the Elder Forced to Change Name," *Salon* (July 7, 1999), at http://www.salon.com/people/col/reit/1999/07/07/billsr/; UW Awards 2000, "William H. Gates, Jr.—Recognition Award," *University Week* 17, no. 29 (May 25, 2000), at http://depts.washington.edu/~uweek/archives/uw_2000/alumni_recognition.html; University of Washington, "Regent William H. Gates," at http://www.washington.edu/regents/gates.html; Paula Bock, "As Activist, Volunteer and Dad, William Gates Sr. Leads by Doing," *Seattle Times,* February 5, 2003; and Bob Thompson, "Sharing the Wealth?" *Washington Post Magazine,* April 13, 2003, p. W08.

For a copy of the "Call to Preserve the Estate Tax Coalition," see https://faireconomy.org/join/et-call-rw.html, and for its signatories, see http://www.responsiblewealth.org/estatetax/ETCall_Signers.html. Also see David Cay Johnston, "Dozens of Rich Americans Join in Fight to Retain the Estate Tax," *New York Times,* February 14, 2001, p. A1; Responsible Wealth Press Release, "Bill Gates, Sr., George Soros, Steven Rockefeller, 100 Others Oppose Estate Tax Repeal" (February 14, 2001), at http://www.responsiblewealth.org/press/2001/estate_tax_call_pr.html; Responsible Wealth Press Release, "400 Millionaires, Small Business Owners Join Estate Tax Supporters" (February 27, 2001), at http://www.responsiblewealth.org/press/2001/estate_tax_bush_sotu.html. For a list of senators targeted by Responsible Wealth on this issue, see http://www.responsiblewealth.org/estatetax/latest_news.html.

On the philosophical case made by Responsible Wealth for the preservation of the estate tax, see the testimony of William H. Gates, Sr., before the Senate Committee on Finance, Subcommittee on Taxation and IRS Oversight, "Preserving and Protecting Family Business Legacies" (March 15, 2001), which can be found in the *Congressional Record Daily Digest* (March 15, 2001): D221, or at http://www.senate.gov/~finance/031501wgtest.pdf. Also see William H. Gates, Sr., "A Tax Break's Unfortunate Legacy," *Washington Post,* May 25, 2001 and William H. Gates, Sr., "The Estate Tax: What's at Stake," *Washington Post,* February 16, 2001, p. A25. Various articles were also published on this issue in the Responsible Wealth newsletter, including, "Tax Fairness Pledge," *Action News* 4, no. 1 (March 2000); "We Won!" *Action News* 4, no. 3 (October 2000); "Turning the Tide," *Action News* 5 no. 1 (April 2001); and "Take the Tax Fairness Pledge," *Action News* 6, no. 1 (March 2002). For a detailed explanation of their arguments to preserve the estate tax, see William Gates, Sr., and Chuck Collins, *Wealth and Our Commonwealth: Why America Should Tax Accumulated Fortunes* (Boston: Beacon Press, 2003), and for a review of that book, see Rich Barlow, "Book Review: A Convincing Case for Keeping 'Death Tax' Alive," *Boston Globe,* July 6, 2003, p. D2.

For the debate on "Death and Taxes" between William Gates, Sr., and Pete

DuPont, see the "Dialogues" section of *Slate* on Wednesday February 21, 2001, at http://slate.msn.com/id/101227/entry/101228/; on March 9, 2001, at http://slate.msn.com/id/101227/entry/102161/; on March 12, 2001, at http://slate.msn.com/id/101227/entry/102265/; on March 14, 2001; at http://slate.msn.com/id/101227/entry/102424/; on March 13, 2001, at http://slate.msn.com/id/101227/entry/102449/; and on March 15, 2001, at http://slate.msn.com/id/101227/entry/102496/. For the transcript of the *Crossfire* debate between Gates, Sr., and Senator Jon Kyl, see "Do Death and Taxes Have to Come Together?" (aired March 15, 2001, 7:30 P.M. EST), at http://www.cnn.com/TRANSCRIPTS/0103/15/cf.00.html. Also see Glenn Kessler, "Gates Sr. Spars with GOP over Estate Tax," *Washington Post*, March 16, 2001.

For additional information on the activities of Responsible Wealth on this issue, see Responsible Wealth Press Release, "Bill Gates, Sr., Marian Wright Edelman, Senator Conrad and Others Rally to Preserve Estate Tax" (May 7, 2001), at http://www.responsiblewealth.org/press/2001/estate_tax_rally_pa.html; Responsible Wealth Press Release, "Senate Tax Cut Bill: 'A Giant Step Towards Economic Apartheid'" (May 21, 2001), at http://www.responsiblewealth.org/press/2001/estate_tax_senate_critics.html; Responsible Wealth Press Release "Estate Tax Repeal Opponents: 'The Battle Isn't Over Yet'" (June 5, 2001), at http://www.responsblewealth.org/press/2001/estate_tax_battle.html. For the NFIB opposition to Gates's efforts see "NFIB Release Challenging the Members of 'BARF,'" *Tax Notes* (May 10, 2001); Kent Hoover, "Bush Still Deeply Committed to Repealing Estate Tax," *Washington Business Journal*, February 23, 2001, at http://www.bizjournals.com/washington/stories/2001/02/26/newscolumn3.html; Hoover, "Classes Clash at Hill Protest over Estate Tax Repeal," *Washington Business Journal*, May 18, 2001, at http://www.bizjournals.com/washington/stories/2001/05/21/newscolumn3.html; and Dan Danner's "Letter to Billionaires (February 20, 2001)," at http://www.nfib.com/cgi-bin/NFIB.dll/jsp/issues/researchStudyDisplay.jsp?BV_SessionID=@@@@0157315657.1078606030@@@@&BV_EngineID=ccddadckjglhjkfcflgcehldffgdhfi.0&contentId=2696545. On the history of billionaires and wealth concentration in American society, see J. Bradford DeLong, "Robber Barons" (January 1, 1998), at http://econ161.berkeley.edu/Econ_Articles/carnegie/delong_moscow_paper2.html. On the support of the wealthy for taxes in American society, see Will Hutton, "Why America's Richest Love Taxes," *Observer*, February 25, 2001.

For background information on Robert Johnson and Black Entertainment Television, see Stacy Gilliam, "Bob Johnson Talks Entrepreneurship," at http://www.bet.com/articles/1,,c6gb1110–1761,00.html; Paul Farhi, "BET Chief Envisions Entertainment Empire of Sports, Concerts, Cable TV—and D.C. Arena," *Washington Post*, August 22, 1994, p. F01; "Brookings' Board of Trustees Gains Six New Members" (May 25, 2000), at http://www.rpi.edu/web/President/press/2000/pressbrookings2.html; Greg Lohr, "Viacom to Acquire BET for $2.5B," *Washington Business Journal*, November 3, 2000; George Curry, "BET

Fades to White," *Palm Beach Gazette,* November 9, 2000; David Plotz, "Robert Johnson: How Did BET's Boss Become the United States' Official Black Tycoon?" *Slate,* November 10, 2000, at http://slate.msn.com/id/93393/; DeWayne Wickham, "Profit Not All That Drives BET Content," *USA Today,* November 27, 2000, at http://www.usatoday.com/news/opinion/columnists/wickham/wick167.htm; Yemi Toure, "The End of Black Entertainment Television," *Media File* 20, no. 1 (January/February 2001), at http://www.media-alliance.org/mediafile/20–1/bet.html; "Governor Jeb Bush and First Lady Columba Bush Display BET Founder Robert L. Johnson's Barnett-Aden Art Collection for Black History Month" (February 3, 2003), at http://www.myflorida.com/myflorida/governorsoffice/black_history/rlj-art-collection.html; and Joseph Perkins, "Death Tax Agonies with Wide Side Effects," *Washington Times,* April 18, 2001, p. A13.

For Johnson's advertisement in support of estate tax repeal, see Jack Kemp, "African American Business Leaders Support Repeal of the Death Tax" (April 6, 2001), at http://www.empoweramerica.org/stories/storyReader$253, and Jack Kemp, "How Minority Entrepreneurs Can Save the Tax Cut" (April 12, 2001), at http://www.townhall.com/columnists/jackkemp/printjk20010412.shtml. For President Bush's mention of Johnson in a White House speech, see "Remarks by the President to U.S. Conference of Mayors National Summit on Investment in the New American City," The Rose Garden (April 5, 2001), at http://www.whitehouse.gov/news/releases/2001/04/20010405-4.html.

For discussion of opposition to Johnson's efforts, see "BET's Black Billionaire Trojan Horse: 'Democrat' Bob Johnson Fronts for GOP," *Black Commentator,* issue 13 (October 3, 2002), http://www.blackcommentator.com/13_thw.html, and Dalton Conley, "How to Widen the Black-White Wealth Gap," *Salon* (April 5, 2001), at http://dir.salon.com/politics/feature/2001/04/05/black_wealth/index.html.

CHAPTER 17: PAINT-BY-NUMBERS LAWMAKING

For a more in-depth analysis of Congress's paint-by-numbers tax lawmaking, see Michael J. Graetz, "Paint-by-Numbers Tax Lawmaking," *Columbia Law Review* 95:609. The 2001 tax bill started with a $1.62 trillion proposal by Bush. See Daniel J. Parks, "Bush May Test Capitol Hill Clout Early with Expedited Tax-Cut Proposal," *CQ Weekly* (January 6, 2001). On Senator Daschle's support of a lower tax cut figure, see Lori Nitschke, "Writing Size of Tax Cut into Budget Looms as an Early Turning Point," *CQ Weekly* (January 27, 2001); Nitschke, "Proposals to Alter Bush's Tax Plan Multiply Despite White House Appeals for Unity," *CQ Weekly* (February 17, 2001); and Nitschke, "The Elusive Middle Ground," *CQ Weekly* (March 3, 2001). Three Republican senators stated concerns about the size of Bush's tax cut proposal, and one Democrat, Zell Miller, supported Bush's plan. See Nitschke, "Proposals to Alter Bush's Tax Plan Multiply Despite White House Appeals for Unity"; and Alison Mitchell, "The President's Budget: The Democratic Response; Democrats Cite Deficit Fears in Opposing Bush's Tax Plan," *New York Times*, February 28, 2001.

A brief description of the interplay between a reconciliation bill and the Byrd Rule can be found at Daniel J. Parks, "Byrd Seeks a Way to Stop Tax Bill from Passing by Simple Majority Vote," *CQ Weekly* (March 10, 2001). Boris Bittker offered the analogy of enacting tax legislation to a dance.

On the first bill to make its way through Bill Thomas's Ways and Means Committee and the full House, including Democratic reaction, see Heidi Glenn, "W&M Approves $958 Billion Rate Cut Bill," *Tax Notes* (March 2, 2001); Nitschke, "The Elusive Middle Ground"; and Nitschke, "Tax-Cut Bipartisanship Down to One Chamber," *CQ Weekly* (March 10, 2001). On the second bill's more bipartisan support in the House, see Nitschke, "House Presses Bush's Tax Agenda While Senate Talks of Stimulus," *CQ Weekly* (March 31, 2001); Nitschke, "Alleviation of 'Marriage Penalty' Hits Bipartisan High Note in House," *CQ Weekly* (March 31, 2001); and David E. Rosenbaum, "House Passes Bill for 2 More Pieces of Bush's Tax Cut," *New York Times*, March 30, 2001. Bill Thomas was quoted as comparing the process to a "buffet," stating that "the smorgasbord has more food out there than you're going to eat," in Lori Nitschke, "Tax Cut's Viability Lies in Deep Dealmaking," *CQ Weekly* (March 17, 2001). For more information on the budget resolution passed in the House, see Daniel J. Parks, "Bush's Budget Now before the Senate, Where Moderates Wield the Critical Votes," *CQ Weekly* (March 31, 2001). On Dick Armey insisting on a larger tax cut, see *Inside Politics* transcript, "Democrats Attack Bush Tax Cut Proposal" (February 6, 2001), at http://www.cnn.com/TRANSCRIPTS/0102/06/ip.00.html, and Scott Lindlaw, "President Sends His Crown Jewel Tax-Cut Plan to Congress," *Portsmouth Herald*, February 8, 2001, at http://www.seacoastonline.com/2001news/2_8_w1.htm.

Lindy Paull's February and March JCT memos to John Buckley can be found, respectively, in "Paull's Feb. Memo to W&M Counsel on Estate and Gift Tax Estimates," *Tax Notes Today* (March 28, 2001) and "Paull's March Memo to W&M Counsel on Estate and Gift Tax Estimates," *Tax Notes Today* (March 28, 2001). Also see the following editorial: "New Cost Estimate Shows Folly of Ending Estate Tax," *Newsday*, March 30, 2001. Florida attorney Lauren Detzel's testimony before the Ways and Means Committee can be found at "Attorney's Testimony at W&M Hearing on Bush Tax Relief," *Tax Notes Today* (March 22, 2001).

An ever-shrinking amount of the $1.62 trillion-dollar pot was left for estate tax repeal. One such competing bill for retirement savings tax incentives won a vote in the House on May 2, 2001; see Lori Nitschke, "House Retirement Measure Unlikely to Gain a Place in Senate Tax Package," *CQ Weekly* (May 5, 2001).

On March 29, the Ways and Means Committee voted to repeal the estate tax mostly along party lines. Lori Nitschke, "House Presses Bush's Tax Agenda While Senate Talks of Stimulus," *CQ Weekly* (March 31, 2001), and John Godfrey, "House Approves Marriage Tax Cuts; Panel Votes to Repeal Estate and Gift Levy," *Washington Times*, March 30, 2001. A description of the bill can found in Martin

A. Sullivan, "Economic Analysis—JCT Estimates Widespread Evasion with Estate Tax Repeal," *Tax Notes* (April 2, 2001).

Democrat Charles Rangel's proposal to increase the estate tax exemption was defeated by a partisan committee vote. See David E. Rosenbaum, "Bush's Tax Plan Gets Lift in House, but Senate Balks," *New York Times*, April 5, 2001; Fred Stokeld, "Treasury's Weinberger Preaches Bush Tax Cut; Rangel Not Convinced," *Tax Notes Today* (April 4, 2001); and Glenn Kessler, "Couples Tax Relief Approved by House; Lawmakers Also Pass Doubled Child Credit," *Washington Post*, March 30, 2001.

Robert Matsui's bill to repeal the estate tax immediately was rejected by both Republicans and Democrats. See Nitschke, "House Presses Bush's Tax Agenda While Senate Talks of Stimulus."

The House voted favorably on the committee's bill on April 4, 2001. See Lori Nitschke, "Estate Tax Phaseout Passes House but May Be Scaled Back in Senate When Finance Panel Begins Work," *CQ Weekly* (April 7, 2001), for the facts and figures, including Amo Houghton's opposition quote. The same day, the Senate voted on its budget resolution. See Daniel J. Parks, "It's the Day of the Centrist as Bush Tax Cut Takes a Hit," *CQ Weekly* (April 7, 2001), which discusses Breaux's compromise maneuver, the budget resolution, and Bush's reaction. Baucus met with the president on April 25, 2001, to discuss the tax cut. See "Baucus Meets with President, Promotes Large Tax Cut That Is Fair, Equitable to Montanans," at http://baucus.senate.gov/~baucus/Press/01/04/2001430438.html (July 16, 2003).

For a quick look at the tax cuts being enacted through a reconciliation bill and Robert Byrd's quote, see Andrew Taylor, "Law Designed for Curbing Deficits Becomes GOP Tool for Cutting Taxes," *CQ Weekly* (April 7, 2001).

On the May 1, 2001, Republican budget agreement, see Scott Shepard, "GOP Floats Tentative Deal on Tax Cuts," *Atlanta Journal-Constitution*, May 2, 2001. For more information on the joint budget resolution, see Daniel J. Parks, "GOP Budget Resolution Squeaks by, but Implementation Will Be Tougher," *CQ Weekly* (May 12, 2001). For the *Wall Street Journal* quote regarding the estate tax repeal as a part of the budget resolution, see Shailagh Murray and Greg Hitt, "Senators Stall over Distributing Tax-Cut Spoils," *Wall Street Journal*, May 11, 2001.

The National Federation of Independent Business launched advertising advocating repeal. See Tom Herman, "Tax Report—A Special Summary and Forecast of Federal and State Tax Developments," *Wall Street Journal*, May 9, 2001. For a description of Bill Gates, Sr.'s, Capitol Hill rally, see Mary Jacoby, "Will Charitable Giving Fall if Estate Tax Does?" *St. Petersburg Times*, May 14, 2001. On the exchange between Gates, Sr., and the National Taxpayers Union Federation with the NFIB, see Deborah McGregor, "Wealthy Americans' Fight for Death Tax on Verge of Defeat: Some Rich People Believe in Merits of Estate Tax but Momentum Grows for Its Repeal," *Financial Times*, May 15, 2001, and Pati Mohr, "Lawmakers, Interest Groups Go to Battle over Estate Taxes," *Tax Notes Today* (May 11, 2001).

The Republicans and Democrats of the Senate Finance Committee worked to apportion the tax cut leaving neither party's leadership satisfied. See David E. Rosenbaum, "Senate Panel May Abandon Gift Tax Repeal," *New York Times,* May 10, 2001, and Richard W. Stevenson and David E. Rosenbaum, "Panel Reaches Deal on Budget Framework," *New York Times,* May 9, 2001. Grassley's quote can be found in Jake Thompson, "Grassley's Influence Set to Soar," *Omaha World Herald,* January 13, 2001. Baucus's quote regarding the timeline on creating a bill and Torricelli's quote regarding the competing tax issues can both be found at Murray and Hitt, "Senators Stall over Distributing Tax-Cut Spoils." Grassley and Baucus came up with a compromise bill, though, on May 11, 2001, as announced on Baucus's and Grassley's webpages: "Baucus, Grassley Release Final Bipartisan Tax Package," at http://baucus.senate.gov/~baucus/Press/01/05/2001515930.html (July 16, 2003; includes Baucus's quote) and http://grassley.senate.gov/releases/2001/p01r5.11b.htm (July 16, 2003). On the details of the bill, see also David E. Rosenbaum, "Close Look Shows the Senate Tax Bill Isn't All That It Seems," *New York Times,* May 15, 2001, and Shailagh Murray, "Compromises Shape Tax Package for Further Fine-Tuning in Senate," *Wall Street Journal,* May 14, 2001. On the temporary nature of some of the cuts, see John D. McKinnon, "Some Taxes Being Cut to Reappear—Discovery Prompts Criticism, Points up Congress's Dilemma," *Wall Street Journal,* May 15, 2001.

The Finance Committee passed out the bill on May 16, 2001. For details on the Committee bill, see Shailagh Murray and David Rogers, "Senate Finance Panel Backs $1.35 Trillion Tax Cut," *Wall Street Journal,* May 16, 2001. Margaret Milner Richardson's quip can be found in Tom Herman, "A Special Summary and Forecast of Federal and State Tax Developments," *Wall Street Journal,* May 9, 2001.

For more information on the Byrd Rule, consult the following: Allen Schick, *The Federal Budget: Politics, Policy, Process* (Washington, D.C.: Brookings Institution, 1995), 85–86; Charles Tiefer, "How to Steal a Trillion: The Uses of Laws about Lawmaking in 2001," *Journal of Law and Politics* 17, no. 409 (2001); Elizabeth Garrett, Symposium: "Law and Political Parties: The Congressional Budget Process: Strengthening the Party-in-Government," *Columbia Law Review* 100 (2000): 702; Anita S. Krishnakumar, "Note: Reconciliation and the Fiscal Constitution: The Anatomy of the 1995–96 Budget 'Train Wreck,'" *Harvard Journal on Legislation* 35, no. 589 (1998): 597–98.

The Committee bill also substantially decreased the credit on state death taxes and eliminated it as of 2005. See Shailagh Murray and Greg Hitt, "Estate Tax Is Flash Point as Tax Bill Heads to Senate," *Wall Street Journal,* May 17, 2001.

To view Grassley's floor statement on the bill in full, see http://grassley.senate .gov/releases/2001/p01r5.17.htm (July 16, 2003). The Senate voted favorably on a bill very similar to the one that came out of Grassley's committee. See Shailagh

Murray and Greg Hitt, "Senate Passes $1.35 Trillion Tax-Cut Bill," *Wall Street Journal,* May 24, 2001; Shailagh Murray and David Rogers, "Democrats Foil Hopes to Sign Tax Bill Soon," *Wall Street Journal,* May 23, 2001; Shailagh Murray, "Tax-Cut Bill Now Faces Big Challenge, with Work on House-Senate Compromise," *Wall Street Journal,* May 22, 2001; and Lori Nitschke, "Senate Tax Bill Trade-offs Leave a Fragile Coalition," *CQ Weekly* (May 19, 2001). For additional descriptions of the many amendments proposed and defeated, see Lori Nitschke, "Tax Cut Deal Reached Quickly as Appetite for Battle Fades," *CQ Weekly* (May 26, 2001). The May 19 *CQ Weekly* article also notes the House's reaffirmation vote to reduce the top income tax rate to 33%.

Chapter 18: The Final Four

Four legislators came together to hash things out and put together the final version of the tax cut bill. The *National Journal* article regarding conference committees can be found in full in Richard E. Cohen, "The Third House Rises," *National Journal,* July 28, 2001.

On Jeffords's defection from the Republican party, see Albert R. Hunt, "A Moveable Majority," *Wall Street Journal,* May 24, 2001, and Greg Hitt and Shailagh Murray, "Special Interests Hitch a Ride on Tax Bill—Commodities Firm with Ties to Breaux Gets a Break; Final Deal Inches Ahead," *Wall Street Journal,* May 25, 2001.

The conference committee included nine Senate conferees and three House conferees. See Heidi Glenn, "Tax Cut Conferees Continue Talks," *Tax Notes* (May 25, 2001), which also contains Hastert's quote. On the domination of the process by Thomas, Grassley, Baucus, and Breaux, see Lori Nitschke, "Tax Cut Deal Reached Quickly as Appetite for Battle Fades," *CQ Weekly* (May 26, 2001).

For more information on Bill Thomas and his chairmanship of Ways and Means, see http://billthomas.house.gov/Bio.asp (August 6, 2003); Katherine M. Stimmel and Elizabeth White, "House GOP Selects Thomas as Chairman and Crane Expected to Continue Lead of Trade," *Daily Tax Report* (January 5, 2001); Juliet Eilperin, "GOP Leader Makes a Choice of Necessity; Many Confident Thomas Can Best Shepherd Bush's Agenda through Ways and Means Panel," *Washington Post,* January 6, 2001 (Thomas is the "son of a union plumber who prides himself on his hardscrabble Welsh ancestry"); and Richard Simon, "Californian Thomas Gets House Ways and Means Chairmanship," *Los Angeles Times,* January 5, 2001.

On the informal Wednesday night meeting, see John Godfrey, "Negotiators Agree on Tax-Cut Package; Final Approval Could Come by Today," *Washington Times,* May 26, 2001.

On John Breaux, see his website at http://breaux.senate.gov/index_breaux .html (August 4, 2003; including the *Times-Picayune's* quote); David Ivanovich, "Bush Arrives for Big Day in Washington; Greenspan Talk Set; Dems Rattle

Sabers," *Houston Chronicle*, December 18, 2000; Matt Bai, "The Cool Cajun to See," *Newsweek*, December 18, 2000; and Eric Pooley, "Can Bush Bring Us Together? It Was a Strange, Troubling Ride to Victory, and It Could Get Bumpier. How Will the New President Heal the Wounds—and Tame the Congress?" *Time Magazine*, December 25, 2000.

For more information on Max Baucus, see http://baucus.senate.gov/aboutmax .html (August 11, 2003); J. Norton and Bill Ghent, "Tax-Cut Kings," *National Journal*, April 21, 2001; "Grassley's No 'Errand Boy' for Bush; New Senate Finance Chairman Won't Take Marching Orders from the White House, but Republican Is Eager to Help Crown Jewels of New President's Legislative Agenda," *Roll Call* (February 12, 2001); and Senator Max Baucus, "Breaking Away from One-Size-Fits-All Mentality," *The Hill* (June 17, 1998). The full *National Journal* article regarding Baucus's reelection concerns can be found in Richard E. Cohen and Marilyn Werber Serafini, "Taxing Times," *National Journal*, December 23, 2000.

To learn more about Charles Grassley, see http://grassley.senate.gov/bio.htm (August 6, 2003); Paul Kane, "All Work, No Play for Finance Chair," *Roll Call* (January 15, 2001; including his eight o'clock meetings and his self-described lack of style); Steven Brostoff, "Industry Wondering What It Can Expect from Bush," *National Underwriter—Life & Health* (January 1, 2001); Norman Jane, "D.C. Learns Iowa's Grassley Is No Rube," *Des Moines Register,* January 7, 2001; Jake Thompson, "Grassley's Influence Set to Soar," *Omaha World-Herald,* January 13, 2001; and Alexander Bolton, "Grassley Says Finance Panel Will Work Closely with House," *The Hill* (January 17, 2001).

On the final days of negotiating between the key players, see David E. Rosenbaum, "Congress Agrees on Final Details for Tax-Cut Bill," *New York Times,* May 26, 2001; Glenn Kessler and Juliet Eilperin, "Hill Negotiators Reach Deal on Tax Cut; Package Offers Refunds This Year: $300 for Singles, $600 for Families," *Washington Post,* May 26, 2001 (including Armey's announcement lawmakers would have an hour to read the bill before debate began); "Victory at a Price," *Economist,* May 26, 2001; John Godfrey, "Negotiators Agree on Tax-Cut Package; Final Approval Could Come by Today," *Washington Times,* May 26, 2001 (including Thomas's quip that a more than trillion dollar bill "doesn't get what it used to"); William Neikirk, "Tax Cuts Near Final Approval; Compromise Bill Offers Lower Rates, Immediate Rebates," *Chicago Tribune,* May 27, 2001 (including Thomas's plea for help to reporters); and Daniel J. Parks and Bill Swindell, "Tax Debate Assured a Long Life as Bush, GOP Press for New Cuts," *CQ Weekly* (June 2, 2001). For Chairman Grassley's comments on the slow pace of negotiations, see Glenn, "Tax Cut Conferees Continue Talks."

On the House Rules Committee changing their one-day waiting period rule, see Heidi Glenn and Warren Rojas, "Senate Passes $1.35 Trillion Reconciliation Tax Bill," *Tax Notes Today* (May 24, 2001).

For Democratic reaction to the bill's passage, see David E. Rosenbaum, "Congress Agrees on Final Details for Tax-Cut Bill," *New York Times,* May 26, 2001 (Daschle and Rangel's reactions); and Glenn Kessler and Juliet Eilperin, "Hill Negotiators Reach Deal on Tax Cut" (including Conrad's reaction).

For Republican reaction, see Senator Charles E. Grassley, "Grassley Release on Final Passage of Tax Bill," *Tax Notes* (May 30, 2001). Bush's reaction from Camp David can be found in Rosenbaum, "Congress Agrees on Final Details for Tax-Cut Bill." Andrew Card's take on Bush's tax cut can be found in Neikirk, "Tax Cuts Near Final Approval."

For more information on the Reagan tax cuts, see Todd S. Purdum, "Remembering a Tax Cut, and Revisiting a Debate," *New York Times,* August 13, 2001. On the tax cut coming through faster than even Reagan managed, see "Victory at a Price," *Economist,* May 26, 2001. On the signing of the bill, see Dana Milbank, "Bush Signs Tax Bill into Law; Lawmakers Spar over Whether to Pare or Extend $1.35 Trillion Cut," *Washington Post,* June 8, 2001 (including immediate partisan bickering on whether the cuts should be made permanent). On Republican frustration with the sunset provision of the law, see Lori Nitschke and Bill Swindell, "Tax Law Signed, Its Sunset Chided," *CQ Weekly* (June 9, 2001; including Marshall Wittmann's comment). For Van Dongen's quote, see Dan Morgan, "Business Backs Bush Tax Cut; under Pressure, Groups Agree to Defer Push for Wider Relief," *Washington Post,* March 4, 2001.

Chapter 19: Winners, Losers, and Uncertainty

For Senator Grassley's claim that the 2001 tax act was a victory for all, see William Neikirk, "Tax Cuts Near Final Approval; Compromise Bill Offers Lower Rates, Immediate Rebates," *Chicago Tribune,* May 27, 2001. Senator Kent Conrad's remarks to Alan Greenspan are reported in Ron Suskind, *The Price of Loyalty* (New York: Simon and Shuster, 2004), 61. See Lori Nitschke, "A Tax Cut Deal Reached Quickly as Appetite for Battle Fades," *CQ Weekly* (May 26, 2001).

More information on the states' unsuccessful fight to scale back effects on state revenue can be found at http://www.nga.org/nga/legislativeUpdate/1,1169,C_LETTER^D_2086,00.html (March 10, 2004; May 23, 2001, letter from the National Governors Association [NGA] to senators Grassley and Baucus and Congressmen Thomas and Rangel); http://www.nga.org/nga/legislativeUpdate/1,1169,C_LETTER^D_2061,00.html (March 10, 2004; May 17, 2001 letter from NGA to all senators); http://www.nga.org/nga/newsRoom/1,1169,C_PRESS_RELEASE^D_2088,00.html (March 10, 2004; May 23, 2001 NGA press release); and Tim Nickens and Alisa Ulferts, "Gov. Bush Warns of Dour Fiscal Prospects," *St. Petersburg Times,* June 12, 2001 (citing Jeb Bush's comments regarding the effect on state revenues). For how the states responded, see Joel Michael, "State Responses to EGTRRA Estate Tax Changes," *Tax Notes* 103 (May 24, 2004): 1023–35

On Senator Bob Graham's effort on behalf of the states, see http://www

.ffis.org/misc/051401.htm (March 10, 2004; Federal Funds Information for States press release); Ryan J. Donmoyer, "Federal Estate-Tax Repeal Would Affect States Too, $4 Billion Difference Is Part of Senate Plan," *Seattle Times,* May 18, 2001; and Kevin Sack, "States Expecting to Lose Billions From Repeal of U.S. Estate Tax," *New York Times,* June 21, 2001. For the NGA letter on March 27, 2003, see http://www.nga.org/nga/legislativeUpdate/1,1169,C_LETTER^D_5232,00.html (March 10, 2004).

For Phil Gramm's take on the estate tax as "bigotry to the successful," see Glenn Kessler, "Panel Aims To Rejigger Tax Relief; Senators Likely to Tilt Cut to Lower Brackets," *Washington Post,* May 6, 2001.

For estate tax data on farmers and small business owners, see Barry W. Johnson and Jacob M. Mikow, "Federal Estate Tax Returns, 1998–2000," at http://www.irs.gov/pub/irs-soi/00esart.pdf.

CHAPTER 20: STORIES TRUMP SCIENCE

For an overview of why President Coolidge and his Secretary of the Treasury Andrew Mellon proposed to repeal the estate tax in the 1920s and why they failed, see "Against Inheritance Tax," *New York Times,* February 16, 1925, p. 5; "Coolidge Would End Inheritance Taxes; Calls It State Field," *New York Times,* February 20, 1925, pp. 1, 4; "Mellon Gives Hint of Tax Program," *New York Times,* March 18, 1925, p. 2; "Coolidge Enlarges Tax Appeals Board," *New York Times,* March 19, 1925, p. 4; "Commerce Leaders Seek Tax Changes," *New York Times,* April 27, 1925, p. 32; "Mellon Urges South to Back Tax Reform; Suggests Deep Cuts," *New York Times,* May 6, 1925, pp. 1, 6; W. M. Kiplinger, "Coolidge Pares Budget to Make Tax Cut," *New York Times,* May 24, 1925, p. 21; "Coolidge Dubious on Estate Taxes," *New York Times,* June 13, 1925, p. 15; "Business on Record for Tax Reforms," *New York Times,* June 22, 1925, p. 19; "Smoot Outlines Coolidge Tax Cut Program," *New York Times,* July 19, 1925, p. 26; "Treasury Favors 20 Percent Surtax," *New York Times,* July 30, 1925, p. 1, 6; "Favors Tax Cuts Exceeding Those Treasury Urges," *New York Times,* August 3, 1925, p. 1; "Mellon to Propose $250,000,000 Tax Cut," *New York Times,* October 15, 1925, p. 25; "Wants Estate Tax Gradually Cut Out," *New York Times,* October 17, 1925, p. 17; "Industrial Board Asks Tax Relief," *New York Times,* October 19, 1925, p. 2; "Mellon Proposes Changes," *New York Times,* October 20, 1925, pp. 1–2; "Iowa Men Attack Green's Tax Views," *New York Times,* October 22, 1925, p. 10; "32 Governors Ask Congress to Ban Inheritance Tax," *New York Times,* October 24, 1925, pp. 1, 8; "Industry Assails Estate Tax Law," *New York Times,* October 26, 1925, p. 8; "Publicity Dropped in New Tax Bill; Estate Tax Levy Stays," *New York Times,* November 7, 1925, pp. 1–2; "Senators to Fight for Tax Publicity and Estate Levies," November 8, 1925, pp. 1, 16; "Tax Retained Despite Opposition," *New York Times,* November 13, 1925, p. 8; "Congress Ready to Cut Income Tax $300,000,000," *New York Times,* November 22, 1925, p. 33; "Democrats to Back Cut in Estate

Taxes," *New York Times,* November 22, 1925, p. 16; "Tax Bill Finished," *New York Times,* November 25, 1925, pp. 1, 6; "Tax Bill Praised as Non-Political," *New York Times,* November 25, 1925, p. 5; "Tax Bill Is Ready to Go to the House with Sweeping Cuts," *New York Times,* December 5, 1925, p. 1, 6; "Full Text of the President's Message to Congress upon the State of the Union," *New York Times,* December 9, 1925, pp. 10, 11; "10 States Protest Estate Tax Split," *New York Times,* December 11, 1925, p. 5; "Estate Tax Cuts Win in the House," *New York Times,* December 17, 1925, pp. 1, 6; "$330,000,000 Tax Cut Now Mellon's Limit," *New York Times,* January 5, 1926, p. 4; "Minority Tax Plan, Rejected, 10 to 1," *New York Times,* January 12, 1926, pp. 1, 4; "Senate Tax Bill Nears Completion," *New York Times,* January 16, 1926, p. 17; "Senate Cuts Surtax More," *New York Times,* January 17, 1926, pp. 1, 2; "Estate Tax Repeal Starts New Fight," *New York Times,* January 18, 1926, p. 23; "Coolidge Questions Estate Tax Repeal," *New York Times,* January 20, 1926, p. 27; Editorial, "The Estate Tax," *New York Times,* January 20, 1926, p. 24; "Coolidge to Accept Estate Tax Repeal," *New York Times,* January 23, 1926, p. 4; "Radicals Map Out Fight on Tax Bill," *New York Times,* January 27, 1926, p. 4; "Federal Estate Tax Repeal Is Opposed," *New York Times,* February 14, 1926; "Declares Tax Cuts of Senate Will Rise to $600,000,000," *New York Times,* February 15, 1926, pp. 1, 4; "The Tax Bill in Conference," *New York Times,* February 15, 1926; "Tax Bill Conferees in Secret Meeting," *New York Times,* February 16, 1926, p. 1; "Conferees Prepare Tax Compromises," *The New York Times,* February 18, 1926, pp. 1, 4; "Tax Bill Agreement Expected Tonight," *New York Times,* February 19, 1926, pp. 1, 10; "Estate Tax Repeal Lost," *New York Times,* February 20, 1926, pp. 1, 2; "Ceremony at White House; Congress Leaders See President Affix His Signature," *New York Times,* February 27, 1926; "Features of Bill Signed by Coolidge," *New York Times,* February 27, 1926, p. 1, 4; and "Prosperous America Cuts Taxes Again," *New York Times,* February 28, 1926.

For more on the legislative history of the act, see John Witte, *The Politics and Development of the Federal Income Tax* (Madison: University of Wisconsin Press, 1985); Louis Eisenstein, "The Rise and Decline of the Estate Tax," *Tax Law Review* 11, no. 223 (1955); Revenue Bill of 1926, HR 1, 69th Cong. 1st Sess. 14–15 (1925); Ways and Means Report, The Revenue Bill of 1926, H.R. Rep., No. 1, 69th Cong. 1st Sess. Calendar No. 1; Committee on Finance Report No. 52, Internal Revenue Bill of 1926, Senate, 69th Cong. 1st Sess. Calendar No. 54; House Roll Call Vote, *Congressional Record* (December 18, 1925): 1164–65; and Senate Roll Call Vote, *Congressional Record* (February 12, 1926): 3896.

For background information on Chairman of the Senate Finance Committee Reed Smoot, who favored repeal, see Biographical Dictionary of the United States Congress, available at http://bioguide.congress.gov/scripts/biodisplay.pl?index=S000644; and Milton Merrill, *Reed Smoot: Apostle in Politics* (Logan: Utah State University Press, 1990); in addition to "High Expenditures Expected by Smoot," *New York Times,* March 18, 1925, p. 5; "Smoot Now in Line for Church Honors," *New York Times,* May 19, 1925, p. 25; "Smoot Fails to Get Mormon Presidency,"

New York Times, June 7, 1925, p. E2; "Fear Smoot Faces Defeat at Polls," *New York Times,* August 31, 1925, p. 3; "Call on the President to Discipline Smoot," *New York Times,* January 8, 1926, p. 18; "Smoot Perturbed, but Likely to Win," *New York Times,* October 22, 1926, p. 3; "Utah," *New York Times,* November 3, 1926, p. 3; and "Tax Reduction Becomes an Issue Once More," *New York Times,* November 14, 1926.

For information on Chairman of the House Ways and Means Committee William Green, who opposed repeal, see Biographical Dictionary of the United States Congress, available at http://bioguide.congress.gov/scripts/biodisplay.pl ?index=G000422; as well as "Scientific Taxation Advocated by Green," *New York Times,* September 22, 1926, p. 39; and "House Will Speed Income Tax Bill," *New York Times,* September 28, 1925.

For background on John Garner, the ranking Democrat on the House Ways and Means Committee, who also opposed repeal, see George Rothwell Brown, *The Speaker: The Romantic Story of John N. Garner* (New York: Putnam, 1932), and Bascon Timmons, *Garner of Texas: A Personal History* (New York: Harper, 1948).

For background on President Calvin Coolidge, see his *Autobiography of Calvin Coolidge* (New York: Little and Ives, 1929); Claude Fuess, *Calvin Coolidge: The Man From Vermont* (Westport, Conn.: Greenwood Press, 1976); Mark Sullivan, *Our Times: The United States 1900–1925* (New York: Scribner, 1935); Donald McCoy, *Calvin Coolidge: The Quiet President* (New York: Macmillan, 1967); Robert Sobel, *Coolidge: An American Enigma* (Washington, D.C.: Regnery Publishing, 1998); and "Coolidge's New Term to Be His Real Test," *New York Times,* March 1, 1925.

For information on Andrew Mellon, see William Mellon, *Judge Mellon's Sons* (Pittsburgh: private printing, 1948); Paul Mellon, *Reflections in a Silver Spoon* (New York: Morrow, 1992); Charles Willis Thompson, "Silent Men Are Finding Their Voices," *New York Times,* February 15, 1925; "Mellon Pays Most in Pittsburgh," *New York Times,* September 2, 1925, p. 17; "Twenty-Five Men Who Head Income Tax List," *New York Times,* September 6, 1925; and "Tax Bill Is Passed by Senate 61 to 10; To Be Signed Today," *New York Times,* February 25, 1926, p. 1.

For examples of the technical discussion regarding the 1926 repeal act, see Testimony before the House Ways and Means Committee, Statement of Dr. Thomas S. Adams, Professor of Political Economy, Yale University, on the estate tax (1924), pp. 461–70; Dr. Thomas S. Adams, Personal Papers, Letter from President of Chamber of Commerce (October 9, 1925); Committee on Taxation, "Digest of Discussion" (October 16, 1925), p. 6; Committee on Taxation, "Digest of Discussion" (November 21, 1925), pp. 19–20; Testimony before the House Ways and Means Committee, Statement of Dr. Edwin Seligman, New York, N.Y., on the estate tax (1925), pp. 477–96. For information on the National Committee on Inheritance Taxation, which favored repeal, see Testimony before the House Ways and Means Committee, Statement of Frederic Delano, Chairman of the National Committee on Inheritance Taxation, on the Estate Tax (1925), pp. 389–91.

For information on the perspective of the states toward repeal, see "Expressions of Opinions by Governors, Officers, and Members of State Legislatures in Opposition to a Federal Inheritance Tax and Particularly to the Inheritance Section of the Revenue Bill Now Pending before Congress," Hearings before the House Ways and Means Committee on the Revenue Act of 1926, pp. 53–64. For the reasons why the American Farm Bureau opposed repeal at the time, see Hearings before the House Ways and Means Committee on the Revenue Act of 1926, pp. 455–59. For information on who pays the tax, see *Statistical Abstract of the United States* (Washington, D.C.: U.S. Government Printing Office, 1939), and Debate on the Floor of the House of Representatives, Congressional Record, H.R. Rep., No. 1, 69th Cong. 1st Sess., December 11, 1925, pp. 717–24.

For an example of the kind of "scientific" argument about the estate tax made by Democrats, see the Brookings Institution report by Bill Gale and Joel Slemrod, *Rethinking Estate and Gift Taxation* (Washington, D.C.: Brookings Institution, 2001). The Center on Budget and Policy Priorities reports on the estate tax issue include Joel Friedman and Andrew Lee, "Permanent Repeal of the Estate Tax Would Be Costly, yet Would Benefit Only a Few, Very Large Estates" (June 17, 2003); Jon Springer, "Fact Sheet: Estate Tax Should Be Reformed, Not Repealed" (June 17, 2003); Springer, "Fact Sheet: Estate Tax Affects Very Few Family Businesses" (June 17, 2003); Springer, "Fact Sheet: Repealing the Estate Tax Would Reduce Charitable Giving" (June 17, 2003); Friedman and Lee, "Permanent Repeal of the Estate Tax Would Be Costly, yet Would Benefit Only a Few, Very Large Estates" (revised June 3, 2002); Friedman, "The Kyl Amendment to Lock In Permanent Repeal of the Estate Tax" (February 5, 2002); Iris Lav, "Estate Tax Repeal and the Top Income Tax Rate Cut: A State-by-State Look at Who Would Benefit" (May 14, 2001); Lav, "If Estate Tax Is Repealed, Repeal of Gift Tax Would Not Be Far Behind" (May 3, 2001); Joel Friedman, "Lower-Cost Estate Tax Repeal Reflects Slow Phase-In" (revised April 4, 2001); Iris Lav and Joel Friedman, "Can Capital Gains Carry-Over Basis Replace The Estate Tax?" (March 15, 2001); Isaac Shapiro, Iris Lav, and Jim Sly, "4,500 Very Large Estates Would Receive as Much in Annual Tax Reductions under Bush Plan as 140 Million Americans" (February 26, 2001); and Friedman, "Estate Tax Repeal: A Costly Windfall for the Wealthiest Americans" (revised February 6, 2001); Elizabeth C. McNichol, Iris J. Lav, and Daniel Tenny, "Repeal of the Federal Estate Tax Would Cost State Governments Billions in Revenue" (December 12, 2000); Lav and Sly, "Estate Tax Repeal: A Windfall for the Wealthiest Americans" (August 30, 2000); Lav, "The Estate Tax, 'Double Taxation,' and Carry-Over Basis," (July 7, 2000); Lav, "Eliminating the Estate Tax: A Costly Benefit for the Wealthiest Americans" (revised July 20, 1999); and Lav, "Estate Tax Cuts Would Benefit Wealthiest Americans: Targeted Changes Could Help Family Businesses and Farms" (April 1997). For an example of stories mixed with economic analysis provided by Republicans on this issue, see Joint Economic Committee Study, "The Economics of the Estate Tax" (1998), at http://www.house.gov/jec/fiscal/tx-grwth/estattax/estattax.htm. For the report published

BIBLIOGRAPHIC ESSAY 349

by Jack Kemp's Tax Reform Commission, see National Commission on Economic Growth and Tax Reform, *Unleashing America's Potential: A Pro-Growth, Pro-Family Tax System for the Twenty-First Century* (New York: St. Martin's/Griffin, 1996).

On the political philosophy of John Dewey, see his *Political Writings*, ed. Debra Morris and Ian Shapiro (Indianapolis: Hackett, 1993). On the philosophy of Max Weber, see his *Protestant Ethic and the Spirit of Capitalism* (New York: Oxford University Press, 1958). On the trade-off between equity and efficiency, see Arthur Okun, *Equality and Efficiency* (Washington, D.C.: Brookings Institution, 1975). On the views of Andrew Carnegie regarding the estate tax, see his *Gospel of Wealth and Other Timely Essays* (New York: Century, 1900). On the importance of the narrative mode to human psychology, see Jerome Bruner, *Actual Minds, Possible Worlds* (Boston: Harvard University Press, 1986). Walter Berns's views can be found in his book, *For Capital Punishment: Crime and Morality of the Death Penalty* (New York: Basic, 1979), which is also excerpted in Walter Berns, "The Morality of Anger," in *The Death Penalty in America,* ed. Hugo Bedau, 3rd ed. (New York and London; Oxford University Press, 1982), 331–41.

For information on the HBO documentary "Born Rich" and its director Jamie Johnson, see its website at http://www.hbo.com/docs/programs/born_rich/index .html. Also see Julia Chaplin, "Biting the Silver Spoon That Feeds Him, on Film," *New York Times,* October 12, 2003; Bill Goodykoontz, "A Rich Kid Examines Rich Kids' (Sigh) Burden," *Arizona Republic,* October 25, 2003; Matthew Gilbert, "'Born Rich' Reveals Privileged Information," *Boston Globe,* October 27, 2003, p. D16; and Andrew Gumbel, "Betrayal; Jamie Johnson Is a Billion Heir. His Friends Are the Super-Rich Kids," *Independent on Sunday,* November 16, 2003, pp. 1–2. For information on the HBO series and MTV's "Rich Girls," see Melanie McFarland, "Poor Little Rich Kids; Wealthy Offspring Flaunt Riches with Little Sympathy," *Houston Chronicle,* October 27, 2003; Monica Collins, "Poor Souls: Inheritance No Cure-All for These Rich Kids," *Boston Herald,* October 26, 2003; Kevin Thompson, "Lifestyles of the Rich and Aimless," *Palm Beach Post,* October 27, 2003; Alessandra Stanley, "Focusing on Residents of Gilded Cages," *New York Times,* October 27, 2003, p. E8; and Maureen Ryan, "Lifestyles of the Rich, Very Rich Kids," *Chicago Tribune,* October 27, 2003.

For background on "The Simple Life" featuring Paris Hilton and Nicole Ritchie, see Alessandra Stanley, "With a Rich Girl Here and a Rich Girl There," *New York Times,* December 2, 2003, pp. E1, E5; David Usborne, "We'll Always Have Paris," *Sunday Age,* December 14, 2003, p. 7; and Denise Flaim, "Will We Always Have Paris? Reasons Why Some Gain Fame Are Hard to Map," *Orlando Sentinel Tribune,* December 14, 2003, p. F7.

CHAPTER 21: MONEY, MONEY, MONEY

Statistics on campaign contributions and lobbying expenditures utilized in this chapter were derived from a search of the Center for Responsive Politics website at http://www.opensecrets.org. A list of the 400 richest Americans and their net worth can be found in September 18, 2003 issue of *Forbes* at http://www.forbes .com/home/2003/09/17/rich400land.html. Information on campaign contributions, lobbying incomes, and expenditures was gleaned from a search of http:// www.opensecrets.org. On the wealth of members of Congress, see Vikki Kratz, "Who Wins with the Estate Tax Repeal?" at http://www.opensecrets.org /newsletter/ ce75/repeal.asp. For more information on former White House Chief of Staff John Podesta and the Center for American Progress, see the liberal think tank's website at http://www.americanprogress.org/site/pp.asp?c=biJRJ8OVF&b=2483. On the influence of rich families in the estate tax debate, see Jonathan Weisman, "Linking Tax to Death May Have Brought about Its Doom," *USA Today,* May 20, 2001, at http://www.usatoday.com/news/washdc/2001-05-21-estate.htm. On the connection between Representative Abercrombie and the Campbell Estate in Hawaii, see Jonathan Weisman, "For a Few, Tax Bill Delivers Special Breaks," *USA Today,* June 5, 2001, at http://www.usatoday.com/news/washington/2001-06-06-tax.htm.

For samples of editorials supporting repeal of the estate tax found in family-owned newspapers, see the *Seattle Times* editorial, "Death and Estate Taxes Rub Raw Family Legacies," April 27, 1997, at http://www.deathtax.com/deathtax/ tstedit.html; Loren Fleckenstein, "Taxes Take Toll on Family-Owned Newspapers in the U.S.," *Press-Enterprise,* June 21, 1997, at http://www.deathtax.com/ deathtax/pressent.html; and John Sturm, "Estate Tax Is Wiping out Family-Owned Newspapers," *San Jose Mercury News,* November 5, 1999 at http:// www.deathtax.com/deathtax/sturm1199.html. Samples of coalition advertisements can be found at http://www.deathtax.com/deathtax/roots.html. On the radio and television ads targeting Democratic senators in the 2002 election, see Carl Hulse, "Ads Push Estate Tax as Issue in Campaigns," *New York Times,* July 14, 2002, section 1, p. 22. Also see Mark Zdechlik, "Ad War Breaks out in Senate Race" (June 28, 2002), at http://news.mpr.org/features/200206/28_zdechlikm_adwatch/ index.shtml; OMB Watch, "Estate Tax Repeal Proponents Launch New Round of Misleading Attack Ads" (June 24, 2002), http://www.ombwatch.org/article/ articleview/865/1/126/; and Laura McCallum, "Attack Ad Goes after Wellstone" (June 21, 2002), at http://news.mpr.org/features/200206/21_mccalluml_adwatch/ index.shtml.

On polling, see testimony of James Martin, "Eliminating the Federal Estate and Inheritance Taxes" (July 14, 1999), at http://www.60plus.org/vitalspeeches .asp?docID=349, and the memo written by Frank Luntz, "The Death Tax & Gay and Lesbian Americans" (April 24, 2001), at http://www.policyandtaxationgroup .com/pdf/GAYANDLESBIANSURVEY.pdf. For information on the Responsible Wealth petition opposing repeal, see David Cay Johnston, "Dozens of Rich Americans Join in the Fight to Retain the Estate Tax," *New York Times,* February 14, 2001, at http://www.responsiblewealth.org/press/rwnews/2001/estate_tax_nytimes.html. A list of the petition's signers can be found at http://www.responsiblewealth.org/

estatetax/ETCall_Signers.html. Salaries of insurance executives of firms that would be hardest hit by the estate tax are from the company's profiles at http:// biz.yahoo.com/p/l/lnc.html and http://biz.yahoo.com/p/J/JP.html. For the argument that campaign contributions were unimportant to the estate tax debate, see Bruce Bartlett, "Public Grasps Estate Tax Clues," *Washington Times,* June 19, 2002, at http://www.washtimes.com/commentary/20020619-32866536.htm. For a view contrary to ours, contending that campaign contributions played a major role in estate tax repeal, see the article by Edward J. McCaffery, Linda Cohen, and Fred McChesney, "Shakedown at Gucci Gulch," manuscript, 2004 (on file with the authors).

For various proposals for campaign finance reform, see Linda Greenhouse, "The Supreme Court; The Ruling; Justices, in a 5 to 4 decision, Back Campaign Finance Law That Curbs Contributions," *New York Times,* December 11, 2003, p. A1; Matthew Miller, *The Two Percent Solution* (New York: Public Affairs, 2003), 172–80; Bruce Ackerman and Ian Ayres, *Voting with Dollars* (New Haven: Yale University Press, 2002); and Ackerman and Ayres, "System Down: McCain-Feingold Helped Doom the Current Model of Public Financing for Campaigns. Fixing It Will Take Some Imagination," *American Prospect,* December 12, 2003. On contributions from the Enron corporation in recent election cycles, see Mark Thomas, "Enron Fallout," *New Statesman* (April 29, 2003), at http://www .drownedinsound.com/articles/3810.html and "Enron and Andersen," (January 24, 2002) at http://www.opensecrets.org/news/enron/index.asp.

CHAPTER 22: MORALS OF THE MYSTERIES

For a discussion of how framing effects influence public opinion, see Amos Tversky and Daniel Kahneman, "The Framing of Decisions and the Rationality of Choice," *Science* 211 (1981): 543–58; and George Lakoff, *Moral Politics: What Conservatives Know that Liberals Don't* (Chicago: University of Chicago Press, 1996). On the multiple dimensions and intensity of public opinion, see John Roemer, "Why the Poor Do Not Expropriate the Rich: An Old Argument in New Garb," *Journal of Public Economics* 70, no. 3 (1998): 339–424; and Roemer, "Does Democracy Engender Justice?" in *Democracy's Value,* ed. Ian Shapiro and Casiano Hacker-Cordon (Cambridge: Cambridge University Press, 1999). On why compromise on ideological issues is harder than on pure distributive issues, see Nicholas Miller, "Majority Rule and Minority Interests," *Political Order: Nomos XXXVIII,* ed. Ian Shapiro and Russell Hardin (New York University Press, 1996), 207–50.

For an examination of the reasons why the poor in democracies do not soak the rich, see Ian Shapiro, *The State of Democratic Theory* (Princeton: Princeton University Press, 2003), 104–45. On the growth of professionals in the Democratic electoral base, see Michael Hout et al., "The Democratic Class Struggle in the United States, 1948–1992," *American Sociological Review* 60 (1995): 805–28, and on the comparatively high income in Democratic constituencies since 1994, see

Jeffrey M. Stonecash, *Class and Party in American Politics* (Boulder, Colo.: Westview Press, 2000).

On political entrepreneurship in Congress, see David Mayhew, *America's Congress: Actions in the Public Sphere, James Madison through Newt Gingrich* (New Haven: Yale University Press, 2000). On the motives for groups to participate in politics, see Mancur Olson, *The Logic of Collective Action* (Cambridge: Harvard University Press, 1969), and on the empirics of collective action, see Donald Green and Ian Shapiro, *Pathologies of Rational Choice Theory* (New Haven: Yale University Press, 1994). For discussion of the logic of the divide-a-dollar game, see Dennis Mueller, *Public Choice II* (Cambridge: Cambridge University Press, 1989), 19–31.

Facts on the history of the Democratic Leadership Council (DLC) were taken from "Profile: Democratic Leadership Council," available at http://rightweb .irc-online.org/org/demleadcoun.php. Robert Reich's quotes are from Robert B. Reich, "Movement Politics," *Boston Review* 29, no. 3–4 (Summer 2004): 18. Garry Wills's comments are from his review of Bill Clinton's *My Life*, "The Tragedy of Bill Clinton," *New York Review* 51, no. 13 (August 15, 2004): 64. Ralph Nader's critique of the DLC's support for tax cuts can be found in his "The Corporatist Democratic Leadership Council," *In the Public Interest* (August 1, 2003), available at http://www.nader.org/interest/080103.html. On Dick Morris's understanding of triangulation, see his "W's Triangulation," *Front Page Magazine* (June 25, 2003), at http://www.frontpagemag.com/Articles/ReadArticle.asp?ID=8564. Quotations from Grover Norquist were taken from Elizabeth Drew, "Bush: The Dream Campaign," *New York Review of Books* (June 10, 2004): 23–25.

Chapter 23: Another Storm Gathering

A review of 1997 estate tax returns from the IRS reveals that estates of $5 million or more accounted for about 5% of taxable estates and paid 49% of estate taxes collected by the federal government. See Internal Revenue Service, SOI Bulletin (Summer 1999). In 1998, estates larger than $5 million accounted for more than half the total revenue collected from the tax, while the estates of small business people constituted only 1.6% of the total number of taxable estates, and those of farmers formed only 1.4% of the total, according to the Internal Revenue Service and Treasury's Office of Tax Analysis. On the cost of estate tax repeal, see Carl Hulse, "House Backs Permanent End to Estate Tax," *New York Times,* June 7, 2002, p. A16. For an example of information regarding the new tax law changes, see the January 22, 2004, letter from Debevoise and Plimpton, LLP, to its clients, entitled "New Estate and Gift Tax Thresholds for 2004."

For an analysis of public support for tax cuts and attitudes about economic inequality, see Larry Bartels, "Homer Gets a Tax Cut: Inequality and Public Policy in the American Mind," prepared for presentation at the Annual Meeting of the American Political Science Association (August 2003). Regarding public opinion on the income tax, see Luntz Research, "National Survey on Taxes and Social Security" (August 1998), Luntz Research, "Americans Talk Taxes" (January 27, 2003), and National Public Radio/Kaiser Family Foundation/Kennedy School of Government, "National Survey of Americans' Views on Taxes" (April 2003). For the relatively low support for corporate tax cuts, see the NBC News Poll, conducted by Hart-Teeter and released July 30, 1998. Former Vice President Dan Quayle's views on the income tax are quoted in George Lakoff, *Moral Politics: What Conservatives Know That Liberals Don't* (Chicago: University of Chicago Press, 1996), 189. John Cassidy's article "Tax Code: Tax Cuts were just the Beginning; the President Is Signaling a Far More Radical Agenda" appeared in *The New Yorker,* September 9, 2004. See also, "Taxes for an Ownership Society," *New York Times,* September 15, 2004, p. A-26; Lawrence B. Lindsay, "Simplify, Simplify, Simplify," *Wall Street Journal,* September 16, 2004, at A16. For the findings of the Kemp Commission, see the Report of the National Commission on Economic Growth and Tax Reform, "Unleashing America's Potential" (January 1996), at http://www.empower.org/kempcommission/kempcommission_toc.htm. On the tax proposals of various candidates in the 1996 presidential campaign, see chapter 1 of Michael J. Graetz, *The U.S. Income Tax* (New York: Norton, 2001). See also http://www.cnn.com/ALLPOLITICS/1996/issues/topics/taxes.shtml.

For President Bush's State of the Union address, see "State of the Union Address" (January 20, 2004), at http://www.whitehouse.gov/news/releases/2004/01/20040120-7.html.

For general information on Americans for Fair Taxation and their proposal to repeal the income tax and replace it with a national sales tax, see http://www.fairtax.org. Also see the various Fair Tax Newsletters: "Linder to Re-Introduce Fair Tax Bill Today" (January 7, 2003) for information on the bill introduced by Congressman Linder; "Grassroots Update February 2003" (February 5, 2003) for information on activities in the states; "House Majority Leader Tom DeLay Has Recently Co-sponsored the Fair Tax" (February 12, 2004) for list of sponsors and cosponsors; "New Executive Director Introduction" (July 24, 2003) for background information on Tom Wright; "Fair Tax Bill Introduced into Senate for the 1st Time!" (August 21, 2003) for the press release by Senators Chambliss and Miller; and "Promote the Fair Tax in the Media" for information on the cost of the campaign (January 30, 2004). Information on House Resolution 141 can be located at http://thomas.loc.gov/cgi-bin/query/z?c108:H.CON.RES.141. For a list of sponsors and cosponsors of the Fair Tax bill, see http://www.fairtaxvolunteer.org/scorecards/sponsors.html. For additional information on the activities of Americans for Fair Taxation, see http://www.fairtaxvolunteer.org/news/.

For more information on the Fair Tax, see Alison Mitchell, "A New Form of Lobbying Puts Public Face on Private Interest," *New York Times,* September 30, 1998; Ryan Donmoyer, "Rich 'Friends of Bill' Archer Propose National Sales Tax," *Tax Notes* (January 8, 1998); "AFR Publication Advocating National Retail Sales

Tax," *Tax Notes* (January 9, 1998); and Edmund Andrews, "White House Floats Idea of Dropping Income Tax," *The New York Times*, February 8, 2003, p. 14.

For a biography of Congressman John Linder, see http://www.johnlinder.com/biography.asp.

For the Drudge Report comments on Denny Hastert's tax ideas, see www.drudgereport.com/mc.htm (last visited August 4, 2004). Hastert's book is Denny Hastert, *Speaker: Lessons for Forty Years in Coaching and Politics* (Washington, D.C.: Regnery, 2004)

For information on Herman Cain, see Tom Baxter and Jim Galloway, "Legislature 2004: TV Ads Aimed at Raising Cain's Public Profile," *Atlanta Journal-Constitution*, February 3, 2004; Fair Tax Newsletter, "Taxpayer, Urgent Call to Action on Floor Vote" (April 9, 2003); Ralph Hallow, "Black Conservative Seeks Seat in Senate," *Washington Times*, June 2, 2003; and Doug Thomas, "Four Midlanders to Join AK Court of Honor," *Omaha World Herald*, October 15, 1995. On Jim DeMint and his run for the Senate, see http://greenvilleonline.com/news/2004/08/16/2004081637220.htm, http://www.demint.house.gov/Biography/, http://jimdemint.com/demint_contents/record/whitepaper_taxreform.pdf, http://www.heritage.org/Research/PoliticalPhilosophy/loader.cfm?url=/commonspot/security/getfile.cfm&PageID=4327 (last visited September 15, 2004). The quotes on taxation were taken from Dan Hoover, "Tax Reform Now Moving Senate Race," *Greenville News*, August 22, 2004, p. 1317A.

For arguments against the move to a national sales tax, see William Gale, "Fantasy Tax," *Washington Post*, February 15, 1998, p. C09, and Robert McIntyre, "The 23 Percent Solution," *New York Times*, January 23, 1998. For the response to such arguments, see Tom Wright, "A Sound Sales-Tax Scheme," *Washington Post*, February 28, 1998, p. A12, and Wright et al., "Viewpoints," *Houston Chronicle*, February 7, 1998.

Dick Cheney's comment that deficits don't matter can be found in Ron Suskind, *The Price of Loyalty* (New York: Simon and Shuster, 2004), p. 291. On 2001 CBO estimates, see CBO, "The Budget and Economic Outlook: Fiscal Years 2002–2011" (January 2001), at http://www.cbo.gov/showdoc.cfm?index=2727&sequence=0&from=0, and "CBO Surplus Projections Fuel Both Sides of Tax Cut Debate," *Tax Notes Today* (February 1, 2001). For estimates of the budget deficit, see Martin Wolk, "Rubin Warns of a Deficit's Ripples," MSNBC News (January 13, 2004), at http://www.msnbc.msn.com/id/3948923/; "No End in Sight to Rising Deficits, Experts Warn" (September 29, 2003), at http://democrats.senate.gov/dpc/hearings/hearing10/greenstein.pdf; and Robert Rubin, Peter Orszag, and Allen Sinai, "Sustained Budget Deficits: Longer-Run U.S. Economic Performance and the Risk of Financial and Fiscal Disarray," presented at the AEA-NAEFA Joint Session, Allied Social Science Associations' Annual Meetings, the Andrew Brimmer Policy Forum, "National Economic and Financial Policies for Growth and Stability" (January 4, 2004), San Diego, Calif., at http://www.brook.edu/dybdocroot/views/papers/orszag/20040105.pdf.

EPILOGUE

The private estimates of forthcoming deficits are reported in Robert E. Rubin, Peter R. Orzag, and Allen Sinai, "Sustained Budget Deficits: Longer-run U.S. Economic Performance and the Risk of Financial and Fiscal Disarray" (paper presented at AEA-NAEFA Joint Session, ASSA Annual Meetings, January 4, 2004, available at http://www.centristpolicynetwork.org/legislative_updates/files_2004/rubin2004 _0105.pdf). For Jon Kyl's and Don Nickles's willingness to compromise, see Jonathan Weisman, "Some GOP Lawmakers Aim to Scale Back Bush Tax Cuts," *Washington Post,* March 2, 2004, and Jonathan Weisman, "Estate Tax Opponents May Be Forced to Compromise," *Washington Post,* October 22, 2003. The advertisement appeared in *Roll Call* on March 9, 2004. Grover Norquist's remarks were reported in Elizabeth Drew, "Bush: The Dream Campaign," *New York Review of Books,* June 10, 2004, pp. 23–25, available at http://www.nybooks.com/articles /17176.

ACKNOWLEDGMENTS

In writing this book we have benefited greatly from the generosity of others. First and foremost, we are indebted to the some 150 people who spoke with us about this book. They gave freely of their time and experience. As a close second, we want to thank the person or persons who really invented the Internet (assuming it wasn't Al Gore). It enabled us to confirm and unearth facts that would have been fugitive in earlier times. Mayling Birney, a Ph.D. candidate in political science at Yale, played a crucial role. She was present for many of the interviews and contributed immeasurably to our understanding of the events that unfolded here. We also had the benefit of extraordinary research assistance from Jeffrey Mueller, a Yale undergraduate and then a Yale Law student, who has contributed to this project from its inception. Adam Haslett, a Yale Law School graduate, who is an extraordinarily talented writer and a good friend, accompanied us on some interviews, giving us the benefits of his keen eye for detail. He also read early drafts of the manuscript and provided invaluable advice about how we might improve it—advice we never failed to take. When it comes to writing, we are his students. Celica Whitaker, who was a professional editor before attending the Yale Law School, also provided editorial assistance and suggestions on the entire manuscript.

David Mayhew, who knows more about Congress than just about anyone, gave us particularly valuable comments. Other colleagues who read the entire manuscript and offered valuable suggestions include Bruce Ackerman, Linc Caplan, Joseph LaPalombara, and Daniel Markovits. Our anonymous referees also offered many helpful ideas for improvements. Sarah Holland managed to pull together our bibliographic essay, with help from Liora Brener, Molly Lewis, and Jeffrey Mueller. Susannah Camic, Jeremy Robbins, and Denise Bertholin also provided excellent research assistance. Paul Nitze and Isabel Reichardt contributed as well. Kris Kavanaugh typed the entire manuscript, retyped it, and then typed it again and again.

Her willingness to meet more than one deadline with unfailing good humor was a great boon to us. Gene Coakley, Scott Matheson, and others of the staff of the Yale Law Library were, as always, enormously helpful. And the deans of the Yale Law School, Tony Kronman and Harold Koh, provided both encouragement and financial support, as did Yale's Institution for Social and Policy Studies. The Carnegie Corporation of New York also provided valuable financial support to Ian Shapiro for this project. His generous Carnegie Scholar award in 2000 funded much of the early research and interviews. We hope that Andrew Carnegie, a key player in an earlier battle over the estate tax, would have liked the result.

Finally, we want to thank our agent, Wendy Strothman, and her associate Dan O'Connell, who helped bring this book to fruition, and Ian Malcolm for shepherding it into print. We had an awesome team at our side.

pointments of, 195, 199; conference negotiations and, 195–201; "death tax"
rhetoric and, 83; final bill comments by,
202–3, 206; profile of, 198–99; reelection campaigns of, 153; reform/repeal
efforts of, 46, 188–92; as "winner" in
tax cuts, 206
Grassley-Baucus bills: (1997), 34, 38;
(2001), 189–92, 210
grassroots mobilization, 39–40, 48, 275
"grasstops" constituents, 4, 105–7; mobilization of, 48–61, 164, 237, 239, 258;
storytelling and, 73, 232; on sunset provisions, 55, 59, 191, 236
Great Britain. *See* United Kingdom
Great Tax Wars, The (Weisman), 74
Green, Joshua, 66, 124
Green, William, 223–24
Greenberg Research, 124–25, 128, 245
Greenspan, Alan, 144–45, 208
Greenstein, Bob, 97–98, 243
Gross, Terry, 213–14

Hagel, Chuck, 59
Halliburton, Inc., 155
Hannay, Roger, 54
Harbert, John, 15, 232, 242
Harkin, Tom, 248
Harrington, Paul, 112
Hart, Gary, 263
Hastert, Dennis "Denny," 145–47, 153,
163, 180–82, 196–97, 206–7, 276
Hatch, Orrin, 195–97
Head Start programs, 75
hearings, congressional, 39, 51, 62–66,
144, 181
Hearst, Patricia, 234
Heinz, Henry, 222
Helms, Jesse, 46
Henderson, Wayne, 68
Heritage Foundation: antitax philosophy
of, 267; budget/expenditures of, 85, 89,
91, 93; funding of, 91, 242–43; men-
tioned, 27, 168; repeal focus of, 94, 98,
228; research-activism of, 15, 85, 89–
96, 241–42, 261; storytelling and, 51
Herrera, George, 70

Hilfiger, Ally, 272
Hill, The, 70, 244
Hilton, Paris, 234
Hispanic Chamber of Commerce, U. S.,
70, 72
Hispanics, 68, 70, 72, 124
Homeland Security Department, 6, 144
Homer, Pete, 70
Hoover, Herbert, 120
Houghton, Amo, 184–85
House of Representatives: legislative agen-
das in, 45, 47, 257; rules and discipline
in, 25, 46, 146, 180, 202; seniority sys-
tem in, 44, 147–48; 1925–26 repeal ef-
forts in, 223–24; 2001 tax cut bills in,
180–85, 194–202, 210
Houston Chronicle, 274
Hubbard, Al, 136–37
Hubbard, Glenn, 88, 138

IMPACTO Group, 72
Imus, Don, 234
income taxes, corporations, 12, 123, 154,
156–57, 162–63, 190, 269, 272–73
income taxes, individual, 46, 269–71; alternative minimum tax and, 183, 189;
charitable giving and, 113, 183; corporate dividends and, 12, 141, 204, 273;
itemized deductions and, 114; rate reductions and, 12, 41, 75, 108, 123,
138–39, 147, 157, 159, 163, 181,
188–89, 193, 200
Independent Sector, 114
Indian Treaty Room meeting, 159–63
inheritance taxation, 83–84, 100, 233–
35, 255–56
Insight, 42, 45
Insurance Agents and Brokers of America,
115
Internal Revenue Service (IRS), 81, 275–76
International Foodservice Distributors Association, 166
Internet, the, 164, 243–44, 244
IRS. *See* Internal Revenue Service
IRS Restructuring and Reform Act (1998),
34–35
Isakson, Johnny, 276